The Space Legislation of the United Kingdom

Studies in Space Law

VOLUME 28

The titles published in this series are listed at *brill.com/slaw*

The Space Legislation of the United Kingdom

By

Alexander Simmonds

BRILL | NIJHOFF

LEIDEN | BOSTON

The Library of Congress Cataloging-in-Publication Data is available online at https://catalog.loc.gov
LC record available at https://lccn.loc.gov/2025021259

Typeface for the Latin, Greek, and Cyrillic scripts: "Brill". See and download: brill.com/brill-typeface.

ISSN 1871-7659
ISBN 978-90-04-73254-4 (hardback)
ISBN 978-90-04-73255-1 (e-book)
DOI 10.1163/9789004732551

This book is printed on acid-free paper and produced in a sustainable manner.

Contents

Acknowledgements

With any undertaking of this nature there are many people that one wishes to thank. It is certainly not possible to list them all here, although I'll try my hardest.

Firstly, I'd like to thank Professor Frans von der Dunk for giving me the opportunity to write a monograph for this prestigious series. I am truly honoured to have been allowed to write the first comprehensive work of its kind on the space legislation of my country and I will be forever grateful for having been able to make this contribution to the academic literature within the fascinating and increasingly important discipline of Space Law. I would also like to thank Professor von der Dunk for his time and patience with the editing process, his consistently constructive and helpful feedback and for always being available to me when I required assistance.

Secondly, I would like to give my sincere thanks to Dr Math Noortmann for initially putting me in touch with Professor von der Dunk back in 2021. If it were not for your thoughtful introduction this work may never have been realised. I am eternally grateful to you for this.

Thirdly, I would like to thank my friends and colleagues at Coventry University for their encouragement and support with my early space law work. In particular, I would like to thank Dr Steve Foster for the opportunity to publish my first articles in the Coventry Law Journal. It was through these initial publications that I was able to develop the body of research which would ultimately lead to this work becoming a reality. I would also like to thank Dr Lorenzo Pasculli, now of University College London, for his consistent support and interest in my research, in addition to Dr Gary Betts, Sukhwinder Chhokar, Aaron Cooper, Professor Stephen Hardy, Dr Mahmoud Masud, Dr Stuart MacLennan, Sandrea Maynard, Dr Tony Meacham, and Dr Ben Stanford along with my former colleagues on the SWUPL Team, Dr Lorraine Barron, Simran Basi and Dr Bingdao Wang for all your encouragement and interest during those formative years. I would also like to thank my current friends and colleagues of the School of Law at the University of Dundee along with my students past and present, particularly those I have had the privilege of teaching on the Space Law module at Dundee Law School.

None of our individual achievements exist in a complete vacuum (excuse the pun). Beneath the surface of any accomplishment there are countless people who support every one of us, both directly and indirectly. To this end, I'd also like to give thanks to my mother, Amanda Simmonds (for everything ...), in addition to the friends, colleagues and teachers who have supported me in so many ways throughout my life and career to date. You too have made this work possible in your own immeasurable ways. In this spirit, I would also like to extend my thanks to the Parlour Café of 58 Westport, Dundee for keeping me caffeinated and fed during my Saturday writing sessions of 2023.

Abbreviations

ADHD	Attention deficit hyperactivity disorder
AEE	Assessment of Environmental Effects
ALARP	'as low as reasonably practicable'
ANO	Air Navigation Order
BBC	British Broadcasting Corporation
BIS	British Interplanetary Society
BSB	British Sky Broadcasting
BNSA	British National Space Centre
CAA	Civil Aviation Authority
CAN	Cornwall Airport Newquay
CAP	Civil Aviation Publication
CBA	Cost Benefit Analysis
CEC	Conditional Expected Casualty
CUKAC	Combined United Kingdom-Australian Long-Range Weapons Committee
CNI	Critical National Infrastructure
COMSAT	Communications Satellite Corporation
CONFERS	Consortium for the Execution of Rendezvous and Servicing
COPUOS	Committee on the Peaceful Uses of Outer Space
COSPAR	Committee on Space Research
CPNI	Centre for Protection of National Infrastructure
CRPD	United Nations Convention on the Rights of Persons with Disabilities
EASA	European Union Aviation Safety Agency
EcIA	Ecological Impact Assessment Guidelines
ECSS	European Cooperation for Space Standardization
EESS	Earth Exploration Satellite Services
ESA	European Space Agency
ESN	Earth Station Network
EU	European Union
EURATOM	European Atomic Energy Community
EGNOS	European Geostationary Navigation Overlay Service
EUTELSAT	European Telecommunications Satellite Organisation
FAA	Federal Aviation Administration
FAA-AST	Office of Commercial Space Transportation
GmbH	Gesellschaft mit beschränkter Haftung (Germany – 'company with limited liability')
GNSS	Global Navigation Satellite System

HAZOPS	Hazard and Operability Study
HCoC	Hague Code of Conduct against Ballistic Missile Proliferation
HFD	Hazard Fragmentation Distance
IADC	Inter-Agency Space Debris Coordination Committee
IEMA	Institute of Environmental Management and Assessment
ICAO	International Civil Aviation Organisation
INMARSAT	International Maritime Satellite Organisation
IMSO	International Mobile Satellite Organization
INTELSAT	International Telecommunications Satellite Organisation
ISO	International Organization for Standardization
ITSO	International Telecommunications Satellite Organization
ITU	International Telecommunications Union
LOA	Letter of Authority
MEL	Minimum Equipment List
MFC	Member of Flight Crew
MFTP	Member of Flight Termination Personnel
MMO	Marine Management Organisation
MOU	Memoranda of Understanding
MPL	Maximum Possible Loss
MR	Master of the Rolls
NASA	National Aeronautics and Space Administration
NASP	National Aviation Safety Plan
NGSO	Non-geostationary orbit
Non-FSS	Non-Fixed Satellite Earth Stations
Non-Geo	Non-Geostationary Earth Stations
NOTAMS	Notices to Airmen
NOTMARS	Notice to Mariners
NTB	1963 Treaty Banning Nuclear Weapon Tests in the Atmosphere, in Outer Space and under Water
OCST	Office of Commercial Space Transportation
OES	Operator of Essential Services
Ofcom	United Kingdom Office of Communications
OMP	Oversight and Monitoring Plan
OSA	Outer Space Act 1986
OST	1967 Outer Space Treaty
PACE	Police and Criminal Evidence Act 1984
PES	Permanent Earth Station
RFA	Rocket Factory Augsburg
ROES	Receive-Only Earth Station
SAIA	Space Accident Investigation Authority

SDA	Space Domain Awareness
SFP	Spaceflight Participant
SHA	Ship Hazard Areas
SIA	Space Industry Act 2018
SIR	Space Industry Regulations 2021
SPLOG	Space Launch and Orbit Group
TES	Transportable Earth Stations
TopSat	Tactical Operational Satellite
TNT	Trinitrotoluene
TSA	UK-US Technology Safeguards Agreement
UAS	unmanned aircraft systems
UCTA	Unfair Contract Terms Act 1977
UN	United Nations
UNCLOS	United Nations Convention on the Law of the Sea
UNESCO	United Nations Educational, Scientific and Cultural Organisation
UNOOSA	United Nations Office for Outer Space Affairs (UNOOSA)

CHAPTER 1

Introduction

There have been many interpretations of what 'space law' is. Doctrinally, International space law could be regarded as 'a branch of general (public) international law, a subset of rules, rights and obligations of states within the latter specifically related to outer space and activities in or with respect to that realm'.[1] When framing domestic space legislation, international space law is where national legislatures must first turn. As Professor von der Dunk has written, in an international law context 'states act both as the 'makers' and the 'breakers' of the law. They are not only the main creators of such rules, rights and obligations, they are usually also the subjects of such rules. This essentially is no different for international space law'.[2]

'Space law' as a discrete category of regulation, could legitimately be regarded as somewhat of a fiction. As has been written:

> It is well to keep in mind at all times that, as lawyers, we speak here not of 'space law' but of national and international law concerning activities in outer space. The problems of human and international relationships are essentially the old and persistent ones; it is the milieu which is new. The interactions of the old problems in the constraints of the new setting are what challenge us.[3]

The 'new setting' described above, refers to the days of the Apollo missions, long before the space shuttle and the International Space Station. Today's 'new setting' consists of the proliferation of private actors in the field of space activities along with various new domestic 'space law' regimes across multiple jurisdictions.[4]

Some of them are unlikely candidates for a fully-fledged space program. They may be offering themselves forth as 'flags of convenience'. As has been written, unlike the law of the sea, international space law does not expressly

1 Frans von der Dunk, *International Space Law*, 29, in Frans von der Dunk, Fabio Tronchetti, *Handbook of Space Law*, (Edward Elgar, 2017).

2 *Ibid*, 30.

3 S. Houston Lay and Howard J. Taubenfeld, *The Law Relating to Activities of Man in Space*, (University of Chicago Press/American Bar Association, 1970).

4 See for example, Australia, Luxembourg, Portugal, the United Arab Emirates, Canada etc.

 | DOI:10.1163/9789004732551_002

provide for a 'genuine link' to be demonstrated in respect of space objects registered with the launching state.[5] To attract foreign investment, such regimes may establish skeletal or even token legal frameworks with limited safety requirements to reduce costs and undercut any competitors.[6] Others are very definite in their national ambitions. The United Kingdom is one of these new jurisdictions which has, over the last 6 years, seen a huge expansion of its domestic space legislation.

As Francis Lyall has pointed out:

> There is a central body of 'space law', but the term should be considered as a label attaching to a bucket that contains many different types of rules and regulations rather than as denoting a conceptually coherent singular form of law.[7]

In the case of the United Kingdom, its addition to the contemporary 'bucket' comes in the form of its licensing and safety provisions which, in some cases represent a partial legal transplant of provisions from the United States of America and an importation of other legislative elements from comparable hazardous industries like oil and gas. It is hoped that this work will offer the first examination of the space legislation of the United Kingdom and also challenge traditional interpretations of the role of domestic legislation in implementing and, indeed, to an extent shaping international space law.

Professor Lyall further stated that:

> 'Space law' is akin to 'family law' or 'environmental law', where many different laws are denoted by what they deal with rather than derived from the rational development of a singular legal concept.[8]

Following a 'dualist', as opposed to a 'monist' tradition, the United Kingdom does not treat international law as part of its body of domestic law

5 See Frans von der Dunk, Towards 'Flags of Convenience' in Space?', in Proceedings of the International Institute of Space Law 2012 (IISL) (2013), 811–30, 815. See also, Bin Cheng, 'The Commercial Development of Space: The Need for New Treaties' (1991) 19 J Space L 17, 38–39.

6 As summarised by Larsen and Lyall: 'The 'corporate veil' should be disregarded where buccaneering entrepreneurs, seeking to avoid the supervision which their real 'home state' might well exercise, try to find a less rigorous 'home' for the licensing and supervision of their activities. In space the highest standards should be required in the interests of all.' N8, infra, 88.

7 Francis Lyall, *Space Law: A Treatise*, (Routledge, 2nd edition), 2.

8 *Ibid.*

from the moment of its inception. Instead, it follows a process of internal accommodation.

As was stated in the judgment of Lord Oliver in the case of *JH Rayner (Mincing Lane) Ltd v Department of Trade and Industry*:

> ... as a matter of the constitutional law of the United Kingdom, the Royal Prerogative, whilst it embraces the making of treaties, does not extend to altering the law or conferring rights upon individuals or depriving individuals of rights which they enjoy in domestic law without the intervention of Parliament. Treaties, as it is sometimes expressed, are not self-executing. Quite simply, a treaty is not part of English law unless and until it has been incorporated into the law by legislation.[9]

In this spirit, the new legislation is very much concerned with implementing the United Kingdom's responsibilities under relevant international law. From a practical perspective the new legislation isn't about 'space' or 'outer space' as such but is concerned with the question of how 'space operators' within the United Kingdom can safely reach this destination in accordance with international law, whilst staying within the confines of existing domestic provisions.

This work will chiefly focus on the legislation relating what could broadly be termed 'spaceflight' itself and reflect upon how the law will facilitate this process in a manner which is conducive both to public safety and the safety of those involved whilst implementing international requirements. It will present a rigorous engagement with both the theoretical and practical aspects of space law- with an emphasis upon the former- and a scrutiny of the key legal instruments and regulations themselves. Where possible it will aim to provide a critical analysis of how they have been implemented in practice along with the experiences of operators and other affected stakeholders. Although 'spaceflight' in the context of this work is taken broadly to mean space activities as defined in the new legislation which also includes 'launch', there will be a particular emphasis later in the work on provisions relating to what could be termed the 'human dimensions' of spaceflight. A novel endeavour in the context of United Kingdom legislation generally, the new Act and Regulations are the first statutory provisions enacted as regards informed consent as regards, in the case of an operator's workforce or his/her agents, potentially hazardous occupations and in the case of a space flight participant, potentially hazardous leisure activities. In addition to matters that could be regarded as having a

9 [1990] 2 A.C. 418, 500 (HoL).

'tortious' or 'delictual' flavour, there will also be consideration given to contractual matters relating to these unique transactions. Additionally, there will be some discussion of provisions relating to sustainability with lessons and observations drawn from recent activities. There will also be some critical analysis of the adequacy of the distinction between 'orbital' and 'sub-orbital' activities as a measure of determining the desirability of an Assessment of Environmental Effects. The distinction between such definitions may not be satisfactory in the context of launch activities falling outside certain parameters, and it will be submitted that, in line with the practice of a number of other jurisdictions, further attention is required here. The role of international law will be considered in the context of the new instruments along with the balancing act of framing safety regulations in the context of fostering legitimate business interests in a 'new' and potentially hazardous area. The work will briefly consider the background to international space law and main constituent instruments, although there will not be an in-depth treatment of them, such an examination being beyond the intended scope. Analysis here will be largely limited to those international instruments that have the most influence and bearing on the United Kingdom's new rules. Matters such as the Artemis Accords[10] are not regarded for the purpose of this work as having a particularly significant impact on recent domestic developments and will not, therefore, be the subject of extensive discussion. The historical context of space activities within the United Kingdom will also be briefly outlined along with the background to the new legislation to give context. Contrary to reasonable assumption, the United Kingdom has a vibrant heritage in space matters, notably the partnership with Australia in the 1950's in addition to the development of the 'Skylark' rocket and its working relationships with the United States. Regard should also be given to the United Kingdom's historical involvement with the European Space Agency (ESA) of which it has been a member since 1975.

The new legislative framework is best understood as an expansive licensing platform, with would-be operators expected to navigate and satisfy a range of requirements under it. The United Kingdom Civil Aviation Authority (CAA), the Regulator under the new rules, has described the licensing application process as having to satisfy 7 legislative tests: '1. National Security, 2. International Obligations, 3. National Interest, 4. Financial, 5. Fit and Proper Persons,

10 NASA, The Artemis Accords; Principles for Cooperation in the Civil Exploration and Use of The Moon, Mars, Comets, and Asteroids for Peaceful Purposes, Adopted October 13, (https://www.nasa.gov/wp-content/uploads/2022/11/Artemis-Accords-signed-13Oct2020.pdf?emrc=653a00) accessed 7 October 2024.

6. Safety Assessment, 7. Environment'.[11] This work will largely consider points 1, 2, 3, 6 and 7 although there will inevitably be some overlaps.

In respect of the overall ambitions for the new legislation, the words of the Department for Business, Energy and Industrial Strategy, submitted to the House of Commons Select Committee for Science and Technology' inquiry into Space Strategy and Satellite Infrastructure, give a succinct but comprehensive overview:

> The UK has adopted an outcome-focused Regulatory approach, set to be one of the most modern pieces of space legislation in the world which assesses Operators on persistent demonstration of safety, security and sustainability and allows Operators to choose the methods for mitigating hazards that work best in their circumstances. The regime is non prescriptive, but takes into account established international best practice, lessons from other high hazard safety case-based industries in the UK and recognised industry standards. This flexible and forward-looking approach is well suited to enable a wide-ranging and rapidly evolving commercial space sector whilst also delivering a robust Regulatory regime.[12]

This is a fair and accurate assessment of the United Kingdom's new regime. The framework is indeed comprehensive, and has borrowed from best practice from other jurisdictions, particularly the United States with some of the rules and regulations in UK law being the apparent result of direct legal transplants. Moreover, the sizeable body of regulatory guidance which exists to support the published legal provisions itself borrows from the United States model in certain respects with some key US documents being incorporated by reference. Given the relative novelty of this new regulation, the guidance documents themselves, of which there have by now been at least two generations in some cases, are of particular importance. Whilst they are not 'law' in the strict sense of the word, they are undoubtedly authoritative, and there will be some discussion of their legal status in the context of the legislation.

---

11 The United Kingdom Civil Aviation Authority, Space Launch and Orbit Group, Launch Session, November 2022, <https://www.caa.co.uk/media/l2mmf5ow/november-splog-master_launch_published.pdf > accessed 7 October 2024.

12 Written Evidence Submitted by the Department for Business, Energy and Industrial Strategy (BEIS) (SPA0026) https://committees.parliament.uk/writtenevidence/37181/pdf/ accessed 7 October 2024.

Following an examination and analysis of the new rules as they both implement existing international obligations and intersect with domestic laws, the final part of this work will compare the new laws to those of the United States as the jurisdiction with by far the most well developed national space legislation,[13] along with a number of other jurisdictions.[14] It is hoped that this exercise will give the work a sense of overall completeness as regards its stated mission to present a rounded examination of the space legislation of the United Kingdom. Importantly, it is hoped that it will spark some intense and lively academic and professional discussions on future developments and ultimately be of interest to decision makers and legislators.

Although the United Kingdom regime is in its infancy, there have been a number of licence applications submitted pursuant to it, and even a launch attempt licenced by the Act since its recent inception. Such matters will make for an illustrative overview of how the rules operate in practice. The Assessment of Environmental Effects submitted by Virgin Orbit in respect of their unsuccessful launch in 2023 is highly comprehensive and praiseworthy, for example, as has been the considerable attention paid to airspace requirements by the regulator. Of concern is the potential for fragmentation in practices followed given some of the approaches adopted by operators. For instance, the adoption of certain US standards in respect of the storage of dangerous materials in addition to what could in some instances be regarded as undue or excessive flexibility granted by the guidance in respect of best practice.

As Lord Justice Megaw stated in the famous Contract Law case, *The Mihalis Angelos*, 'One of the essential elements of law is some measure of uniformity. One of the important elements of the law is predictability',[15] and moreover 'Where justice does not require greater flexibility, there is everything to be said for, and nothing against, a degree of rigidity in legal principle.'[16] However, as stated in a COPUOS 2024 working paper on long-term sustainability of outer

---

13 So marked is the difference in the volume of published rules and guidance, that it would not be surprising if as much United States domestic space law existed as the sum-total of the next 3, 4 or even 5 comparable jurisdictions put together.

14 For example, Sweden and Portugal have established regulatory frameworks in this sphere in recent times; see *e.g. Lag om rymdverksamhet*, 1982: 963, 18 November 1982; *National Space Legislation of the World*, VOL. I (2001), at 398; *Space Law – Basic Legal Documents*, E.II.1; 36 *Zeitschrift für Luft- und Weltraumrecht* (1987), at 11; resp. Decree-Law No. 16/2019 (hereafter Portuguese Law on Space Activities), of 22 January 2019; *Official Journal, 1st Series – No. 15*, of 22 January 2019; <https://www.vda.pt/xms/files/05_Publicacoes/2019/Flashes_Newsletters/Portuguese_Space_Act.pdf.> accessed 7 October 2024.

15 *Maredelanto Compania Naviera S.A. v Bergbau-Handel G.M.B.H* (*The Mihalis Angelos*) [1971] 1 Q.B. (EWCA) 164, 205 (Megaw LJ).

16 *Ibid.*

space activities, 'A non-prescriptive, outcome-based authorization regime provides flexibility by design. This flexibility, alongside proactive engagement with the space industry and the broader community, will be key to ensuring that the rapid pace of change in technology and operational practice can be adequately taken into account'[17] In respect of the United Kingdom's fledgling space industry, whilst a significant degree of flexibility is certainly desirable, it is likewise important for reasons of practical and legal certainty along with considerations of safety that a uniform approach is taken in some crucial areas, and, further, that some degree of rigidity be imported to ensure the maintenance of high standards.

At the time of writing, those involved with the space industry in its many guises are still awaiting the government's response to the September 2023 Consultation on Orbital Liabilities, Insurance, Charging and Space Sustainability.[18] Indeed, the author, and Dr Nicholas Ross of Niparo[19] submitted evidence to the consultation on legal issues relating to sustainability, some of which will be detailed later.[20] The changes arising from the consultation could be far reaching and impact on some of the areas covered within this work, and, it is to be hoped, resemble some of the examples of good practice examined in other jurisdictions.

1 The British Space Program – a Brief History

The United Kingdom's involvement with spaceflight can be dated at least as far back as 1932 with the inception of the British Interplanetary Society (BIS)

17 Committee on the Peaceful Uses of Outer Space Scientific and Technical Subcommittee Long-term sustainability of outer space activities: implementation experiences, opportunities for capacity-building and challenges, Working paper by the Chair of the Working Group on the Long-term Sustainability of Outer Space Activities, A/AC.105/C.1/L.410/REV.1, 7 May 2024, para 15, <https://www.unoosa.org/res/oosadoc/data/documents/2024/aac_105c_1l/aac_105c_1l_410rev_1_0_html/AC105_C1_L410Rev01E.pdf> accessed 4 October 2024.

18 United Kingdom Space Agency, Consultation on Orbital Liabilities, Insurance, Charging and Space Sustainability, 14 September 2023, <https://www.gov.uk/government/consultations/consultation-on-orbital-liabilities-insurance-charging-and-space-sustainability/consultation-on-orbital-liabilities-insurance-charging-and-space-sustainability> accessed 10 October 2024.

19 From the Niparo website: 'Niparo is the U.K.'s first sustainable space consultancy and works at the Science-Policy-Industry interface' <https://niparo.org/> accessed 10 October 2024.

20 See chapter 9 and throughout.

who advocated the use of rocket technology for space exploration, a radical idea at the time.[21] A leading pioneer, the BIS made considerable efforts during the 1930s to expand and collaborate with other rocketry inspired groups internationally, including an effort to establish radio communication links between such bodies for the purpose of exchanging ideas in an attempt to foster 'a free exchange of vital information between the rocket societies of the world'.[22] An interesting sidenote here is that legislation regarding actual rockets was on United Kingdom statute books as far back as 1875 in the form of the Explosives Act which outlawed the use of experimental rockets under section 3.[23]

Although early governmental efforts were 'ad hoc' and 'disjointed',[24] the United Kingdom as a state has been directly involved in space activities as far back as 1946, being 'amongst the first group of countries to pioneer space systems'.[25] 1946 also saw representatives of the United States and the United Kingdom travel to Germany to observe the effective capabilities of the notorious V2 missile which had wreaked havoc on London – and other parts of Britain – during the Second World War.[26] Known as 'Operation 'Backfire''[27] this military initiative was the first of many for the United Kingdom during the early years of the Cold War.

Negotiations with the Government of Australia then lead to the establishment of the Combined United Kingdom-Australian Long Range Weapons Committee (CUKAC) which ultimately lead to the establishment of a joint-launching facility at Woomera, Australia.[28] This facility was used for both military and scientific purposes and led to the launch of more than 100 'Skylark' rockets, with the first being launched on the 13th of February 1957.[29] The boosted vehicles launched atop the Skylark rocket were capable of reaching

---

21 Oliver Dunnett, 'Geopolitical Cultures of Outer Space: The British Interplanetary Society, 1933–1965' Geopolitics, 22(2), (2017), 452, 460.

22 *Ibid*, 459.

23 C. 17, 38 and 39 Vict, see s3.

24 James Eberle and Helen Wallace, 'British Space Policy And International Collaboration', Royal Institute of International Affairs, (Routledge 1987), 5.

25 *Ibid*, 15.

26 The War Office, 'Report on 'Operation Backfire''(1946) Volume 1, 4.

27 *Ibid.*

28 Peter Morton, 'Fire Across the Desert; Woomera and the Anglo Australian Joint Project' (1989) Commonwealth of Australia, Defence Science and Technology, 18, < https://www.dst.defence.gov.au/sites/default/files/publications/documents/Fire%20Across%20the%20Desert.pdf> accessed 11 October 2024.

29 *Ibid*, 397.

between 205 and 270 kilometers[30] and some 6 launches were procured by NASA to investigate matters relating to ultra-violet radiation.[31]

Notably, the United Kingdom did not have any legislation relating to actual launch or launch procurement on its statute books at that time. This was, it may be speculated, due to the initial military nature of such operations hence lying within the broad domain of national security without the need or desire for specific rules. Moreover, the prospect of private actors becoming involved in the domain of spaceflight was a remote, if not non-existent, possibility. Indeed, the construction of powerful rockets was originally for the purpose of launching nuclear warheads in light of threats – perceived or otherwise – from the Soviet Union, such powers being derived from established institutional relationships. As has been written by Charles Hill on such rocket projects as the 'Blue Streak' missile delivery system:

> When a need for a particular weapon had been clarified, the Ministry of Defence or the Air Ministry issued an Operational Requirement, or OR. Thus, Blue Streak was OR 1139, the warhead Orange Herald was OR 1142, and so on. The OR could be very specific about some of the requirements: thus, for aircraft it might specify range, altitude, speed, maximum weight, and other such details. The OR would then be circulated to various private firms who would produce appropriate designs. The Ministry would then evaluate rival designs and award the contract to a particular manufacturer. Development was the responsibility of the Ministry of Supply, who dealt directly with the firms concerned. When the winning design had been selected, it would look after the timetable, finances and so on for the project.[32]

The need for specific space legislation was, therefore, largely bypassed with no Parliamentary rules being set down. The risk management and range control functions for the Woomera launches appear to have come within the exclusive remit of the Australian weapons research establishment[33] whereas today rules in respect of such functions are comprehensively detailed under the new legislation. Contemporaneously with these instruments, rocket launches have been

30 *Ibid.*

31 *Ibid*, 399.

32 Charles N. Hill *Vertical Empire, A: History Of The British Rocketry Programme*, (World Scientific Publishing Company 2nd Ed, 2011), 15.

33 N29, 399.

conducted within the United Kingdom[34] in addition to static testing.[35] Owing to limitations on their ceiling,[36] the launches themselves did not trigger the licensing requirements of the Act and Regulations. Nevertheless, these activities justify the need for the new legislation, and, just as importantly, that such legislation be accordingly informed by both industry requirements and the overarching needs of sustainability and public safety.

Regarding other joint ventures, in 1962 the United Kingdom worked in partnership with the United States in the construction and launch of the Ariel 1 satellite which was built by NASA but contained 7 experiments created by United Kingdom universities and industry.[37] Ariel 1 was followed by 5 more in the series culminating in Ariel 6 in 1979.[38] The United Kingdom was engaged in other multilateral endeavours as regards satellites. The Skynet military communications satellite program was developed by Britain in the 1960's,[39] the initial satellites themselves were developed and launched from the United States where the first of which, Skynet 1A launched in November 1969, went into a geostationary orbit over the Indian Ocean to relay messaging to the British Armed Forces.[40] British built satellites later followed[41] including some which were placed into orbit via the space shuttle.[42] There was mixed success regarding the launch of others, some of which did not make it out of the atmosphere.[43] In connection with the Skynet project, 4 British Astronauts were selected for

---

34 Paul Rodger, 'Skylark Nano: Shetland propelled into the rocket age with first launch', The Times, June 16 2020, <https://www.thetimes.com/uk/scotland/article/skylark-nano-shetland-propelled-into-the-rocket-age-with-first-launch-mvptwtdll> accessed 1 October 2024, Eastern Daily Press, 'Norfolk-built rocket launches from Outer Hebrides', 27 August 2021, <https://www.edp24.co.uk/news/20644373.norfolk-built-rocket-launches-outer-hebrides/> accessed 1 October 2024. As discussed later in this work, rocket launches not exceeding a 47km altitude are the subject of Large Rocket Permissions under the Air Navigation Order 2016 as opposed to the Space Industry Act 2018.

35 UK Parliament, Early Day Motions, 'Skyrora and UK's first rocket launch test in 50 years', 20 May 2020, <https://edm.parliament.uk/early-day-motion/57003/skyrora-and-uks-first-rocket-launch-test-in-50-years> accessed. 1 October 2024.

36 N34.

37 Douglas Millard, 'An Overview of United Kingdom Space Activity 1957–1987', 9, (2005) European Space Agency, Publications Division, online at <https://www.esa.int/esapub/hsr/HSR_36.pdf > accessed 10 October 2024.

38 N25.

39 Colin Burgess, *Shattered Dreams: The Lost and Cancelled Space Missions*, (Lincoln, University of Nebraska Press 2019) 147.

40 *Ibid.*

41 *Ibid.*

42 *Ibid*, 148.

43 *Ibid.*

flight on a shuttle mission in connection with the Skynet payload.[44] Unfortunately, their mission was put on hold and eventually cancelled in the wake of the *Challenger* disaster.[45]

The United Kingdom has also been an important part of the European Space Agency[46] and, besides launches, has been involved with many scientific space-related activities. As the United Kingdom Registry of Space Objects attests, satellites originating – at least in part – from the United Kingdom have been launched from locations worldwide such as Kenya, French Guiana and Cape Canaveral on a regular basis since the 1980's.[47] The purpose of such satellites ranges from military communications through to the purely scientific with a wide range of stakeholders from the security, academic and commercial sectors.

In 1985, the now defunct British National Space Centre (BNSC) was established to coordinate national space matters.[48] Rather than functioning as an authoritative entity in its own right, the BNSC was essentially a pivot round which other governmental departments and organisations could center their space activities. As of 1996, the BNSC was working in partnership with a range of governmental bodies such as the Department of Trade and Industry, the Office of Science and Technology, the Ministry of Defence and the Met Office in addition to others.[49] It was not until a year after the establishment of the council that the first piece of space legislation was enshrined in the form of the Outer Space Act 1986.[50] Although the BNSC had wide-ranging ambitions, the government of the day was not prepared to offer the required funding which ultimately led to the scrapping of other plans, including 'Project Zicron', a rumoured spy-satellite program proposed by the Ministry of Defence.[51] The Prime Minister of the day, Margaret Thatcher, had also made a statement to the House of Commons that no further resources could be found for the British

44 *Ibid*, 157.

45 *Ibid*, 165.

46 Convention for the Establishment of a European Space Agency (CSE/CS(73)19, rev.7) 31 December 1975.

47 The United Kingdom Space Agency, 'UK Registry of Space Objects; To comply with international obligations and section 7 of the Outer Space Act 1986' May 2021, <https://assets.publishing.service.gov.uk/media/60a66d4fe90e071b5a7c001a/UK_Registry_of_Space_Objects_May_2021.pdf> accessed 11 October 2024.

48 N38, 3.

49 The British National Space Centre, 'A Forward Plan for Space in the UK', Space Policy, November 1996, 291.

50 The Outer Space Act 1986 c.38.

51 N25, 7.

Space Programme.[52] Other potentially interesting prospects were also lost owing to this reluctance, including a direct broadcasting satellite contract to the United States.[53]

The United Kingdom was, during this time, nonetheless, very much involved as a collaborative partner in respect of space ventures being a signatory to various satellite agreements. INMARSAT, for example, established for maritime satellite communications was based in London where its office remains today.[54] There were also at this time, other collaborative links such as those to EUTELSAT and INTELSAT as regards international communication channels such as telephone and telex.[55] The United Kingdom mostly contributed to space activities and programs through their membership within the European Space Agency during the 1980's, with up to 85% of the civilian space budget going towards associated projects.[56] It is worth noting that British contributions to ESA were among the lowest in 1986 – a 13.1% contribution in total – compared with 27.2% from France and 24.4% from Germany and only a 3.7% workshare in the Ariane 5 rocket program as opposed to 57% from France and 18.2% from Germany[57] which show a less than enthusiastic participation in these initiatives.

There were also a number of other ventures involving the United Kingdom as a 'prime contractor' throughout the 1980's. These included the Inmarsat 2, Olympus, Giotto, ECS 1–5 and Marecs A, and B2 satellites for communication and scientific endeavour,[58] British Aerospace (as it then was) serving as prime contractor for many of these ventures.[59] In terms of military space activity, the United Kingdom was in the 1980's a user of the Skynet system of military communications satellites.[60] The United Kingdom, during this time, was very much an international participant rather than a key stand-alone player, although its previous impact on the world of space telecommunications should not be understated and will be elaborated on later within this work.[61]

As of 1996, the United Kingdom had a wide range of space ambitions which it sought to fulfil with varying degrees of success over the following decade

52 *Ibid*, 8.
53 *Ibid*, 7.
54 *Ibid*, 10.
55 *Ibid*, 10.
56 *Ibid*, 13.
57 *Ibid*, 68.
58 *Ibid*, 69.
59 *Ibid*, 27.
60 *Ibid*, 14.
61 See Chapter 7.

or so. In addition to Earth Observation, ensuring equitable treatment of UK stakeholders in satellite and communications programs and becoming a more prominent player in the European Global Navigation Satellite System were also priorities.[62] There were still no plans to establish an independent launching capability, and further reliance on ESA and extended participation in the Ariane 5 program was instead favoured.[63] A number of other ambitions were the focus of lobbying ESA as opposed to direct action.[64] The overall ethos during the 1990s was said to be 'Putting Space to Work'.[65] As was reported at the time, in fact, 'With the exception of military space communications, public involvement in the UK is confined to support for science applications programmes within the framework of ESA'.[66] As stated, the United Kingdom did not initially devote as many resources to the Ariane project as France or Germany, and by the mid-1990's the feeling was that the achievements of Ariane did not really reflect upon the prowess of the United Kingdom and, at the same time, there was no fruitful cooperation between the United Kingdom and the United States via the often cited 'special relationship'.[67]

As of 2009, the United Kingdom's position was broadly the same, the main fields of activity being classed as 'space science, Earth observation systems (Topsat), military and commercial communications systems and microsatellites'[68] with no domestic launch capability. On the 1st of April 2010 the United Kingdom Space Agency was established,[69] becoming the United Kingdom's designated body for space activities, taking over a number of existing partnerships and agreements with international bodies such as NASA and the ESA and taking charge of the administration of grants.[70] In the words of Lord Drayson, the hope was that it would:

> make the decision-making by government in all aspects of space policy much more joined up, better co-ordinated – a single point within

62 N51, 291.

63 *Ibid*, 292.

64 *Ibid.*

65 Bertrand de Montluc, 'The Changing Face of the European Sector: The policies of Germany, Italy and the United Kingdom' Space Policy 1997 13(1), 10.

66 *Ibid*, 11.

67 *Ibid.*

68 European Space Policy Institute, *Yearbook on Space Policy; 2008.2009: Setting New Trends*, SpringerWienNewYork, 2010, 324.

69 Jonathan Amos, "Muscular' United Kingdom Space Agency Launched', BBC News, 23 March 2010, <http://news.bbc.co.uk/1/hi/sci/tech/8579270.stm> accessed 7 October 2024.

70 The United Kingdom Space Agency (Transfer of Property etc.) Order 2011 No. 822, Article 3, Part 1–2.

> government which has responsibility for making sure that we get everything in alignment such that the space research we do, the space industry that we're building, fulfils its true potential.[71]

The ambitious plans were initially underscored by the delivery of around £230 million pounds a year in funding.[72]

Presently, the United Kingdom space industry is in a healthy position, with a total industry income of £18.9 billion in 2023[73] with the one of the largest shares thereof coming from Direct to Home Broadcasting at 47% of the total income.[74] There was also growth of £673 million in the Space Manufacturing and Space Operations although there was a larger decline of £782 million in the Space Applications and Ancillary Services sectors.[75]

The most high-profile recent developments have come in the form of the establishment of spaceports around the United Kingdom, notably the vertical launch facilities of SaxaVord in the Shetland Islands[76] and SpaceHub Sutherland[77] in addition to the unsuccessful Virgin Orbit Spaceport in Cornwall.[78] In addition to these well-publicised examples, there is also Spaceport 1 based on North Uist, a vertical space port, in addition to Spaceport Machrihanish in Campbelltown, Argyll, set to operate both horizontal and vertical launches along with Glasgow Prestwick set to offer horizontal launch capability.[79] Wales is also represented by Spaceport Snowdonia, which purports to offer horizontal, vertical and rail launches.[80] The United Kingdom space industry is presently strong in areas other than domestic launch, with a number of satellite

---

71 N74.

72 *Ibid.*

73 United Kingdom Space Agency, Corporate report, 'Size and Health of the UK Space Industry 2023, 26 July 2024, <https://www.gov.uk/government/publications/the-size-and-health-of-the-uk-space-industry-2023/size-and-health-of-the-uk-space-industry-2023#state-of-the-uk-space-industry> accessed 11 October 2024.

74 *Ibid.*

75 *Ibid.*

76 Saxa Vord UK Spaceport, <https://saxavord.com/> accessed 18 November 2023.

77 United Kingdom Space Agency, United Kingdom Space Agency Blog <https://space.blog.gov.uk/2022/03/16/on-the-ground-with-space-hub-sutherland-and-orbex/> accessed 7 October 2024.

78 Jonathon Amos, 'UK Space Launch: Historic Cornwall Rocket Launch Ends in Failure' 10 January 2023, <https://www.bbc.co.uk/news/science-environment-64218883> accessed 7 October 2024.

79 Department for Transport, Corporate report, 'A Guide to UK spaceports' 18 April 2018, <https://www.gov.uk/government/publications/brochure-a-guide-to-the-uks-commercial-spaceports/a-guide-to-the-uks-commercial-spaceports> accessed 11 October 2024.

80 *Ibid.*

operators such as OneWeb[81] a telecommunications company which specialises in providing broadband satellite services with a significant number of orbiting units in addition to other satellite and communications providers. There are also interesting developments in innovative fields such as space debris removal which accords with the United Kingdom's signature to the COPUOS[82] and ESA Guidelines[83] relating to debris mitigation. ClearSpace UK[84] and Astroscale[85] are examples of such initiatives. These companies were also granted funding by the United Kingdom Space Agency.[86]

In addition to private sector activity, the United Kingdom government has been active in respect of developing relations with other states as regards space activities and has space partnerships with the United States,[87] Japan[88] and India.[89] The United Kingdom has also partnered with Australia under the 'Space Bridge'[90] agreement which, it is hoped, will advance both nations space

---

81 Website of Eutelsat Oneweb <https://oneweb.net/> accessed 7 October 2024, see also N1119.

82 United Kingdom Government, Committee on the Peaceful Uses of Outer Space (COPUOS): UK statement on legal mechanisms relating to space debris and remediation measures at the 61st Legal Sub-committee, <https://www.gov.uk/government/speeches/uk-statement-on-legal-mechanisms-relating-to-space-debris-and-remediation-measures-at-the-61st-legal-sub-committee-of-copuos> accessed 7 October 2024.

83 The European Space Agency, 'Space Debris by the Numbers' <https://www.esa.int/Space_Safety/Space_Debris/Space_debris_by_the_numbers> accessed 17 October 2024.

84 Clearspace, 'The Clear Mission', <https://clearspace.today/missions/clear> accessed 17 October 2024.

85 Astroscale, 'Building the Future of Space, Sustainably', <https://astroscale.com/> accessed 17 October 2024.

86 United Kingdom Space Agency, 'UK working with global partners to clear up dangerous space debris' 26 October 2021, <https://www.gov.uk/government/news/uk-working-with-global-partners-to-clear-up-dangerous-space-debris> accessed 17 October 2024.

87 Agreement in the form of an exchange of notes between the government of the United Kingdom of Great Britain and Northern Ireland and the government of the United States of America on technology safeguards associated with United States participation in space launches from the United Kingdom, Washington 16 June 2020 <https://assets.publishing.service.gov.uk/media/5f886c5b8fa8f504267c453b/CS_UK_USA_1.2020_USA_Techno_Safeguards_Space_Launches.pdf> accessed 17 October 2024.

88 United Kingdom Space Agency, 'Strengthening Space Ties between the UK and Japan,' 25 June 2021, <https://space.blog.gov.uk/2021/06/25/strengthening-space-ties-between-the-uk-and-japan/> accessed 17 October 2024.

89 Thomas Seal, 'U.K. Launches First Satellites With New Space Partner India,' BloombergQuint, December 18, 2020, <https://www.newsindiatimes.com/u-k-launches-first-satellites-with-new-space-partner-india/.> accessed 17 October 2024.

90 UK–Australia Space Bridge Framework Agreement, 23 February 2021, <https://www.space.gov.au/sites/default/files/media-documents/2024-01/australian-space-agency-uk-space-bridge.pdf> accessed 17 October 2024.

ambitions in future[91] by facilitating 'knowledge exchange' and 'investment'. For the sake of completeness, it is worth pointing out that the United Kingdom has agreements with other states in respect of various other space activities. These include the Memorandum of Understanding (MOU) between the Government of Great Britain and Northern Ireland And the Government of the Faroe Islands On Cooperation on Space Launches From the United Kingdom of Great Britain and Northern Ireland.[92] This is an agreement pursuant and cognizant of international space law and the treaties binding both parties whereby, inter alia, under Article 1 of Paragraph 2, the United Kingdom Government undertakes to ensure that commercial space operators keep the government of the Faroe Islands informed about any space activities which may impact their territory. Under Article 2 operators will also carry out checks on whether any seasonal fishing is taking place in potential drop zones prior to launch activities. Whilst this MOU may seem obscure, it could have particular significance and indeed be acted upon as a result of the operations of SaxaVord in the Shetland Islands whose launch operations may indeed cross over the territory of the Faroe Islands in order to reach a polar-synchronous orbit. This MOU is additional to a whole raft of others signed with Algeria,[93] Argentina[94] and Saudi Arabia.[95] The subjects covered range anywhere from

91 United Kingdom Government, 'Space Bridge' across the world will help UK and Australia get ahead in global space race, 23 February 2021 <https://www.gov.uk/government/news/space-bridge-across-the-world-will-help-uk-and-australia-get-ahead-in-global-space-race> accessed 17 October 2024.

92 Memorandum of Understanding between the Government of Great Britain and Northern Ireland And the Government of the Faroe Islands On Cooperation on Space Launches From the United Kingdom of Great Britain and Northern Ireland, 4 June 2020 London <https://assets.publishing.service.gov.uk/government/uploads/system/uploads/attachment_data/file/914515/Faroe_Islands_Memoranda_of_understanding.pdf> accessed 17 October 2024.

93 Memorandum of Understanding between The United Kingdom Space Agency of the Government of the United Kingdom and the Algerian Space Agency of the Government of the People's Democratic Republic of Algeria Concerning Collaboration on Civil Space Activities, 17 March 2014, Algiers, <https://assets.publishing.service.gov.uk/government/uploads/system/uploads/attachment_data/file/356054/MOU_Algeria_2014.pdf> accessed 17 October 2024.

94 Memorandum of Understanding between the Comision Nacional de Actividades Espaciales and the British National Space Centre on co-operation in the field of space activities, 27 October 1998, London, <https://assets.publishing.service.gov.uk/government/uploads/system/uploads/attachment_data/file/304217/argentina-bnsc-mou.pdf> accessed 17 October 2024.

95 Memorandum of Understanding Between the Saudi Space Commission in Saudi Arabia And United Kingdom Space Agency in the United Kingdom of Great Britain and Northern Ireland on Peaceful Uses of Outer Space, Riyadh, 27 June 2022, <https://assets.publishing

upholding the commitment to the peaceful uses of outer space, to intellectual property matters to guarantees and/or agreements relating to financial or technical assistance or collaboration in general.

The present picture, then, gives a clear indication of the likely future. There is strong governmental support for an active space industry, enthusiasm and involvement from the private sector and a healthy level of activity at the national/supra national level. The central question posed by this work is the extent to which the new legislative regime will see these ambitions realised and whether the approach is adequate without being unnecessarily suffocating to commercial interests. In some respects, as will be seen, the legislative measures adopted are sound. In others there are areas that require improvement. In nearly all areas, consideration should be given to the approach taken by the United States in addition to the work of other legislatures in what is still relatively unknown territory.

.service.gov.uk/government/uploads/system/uploads/attachment_data/file/1065875/ssc-UKSA-mou.pdf> accessed 17 October 2024.

CHAPTER 2

International Space Law

1 A Brief History of Early Space Law

Before discussing the United Kingdom regime in depth, it is important to establish an overview of the larger international context the domestic law lies within. For the purposes of this work, not all aspects of international space law – or the regulation of space generally – are relevant, and there are many more comprehensive works than this one should the reader seek an appraisal of this area.[96] Resultantly, there will be particular focus here on the Liability Convention[97] and the Rescue Agreement[98] in addition to the seminal Outer Space Treaty 1967.[99]

By way of historical context, the need to regulate the use of space was theorised almost 100 years ago by Vladimir Mandl, who correctly anticipated that rocketry systems would not be well-served by a framework of air law.[100] Years later against the backdrop of the Cold War and burgeoning arms race, the overriding need for an international system of space law was succinctly enunciated by J.E.C. Fawcett:

> a vast expansion of scientific research, engineering techniques, industrial capacity and military ambitions; and the multiplier effects of all of these factors operating together. Overriding all is the need that the uses of outer space be for peace not war.[101]

---

96 See, for example, 'The Handbook of Space Law' by Frans von der Dunk and Fabio Tronchetti or Francis Lyall's 'A Treatise on Space Law'.

97 Convention on International Liability for Damage Caused by Space Objects ('Liability Convention'), UNGA Res 2777 (XXVI) (29 Mar 1972); 961 UNTS 187; TIAS 7762; 24 UST 2389; UKTS 1974 No. 16; Cmnd. 5068; ATS 1975 No. 5; 10 ILM 965 (1971).

98 Agreement on the Rescue of Astronauts, the Return of Astronauts and the Return of Objects Launched into Outer Space ('Rescue Agreement'), UNGA Res 2345 (XXII) (22 Apr 1968); 672 UNTS 119; TIAS 6599; 19 UST 7570; UKTS 1969 No. 56; Cmnd. 3786; ATS 1986 No. 8; 7 ILM 151 (1968).

99 Treaty on Principles Governing the Activities of States in Exploration and Use of Outer Space, including the Moon and Other Celestial Bodies, (adopted 27 Jan. 1967, entered into force 10 Oct 1967) 610 UNTS 205.

100 Peter Jankowitsch, *The Background and History of Space Law*, in Frans von der Dunk and Fabio Tronchetti, (eds), *The Handbook of Space Law* (Edward Elgar, 2015) 1.

101 J.E.C. Fawcett, *International Law and the Uses of Outer Space*, Manchester University Press, 1968, 1.

 | DOI:10.1163/9789004732551_003

Fawcett also pointed out that, although space law could be viewed as a rapidly expanding area, it had this in common with other areas at the time. But for its novel subject matter, it could hardly be regarded as unique:

> The uses of outer space have come in a bare decade to be governed by a number of rules of law. In this, they are not alone. The continental shelf, the legal personality of international organisations, and the international protection of human rights, have all exhibited in very different fields, the same kind of rapid evolution ... [102]

Just as it has been written that the Wright Brothers first engine-powered flight in 1903 – a significant technological development – was the catalyst for global discussion, policy-making and adoption of the first international conventions on aviation, namely the Paris Convention of 1919[103] and Chicago Convention of 1944,[104] it was the seminal launch of Sputnik 1- the first human-made satellite to orbit the earth – in 1957, which proved the ultimate catalyst for space law to become a true public international discipline. In Sputnik's wake, UN General Assembly Resolution 1348 of 1958 put forth the 'Question of the Peaceful Use of Outer space'.[105] This was then followed by UN General Assembly Resolution 1472 in December 1959 – on 'International co-operation in the Peaceful uses of Outer Space'.[106] These instruments were advanced by the United Nations Office for Outer Space Affairs (UNOOSA) and the Committee on the Peaceful Uses of Outer Space (COPUOUS), created by UN Resolution.[107] These bodies ensured that the political and legal ramifications of space exploration and usage were kept under debate until formal legal intervention was established. This ultimately prompted the 'Declaration of Legal Principles Governing the Activities of States in the Exploration and Use of Outer Space' as a result of such discourse which ultimately led to the seminal 1967 Outer Space Treaty.

---

102 *Ibid.*

103 Convention relating to the regulation of Aerial Navigation (with additional Protocol), signed at Paris, October 13, 1919; 11 LNTS 173; UKTS 1922 No. 2; ATS 1922 No. 6.

104 Convention on International Civil Aviation, signed at Chicago, 7 December 1944; 15 UNTS 295; TIAS 1591; 61 Stat. 1180; Cmd. 6614; UKTS 1953 No. 8; ATS 1957 No. 5; ICAO Doc. 7300. See also I.H.P. Diederiks-Verschoor, V. Kopal, *Introduction to Space Law* (3rd Ed, 2008) 2, cited in Peter Jankowitsch, *The Background and History of Space Law*, in Frans Von Der Dunk, Fabio Tronchetti, *Handbook of Space Law*, (Edward Elgar, 2017), 4.

105 General Assembly 13th Session, Question of the Peaceful Use of Outer Space, UNGA Res 1348 (XIII) 13 December 1958.

106 General Assembly 14th Session, Convention on International Co-operation in the Peaceful Uses of Outer Space, UNGA Res 1472 (XIV) 12 December 1959.

107 Ibid.

2 Significant International Instruments

The Outer Space Treaty was the first attempt to establish an international framework for space law and is still the most important international instrument on space law to this day. Some have termed it the 'Magna Carta' of Space Law but as Francis Lyall has pointed out, those who use this description betray a poor understanding of the Magna Carta itself.[108] One significant aspect of the Treaty as noted by Jankowitsch,[109] is that unlike terrestrial lands along with the seas as discovered years ago by the advancing armies and navies of nation states, the Outer Space Treaty 'creates a new ethic and an entirely new spirit in the cold relations between states ... outer space, including the moon and all other celestial bodies, is not subject to national appropriation'.[110]

The extent to which this remains true has become hotly debated in more recent times with the proliferation of commercial actors moving into this field and interest in ventures such as asteroid mining and exploitation of the moon's resources.[111] Some of the broader provisions of the Treaty are not directly relevant to this work, but it suffices to say that they also extend to preventing the orbiting of weapons of mass destruction in an effort to safeguard and promote the peaceful uses of outer space. The Treaty remains the most widely endorsed space law instrument with 112 parties and 24 signatories[112] to date. For states undertaking space activities of any sort, the 1967 treaty is a very important agreement. Regardless of the extent of a state's ambitions, the most important overall provision for national legislatures is Article VI:

> States Parties to the Treaty shall bear international responsibility for national activities in outer space, including the moon and other celestial bodies, whether such activities are carried on by governmental agencies or by non-governmental entities, and for assuring that national activities are carried out in conformity with the provisions set forth in the present Treaty. The activities of non-governmental entities in outer space,

108 N8, 49.

109 N105.

110 *Ibid*, 5.

111 See Fabio Tronchetti, *The exploitation of natural resources of the moon and other celestial bodies: a proposal for a legal regime* (Nijdorff, Boston, 2009).

112 United Nations Office for Disarmament Affairs, Treaties, Treaty on Principles Governing the Activities of States in the Exploration and Use of Outer Space, including the Moon and Other Celestial Bodies <https://treaties.unoda.org/t/outer_space> accessed 18 November 2023; AC105_C2_2023_CRP03E.pdf (unoosa.org).

> including the moon and other celestial bodies, shall require authorization and continuing supervision by the appropriate State Party to the Treaty.[113]

The United Kingdom's new licensing regime, therefore, represents an effort to safeguard international obligations under the treaty by ensuring that 'non-governmental entities' – private actors etc – act in accordance with the treaty itself. Also, as under Article VII, the state is strictly liable for damage occasioned to another state as a result of space activities carried out within the launching state.

Article VI appears to have had the most impact on the United Kingdom's legislative agenda with most focus seemingly being brought to bear on the licensing provisions. There are other significant Treaty aims which also appear to have been actioned by the recent raft of legislation too. Efforts to safeguard the 'peaceful use of outer space' have been seemingly advanced by the provisions relating to security at spaceports in pursuance of other obligations such as export controls regarding weapons of mass destruction or their potential components.[114] Moreover, launched payloads are ultimately subject to the authorisation of the Secretary of State and there are extensive monitoring and enforcement provisions with inspectors having broad powers which could, theoretically, avoid the launch of materials deemed contrary to the Articles aims.

In addition to the broad safety requirements imparted by the Treaty, there is also a more limited environmental dimension under Article IX which requires states to avoid 'adverse changes in the environment of the earth resulting from the introduction of extraterrestrial matter and, where necessary, (…) adopt appropriate measures for this purpose.'. It is highly debatable as to whether this provision requires launching states to adopt measures to avoid harm to the environment of earth that does not result from the introduction of such 'extra-terrestrial matter'. In any case, there are more immediately pressing environmental concerns arising from terrestrial greenhouse gas emissions. Its observance is still required by national legislatures, and it is of interest to note that no UK provision satisfactorily addresses this requirement as will be discussed.

It should also be noted that the 1967 Treaty was not the first binding international instrument to mention outer space. Regard should be had to the Partial

113 N104, Art 6.

114 United Nations Security Council Resolution 1540, 28 April 2004 (S/RES/1540), see also the Missile Technology Control Regime <https://mtcr.info/> accessed 18 November 2023.

Nuclear Test Ban Treaty of 1963[115] under which parties agreed to prohibit the testing of nuclear weapons, *inter alia*, in outer space. In a peripheral sense, the security measures within the United Kingdom's space legislation could also be said to give effect to these obligations.

The Outer Space Treaty was followed by the 1968 Agreement on the Rescue of Astronauts, the Return of Astronauts and the Return of Objects Launched into Outer Space[116] (the 'Rescue Agreement') which obliged states to render assistance to both those in peril beyond the atmosphere and undertake the prompt return of any space object (or part thereof) that may inadvertently find its way into their territory. The 1972 Convention on International Liability for Damage Caused by Space Objects[117] (the 'Liability Convention') followed. Importantly, this instrument established the principle that 'A launching State shall be absolutely liable to pay compensation for damage caused by its space object on the surface of the Earth or to aircraft in flight.'[118] This provision, with encouragement from the 2013 United Nations Resolution on national space legislation,[119] has had much influence on national legislatures as private actors seek to take to the skies and beyond, generating the need for governments to ensure that there are protections in place for their own citizens in addition to those from other jurisdictions as provided for in the Convention. Although the wording of Article II is extremely broad, its application is tapered by Article VII which, underscoring the 'inter-state' nature of the Convention, excludes 'damage caused by a space object of a launching State to: (a) nationals of that launching State' and under Article VII (b), participating foreign nationals.

This in turn has led to many different attempts to grapple with the question of liability for domestic space operators – should there be a monetary cap in place and to what extent should the state be on hold to 'bail out' operators in the event of an unfortunate mishap? The question is not easy to resolve – if the law states that there is unlimited liability on the part of the operator this could scare potential investors or have the effect of making insurance difficult to obtain or impossible if a space activity is deemed high risk. As will be shown later in this work, space faring states – or at least those with domestic legal

115 Treaty banning nuclear weapon tests in the atmosphere, in outer space and under water, No 6964 Moscow, 10 October 1963; 480 UNTS 43; TIAS 5433; 14 UST 1313; UKTS 1964 No. 3; ATS 1963 No. 26.

116 N103.

117 N102.

118 *Ibid*, Art 2.

119 Resolution 68/74 adopted by the General Assembly on 11 December 2013, Recommendations on national legislation relevant to the peaceful exploration and use of outer space.

infrastructure pertaining to space travel – do not take a uniform approach to this matter.

Next came the 1975 Convention on Registration of Objects Launched into Outer Space[120] (the 'Registration Convention') requiring that all states party establish a registry for objects launched or procured for launch into space. This was implemented in the United Kingdom via the Outer Space Act 1986 which required the establishment of a registry of space objects under Section 7. In anticipation of local space activities, Section 7 was amended by the Space Industry Act 2018[121] to include space objects launched from both within and outside the United Kingdom.[122] The local catalogue of UK space objects is maintained by the United Kingdom Space Agency and can be perused online[123] whilst the United Nations Office for Outer Space Affairs maintains an online database of such objects pursuant to the treaty.[124]

Lastly in the treaty series came the 1979 Agreement Governing the Activities of States on the Moon and Other Celestial Bodies(the 'Moon Agreement').[125] Of little particular relevance to the United Kingdom's new space legislation, it is also the least widely ratified of the core instruments. In addition, there are a raft of other international agreements on the use of outer space which have been ratified by the United Kingdom,[126] including the 1963 Treaty Banning Nuclear Weapon Tests in the Atmosphere, in Outer Space and under Water (NTB), the 1971 Agreement Relating to the International Telecommunications Satellite Organization (ITSO),[127] the 1975 Convention for the Establishment of a European Space Agency (ESA),[128] the 1976 Convention on the International

---

120 Convention on Registration of Objects Launched into Outer Space, UNGA Res 3235 (XXIX) (14 January 1975).

121 The Space Industry Act 2018 c.5.

122 *Ibid*, s70(1).

123 N49.

124 United Nations Office for Outer Space Affairs, 'Online Index of Objects Launched into Outer Space', <https://www.unoosa.org/oosa/osoindex/search-ng.jspx?lf_id=> accessed 27 November 2023.

125 UNGA Res 34/68 (5 December 1979).

126 United Nations Office for Outer Space Affairs 'Status of International Agreements Relating To Activities in Outer Space As At 1 January 2020', (2020) United Nations, 10, <https://www.unoosa.org/documents/pdf/spacelaw/treatystatus/TreatiesStatus-2020E.pdf> accessed 3 June 2021.

127 Agreement relating to the International Telecommunications Satellite Organization, Washington, 20 August 1971; 1220 UNTS 21; TIAS 7532; 23 UST 3813; UKTS 1973 No. 80; Cmnd. 4799; ATS 1973 No. 6; 10 ILM 909 (1971).

128 Convention for the establishment of a European Space Agency (CSE/CS (73)19, rev.7), Paris, 30 May 1975; 1297 UNTS 161; UKTS 1981 No. 30; Cmnd. 8200; 14 ILM 864 (1975); *Space Law – Basic Legal Documents*, C.I.1.

Maritime Satellite Organization (IMSO),[129] the 1982 Convention Establishing the European Telecommunications Satellite Organization (EUTELSAT),[130] the 1983 Convention for the Establishment of a European Organization for the Exploitation of Meteorological Satellites (EUMETSAT)[131] and the 1992 International Telecommunication Constitution and Convention.[132] Similarly there have been many other principles adopted by the UN General Assembly, namely the 'Broadcasting Principles,'[133] the 'Remote Sensing Principles,'[134] the 'Nuclear Power Sources Principles'[135] and the 'Benefits Declaration',[136] none of which have a significant bearing on this work although there will be some discussion of the Broadcasting Principles in relation to telecommunications law.

Besides the formal treaties and other related instruments, space law, as a corpus, consists of domestic space law regimes along with other soft-law provisions such as Memoranda of Understanding and Working Arrangements/informal standards.[137] The most recent instrument to join the growing plethora of Space-related provisions are the Artemis Accords,[138] described on their face as 'Principles for Cooperation in the Civil Exploration and Use of the Moon, Mars, Comets And Asteroids for Peaceful Purposes'. As set out in section 1, 'The principles set out in these Accords are intended to apply to civil space activities

---

129 Convention on the International Maritime Satellite Organisation, London, 3 September 1976; 1143 UNTS 105; TIAS 9605; 31 UST 1; UKTS 1979 No. 94; Cmnd. 6822; ATS 1979 No. 10; 15 ILM 1052 (1976).

130 Convention Establishing the European Telecommunications Satellite Organization, Paris, 15 July 1982; UKTS 1990 No. 15; Cm. 956; Cmnd. 9069; *Space Law – Basic Legal Documents*, C.II.1.

131 Convention for the establishment of a European organisation for the exploitation of meteorological satellites ('EUMETSAT'), Geneva, 24 May 1983; 1434 UNTS 3.

132 Constitution and Convention of the International Telecommunication Union, Geneva, 22 December 1992; 1825 UNTS 1; UKTS 1996 No. 24; Cm. 2539; ATS 1994 No. 28; Final Acts of the Additional Plenipotentiary.
Conference, Geneva, 1992 (1993), at 1; resp. 1825 UNTS 1; UKTS 1996 No. 24; Cm. 2539; ATS 1994 No. 28; Final Acts of the Additional Plenipotentiary Conference, Geneva, 1992 (1993), at 71.

133 'The Principles Governing the Use by States of Artificial Earth Satellites for International Direct Television Broadcasting', UNGA Res 37/92 (10 December 1982).

134 'The Principles Relating to Remote Sensing of the Earth from Outer Space', UNGA Res 41/65 (3 December 1986).

135 'The Principles Relevant to the Use of Nuclear Power Sources in Outer Space', UNGA Res 47/68 (14 December 1992).

136 'The Declaration on International Cooperation in the Exploration and Use of Outer Space for the Benefit and in the Interest of All States, Taking into Particular Account the Needs of Developing Countries', UNGA Res 51/122 (13 December 1996).

137 N77, 80.

138 N11.

conducted by the civil space agencies of each Signatory. These activities may take place on the Moon, Mars, comets, and asteroids, including their surfaces and subsurfaces, as well as in orbit of the Moon or Mars, in the Lagrangian points for the Earth-Moon system, and in transit between these celestial bodies and locations.'[139] Resultantly, there is very little effect on national legislatures in respect of establishing or maintaining their earth-bound space infrastructure, particularly those who are unlikely in the immediate term to be undertaking the expected kind of 'Langrangian' operations envisaged.

In light of recent significant political changes within the United Kingdom, specifically the decision to leave the European Union, whilst the United Kingdom was ejected from the Galileo satellite navigation system[140] and EGNOS satellite,[141] post Brexit it has since been welcomed back in to such ventures and remains committed to future membership of the European Space Agency.[142]

In summary, the most important international standards as regards the United Kingdom's legislative aims are the Outer Space Treaty 1967 and the Liability Convention and, to a somewhat lesser extent, the Rescue Agreement. Whilst other agreements are no doubt vital, where required, this work will focus largely upon the transposition of the more significant treaty provisions outlined. Regard will also be had where relevant to items such as the COPUOS Space Debris Mitigation Guidelines[143]and the extent to which this has impacted upon on the ways in which the legislature have framed its approach.

---

139 *Ibid.*

140 Jonathon Amos, BBC News, 'The UK bids farewell to EU's Galileo System', 14 January 2021, <https://www.bbc.co.uk/news/science-environment-55665537> accessed 11 October 2024.

141 Royal Institute of Navigation, 'Withdrawal of EGNOS for UK Users', 11 July 2021, <https://rin.org.uk/news/572850/Withdrawal-of-EGNOS-for-UK-users.htm> accessed 11 October 2024.

142 The Institution of Engineering & Technology, 'UK Commits to Continuing Membership of European Space Agency,' The Institution of Engineering & Technology, November 29, 2019.

143 Space Debris Mitigation Guidelines of the Committee on the Peaceful Uses of Outer Space, UNOOSA, 2007, endorsed by the United Nations General Assembly by Resolution 62/217.

CHAPTER 3

The Legislative Framework Underpinning the United Kingdom Space Industry – an Introduction to Its Composition and Regulatory Ethos

The Space Industry Act and accompanying Regulations were brought into being primarily to facilitate the emergence of a new industry within the United Kingdom. As set out, these provisions were designed in such a way as to, primarily, give life to the United Kingdom's international obligations and, further, to ensure public safety. Three of the most important facets of the new rules are the licensing measures, the proliferation of guidance documents and the role of the regulator – in this case, the CAA. This chapter will seek to give an overview of these matters in their domestic law context as they form an important background for the discussion of the legislation more specifically.

In the context of United Kingdom space law, licensing is where the rubber meets the road. Licensing, in this context, represents the manner in which the government controls and monitors the ways in which private entities conduct space activities from within, and outside of, the United Kingdom.[144] In addition to provisions relating to launching activities specifically, it is also how the United Kingdom ensures compliance with other dimensions of the Outer Space Treaty, such as ensuring the peaceful uses of outer space through ground-based security measures.

The licensing structure is itself buttressed by monitoring and enforcement measures which are also provided for within the domestic constituent instruments and will be examined in more detail later in this work. Whilst the power of inspectors as regards enforcement and monitoring could be regarded as prescriptive, the consequences for operators of breaching any of the rules is often at the discretion of the Secretary of State. Such consequences can extend to the revocation of licences completely or the imposition of further conditions. The desirability of having a more prescriptive regime is questionable since, whilst this may provide certainty, it could unduly curtail the powers of the regulator and possibly incentivise rule-breaking, if, say, on a certain economic analysis, the paying of a set fine would be more desirable than following instructions.

The rules themselves are helpfully fleshed out with reference to a number of comprehensive guidance documents available via the regulator's website. To

144 UK nationals undertaking space activities outside the United Kingdom are licenced under the Outer Space Act 1986, N53, s1(2).

 | DOI:10.1163/9789004732551_004

make sense of the importance of these documents, it is valuable to understand their legal context as 'soft law'. Whilst it has been written that soft law does not have any agreed definition,[145] in international law it has been described as 'binding legal norms that are vague and open-ended and therefore (arguably) neither justiciable nor enforceable; non-binding norms, such as political or moral obligations, adopted by states; and norms promulgated by non-state actors'.[146] For the purposes of this analysis of UK space legislation, the working definition of 'soft law' will broadly be framed as guidance and other standards falling out with the core legislative enactments, but which could still have significant legal impact. At surface level, the CAA guidance documents provide a useful best-practice repository. An unintended consequence could be the fragmentation of practice amongst operators if the effect is to allow them to pick and choose which rules to follow. Whilst this may seem desirable from an operational and commercial standpoint, it should not be allowed to stand in the way of any relevant safety concerns or otherwise come at the expense of sustainability. The legal status of these documents will be briefly outlined in this chapter. The reader is encouraged to have regard to the approach of the United States whereby relevant rules of the Federal Aviation Administration (FAA) are incorporated into national legislation.

Finally, the role of the CAA as the regulator of the industry will be considered. In the early days of the new legislation, there was some degree of uncertainty as to which body would be appointed as the regulator but the 2021 Space Industry Regulations confirmed the CAA as such. Previously responsible for aviation matters alone, the CAA seems a logical choice owing to its experience in such related matters and have certainly embraced their new responsibilities with a great degree of enthusiasm. There are several specialist space teams at the CAA and, so far, there seem to have been no serious operational issues but there will be further discussions of this later in this work.

1 Licensing – Where the Rubber Meets the Road

Before looking at the domestic instruments in detail, it is important to establish some of the rules which pertain to 'licences' generally to understand the significance (and limitations) of UK space law specifically.

145 Barnali Choudhury, 'Balancing Soft and Hard Law for Business and Human Rights' International and Comparative Law Quarterly 67, 2018, 961–986 at 964.

146 Jaye Ellis, 'Shades of Grey: Soft Law and the Validity of Public International Law' Leiden Journal of International Law, 25 (2012), 313–334, 316.

The earliest type of licensing in the United Kingdom was in relation to alcohol and has been said to have come about in 1552.[147] The main justification for licensing of all types has consistently been for the avoidance of harm, most usually physical harm.[148] The best-known form of licensing across many jurisdictions is likely to be licences provided in respect of driving. The justification for state intervention in this respect was stated by Street to be as follows:

> If a motorist drives dangerously, no doubt he can be fined, or even imprisoned, under the criminal law. If he disables a pedestrian through his careless driving, of course that pedestrian can sue in the courts for damages. But that is not enough; we want to keep down the number of road accidents. And so we licence drivers; we won't let them drive without a licence, and we require them to pass a test before they can have the licence. We believe that we will reduce the number of accidents if drivers have to prove their competence before they drive alone – we are not content to leave it to the law to punish and redress grievances after harm has been done.[149]

In addition to the sale of alcohol and road usage, Street cites other examples of activities and establishments which legally require licences such as passenger-carrying aircraft, boat tours,[150] nursing homes, theatres, riding stables, children's homes, taxis,[151] hypnotists,[152] usage of firearms[153] and even 'ice cream manufacturing'.[154] With the exception of passenger-carrying aircraft – in an extrinsic sense – such activities could be regarded as completely different in nature and scope to those associated with space activity, but the rationale for imposing a licensing regime is essentially the same – the avoidance of harm by taking proactive measures and the imposition of standards.

Many activities which require licensing are directly related to the livelihood of applicants. Sometimes the applicant's sole source of income might be

147 Harry Street, 'Justice in the Welfare State', (2nd edn, 1985) Hamlyn Lectures; Williams 'Control by Licensing' (1967) CLP, 70.

148 *Ibid*. 71.

149 *Ibid*.

150 *Ibid*.

151 *Ibid*. 77.

152 *Ibid*. 77.

153 *Ibid*. 79.

154 *Ibid*. 72.

dependent upon the holding of a certain licence, taxi drivers, for example.[155] Resultantly, any interference with a licence or a refusal to grant one could have serious consequences. Therefore, licensing can involve significant public law dimensions such as 'legitimate expectation'[156] and, given the potential importance of such activities, decisions relating to licensing can be protected by rules of 'natural justice'. Given its centrality to licensing decisions, it is perhaps instructive to observe briefly the parameters of this concept as it applies to relevant hearings.

'Natural justice' – or 'procedural fairness' as it is often interchangeably referred to was defined in *Byrne v Kinematograph Renters Society Ltd*:[157]

> ... the person accused should know the nature of the accusation made; secondly that he should be given an opportunity to state his case; and thirdly, of course, that the tribunal should act in good faith.

Mr Justice Megarry also stated these rules succinctly in the case of *Fountaine v Chesterton*[158] as being:

1. The right to be heard by an unbiased tribunal.
2. The right to have notice of the charged misconduct.
3. The right to be heard in answer to those charges.

The case of *R v Barnsley Metropolitan Borough Council, ex p Hook*[159] presents a cogent example of this whereby a market stall-holder was 'banned for life' from trading under an oral licence at Barnsley Market in South Yorkshire. It was held that this decision, given that it was important *inter alia* to respect the applicant's right to earn a living, attracted the rules of natural justice and that such rules had been breached – in particular the first rule set out by Mr Justice Megarry, often expressed in Latin as *nemo debet esse judex in causa propria*[160] – since the market manager had acted in a role akin to a 'prosecutor' against Mr Hook in this matter and, crucially, was also at least partly responsible for making the decision against him.[161] The body making the decision, therefore, had offended the common law rule against bias.

---

155 See also *Southampton Port Health Authority v Seahawk Marine Foods* [2002] EWCA Civ 54, [2002] EHLR 15.

156 See *McInnes v Onslow Fane* [1978] 1 WLR 1520 (EWHC).

157 [1958] 1 WLR 762 (EWHC).

158 (1968) 112 Sol Jo 690.

159 [1976] 1 WLR 1052 (EWCA).

160 *Ibid*, 1060.

161 *Ibid*, 1057.

This has significant implications for the new space industry rules. It imports a considerable public law aspect which applicants and licencees could potentially find themselves availing themselves of should one of the licensing requirements or conditions be called into question. Of course, there are the Space Industry (Appeals) Regulations[162] which were created under the Space Industry Act to specifically cater for such matters but by no means does this extinguish the right of an applicant to have a particular decision judicially reviewed. Providing that the decision maker is a public body, such a review could be brought upon the basis of an infringement of a rule of natural justice or the denial of a 'legitimate expectation' to carry out (or continue carrying out) an activity subject to licensing rules should the required conditions be satisfied.

As stated at the outset of this work, whilst the new space instruments are concerned with a novel subject matter, the instruments and their 'guardian', the CAA, are by no means a unique model of execution. Licensing authorities that could be said to be similar to the one servicing the space industry are the Oil and Gas Authority established under the Energy Act 2016[163] which has the power to grant licences in addition to regulatory functions, so the legal landscape as it pertains to the space industry is far from unique. It is worth considering that there were other means by which the space industry could have been licenced. The Petroleum Act 1998,[164] for example, required the insertion of 'model clauses' under section 4 – at the regulator's discretion – which were comprehensively set out under Schedule 1. Operating in a similar way to an implied term, such clauses may become a requirement of space legislation as time goes by and commercial practices become realised. Such crystallization within the industry will inevitably bring regulatory refinement in some form or another – the petrol industry predates the space industry by many years, particularly in the United Kingdom – and Model Clauses were a feature of legislation dating back to 1935.[165]

All space activities under the Act and Regulations must be licenced, and the type of licence granted depends on the type of activity the prospective licencee wishes to conduct. The licences available are a 'Launch Operator Licence', a 'Spaceport Licence', a 'Range Control Licence' or a 'Return Operator Licence'.[166]

162 SI 2021 816.
163 C20 Part 1.
164 C17.
165 See s6(1)(d).
166 N127, Part 1.

Under Regulation 6 of the Space Industry Regulations 2021,[167] certain individuals are ineligible to apply for such licences, specifically undischarged bankrupts or those under related sanctions, individuals disqualified from being a company director and those convicted of certain criminal offences.[168]

As a condition of such licences being granted, the licencee must subsequently appoint a range of management staff to ensure the safe and effective running of the licenced activity. These are an 'accountable manager', a 'safety manager' and a 'security manager'.[169] This is similar for Range Control Licencees who must appoint a 'range safety manager' a 'range operations manager', an 'accountable manager', a 'security manager' and a 'training manager'. These managers must also meet the same eligibility criteria as the licencee under Regulation 5(1)(b) and (c). Under Regulation 12, licencees are responsible for ensuring that the appointees 'have the necessary resources and means to carry out their duties'. As would be expected, this is a standard provision which is reflected in a number of other jurisdictions. Luxembourg, for example provides that, specifically as regards 'exploitation' of Space Resources, that:

> The Operator to be authorised shall have a robust scheme of financial, technical and statutory procedures and arrangements through which the exploration and utilization mission, including the commercialisation of space resources are planned and implemented. The Operator to be authorised shall furthermore have a robust internal governance scheme, which includes in particular a clear organisational structure with well defined, transparent and consistent lines of responsibility, effective processes to identify, manage, monitor and report the risks it is or might be exposed to, and adequate internal control mechanisms, including sound administrative and accounting procedures, as well as control and security arrangements for its technical systems and applications.[170]

Whilst it is perhaps surprising to learn that Luxembourg has any degree of space regulation given its size and absence of any visibly significant space activity, the rest of its legal provisions are basic and do not come close to

167 The Space Industry Regulations 2021 No. 792.

168 R6(1)(a).

169 R7(1), (a)–(c).

170 Law of 20 July 2017 on the Exploitation and Use of Space Resources (Luxembourg), Article 7(2).

approximating the degree of specificity or volume of the UK Space Industry Act and the accompanying Regulations.[171]

In respect of the exploitation of space resources more generally, it is perhaps important to note that the United Kingdom has not specifically legislated for this. Whilst for many years there were various questions regarding whether such exploitation was permitted under the terms of the 1967 Treaty, the United States in 2015 passed its Commercial Space Launch Competitiveness Act[172] in respect of the same.

Regarding the teeth behind the licensing regime, as will be covered in more detail later, there are numerous powers of inspection and enforcement. If certain circumstances change, licencees must, under pain of criminal conviction, inform the regulator of any changes regarding the status of such appointees such as death or having left their employ.[173]

The licensing rules imported by these recent developments, therefore, intersect with a wider common law heritage. Licences provided to operators have the potential to be exposed to actions at common law should certain procedural elements not be followed. Just as importantly, public law challenges could emanate from other individuals deemed to have 'standing'. Judicial review actions could also be brought in respect of certain licensing decisions too which could prove challenging.

2 Status of the Official Guidance Documents

As stated at the outset of this chapter, one defining aspect of the United Kingdom's new legislation is its extensive reliance on guidance documents to support operators. For example, Part 4 of the Space Industry Regulations deals specifically with risk in the licensing context, in particular risks to those not directly involved in spaceflight activities – that is, not crew or spaceflight participants. Section 1 of Chapter 2 also imposes a positive obligation on the applicant to take steps to 'ensure that risks are as low as reasonably practicable'. There is extensive guidance[174] on this matter which, in and of itself, will be examined at a later stage.

171 See also the Law of 15 December 2020 on Space Activities (Luxembourg) for example.

172 Commercial Space Launch Competitiveness Act 51 USC 10101(US).

173 R 14 (1)–(2).

174 The United Kingdom Civil Aviation Authority, 'Guidance and Resources', <https://www.caa.co.uk/space/guidance/> accessed 12 October 2024.

Since the issued guidance is so crucial to the lawful facilitation of space activities, a significant question is the extent to which such guidance can be said to be legally binding. There are a range of instructive cases that assess the status of guidance which may be useful in arriving at an informed understanding of where they fit into the regulatory regime. The status of guidance under section 7 of the Local Authority and Social Services Act 1970[175] was considered by Sedley J in the case of *R v Islington Borough Council, ex parte Rixon*[176]

> Clearly guidance is less than direction, and the word 'general' emphasises the non-prescriptive nature of what is envisaged ... In my judgment Parliament ... did not intend local authorities to whom ministerial guidance was given to be free, having considered it, to take it or leave it. Such a construction would put this kind of statutory guidance on a par with the many forms of non-statutory guidance issued by departments of state. ... in my view Parliament by section 7(1) has required local authorities to follow the path charted by the Secretary of State's guidance, with liberty to deviate from it where the local authority judges on admissible grounds that there is good reason to do so, but without freedom to take a substantially different course.

This would indicate that there is a distinction to be drawn between guidance of the Secretary of State and other types of guidance. Guidance issued by the CAA, not being of the former type, may be said to fall within the latter category.

The statements of Lord Bingham and Lord Hope of Craighead in *R (Munjaz) v. Mersey Care NHS Trust*[177] are also important. This case regarded a Code issued under section 118 of the Mental Health Act 1983 relating to the seclusion of psychiatric patients rather than the statutory guidance as was considered in the *Rixon* decision. At paragraph 21 Lord Bingham said:

> It is in my view plain that the Code does not have the binding effect which a statutory provision or a statutory instrument would have. It is what it purports to be, guidance and not instruction ... It is not instruction, but it is much more than mere advice which an addressee is free to follow or not as it chooses. It is guidance which any hospital should consider with great care, and from which it should depart only if it has cogent reasons for doing so. Where, which is not this case, the guidance

175 C 42.
176 (1998) 1 CCLR 119, [23] (Sedley J) (EWCA).
177 [2005] UKHL 58, [2006] 2 A.C. 148 [21] (Bingham LJ).

> addresses a matter covered by section 118(2), any departure would call for even stronger reasons. In reviewing any challenge to a departure from the Code, the court should scrutinise the reasons given by the hospital for departure with the intensity which the importance and sensitivity of the subject matter requires.

Departure from guidance not originating from the Secretary of State but still being of great importance, therefore, would still have to be reasonable in the circumstances. Going further, at Paragraph 69 Lord Hope of Craighead stated:

> The Court of Appeal said in para 76 of its judgment that the Code is something that those to whom it is addressed are expected to follow unless they have good reason for not doing so: see R v Islington London Borough Council, ex p Rixon (1996) 1 CCLR 119, per Sedley J at p 123. Like my noble and learned friend Lord Bingham of Cornhill I would go further. They must give cogent reasons if in any respect they decide not to follow it. These reasons must be spelled out clearly, logically and convincingly. I would emphatically reject any suggestion that they have a discretion to depart from the Code as they see fit. Parliament by enacting section 118(1) has made it clear that it expects that the persons to whom the Code is addressed will follow it, unless they can demonstrate that they have a cogent reason for not doing so. This expectation extends to the Code as a whole, from its statement of the guiding principles to all the detail that it gives with regard to admission and to treatment and care in hospital, except for those parts of it which specify forms of medical treatment requiring consent falling within section 118(2) where the treatment may not be given at all unless the conditions which it sets out are satisfied.

In the opinion of Lord Hope, therefore, adherence to the code in question meant 'global' adherence in the sense that the letter and spirit should be followed in the absence of good reasons.

The situation in respect of such a departure from guidance was also the subject of a more recent judicial pronouncement in *R. (on the application of X) v Tower Hamlets*[178] which seems to support this interpretation:

> In summary, therefore, the guidance does not have the binding effect of secondary legislation and a local authority is free to depart from it, even

178 *R. (on the application of X) v Tower Hamlets LBC*, 2013 WL 617504 at para 35 (EWHC).

> 'substantially'. But a departure from the guidance will be unlawful unless there is a cogent reason for it, and the greater the departure, the more compelling must that reason be. Conversely a minor departure from the letter of the guidance while remaining true to its spirit may well be easy to justify or may not even be regarded as a departure at all.

The guidance in this matter was issued by the Royal College of Paediatrics and Child Health, not the Secretary of State as was the case in *Rixxon*. Further explanation was given at paragraph 40:

> The President of the Royal College of Paediatrics and Child Health has issued from time to time guidance entitled 'Making Decisions to Limit Treatment in Life-limiting and Life-threatening Conditions in Children; a Framework for Practice' (the Guidance). This guidance was updated in March 2015 and is, as it is described in the foreword, 'A live document and not an end point for discussion and learning'. The Guidance is exactly that. It is not binding on a court and has no legal force. Nevertheless, in reality it forms the backdrop against which multidisciplinary medical teams conduct their assessments when they address what is described in the Guidance as 'the complexity, challenge and pain of that most difficult of decisions: is the treatment we are providing no longer in the best interests of the child'. Each of the experts has used the Guidance in this case.

The situation, therefore, is more complicated than may at first be appreciated. Different cases concerning diverse types of guidance are guided by the same golden thread; that whilst not legally binding, guidance should be adhered to unless there is some objectively justifiable reason which legitimises a departure. The guidance documents for the space industry regime were jointly issued by the Department for Transport and the United Kingdom Space Agency. It now comes within the ambit of the CAA. It has to be assumed, therefore, that it will be binding to a certain degree or, as with *Tower Hamlets*,[179] a reasonable argument would have to be made to justify a departure.

As a matter of interpretation, it should be noted that the space industry guidance does not have an 'imperative' or 'mandatory' flavour to it. It is not overtly suggested that breaching the guidance could result in legal consequences other than where such a breach would involve a breach of the Act or Regulations, but it is likely that such a decision will be dependent upon the results

179 *Ibid.*

– or potential results – of such a breach and whether or not there was a reasonable reason for departure. As has been previously argued, the approach taken in the United States may be a more worthwhile method of implementation of such rules. Such an approach may enhance legal certainty by transforming 'soft' legal provisions into concrete ones. Whilst a wholesale importation of the guidance documents may prove cumbersome and out of step with the legislative culture of the United Kingdom, some of the more 'safety critical' aspects may be worthy of such transportation to avoid fragmentation of approach on such matters. Another pertinent issue may be the fragmentation of the guidance itself. As will be noted throughout this work, there have been at least two iterations of the official guidance. In many, if not all, cases, all versions of the same document are hosted online on official portals. The documents are sometimes contradictory in nature, but it is to be presumed that the later versions supplant the earlier. The older documents contain very valid and useful statements regarding examples of best practice, however, and they would be theoretically admissible as evidence.

3 The Regulator

As it is important to set out the status of the accompanying guidance, it is also important to establish the status of the regulator. Under Regulation 3, the appointed Regulator for space activities is the CAA. The CAA was established by Section 1 of the 1971 Civil Aviation Act[180] thereby replacing the Air Regulation Board.

Initially its functions extended to:

> ... licensing of air transport, the licensing of the provision of accommodation in aircraft, the provision of air navigation services, the operation of aerodromes and the provision of assistance and information ... [181]

in addition to:

> ... such functions as are for the time being conferred on it by or under Air Navigation Orders with respect to the registration of aircraft, the safety of air navigation and aircraft (including airworthiness), the control of air

180 C 75.
181 s2(b).

> traffic, the certification of operators of aircraft and the licensing of air crews and aerodromes.[182]

Its role has been altered to varying degrees with the passage of other enactments such as the 1982 Civil Aviation Act,[183] now the key piece of legislation regarding aviation matters in the United Kingdom (and the privatisation of air traffic control functions) but it performs substantially the same duties. The remit of the CAA is liable to both expansion and contraction by virtue of Section 2(d) of its constituent instrument, the 1971 Act which determines that it must carry out: 'such other functions as are for the time being conferred on it by virtue of this Act or any other enactment.' Regulation 3 of the Space Industry Regulations does just this by expanding its remit into the United Kingdom's Space Affairs. It is worth recalling that the designation of the Regulator was initially unclear – the Space Industry Act did not specify which body would take charge and although it was anticipated that the CAA would have some role to play, the extent of its duties was speculative. It was even surmised in the House of Commons that:

> The Regulator is likely to be the Civil Aviation Authority for horizontal take-off and sub-orbital, and the UK Space Agency for vertical take-off and orbital or outer space missions.[184]

Ultimately there was no such demarcation of responsibility and whilst this may mean a significant amount of additional work for the CAA this may be preferable to the likely fragmentation that could occur. The scenario speculated upon in the House of Commons could also have proven to be unnecessarily confusing – a sub-orbital mission could have used a vertical take-off method and an orbital mission could have used a horizontal one. Would the same regulator be responsible for all components of these missions? This question has now been answered in the affirmative, and the CAA to date appears to have satisfactorily discharged the duties placed upon it.

Besides matters of aviation, it is worth also noting the broader regulatory context the CAA operates within. When discharging such duties, they are bound to have regard to the 'Regulators Code'[185] in the development of policies

182 s2(c).

183 C 16.

184 HC Deb 15 January 2018 Volume 634 col 660.

185 Department for Business, Innovation and Skills, Better Regulation Delivery Office, 'Regulators Code', April 2014, <https://assets.publishing.service.gov.uk/media/5f4e14e2e90e071c745ff2df/14-705-regulators-code.pdf> accessed 11 October 2024.

and procedures and, ultimately, their associated regulatory activities. This is a requirement of the Legislative and Regulatory Reform Act 2006.[186] The core principles of the Regulators Code are as follows: 'Proportionality – Regulators should intervene only when necessary; remedies should be appropriate to the risk posed, and costs identified and minimised. Accountability – Regulators should be able to justify decisions and be subject to public scrutiny. Consistency – Government rules and standards must be joined up and implemented fairly. Transparency – Regulators should be open and keep regulations simple and user-friendly. Targeting – Regulation should be focused on the problem and minimise side effects.'[187] Instructively for space industry matters, there is a considerable emphasis on regulatory activities being based around 'risk' within the code, with the following provisions being notable:

> 3.2 Regulators should consider risk at every stage of their decision-making processes, including choosing the most appropriate type of intervention or way of working with those regulated; targeting checks on compliance; and when taking enforcement action.

And:

> 3.5 Regulators should review the effectiveness of their chosen Regulatory activities in delivering the desired outcomes and make any necessary adjustments accordingly.[188]

Hence, every decision made under the Regulations and Act as regards licensing will be strongly – if not primarily – influenced by the respective levels of 'risk'. Moreover, the requirement to keep 'effectiveness' of regulatory activities under review should be looked upon as encouraging from the perspective of reducing administrative burden. This is related to paragraph 4.1 of the Code which states:

> 4.1 Regulators should collectively follow the principle of 'collect once, use many times' when requesting information from those they regulate.

186 C 51.
187 N191.
188 *Ibid.*

Whilst this may seem somewhat lenient towards regulated bodies – the need to present information once is surely more efficient – it must be read in conjunction with the principles in the regulations as regards updating the Regulator of any material changes to a licencee's activities. This may seem particularly relevant as regards the provision of environmental assessments which, as the regulations state, can be used for more than one launch. This is only insofar as there have not been changes taking place between the submission of the initial assessment and the subsequent launch activity.

The CAA must also 'have regard' to the 'growth duty'[189] imposed under the Deregulation Act 2015.[190] The prevailing philosophy as regards regulation is encapsulated by section 108 (1):

> A person exercising a Regulatory function to which this section applies must, in the exercise of the function, have regard to the desirability of promoting economic growth.

As stated in section 108(2)(b), a person exercising Regulatory functions:

> must consider the importance for the promotion of economic growth of exercising the Regulatory function in a way which ensures that—
> a. Regulatory action is taken only when it is needed, and
> b. any action taken is proportionate.

Whilst this may be an important statutory objective for the legislator, the principle of 'proportionality' in this context must surely be judged by the potential safety implications if regulatory action is not taken when needed. As stated in paragraph 1.5 of the statutory guidance on the 'growth duty':

> The purpose is to ensure that specified Regulators give appropriate consideration to the potential impact of their activities and their decisions on economic growth, both for individual businesses and more widely for sectors or groups that they regulate, alongside their consideration of their other statutory duties.[191]

189 The United Kingdom Civil Aviation Authority, 'Our Regulatory Principles', (CAP2185) <https://www.caa.co.uk/publication/download/18804> accessed 11 October 2024.

190 C20.

191 Department for Business, Energy and Industrial Strategy, 'Growth Duty: Statutory Guidance, Statutory Guidance under Section 110(6) of The Deregulation Act 2015', <https://assets.publishing.service.gov.uk/government/uploads/system/uploads/attachment_data/file/603743/growth-duty-statutory-guidance.pdf> accessed 11 October 2024.

It is hoped that such consideration will not prejudice the need to also consider implications of safety in respect of the general public in addition to those working on behalf of operators. As regards the work of the CAA so far in granting licences in respect of space activities there is not much to observe but, from the ones that are available, it would be difficult to suggest that they were not proportionate to the risks as regards the prevailing conditions. A glance at the spaceport licence granted to Cornwall Airport confirms this as regards the condition preventing them from storing propellants until the launch operator had been granted a licence[192] and requiring them to establish a 'safety clear zone'[193] in respect of what may have been the proposed launch by Virgin Orbit. For the sake of completeness, the full text reads as follows:

> Before HAZOPS 1 and HAZOPS 2 can take place, the Licencee must demonstrate to the satisfaction of the Regulator that the Licencee is able to put in place an appropriate safety clear zone and that the Licencee is able to comply with the requirements of Regulation 157.[194]

'HAZOPS 1' and 'HAZOPS 2' – an abbreviation of 'Hazard and Operability Study' – are stated to have 'the same meanings as in the Safety Case' under paragraph 2.1.4. of the Licences' Interpretation section. Whilst this may be opaque, it is reasonable to assume that this is related to the proposed launch activities.

Regulation 157(3) designates the licencee's responsibilities for 'safety clear zones':

> A spaceport licencee must—
> a. promulgate the times at which a safety clear zone is in place,
> b. promulgate the area that comprises the safety clear zone,
> c. ensure that the safety clear zone is monitored at all times, and
> d. secure that arrangements are in place to ensure that no person is inside the safety clear zone unless the person's presence there is essential for the carrying out of spaceflight activities or for the performance of duties connected with such activities.

192 The United Kingdom Civil Aviation Authority, Spaceport Licence Granted to Cornwall Airport, 15 November 2022, para 3.2 <https://www.caa.co.uk/publication/download/20107> accessed 11 October 2024.

193 *Ibid.*

194 *Ibid.*

It is worth considering whether what may have actually happened as regards the proposed 'safety clear zone' matches any assurances given under the licence or any promulgation. As previously mentioned, written evidence given to the House of Commons Select Committee on Science and Technology by Newton Launch Systems[195] stated the following:

> Video evidence from the January 2023 Virgin Orbit launch shows significant numbers of people, including members of the public, in close proximity to the aircraft and its fully-fuelled rocket as it taxied to the runway – for example, photographs published by the Guardian newspaper showing spectators well within this radius crowded around the site's perimeter fence. Although the risk of the rocket exploding while on the ground is quite low, if the FAA recommendations had been applied, CEC[196] would clearly have been greater than in this case, i.e. had the rocket exploded, people would have been killed.

As detailed elsewhere in this work, the FAA regime is much more elaborate and extensive than its UK counterpart – exacting details are required regarding launch activities over and above what appears to be required domestically. For example, under rule 415.109(d) of the US Code of Federal Regulations, drawings must be provided of the vehicle's flightpath and there is even a positive obligation placed on operators to ensure that rules are made regarding rest-breaks and fatigue amongst key personnel.[197] The photograph from the Guardian newspaper – as mentioned – does indeed show a crowd in – relatively – close proximity to the rocket and carrier aircraft just prior to launch[198] and how the safety clear zone was calculated by the licencee is not apparent. If, as the evidence submitted suggests, it fell below what would have been expected by the FAA, it would be a wise move on the part of the legislator to consider mandating firmer statutory rules as regards how safety clear zones are established. As the evidence stated, whilst the chance of a mishap would have been low, the loss of life involved would have been catastrophic in the event of such a mishap occurring. It will be interesting to see exactly how the monitoring

195 Science and Technology Space Strategy Sub-Committee,Written Evidence Submitted by Newton Launch Systems, (SPA0107), 2 <committees.parliament.uk/writtenevidence/119106/pdf/>, accessed 11 October 2024.

196 *Ibid*, 1, 'Conditional Expected Casualty',

197 CFR (US) 417.113 (f).

198 Steven Morris, *UK air accident officials to investigate failure to get satellites into orbit*, The Guardian, 10 January 2023, <https://www.theguardian.com/science/2023/jan/10/uk-rocket-launch-failure-virgin-orbit-second-mission> accessed 11 October 2024.

and enforcement methods are executed in respect of transgressions involving health and safety matters. As has been outlined, the CAA is under a number of duties which appear to lean towards non-intervention so as to safeguard growth and not prove burdensome to business interests. These duties will need to be balanced sensibly with the overriding priority of public safety.

The CAA's policy as regards monitoring and oversight includes the carrying out of periodic reviews, carrying out 'annual checks on all UK licenced spacecraft to meet our obligations under the UN treaties to monitor and supervise the activities of nationals, most notably Article VI of the Outer Space Treaty'.[199] Its power to conduct inspections derives from Section 26 of the Space Industry Act.

Other functions of the CAA include administering charges in respect of licensing activities. Licences sought under the Space Industry Act were provided free of charge before 2024 to encourage as much activity as possible to nurture the fledgling space industry[200] with a charging scheme due to materialise over the coming years. Orbital licences sought for activities abroad under the Outer Space Act 1986 are subject to a schedule of charges maintained by the CAA[201] which was established under Section 62 and Schedule 11 of the Space Industry Act 2018. At the time of writing, the current charge for a Satellite Operator Licence is £6500.[202] For jointly issued licences under the Space Industry Act and Outer Space Act, a single charge will apply.[203] The scheme does allow for refunds whereby an operator applies for over 99 licences in a 12-month rolling period with the refund amount increasing in line with the number of licences. Interestingly, such refunds are issued by the United Kingdom Space Agency where the licence has been obtained under the Outer Space Act 1986 – or jointly under the Outer Space Act and Space Industry Act, whereas the CAA is responsible in cases where the licence was obtained under the Space Industry Act alone. Under section 4.2 it is stated that refunds can be refused if:

199 The United Kingdom Civil Aviation Authority, 'Monitoring and Oversight', <https://www.caa.co.uk/space/what-happens-next/monitoring/> accessed 11 October 2024.

200 The United Kingdom Civil Aviation Authority, CAA Regulation, Space, 'Space Licensing in the UK', 7 <https://www.caa.co.uk/media/kbfjgbxo/space-licensing-in-the-uk.pdf#:~:text=There%20are%20no%20fees%20for%20spaceport%2C%20range%2C%20launch,no%20current%20charging%20scheme%20for%20these%20licensing%20activities.> accessed 11 October 2024.

201 See Section 62 and Schedule 11 of the Space Industry Act 2018.

202 N206.

203 *Ibid.*

a. There are material changes to the satellite platforms or their concept of operations. This reflects changes in either design, manufacture, or how they are used.
b. The satellites do not perform as anticipated when the licences were first issued. Licences are issued on the assumption of certain satellite performance and reliability. If systemic problems with the design, manufacture, or operations of the satellite are to be discovered, this will require greater overhead of monitoring.

This is encouraging, but in order to achieve sustainability objectives and environmental targets a potential improvement would be to offer an enhanced refund if certain additional mitigation measures could be shown to have been taken by the operator or in recognition of other offsetting methods. It is disappointing that this appears not to have been factored into the pricing structure, particularly given that the document was made under the Space Industry Act which was drafted with at least a degree of environmental concern.

Overall, the CAA appears to be more than equal to the challenge posed by its new role. There has been the establishment of a spaceflight specific department catering for all regulatory aspects as set out by the new instruments in addition to the focus groups and the constructive work undertaken as regards airspace. In respect of the latter, little or no legislative guidance was given on how the use of airspace for space activity was to be governed or processed. The CAA has undertaken much work to ensure that the proposed flights from Saxa-Vord run as smoothly as possible as regards airspace usage which is detailed later. It is perhaps too early to speculate whether or not the CAA is the body best placed to regulate space activities. It is maybe instructive to note that there has been at least a level of dissatisfaction with the role of the Federal Aviation Administration in the United States as regards its handling of spaceflight matters[204] which could potentially call into question the practice of aviation regulators taking responsibility for all matters involving flight including space flight should Congress be so moved. Importantly, it should be borne in mind that commercial spaceflight is handled internally within the FAA by the Office of Commercial Space Transportation (OCST), as established by the Commercial Space Launch Act of 1984.[205] The office is responsible for regulatory matters

204 Jeff Foust, 'Launch Industry asks Congress for Regulatory Reforms', Spacenews, October 19, 2023 <https://spacenews.com/launch-industry-asks-congress-for-Regulatory-reforms/#:~:text=Gerstenmaier%20and%20other%20witnesses%20called,to%20the%20office> accessed 11 October 2024.

205 51 USC Ch. 509, 50923 (US).

and licensing for space activities within the FAA.[206] To a certain extent, this reflects practice at the CAA whereby space matters come under the auspices of a separate division.[207] This in turn is supported by the Space Launch and Orbit Group which assists in regulatory matters, providing a link between stakeholders such as those licenced to undertake activities under the Space Industry Act 2018.[208] Alongside this, the Department for Transport runs the Spaceflight Safety and Regulatory Council comprised of key governmental and industry figures with the remit of recommending suitable legislative changes. Whilst there is not the clear demarcation between the CAA's 'space team' and the rest of the organisation as is the case with the FAA and OCST, it nevertheless operates as a discrete and dedicated offshoot with a narrow ambit.

In the relatively short space of time since the CAA was appointed as Regulator, it has grappled commendably with the new responsibilities bestowed upon it. It is important to bear in mind that, in discharging its duties under the Space Industry Act and Regulations, it is also bound by other instruments in terms of how it discharges its obligations. The general growth duty under the Deregulation Act 2015 in addition to requirements of proportionality under the Regulators Code are two such instruments. Time will tell whether the CAA successfully observes this balancing act. It is important to also consider that the guidance documents now deposited with the CAA were largely – if not entirely – drafted prior to its appointment as Regulator although many have been updated since. This could be significant in a drafting sense but even if not, it is certainly worth considering whether the guidance should be worded more strongly given the arising safety implications.

---

206 The Federal Aviation Administration, 'About the Office of Commercial Space Transportation', <https://www.faa.gov/about/office_org/headquarters_offices/ast> accessed 11 October 2024.

207 The United Kingdom Civil Aviation Authority, 'Space; Information on rocket launches, space flight and associated activities', <https://www.caa.co.uk/space> accessed 11 October 2024.

208 The United Kingdom Civil Aviation Authority, 'Space Launch and Orbit Group (SPLOG), remit, members and terms of reference' <https://www.caa.co.uk/space/about-the-space-team/space-launch-and-orbit-group-splog/> accessed 11 October 2024.

CHAPTER 4

The Space Legislation of the United Kingdom

The recent instruments – the 2018 Space Industry Act and 2021 Space Industry Regulations – represent a new foray into space law for the United Kingdom. Whilst they drastically expand the legal landscape within this sphere, the genesis of UK space legislation was a number of years prior in the shape of the Outer Space Act 1986. This was at a time when a domestic United Kingdom space launch infrastructure was not much of a possibility, although as has been previously outlined, the United Kingdom was still somewhat of a relatively minor – but not insignificant – player in the field of space activities internationally. The main effect of the 1986 Act was to give life to the provisions of the Registration and Liability Conventions by ensuring the United Kingdom's international treaty obligations were catered for in the spirit of its dualist approach.[209] Space as a legislative field was completely dormant until the 2018 Space Industry Act arose, providing ample scaffolding from which 2021 Space Industry Regulations hung the finer regulatory details. Driven by entirely different legislative aims, the latter two instruments have very little in common with the Outer Space Act, which almost feels like it was begrudgingly created by means of a check-box exercise to accommodate international obligations and establish a rudimentary licensing regime. Since this work aims to assess the corpus of United Kingdom space law, the Outer Space Act 1986 marks the most logical starting point. It is also still a very important piece of legislation for the functioning of the United Kingdom's space industry, and given the volume of activities licenced under it, possibly the most important.

1 The Outer Space Act 1986 – One Small Step …

To restate, the Outer Space Act 1986[210] was created in light of the United Kingdom's treaty obligations,[211] and also to clarify and formally establish a legislative

209 See The Outer Space Act 1986, s7 'Register of Space Objects' and s10 'Obligation to indemnify government against claims'.

210 C38.

211 The Department for Business, Innovation and Skills, The United Kingdom Space Agency, 'Review of the Outer Space Act 1986', Impact Assessment, 20 June 2013, 6 <https://assets.publishing.service.gov.uk/government/uploads/system/uploads/attachment_data/file/493187/OSA_Impact_Assessment_FINAL_BIS0067.pdf> accessed 12 October 2024.

 DOI:10.1163/9789004732551_005

regime in this area. Lord Lucas of Chilworth articulated the necessity for such a measure in the House of Lords during the Bill's passage through Parliament:

> This Bill is an important one. It is intended to enable us to fulfil a number of international obligations concerning the use of outer space. These obligations arise from a series of United Nations conventions, the first and most important of which is the Treaty on Principles Governing the Activities of States in the Exploration and Use of Outer Space including the Moon and Other Celestial Bodies – the Outer Space Treaty for short. We signed this treaty in 1967, the year it entered into force. But there are two other conventions which are dealt with in the Bill: the 1972 Convention on International Liability for Damage Caused by Space Objects—which I shall refer to as the 'Liability Convention'—and the 1975 Convention on Registration of Objects Launched into Outer Space—or the Registration Convention for short.[212]

And, further still, foreshadowing the emergence of private actors:

> Some noble Lords might wonder how we have managed to meet our obligations in the almost 20-year period since the Outer Space Treaty was signed. Simply put, the answer is that we have had little difficulty, since all the outer space activities for which we have international responsibility have been carried on in the public sector.[213]

Such legislation was also needed owing to the increase in space activities other than domestic launch undertaken by United Kingdom nationals.[214] Licences were granted under the Act to such nationals in respect of satellite launches, but these took place exclusively outside United Kingdom territory.[215] As shown by the UK Registry of Space Objects,[216] the majority, if not all owner operators of UK satellites are based in the United Kingdom with launches since the enactment taking place at various launch sites around the world from French Guiana to the former Cape Canaveral in the United States.[217]

212 Hansard Volume 470: debated on Tuesday 4 February 1986, Column 1097.

213 *Ibid.*

214 Annette Froehlich, Vincent Seffinga, *National Space Legislation,* Springer, (2018), 22.

215 *Ibid.*

216 N49.

217 *Ibid*, 15, 24. See the satellite Skynet 4-B owned and operated by the Ministry of Defence launched from French Guiana in 1988 and Orion 1 owned and operated by British Aerospace Space Systems Ltd launched from Cape Canaveral in 1994. It is worth noting that

Accordingly, the Act itself states that its purpose is:

> ... to confer licensing and other powers on the Secretary of State to secure compliance with the international obligations of the United Kingdom with respect to the launching and operation of space objects and the carrying on of other activities in outer space by persons connected with this country.[218]

Section 4 of the Act broadly caters for the safeguarding of obligations under Article VI of the Outer Space Treaty.[219] As the Treaty states, the United Kingdom 'bears international responsibility for national activities in outer space.'[220] Before the 1986 Act, these responsibilities were met by 'government agencies or by nongovernmental bodies of a public character such as the Science and Engineering Research Council.'[221] 'National activities', as defined by the Act, are 'the launching and operation of space objects and the carrying on of other activities in outer space by persons connected with this country'.[222] Consequently, the scope *rationae personae* of the Act applies to space activities carried out by United Kingdom nationals anywhere in the world. As referred to later in this chapter, the 1986 Act now applies exclusively to space activities carried on *outside* the United Kingdom, with space activities carried on *within* falling under the Space Industry Act 2018. To this extent, the concept of 'national' space activities under UK law is somewhat bifurcated and could thusly be defined as 'any space activity carried out either by a United Kingdom

---

military satellites may not come within the ambit of the Act if the Ministry of Defence is not considered a 'body incorporated under the law of the United Kingdom'. It would not seem to fulfil the definition of a 'body corporate' under s1173 of the Companies Act 2006, and nor presumably could it be considered a UK national or [Scottish Firm] under s2 of the Outer Space Act. However, Defence-related activities in general do come within the Space Industry Act 2018. See the recent consultation of 16 September 2024 for 'Draft proposals for exempting defence-related activities from the Space Industry Act 2018' <https://www.gov.uk/government/consultations/draft-policy-proposals-for-exempting-defence-related-activities-from-the-space-industry-act-2018/draft-policy-proposals-for-exempting-defence-related-activities-from-the-space-industry-act-2018#:~:text=Open%20consultation.%20Draft%20policy> accessed 1 October 2024. Millitary rockets are also presently excluded from the requirement for a permission under the Air Navigation Order 2016, s96(2)(b).

218 N53, Introductory Text.

219 N104.

220 *Ibid*, Article 4.

221 Colin Warbrick, Robin Churchill, Robin White, John Woodliffe and Brian Yeomans, 'The Outer Space Act 1986' (1986) 35(4) ICLQ 986.

222 N194, long title.

national abroad or by an individual of any nationality from within the United Kingdom'.[223]

Section 7 provides for the creation of a 'Register of Space Objects' – reflecting the United Kingdom's obligations under the Registration Convention.[224] (this is not to be confused with the register of launches which is provided for under the Space Industry Act 2018 under section 61(1)). Whilst the Register of Space Objects is a database of all *space objects* launched in the United Kingdom or elsewhere (in cases where the space activity has been carried on by a United Kingdom national abroad as discussed above), the register of launches requires that records are kept of *launches* from United Kingdom spaceports.[225] Launches which must be registered include only those where objects are launched beyond the stratosphere[226] or, in the case of a balloon carrying crew or passengers, those that reach the stratosphere.[227] As with responsibility for other international obligations, such matters were handled on a voluntary basis by the now defunct[228] British National Space Centre.[229] Under the Act, the granting of licences in connection with space activity is contingent upon the Secretary of State's approval. The Secretary of State may refuse to grant a licence if it is deemed that the activities may jeopardise 'public health or the safety of persons or property', be deemed inconsistent with 'international obligations of the United Kingdom,' or 'impair the national security of the United Kingdom.'[230] Section 5 (on Terms of Licence) was largely imported into the Space Industry Act 2018 by virtue of Schedule 1. In turn, the 2018 Act inserted section 3ZA and section 3A into the 1986 Act in relation to the granting of exemptions by the Secretary of State as regards licences. This specifies the Secretary of State's powers to make various provisions, together with section 4A on the Secretary of State's powers to make a scheme by statutory instrument for determining charges in respect of functions under section 4 in relation to the granting of such licences.

---

223 For an informative discussion on national space law generally, see Frans von der Dunk, 'The third ring: national space legislation' *Advanced Introduction to Space Law* (2020), Cheltenham, UK, Edward Elgar Publishing, 122–123.

224 N126.

225 N127, s61(1).

226 *Ibid*, s61(2)(a).

227 *Ibid*, s61(2)(b).

228 N74.

229 Ibid.

230 s4(2)(a)–(c).

Prior to the Space Industry Act, the Deregulation Act 2015[231] also amended various aspects of the 1986 Act. These included, chiefly, excluding those who may not be performing activities so governed by the Act from the requirement to indemnify the government and granting the Secretary of State the power to specify the maximum amount of an individual's liability when undertaking activities that do not require a licence.[232] In the case of licenced activities the Act was amended to require that the terms of any licence *must* specify the maximum amount of the licencee's liability.[233] This is supported by the amendment made to Section 10 which provides that the obligation to indemnify the government is subject to the amount specified in the licence or any order made under section 3(3) – which would imply that in some circumstances licencees may, at the discretion of the Secretary of State, be absolved from all liability under the 1986 Act, though what this would depend upon is not clear. Overall, the reforms to the 1986 Act would appear to be welcome ones from the perspective of industry should they wish to launch from outside the United Kingdom. A common complaint with other legislative provisions is that the absence of limits on liability can have the effect of driving up costs or making insurance much harder to obtain.[234]

Prior to amendment by the Deregulation Act 2015, section 10 of the 1986 Act laid down the obligation of private operators to indemnify the government against claims arising out of loss or damage connected with space activities. According to the Department for Transport's impact assessment – a relatively routine procedure in UK law whereby government departments attempt to assess the likely consequences of legislative change across a range of areas – in respect of the Space Industry Bill (which ultimately became the Space Industry Act 2018), this was an anti-competitive clause since it required excessive insurance premiums to be obtained by satellite operators where this was not the case in other countries.[235] As previously outlined, the Deregulation Act 2015 made such an indemnity subject to a liability cap which could be specified in a licence condition. On this point, it is important to note that the subject of liability under UK space law more generally is, at the time of writing, under

231 N196.

232 s3A(b).

233 s5(3).

234 See, for example, objections raised by various stakeholders in the evidence given to the recent consultation on orbital liabilities, N19. There will be a further discussion of such matters in the conclusion to this work.

235 N217.

review as part of the Consultation on Orbital Liabilities, Insurance, Charging and Space Sustainability.[236]

Further, in respect of insurance, Brian Yeomans writes of a potential issue not covered by the 1986 Act:

> Many of the commercial spacecraft to which the UK Act will apply are unlikely to return to earth for many thousands, if not millions, of years and it is interesting to reflect on a potential situation in, say, 50 years' time, where 20 or perhaps 30 derelict and uninsured spacecraft under UK registry may become hazardous and incur a liability. Unless the government has taken action to preserve the insurance, it may well find it difficult to proceed against former licencees which may have disposed of all rights to those spacecraft or, indeed, have ceased operations altogether.[237]

The above statement was made almost a decade before space debris even became a faint priority for supranational lawmakers.[238] Since this time, efforts to curtail the threat of space debris have multiplied, with the COPOUS Space Debris Mitigation Guidelines being endorsed by the United Nations General Assembly in 2007.[239] These have since been adopted by a number of states to various extents, including Russia and the United States.[240] Under the definition endorsed by both the Inter-Agency Space Debris Coordination Committee (IADC), COPUOS and the EU Code of Conduct for Outer Space Activities, the 'derelict and uninsured spacecraft' referred to by Yeomans, having ceased to be functional, would themselves become space debris.[241] Since the Outer Space Act 1986, UK space law has also endorsed the space debris mitigation guidelines under section 2(2)(h) of the Space Industry Act 2018, which compels the

236 N19.

237 N227, 988–989.

238 Lotta Viikari, Environmental Aspects of Space Activities, in Frans von der Dunk and Fabio Tronchetti, (eds), 'Handbook of Space Law' (Edward Elgar, 2015), 742.

239 N149.

240 United Nations Office for Outer Space Affairs, 'Compendium of space debris mitigation standards adopted by States and international organizations', <https://www.unoosa.org/oosa/en/ourwork/topics/space-debris/compendium.html> accessed 12 October 2024.

241 Committee on the Peaceful Uses of Outer Space (COPUOS) Scientific and Technical Subcommittee, Forty-ninth session, Vienna, 6–17 February 2012, 'Active Debris Removal – An Essential Mechanism for Ensuring the Safety and Sustainability of Outer Space. A Report of the Interntional Interdisciplinary Congress on Space Debris Remediation and On-Orbit Satellite Servicing, 30–31, <https://www.unoosa.org/pdf/limited/c1/AC105_C1_2012_CRP16E.pdf> accessed 12 October 2024.

regulator to take them into account when exercising its functions thereunder.[242] In comparison to a number of other jurisdictions, these measures do not seem to go far enough, but it is worth noting that change may come at the conclusion of the recent consultative exercise.[243]

It has also been written that the Act left another void:

> … the concept of national space activities in the UK is defined through the nationality of the person conducting the activity. Therefore, any person, natural or juridical, with a foreign nationality conducting space activities from the territory of the UK does not fall within the scope of the Act.[244]

This is no longer a live issue since such individuals would now be required to be licenced under the Space Industry Act 2018 as previously outlined. The United Kingdom now has what the author has termed a 'bifurcated' definition of national space activities. It is important to note that since the Outer Space Act 1986, the international obligations pertaining to the internal regulatory affairs of states as regards their national space activities have become more acute. The UN Resolution on National Space Legislation of 2013[245] made some general yet comprehensive recommendations in respect of how this should be managed, in respect of both space activities carried out within a state's territory and those under its 'jurisdiction and/or control'.[246] The Space Industry Act 2018 closes the pre-existing gap and as will be outlined later, addresses other of these recommendations.

In addition to the larger regulatory picture, the Act also defines 'outer space' as 'including the moon and other celestial bodies' and a 'space object' as including 'the component parts of a space object, its launch vehicle and the component parts of that' echoing the Liability Convention under section 13(1). It is also interesting to note that, in common with a number of other national legislatures there are no distinctions drawn as to the size or purpose of any such space object.[247] Regarding activities pertaining to such objects and outer space, section 13(2) states that 'For the purposes of this Act a person carries on

242 N127, s2(2).

243 N187.

244 N19, 23. See also Chapter 10 on comparative perspectives for a discussion of the rules of other jurisdictions in relation to Space Debris.

245 N125.

246 *Ibid*, 2. This question is also kept under constant review during the yearly meetings of the UNCOPUOS Legal Subcommittee.

247 Frans von der Dunk, 'Liability for Damage Caused by Small Satellites – A Non-Issue?' (2016) *Space, Cyber and Telecommunications Law Program Faculty Publications*, 99, 10.

an activity if he causes it to occur or is responsible for its continuing.' There is no guidance within the Act as to who may be classified as 'causing to occur' or being 'responsible for (a space activity) continuing'. In addition to United Kingdom nationals as previously discussed, the Act states, further, that it also applies to 'Scottishfirms('Scottish Firms')' and 'bodies incorporated under the law of any part of the United Kingdom'[248] which widens the category of exactly who may require a licence under the Act or at any rate refines it. It is important to note that the Act also applies to the 'procuring' of the launch of a space object under section 1(a). Individuals wishing to 'procure' the use of a space object such as a satellite, as set out within the guidance for licence applications under the Space Industry Act 2018, would not require a *launch* licence as such, but would instead be required to obtain an orbital operator licence.[249] In the case of those wishing to procure the use of a space object launched outside the United Kingdom, the correct avenue would be to obtain such a licence under the Outer Space Act 1986. Whilst individuals and other legal entities directly involved with either procurement or launch will clearly need to obtain a licence, there is no indication within the existing United Kingdom space instruments themselves as to where the line is to be drawn as regards those who may be a step or two removed from this process. For example, there is no indication given as to the extent to which a non-governmental entity responsible for actually funding a particular satellite operation or launch – but not necessarily directly involved with either or both activities – would require a licence. It could be determined at the application stage under the Regulators Licensing Rules, that an 'agency' relationship exists between such entities and a licensing decision made on that basis accordingly.[250] Section 5(2)(e) also paves the way for environmental protection, later elaborated upon in the Space Industry Act 2018 – a licencee can be required to perform their duties in 'such a way as to ... prevent the contamination of outer space or adverse changes in the environment of the earth'.

Far from being a dead letter, the Outer Space Act 1986 still serves a very valuable role. It provides for space activities taking place outside the United Kingdom whereas activities within the United Kingdom are provided for by the more recent legislative provisions. The Act also remains highly relevant as

248 s2(1).

249 United Kingdom Space Agency and United Kingdom Civil Aviation Authority, 'Applying for a licence under the Space Industry Act 2018', 29 July 2021, <https://www.caa.co.uk/publication/download/18919> accessed 12 October 2024, 10.

250 The Regulators Licensing Rules, 2 July 2020, 8, Table A, <https://assets.publishing.service.gov.uk/government/uploads/system/uploads/attachment_data/file/904463/the-regulators-licensing-rules.pdf> accessed 12 October 2024.

regards certain satellite payloads. As was stated in the first edition of Regulatory guidance for launch and return Operator licences:[251]

'Where the launch payload manifest includes a satellite which will be operated from outside the UK by a UK entity, the Operator of the payload will need to apply for a licence under the Outer Space Act 1986.'[252] However if a satellite is to be operated from the United Kingdom as opposed to abroad, the operator is still required to obtain an orbital operator licence under the Space Industry Act even if they themselves are not United Kingdom-based.[253]

Whilst the 1986 Act was seemingly born of necessity, it still retains value today for the reasons outlined, albeit in a marginally more geographically limited sense. Its contribution to the body of UK space law should not be completely understated since it was the first enactment to attempt to implement the United Kingdom's international obligations in this new field and was welcomed on inception for addressing a glaring omission in this this respect.[254] In spite of being overshadowed in terms of volume and scope by subsequent instruments, it is important to observe that many licences in respect of successful operations have been granted under the Outer Space Act in respect of launches overseas as now remains its stated purpose.[255] Although its content and scope are limited by the later enactments, it is important to recognise the different contexts in which the latter instruments came about. At the time of the Outer Space Act 1986, there was no equivalent to the 2013 National Space Legislation Resolution[256] effectively prompting states to create a legislative framework for such activities in contrast to the contemporary era.[257] Whilst this work focuses primarily on the later instruments, frequent reference will be made to the Outer Space Act as its importance continues to resonate for United Kingdom space activities and is likely to do so for the foreseeable future.

---

251 The United Kingdom Civil Aviation Authority, 'Guidance for Launch Operator and Return Operator Licence Applicants and Licencees' 1st edition, 21, <https://www.legislation.gov.uk/ukdsi/2021/9780348223682/pdfs/ukdsiod_9780348223682_en_003.pdf> accessed 12 October 2024.

252 *Ibid*, 20.

253 *Ibid.*

254 Prior to 1986, the UK was involved in various space activities as outlined, but there was no coherent licensing mechanism.

255 See the UK Register of Space Objects, *supra* at N49.

256 N125.

257 N125, the Resolution on national space legislation can be viewed as a response of the international community to the increased levels of interest and activity in recent years in the commercial utilisation of space by private actors.

2 The Space Industry Act 2018 – One Giant Leap ...

As the United Kingdom's sole licensing instrument, the Outer Space Act 1986 lay dormant in the statute books for many years, at least as far as domestic operations were concerned. This was until interest began swelling in respect of the United Kingdom's potential as a player in respect of commercial space launch. With satellite data gaining increasing importance in the electronic age, decreasing costs in small satellite services, and governmental ambitions to corner 10% of the market for space[258] it was decided that new legislative measures were required to stimulate the market.[259] The recommendations of the National Space Legislation Resolution also provided a sense of legislative urgency.[260] In the wake of this decision, the Outer Space Act 1986 was not repealed, but amended so as to cover launches overseas[261] whilst in order to facilitate lofty ambitions, the legislator looked towards previously unchartered territory; the Outer Space Act 1986 was not conducive to the forecast development within the space sector or the Government's target of a '£40 billion Space Sector by 2030'.[262] The provisions were neither adequate nor comprehensive enough to facilitate commercial space activities from within the United Kingdom or meet revised international requirements as outlined.

As was set out in the impact assessment for the new Space Industry Act:

> There is currently no regulation to enable commercial powers to licence spaceports, spaceflight Operators and operations, vehicles and crew and powers on liability. Although regulations to allow spaceflight to exist, the lack of a wider comprehensive framework effectively makes it impossible, as without rules on risk, safety and liability firms are unwilling to invest and begin operations.[263]

---

258 Georgina Hutton, 'The Space Industry Bill 2017–2019' (2018) Briefing Paper Number CBP 8197, online <https://commonslibrary.parliament.uk/research-briefings/cbp-8197/> accessed 12 October 2024.

259 Space Industry Bill [HL] Explanatory Notes, 29 November 2017, 4, <https://publications.parliament.uk/pa/bills/cbill/2017-2019/0137/en/18137en.pdf> accessed 12 October 2024.

260 N125.

261 The Space Industry Act 2018, s1(3).

262 Department for Transport, Space Industry Bill, Spaceflight Impact Assessment, 30 September 2016 <https://www.legislation.gov.uk/ukpga/2018/5/pdfs/ukpgaod_20180005_en_001.pdf> accessed 12 October 2024.

263 *Ibid*, 5.

Resultantly, the Space Industry Act 2018 was launched on March 15th, 2018, with the intention that the United Kingdom could, in its wake, 'once more reach for the stars ... in the best spirit of British innovation ... by enabling commercial markets for small-satellite launch and suborbital flight from UK spaceports'.[264] In legislative terms it was an Act of seismic proportions. Combined with the later Space Industry Regulations 2021, arguably the Act is to UK-based space activities what the 1984 Police and Criminal Evidence Act (PACE)[265] was to UK policing, short of the elements of codification and controversy.[266] Whilst not concerned with licensing, PACE is a comprehensive procedural statute delineating various aspects of police authority across a series of chapters. It is also supported by routinely updated codes of practice[267] and was the first wide-ranging statute of its kind in the field of policing, bringing a new approach to the regulation of police investigatory powers.[268] It has served as the main source of power in this regard since its creation.

The Space Industry Act drastically expanded the domestic legislative framework, containing 72 sections and 12 schedules as compared to the Outer Space Act 1986 which had just 15 sections. Covering important issues of liability in addition to space flight and spaceports, the 2018 Act also covered safety and security and emergent powers in respect of human spaceflight and the groundwork was set for a comprehensive licensing regime.

Whilst there is considerable overlap between the licence application processes, there are key differences between the licencees and the expectations the legislation puts on them. The broad categories of licence are 'Operator licences' and 'Spaceport licences'.[269]

Spaceflight itself is given substantive treatment within the Act from the very outset – section1(1) distinguishes 'suborbital' and 'space activities'. Under Section 1(4)(c) 'space activities' are 'any activity in outer space' whilst 'suborbital activity' means 'launching, procuring the launch of, operating or procuring the return to earth of—(a) a craft to which ss.(5) applies, or (b) an aircraft carrying such a craft, but does not include space activity'. However, suborbital activities are still classed as 'spaceflight activities',[270] and whilst a suborbital activity is not classed as a 'space activity', it nevertheless includes the 'launching,

264 HC Deb 15 January 2018, Vol 634, Column 651.

265 C60.

266 Stephen Jones, 'The Police and Criminal Evidence Act 1984', Modern Law Review, 1985–11, Vol 48(6), 679.

267 N246 s66.

268 Ed Cape, 'Modernising Police Powers – again?', Crim. L.R. 2007, Dec, 934.

269 ss8–15.

270 S1(6).

procuring the launch of, operating or procuring the return to earth of … a rocket or other craft that is capable of operating above the stratosphere'.[271] A rocket capable of operating above the stratosphere, almost by definition, is capable of reaching 'outer space' – definitions of this contested term 'will be discussed later. The definition of 'space activity' includes 'launching or procuring the launch (or return) of a space object or of an aircraft carrying a space object'.[272] It also includes 'operating a space object'[273] or 'any activity in outer space'.[274] As mentioned, suborbital activities are said not to include space activities[275] but can include activities involving craft that are at least capable of reaching outer space. This state of affairs within the legislation appears to be unnecessarily confusing. Perhaps a more precise technique would be to refine the definition of 'space activities' by distinguishing those taking place above the stratosphere which do not achieve orbit and those that do. The details of what was discussed at the drafting stage here are not apparent, but it would be of interest to learn why the present approach was adopted.

No distinction is drawn between 'horizontal' and 'vertical' launch systems in this respect. The legislation also seeks to demarcate, in its own way, the place where air space ends and outer space technically begins by means of subsection 5 which refers to '(a) a rocket or other craft that is capable of operating above the stratosphere; (b) a balloon that is capable of reaching the stratosphere carrying crew or passengers.'

There is, famously, no agreed limit under international law as to where space actually begins[276] and where the 'stratosphere' ends may also be something which is up for debate to some degree but according to the Center for Science Education[277] the Stratosphere ends 30 miles (50 km) about the earth's surface. This is interesting since there is cause to believe that, under customary international law, soon anything about 95–110 km could be classified as 'outer space'.[278] The most famous scientific demarcation of where space begins is at

271 S1(4) (a), s1(5)(a).
272 S1(4)(a).
273 S1(4)(b).
274 S1(4)(c).
275 S1(4).
276 Stephan Hobe, 'Legal Aspects of Space Tourism' 86 (2007) Neb. L. Rev. 441, see also Thomas Gangale, *How High The Sky?* (Brill Nijhoff 2018).
277 Center for Science Education, 'The Stratosphere' <https://scied.ucar.edu/learning-zone/atmosphere/stratosphere> accessed 21 November 2023.
278 N105, 4.

the Karman line[279] at 62 miles above the earth's surface but there is, as of yet, no overall consensus on this matter. It is important to note that the correct attribution of this figure – and even the figure itself – is widely disputed across a range of scientific and academic disciplines and, hence, should not by any means be treated as an authoritative or conclusive definition.[280] The statutory position in the United States is vague:[281] 'the areas outside the Earth's atmosphere'. A glance at a range of national space legislation will inevitably furnish a range of definitions. The South African Space Affairs Act, for example, delineates outer space as 'the space above the surface of the Earth from a height at which it is in practice possible to operate an object in an orbit around the Earth.'[282] In the United Kingdom context, the working definition of the 'stratosphere' was updated by means of the first generation of written guidance brought out to supplement the Act which states:

> … the Regulator proposes to use the International Standard Atmosphere (47 km) as the stratopause (i.e. the upper limit of the stratosphere) for the purposes of determining whether an activity is 'suborbital'[283]

Revisiting the definition of 'suborbital', there are various other positions on this taken by other entities. The Council of the International Civil Aviation Organisation (ICAO) in a working paper suggested that a suborbital flight could be defined, somewhat vaguely, as 'a flight up to a very high altitude which does not involve sending the vehicle into orbit.'[284] The United States' definition is furnished with more scientific gloss: 'The intentional flight path of a launch

---

279 Andrew G. Haley, 'Space Exploration: The Problems of Today, Tomorrow and in the Future', 2 PROC. ON THE L. OF OUTER SPACE (1959) 49, see also, Eric Betz, 'The Karman Line: Where does Space Begin?' (Astronomy.com, March 5 2021) <https://www.astronomy.com/space-exploration/the-karman-line-where-does-space-begin/> accessed 12 October 2024.

280 See Thomas Gangale, 'The Non Karman Line: An Urban Legend of the Space Age', 41 J. Space L. 151 (2017).

281 National Aeronautics and Space Act, Section 51, USC S 40302 (5) 2010 (US).

282 Space Affairs Act 1993 [No. 84 of 1993] G 14917. S.1 (xv) (SA).

283 The United Kingdom Civil Aviation Authority, Guidance on Applying for a Licence' 1st edition, <https://assets.publishing.service.gov.uk/government/uploads/system/uploads/attachment_data/file/904285/guidance-on-applying-for-a-licence.pdf> accessed 12 October 2024.

284 Council of the International Civil Aviation Organisation, 36th Session, Legal Committee Working Paper on Commercial Space Flights, Montréal, 30 November to 3 December 2015, 1 <https://www.icao.int/Meetings/LC36/Working%20Papers/LC%2036%20-%20WP%203-2.en.pdf> accessed 12 October 2024.

vehicle, re-entry vehicle, or any portion thereof, whose vacuum instantaneous impact point does not leave the surface of the Earth.'[285] Other jurisdictions such as that of the United Arab Emirates attempt to place a statutory ceiling on the precise height that defines 'suborbital' flight – in the case of the United Arab Emirates it is defined as 'Any area above eighty kilometres or more than the average sea level', a suborbital flight being, therefore, 'A Spaceflight with the intent to enter the Specified Area without the intention of completing an orbit around the Earth'.[286] The United Kingdom's definition, therefore, seems very wide as it encapsulates, under section 1(4), not only launching but 'procuring' a launch and even aircraft carrying rockets can be deemed 'suborbital activities'. On the topic of 'procurement', as discussed previously, there is no definition of this term within UK space legislation. It is imported directly from the Liability Convention which, as mentioned, was the partial impetus for the Outer Space Act 1986. It is instructive to observe how it has been interpreted amongst other states in the establishment of their own national space legislation pursuant to the treaties. Its translation by various legislators has led to interpretations such as 'to make happen', 'initiate', 'prompt' and 'promote'.[287] The position of the United Kingdom in practice seems to be to make 'licensing' synonymous with acceptance of the moniker of 'launching state' for the purposes of the Liability Convention.[288] Moreover, the United Kingdom does not regard itself as the 'launching state' in respect of satellites in orbit whereby the launch was procured by a private operator *before* that private operator subsequently became a UK company.[289] This raises interesting questions. Consider, for example, a satellite launched from a state other than the United Kingdom on being procured by a non-UK private actor, which then becomes subject to a claim under the Liability Convention after the private actor has become or taken over by a UK company. Where would liability fall to be apportioned here given that the launching state is no longer in control of the satellite causing the damage? Whilst the Liability Convention is clear in this respect – that the 'launching state' is the liable state, the fact that a space object which is no longer within the control of the actual launching state could nevertheless still render the launching state accountable does not seem satisfactory.

285 *Ibid.*

286 Federal Law No. (12) of 2019 Issued on 19/12/2019 (UAE), On The Regulation of the Space Sector, Chapter 1 - definitions.

287 Peter van Fenema, Legal Aspects of Launch Services and Space Transportation, in Frans von der Dunk and Fabio Tronchetti, (eds), 'Handbook of Space Law' (Edward Elgar, 2015), 398.

288 *Ibid*, 399 – see fn 60.

289 *Ibid.*

The United Kingdom position seems to be that it would not accept liability in such instances and there would not appear to be any question of joint or severable liability on a literal approach to the Liability Convention in such circumstances. As per Article II (2) of the Registration Convention, appropriate agreements between launching states can be concluded as to the control of in-orbit space objects. There is also some precedent in this area regarding the practice of the United Kingdom as regards transfer between states which came about as a result of the transfer of sovereignty over Hong Kong to China in 1997.[290] Note that in this instance, China was the launching state[291] for the purpose of the Liability Convention. A further instance involving the United Kingdom and an on-orbit transfer involved the BSB-1A British Sky Broadcasting satellite which was owned and operated by a British Company and launched from the United States. The satellite was later purchased by a Swedish company but Sweden could not register the satellite as it was not a launching state. It could be assumed in such instances that the state of the transferee automatically assumes the status of launching state but there are no hard international obligations regarding this.[292] UN Resolution 59/115 on the Application of the concept of the 'launching State'[293] was adopted following discussions of the COPUOS Legal Subcommittee on issues such as these in its 41st session. Foreshadowing the later 2013 Resolution on National Space Legislation, it was suggested that states implement national laws to provide for continuous supervision of space activities carried out by private actors, but stopped short of suggesting a framework for the handling of on-orbit sales or other transfers of space objects. Instead, states were encouraged, as echoed in the Registration Convention, to reach agreements between themselves on such matters, in spite of the Resolution itself setting out that there would be a proliferation of these scenarios in future. UK legislation does not currently provide any contingency for on-orbit transfer of space objects but it is perhaps more appropriate for such matters to be agreed upon in the form of a resolution or convention at

290 Ram Jakhu, Bhupendra Jasani, Jonathan McDowell, 'Critical Issues Related to Registration of Space Objects and Transparency of Space Activities', Acta Astronautica 143 (2018) 406, 412. See also Note verbale dated 27 March 1998 from the Permanent Mission of the United Kingdom of Great Britain and Northern Ireland to the United Nations (Vienna) addressed to the Secretary-general, UN Doc ST/SG/SER.E/333.

291 *Ibid.*

292 *Ibid* 412–413. See also Application of the Concept of the 'launching State', UN Doc A/RES/59/115.

293 Application of the Concept of the 'launching State', UN Doc A/RES/59/115.

some future date so as to promote a relative degree of uniformity in what will surely become a more contested area.[294]

Regarding suborbital activities, in law, the unsuccessful Virgin Orbit launch[295] could have been regarded as a 'suborbital activity' even if the rocket carried by the aircraft 'Cosmic Girl' was not released from the aircraft as a result of a technical error. Going a step or two back, it could even be argued that the very procurement of the launch itself was in its own right a 'suborbital activity' based upon this legislative definition. It is also important to note that the Space Industry Act definition of 'suborbital' may currently run contrary to sustainability goals as, presently, a suborbital activity which involves going no higher than 47 km is not licenced under the Act, but instead under the Air Navigation Order 2016.[296] As previously outlined, any space activity above 47 km is classified as suborbital and hence requires a licence. Unlike the requirements of the Space Industry Act for an Assessment of Environmental Effects, there is no such requirement under the Air Navigation Order. Further attention will be given to this later.

The airspace/outer space conundrum can make choosing a regulator difficult. Under the regulations as outlined, the CAA was designated as the official Regulator[297] drawing a close to the speculation which had arisen among lawmakers.[298] As previously written, it was initially thought that the responsibility could be divided between the United Kingdom Space Agency and the CAA. The fact that no overall distinction is drawn between these two modes of flight as regards who bears regulatory responsibility is perhaps a matter of convenience and to save complication and duplication. Looking elsewhere, the German Aviation Code deals with this problem in a logical way insofar as 'space vehicles, rockets and similar flight objects are treated as aircraft as long as they are in air space.'[299] The question arising is thus: 'what is it and where can it be taken as beginning and ending?'.[300] A system of dual regulatory responsibility could bring a significant degree of jurisdictional confusion. Considering matters of sustainability in respect of launch activities which do not surpass the 47 km threshold, attention should be given to whether there ought be a separate regulatory body or whether the definition of 'suborbital' ought to be expanded.

---

294 See UNCOPUOS, AC.105/891, Report of the Legal Subcommittee on its forty-sixth session held in Vienna from 26 March to 5 April 2007, para 126–127.
295 N83.
296 SI 2016 no. 765.
297 N173, Regulation 3.
298 HC Debate 15 January 2018 Volume 634 col 660.
299 As stated by Peter van Femema, N293, 411–412.
300 For a discussion of this eternal conundrum, see Gangale, 'How High the Sky?' N282.

So far, the CAA appears to be discharging its regulatory functions as to spaceflight commendably in spite of not having an expressly dedicated office such as with the FAA model.[301] The division of labour within the CAA appears to be commensurate with the United Kingdom's current level of space activity so perhaps there is not presently a call for such a drastic measure. It is likewise evident that the CAA is taking its role seriously as regards matters peripheral to environmental protection in relation to its statutory duties for monitoring and enforcement.[302] This being written, it is clear that the complete absence of any environmental assessment for certain categories of 'space' activity is not a desirable state of affairs. In conjunction with Dr Nicolas Ross of Niparo, the United Kingdom's first sustainable space consultancy, the author submitted joint evidence to the recent United Kingdom Space Agency consultation on Space Sustainability. One of the issues arising was that the aforementioned substantial enforcement and monitoring provisions can be bypassed on the basis that activities falling short of the 47 km threshold do not require licensing under the Space Industry Act although they are clearly related activities.

2.1 *Licences*

As previously discussed, licensing is the essential component of the Space Industry Act 2018. The Act significantly expands the limited provisions of the Outer Space Act 1986. Sections 8–15 of the Act lay the foundations from which licensing matters are assessed and seeks to lay down a framework for the purpose of licensing appropriately qualified private individuals or other legal entities to undertake and administer the United Kingdom's space programme. It is worth noting that whilst specific licences are required for certain activities, some licence conditions will apply to all applicants such as the requirement to be a fit and proper person to conduct such activities and other matters relating to personnel and financial resources.

At the core, under Section 9, is 'Safety', whereby the onus is placed on individuals applying for licences under the Act to have performed appropriate safety assessments as required throughout. The general principles which guide the granting of any such licence are captured within Schedule 1[303] and are:

---

301 See *supra* at page 43.

302 Sarah Knapton, 'Meet the British 'space inspectors' working for a safe blast-off', The Telegraph, 9 March 2024, <https://www.telegraph.co.uk/news/2024/03/09/space-inspectors-rocket-shetland-technology-caa-economy/> accessed 12 October 2024. This page may be behind a paywall for some readers.

303 The Space Industry Act 2018, Sch 1.

a. safety requirements regarding the design and operation of spacecraft, carrier aircraft and payloads;
b. requirements regarding the assembling, integration and fuelling of spacecraft or carrier aircraft, mating of spacecraft or carrier aircraft to their payloads and fuelling of payloads;
c. requirements for handling strategies relating to the security and integrity of payloads;
d. requirements relating to range, tracking, surveillance, risk management, weather measurement and meteorological forecasting;
e. requirements for the protection of persons whose health or safety could be put at risk by spaceflight activities carried out by the licencee, or at or from a spaceport operated by the licencee;
f. requirements for the protection of sensitive or restricted information, technology or items; [and]
g. space debris mitigation guidelines.[304]

There are 38 further types of conditions that may be included in licences.[305] These range from Operator or spaceport licences being granted subject to the applicant submitting an 'assessment of environmental effects ... of launching spacecraft either from a spaceport directly or from a carrier aircraft.'[306] Section 11(6) requires that the Regulator *must* issue guidance on the form and level of detail required for such assessments. Licences that have been issued under the Act are instructive as to what such conditions may look like in practice. The Spaceport Licence for Cornwall Airport[307] included conditions as to the appointment of certain managers and a requirement for a restricted area to be established and a condition not to store hazardous fuels on behalf of the launch operator until the launch operator had, in fact, been granted a licence itself for its own operations.[308]

Schedule 1 and section 4 of the Act state that licences may be granted subject to the limitation of 'the contamination of outer space or adverse changes in the environment of earth.' This was deftly incorporated into the Spaceport licence granted to Cornwall Airport in the following terms:

> The Licencee must use best endeavours to achieve its target of being a carbon neutral spaceport by 2030, as set out in its Assessment of

304 Schedule 1 para 1.
305 Sch 1, para 2–39.
306 *Ibid.*
307 N198.
308 *Ibid*, 3–6.

> Environmental Effects. The Licencee must provide the Regulator with such information as it may reasonably require to ensure compliance with this condition.[309]

As will be discussed as regards aspects of sustainability later in this work, there are certain anomalies regarding the requirement for an Assessment of Environmental Effects, particularly as it applies (or not) to large rockets incapable of operating above the 'stratosphere'. Whilst the stratosphere may seem like a reasonable cut-off point for the purposes of the Act, such launches are still classified as 'suborbital' activities, and, further, they still have the potential to effect 'adverse changes in the environment of earth' as per the statutory language.

Section 2 of the Act requires that space debris mitigation guidelines be adhered to, at least to a degree: 'The Regulator must exercise the Regulator's functions under this Act in the way that the Regulator thinks best calculated to take into account ... (h) any space debris mitigation guidelines issued by an international organisation in which the government of the United Kingdom is represented.' The most significant agreement the United Kingdom is party to in respect of the latter would be the Space Debris Mitigation Guidelines of the Committee of the Peaceful Uses of Outer Space[310] and United Nations General Assembly.[311] There are numerous provisions within the guidelines intended to be regarded by national legislatures when forming domestic rules as to space activities and the design of spacecraft. As a basic requirement, 'Space systems should be designed not to release debris during normal operations.'[312] And various components such as 'sensor covers, separation mechanisms and deployment articles,' should be designed accordingly with regard also given to 'passivation measures' regarding unused stored energy.[313] As will be discussed later in the chapter on monitoring and enforcement, the regulator has very broad powers as regards the inspection of space sites, launch facilities and equipment. Whether or not this will extend to investigating the extent to which debris mitigation measures have been implemented is yet to be seen.

More consideration will be given to this aspect of the legislation when focus shifts to sustainability and comparative evidence but the serious issue presented by space debris should not be taken lightly. It has been said that even 'orbital debris in the 1 mm – 1 cm size range though too small to be tracked by

309 *Ibid*, 4.

310 N149.

311 UNGA Res 62/271 (21 December 2007).

312 N149, Guideline 1.

313 *Ibid.* Guideline 2.

operational systems and to be sensed by most ground systems, are large enough to cause catastrophic damage to many satellites'.[314] Such requirements should, therefore, be a matter of priority for the regulator. What remains to be seen is the extent to which the regulator will balance these requirements against the other forces acting upon it such as the previously mentioned 'growth duty'[315] requiring that any measures taken by the regulator should be sensitive to considerations of economic development. The question of when the consideration of growth and cutting of expenditure yield to the requirements to reduce space debris is yet to be answered, but with such considerations becoming increasingly important within both academic and supranational circles[316] the answer will be of great interest within the context of the United Kingdom space programme.

Wheeler[317] has outlined that, in addition to local requirements within the rules, other international standards likewise are a significant part of an application process, including 'various international space systems' standards defined by the International Organization for Standardization, international guidelines related to space debris mitigation defined by the Inter-Agency Space Debris Coordination Committee and safety standards defined at the European level by the European Cooperation for Space Standardization.'[318] It is yet to be seen whether such instruments will serve to be a persuasive counterbalance to the other duties of the regulator which fall outside of the space domain.

Recently published guidance on licensing from the CAA sets out the information required for the licensing process for each particular licence type and cross-references the guidance documents in a useful format.[319] Besides its role

---

314 Walter Flury, Jean-Michel Contant, 'IAA Position Paper on Orbital Debris, Proceedings of the Third European Conference on Space Debris', 19–21 March 2001 <https://conference.sdo.esoc.esa.int/proceedings/sdc3/paper/7/SDC3-paper7.pdf> accessed 12 October 2024.

315 N195.

316 See Darrell Martin-Lawson, Stefania Paladini, Krishnendu Saha and Erez Yerushalmi, 'The cost of (Un)regulation: Shrinking Earth's orbits and the need for sustainable space governance', (2024) Journal of Environmental Management, 349.

317 Joanne Wheeler, 'The Space Law Review: United Kingdom' in Joanne Wheeler (ed), *The Space Law Review* (3rd, The Law Review 2021). This source was available at the time of writing but appears to presently inaccessible due to being behind a paywall.

318 Joanne Wheeler, 'In review: space law, regulation and policy in United Kingdom', Lexology, online <https://www.lexology.com/library/detail.aspx?g=ae61ea3b-c17c-4c60-8a7c-2364f7b60f1c> accessed 12 October 2024.

319 The Department for Transport, The Department for Science, Innovation and Technology, The United Kingdom Space Agency and The United Kingdom Civil Aviation Authority, 'CAP2221: Regulator's licensing rules', <https://www.caa.co.uk/publication/download/18933> accessed 12 October 2024.

as the custodian of such documents, it is also interesting to note the internal feedback from the CAA itself in respect of how the licensing program has run so far. According to the November and July 'Launch Sessions' of the Civil Aviation Space Launch and Orbit Group, the regulator has 'seen applications that have appeared to have been rushed, with required information not included. It is essential enough time is planned for the submission to be complete and of sufficient quality to avoid applications being put on hold'.[320] This must be viewed against the backdrop of the licensing regime as a whole which, as of March 2023, had 1 Spaceport, Launch and Range Licencee in addition to 669 active operator licences and 86 ongoing licence applications.[321]

2.2 *Range Control*

'Range Control' services are defined under Section 6 of the Act as '… identifying an appropriate range for particular spaceflight activities …'[322] and the associated responsibilities such as monitoring and issuing notifications to those who might be at risk from space activities. The associated guidance document for Range Control activities essentially delineates such responsibilities as may arise under this type of licence as 'tracking' and 'surveillance' of any potentially affected areas in line with a launch operator's safety case in addition to notifications as mentioned. Such notifications may include Notices to Airmen (NOTAMs) by way of ensuring that relevant individuals know of any potential risks as may arise in line with the operator's activities.[323] Notification responsibilities can also include foreign governments[324] where the predicted trajectory crosses into their territory or territorial waters. These matters will be discussed later as regards the law relating to the use of airspace.[325]

'Range' is defined as 'a zone which … is subject to restrictions, exclusions or warnings for keeping it clear, at the relevant times, of: (a) persons or things that might pose a hazard to spaceflight activities; and (b) persons or things

320 The United Kingdom Civil Aviation Authority Space Launch and Orbit Group, Launch Sessions July and November 2022, <https://www.caa.co.uk/media/l2mmf5ow/november-splog-master_launch_published.pdf,> accessed 12 October 2024.

321 The United Kingdom Civil Aviation Authority Space Launch and Orbit Group, Launch Session March 2023 <https://www.caa.co.uk/media/xm4budqo/march-2023-launch.pdf> accessed 12 October 2024.

322 s6(a).

323 The United Kingdom Civil Aviation Authority, Guidance for Range Control Applicants and Licencees, 14 <https://assets.publishing.service.gov.uk/government/uploads/system/uploads/attachment_data/file/904472/guidance-for-range-control-licence-applicants-and-licencees.pdf> accessed 13 October 2024.

324 *Ibid*, para 4.26.

325 See chapter 4.6.1 *infra*.

to which spaceflight activities might pose a hazard. 'Zone' here means a volume of airspace or an area of land or sea.'[326] Under section 2 'Regulations may make provision about the range for spaceflight activities'. Other responsibilities extent to co-ordination of different associated functions and identification of hazards.[327] On application for a Range Control licence, a licencee is assessed against a table of criteria which includes the competencies to carry out the functions previously mentioned which also includes graphical depictions of the systems they will employ.[328]

Regarding the Range Control licencee's relationship with other licencees under the Act, the overall responsibility for the launch lies with the launch operator[329] and no separate safety case is required for this licence. Such licences can also be granted independently of an identified launch operator so that 'The range control licencee can establish its operation, and then negotiate with one or more launch operators in order to provide range control services to them'.[330] The flow chart within the first iteration of the official guidance shows that the Regulator will assess 'if range control applicant can deliver mitigations specified in the launch safety case' only when the launch operator licencee is 'known'.[331] Conversely, where the launch operator is not known, the diagram does not show the same level of involvement, instead stating 'all specified criteria met by applicant'[332] as opposed to being assessed in relation to a specific launch safety case. It does not appear that the services are assessed in relation to the safety case thereafter, instead the regulator assesses 'whether the range control licencee can deliver the specified mitigations during (the) launch licensing process'.[333] It is to be hoped that alongside such details the launch safety case will also be considered and that its omission here is a simple oversight.

2.3 *Spaceport Licences*

Spaceport licences are what enable operators to run 'sites from which spacecraft or carrier aircraft are launched or (as the case may be) are to be launched'.[334] Spaceport licences are also required for areas where spacecraft

326 The Space Industry Act 2018, s5(1).
327 See N173, Regulations 49–51.
328 N329, 23.
329 *Ibid*, 29.
330 *Ibid*, 30.
331 *Ibid*, 31
332 *Ibid.*
333 *Ibid.*
334 s3(2)(a).

are intended to land.[335] In what is a somewhat striking omission, there is no provision for sea-based launches.[336] In respect of launches from the sea, there is still a requirement to comply with other elements of the Act save for the rules relating to spaceports. Whilst the official guidance states that an operator wishing to launch from the sea is advised to contact the Regulator prior to any activities,[337] it is submitted that further authoritative rules should be provided in respect of how and where sea launches can be facilitated. What sort of vessel, for example, should be used for a sea launch and what agreements should be in place regarding proximity to coastlines and other potentially affected areas? A further important question is the extent to which the Space Industry Act would apply to sea launches outside of the United Kingdom's territorial waters given that it applies exclusively to activities 'carried out in the United Kingdom'.[338] It is likely that such launches carried out by United Kingdom nationals would come within section 2(2) of the Outer Space Act 1986 and stand to be licenced thereunder, hence avoiding the additional regulatory matters under the 2018 Act and subsequent Regulations. Whether or not such launches are likely to be commonplace is another matter entirely, but further consideration of this point would be worthwhile.[339] Spaceport licences are granted subject to a range of conditions, first of which is a guarantee of safety under section 10, whereby a licence will not be granted unless 'the applicant has taken all reasonable steps to ensure that risks to public safety arising from the operation of the spaceport are as low as reasonably practicable'.[340] The 'as low as reasonably practicable' principle – or 'ALARP' – is discussed later in this work.[341] In addition to safety considerations, an assessment of environmental effects is also required for a Spaceport licence.[342] Underscoring the need for further legislation or at least guidance here is the presumption that such an

335 s3(2)(b).

336 s3(3).

337 The United Kingdom Civil Aviation Authority, Guidance for Spaceport Licence Applicants and Licencees, 6 <https://www.caa.co.uk/our-work/publications/documents/content/cap2212/> accessed 13 October 2024.

338 S1(1).

339 It should be noted that the British company Skyrora have attempted launches from Iceland. See Skyrora, 'Skyrora attempts first rocket launch to space with Icelandic mobile spaceport' <https://skyrora.com/skyrora-attempts-first-rocket-launch-to-space-with-icelandic-mobile-spaceport/#:~:text=Langanes%2C%2008%20October%202022%20-%20Skyrora%20has%20attempted,vertical%20orbital%20launch%20from%20UK%20soil%20in%202023.> accessed 13 October 2024.

340 S10(1).

341 See chapter 9 in particular.

342 s11.

assessment may not be so required for a sea launch in spite of the obvious environmental impact which could arise. This is even clearer on inspection of the requirements of Regulation 36(4)(c) which, as part of the licensing process, requires the applicant to provide a description of the natural environment around the site – the sea is patently part of the natural environment and should not be excluded from such matters.

There are also safety case requirements for Spaceport licencees under Part 5 of the Space Industry Regulations and it is also important to observe the fact that the safety case is a live document and hence subject to ongoing monitoring under Part 10. The official guidance also highlights the fact that such licences are also subject to other legal provisions such as the Civil Contingencies Act 2004[343] which, in the words of the guidance, along with its associated regulations, 'set out rules and responsibilities for organisations involved in the preparation for and response to emergencies'[344] It is interesting to note that the Act does not set out any particular framework for the handling of emergencies but places a duty upon certain persons or bodies to assess risk and plan for it.[345] This does not appear to be a particularly substantive development on the duties already applicable under the space industry regime itself.

Although Spaceport licences cover both vertical and horizontal spaceports, Regulation 35 requires horizontal spaceports – that is, those which require use of a runway – be situated at CAA approved aerodromes.[346] This does not appear to apply to vertical spaceports.[347] There will be more discussion of spaceport licences when the 2021 Regulations are examined later in this work.

2.4 *Launch and Return Operator Licences*

The strict requirements applicable to Launch licences are expanded on considerably under the Regulations, with the Act being much more skeletal. In respect of implementing the United Kingdom's obligations under international law, aspects of the Acts provisions on launch activities are highly significant. Section 61(1) provides that a register of launches must be established by the Secretary of State. This is a requirement of the 1975 Registration Convention to which the United Kingdom is a party. Under Article 2, the Convention requires that space objects launched into earth orbit or beyond are both registered domestically and brought to the attention of the Secretary General of the

343 C36.
344 N343.
345 N323, S2(1).
346 N173.
347 Vertical space ports are not mentioned in the 2021 Regulations.

United Nations. Section 61 likewise only requires objects launched beyond the stratosphere to be registered although, where the UK requirements go beyond that strictly required by the Convention, is by means of section 61(1) which requires that suborbital launches are also registered. This is without prejudice to the existing responsibilities of the Secretary of State under the Outer Space Act as previously outlined. The details of the space object required under Article IV of the Registration Convention as to its orbital parameters, apogee and perigee and other such, are recorded in the United Kingdom Registry of Space Objects.[348]

Whilst these licence types are explored elsewhere in this work, it is worth clarifying that launch operators or return operators are referred to under the Regulations as 'Spaceflight Operators' and thus, required to observe all the requirements within the rules that apply as regards that role.[349] A 'Launch Operator Licencee' is defined under the Regulations as a holder of 'an Operator licence ... which authorises a person to carry out spaceflight activities that include launching a launch vehicle or launching a carrier aircraft and a launch vehicle'[350] whereas a 'Return Operator Licencee' is a holder of a licence authorising the operation of 'a launch vehicle, launched elsewhere than the United Kingdom, in order to cause that vehicle to land in the United Kingdom'.

2.5 *Individuals Taking Part in Spaceflight Activities*

Underscoring the vibrant ambitions for the United Kingdom space industry, provision is made in the Act for 'Individuals taking part in spaceflight activities.' Such individuals are covered under sections 17 and 18 and look to cover fee-paying 'space tourists' in addition to those in other roles. This part of the Act covers the 'informed consent' rules in addition to medical and fitness requirements for space-faring individuals. Terms such as 'astronaut' are not used anywhere within the Act or the associated regulations. Whether this affects the requirement for assistance rendered to space-faring personnel in the event of crises is unclear. Under Article V of the Outer Space Treaty it is stated that:

> States Parties to the Treaty shall regard astronauts as envoys of mankind in outer space and shall render to them all possible assistance in the event of accident, distress, or emergency landing on the territory of another State Party or on the high seas. When astronauts make such a

348 N49.

349 See Regulation 9 of the Space Industry Regulations 2021.

350 SIR 2021, Interpretation Part 1, 2 (1).

> landing, they shall be safely and promptly returned to the State of registry of their space vehicle.[351]

Should all those – including fee-paying tourists – be regarded as 'envoys of mankind' and, thus, be granted international protections as per the Outer Space Treaty? As regards the precise terminology used to describe space-faring individuals, potentially not, but it is worthy of note that the Rescue Agreement of 1968 is broader in scope:

> Each Contracting Party which receives information or discovers that the personnel of a spacecraft have suffered accident or are experiencing conditions of distress or have made an emergency or unintended landing in territory under its jurisdiction or on the high seas or in any other place not under the jurisdiction of any State shall immediately:
>
> a. notify the launching authority or, if it cannot identify and immediately communicate with the launching authority, immediately make a public announcement by all appropriate means of communication at its disposal;
>
> b. notify the Secretary-General of the United Nations, who should disseminate the information without delay by all appropriate means of communication at his disposal.[352]

A relevant question would whether or not the term 'personnel' would include all those aboard or just those with operational roles. Professor von der Dunk has argued that this is a moot point:

> Existing general humanitarian obligations to assist humans in distress already would cover what is necessary and justified for spaceflight participants, without the added 'entitlements' under the Rescue Agreement, or even Article V of the Outer Space Treaty's qualification as 'envoys of mankind'. After all, this is presently the case with tourists in the high mountains or similar realms, where the inherent dangers accepted willingly and only for the pleasure derived therefrom should not translate into a blanket licence to have others risk their lives or their funds if the risks unfortunately translate into reality.[353]

351 N104.

352 N103, Article 1.

353 Frans Von Der Dunk, *Legal Aspects of Private Manned Spaceflight*, in Frans Von Der Dunk and Fabio Tronchetti, (eds), *Handbook of Space Law* (Edward Elgar, 2015), 711–712.

The exact terminology deployed in national instruments such as the Space Industry Act 2018 therefore, may have little or no bearing on the international status of individuals participating in space activities should they encounter distress.

The rules cover informed consent and matters of training, qualifications and medical fitness. As will be elaborated later on in this work, the informed consent rules are, to a degree, porous, and there needs to be some greater clarity on the relationship between medical fitness and informed consent as per the rules themselves, particularly where this concerns mental capacity and the ability – or not – to actually give informed consent in such circumstances.

'Informed Consent' in the context of the Act, requires that a licencee does not allow an individual to take part in space flight activities unless they have signified their consent to accept the risks involved.[354] This section was greatly expanded upon in the 2021 Regulations as per the direction given by section 17(3) and will be the subject of more elaboration later on in this work. As a comparative point, it is interesting to note that the regulations made under the Act in this regard strongly echo the spirit – and in many cases, the letter – of the United States guidelines put forward by the Federal Aviation Administration[355] and the Code of Federal Regulations.[356]

It is stated therein that

'... An operator must inform space flight participants in writing about the risks of the launch and re-entry, including known hazards and the potential for unknown hazards. The operator must identify the risks and hazards that could result in serious injury, death, disability, or total or partial loss of physical and mental function to the space flight participant and may do so with a hazard analysis';[357] and that, also, the information should be able to be readily understood by those without specialist education or training in the relevant area.[358]

The need to inform participants of the potentially fatal risks inherent in touristic space travel – which is essentially a hazardous journey on what

354 s17(1)(a).

355 Federal Aviation Administration Office of Commercial Space Transportation, Guidance on Informing Crew and Spaceflight /headquarters_offices/ast/regulations/media/ Guidance_on_Informing Participants of Risk, (Version 1.1 Arpil 4 2017). <https://www.faa.gov/about/office_org/headquarters_offices/ast/regulations/media /Guidance_on_Informing_Crew_and_Space_Flight_Participants_of_Risk.pdf> accessed 14 October 2024.

356 51 U.S.C. 50901–50923, Code of Federal Regulations (US) Part 460.9, Human Space Flight Requirements.

357 *Ibid.* 3.

358 *Ibid.* 4. Further guidance is given as to what level of 'technical detail' should be disclosed.

amounts to an experimental aircraft, or, indeed, spacecraft – has prompted the design of waivers by various states across the United States, including this one which was the subject of discussion by O'Brien in an article from 2017. The example was used therein from the State of Virginia's Space Law:

> WARNING AND ACKNOWLEDGEMENT: I understand and acknowledge that, under Virginia law, there is no civil liability for bodily injury, including death, emotional injury, or property damage sustained by a participant in spaceflight activities provided by a spaceflight entity if such injury or damage results from the risks of the spaceflight activity .... I understand and acknowledge that I am participating in spaceflight activities at my own risk. I have been given the opportunity to consult with an attorney before signing this statement.[359]

It is to be noted that section 7 of the 2015 Commercial Space Launch Competitiveness Act[360] made it a requirement for reciprocal cross-waivers of liability between the licencee, spaceflight participants and the FAA to be a condition of private spaceflight transactions. This somewhat reduces the significance of statutes such as this made by states themselves.

This is mirrored to some degree in the draft sample consent form which was included in the original guidance for launch and return operators in the United Kingdom, which included the following statement:

'I accept and understand that the operator's spaceflight activities carry an inherent risk of danger and in particular that—

- the activities may result in death or injury,
- the Regulator has not certified that the launch vehicle complies with any national or international safety standards, and
- the provisions relating to section 34(2) of the Space Industry Act 2018 (which provides for damages to be recovered without proof of negligence or intention or other cause of action, as if the injury had been caused by the wilful act, neglect, or default of the spaceflight operator), and section 35(3) of the Space Industry Act 2018 (which provides for an indemnity from the Secretary of State to the claimant in the circumstances mentioned in that subsection), will not apply in the event of me dying or sustaining injury by

359 Zeledine Niamh O'Brien, 'To boldly go? Private contracts for the carriage of persons in space, exclusion clauses and inter-party waivers of tortious liability' (2007) 29 D.U.L.J., 341.

360 N178.

taking part in the operator's spaceflight activities'.[361] It is interesting to note that the updated guidance published on 31 May 2024 does not include the sample consent form, instead stating that an example consent form can be obtained by emailing the CAA's commercial spaceflight team.[362] Whether the sample consent form is identical to the one published in the initial guidance is unknown.

This statutory informed consent regime is the first of its kind in the United Kingdom for high-risk leisure activities. One very interesting dimension is that it is also apparently deemed to apply to employees of an operator's enterprise in addition to those who may be there on more of a voluntary basis as spectators or even space tourists. The effect of valid informed consent being given is to deprive the person giving such consent of the benefit of the strict liability regime for compensation as provided for elsewhere in the Act. The Act requires individuals acting in a 'prescribed role' to have given informed consent.[363] Crew members are designated as acting within prescribed roles under Regulation 204(a) for the purposes of informed consent while 'space flight participants' are designated as acting within a 'prescribed capacity'. This distinction appears insignificant as regards the need for informed consent to be obtained but still indicates a formal distinction which is to be welcomed. Whilst it is understandable that those who voluntarily place themselves in close proximity to such hazardous activities naturally assume some risk, it is more difficult to see how this can be justified in relation to employees of an operator, even if the only effect is to deprive such individuals of the benefit of the strict liability regime. It should be stressed that giving of informed consent does not abrogate an individual employee's rights under other workplace safety enactments such as the Health and Safety at Work Act 1974[364] and it must be borne in mind, that notwithstanding the consent provisions of the Act and Regulations, there remains the prospect of an action in negligence being raised at common law. Such compulsory individual surrenders of such rights could prove, in and of themselves, to be controversial. Situations such as this are not the subject of

361 Guidance for Launch and Return Operators and Licence Applicants, 1st edition, Annex A, draft sample consent form and information to be provided, 83. <https://assets.publishing.service.gov.uk/government/uploads/system/uploads/attachment_data/file/904911/guidance-for-launch-and-return-operator-licence-applicants-and-licensees.pdf > accessed 14 October 2024.

362 The United Kingdom Civil Aviation Authority, Guidance for Launch and Return Operator Licence Applicants and Licencees, CAP2213, 2ND Edition, 31 May 2024, 83, <https://www.caa.co.uk/publication/download/18943> accessed 14 October 2024.

363 Space Industry Act s17(1)(a).

364 C37.

extensive judicial treatment although in one case a similar provision – albeit a contractual matter as opposed to a statutory imposition – was regarded by the High Court to potentially offend the Unfair Contract Terms Act 1977[365] as will be discussed later.

2.6 *Liability and Insurance*

A crucial dimension of space law on both the national and international scale is liability – in the event of things going wrong, who pays for what. In UK space law, liability is handled across the 3 main instruments – the Outer Space Act, the Space Industry Act 2018 and the Space Industry Regulations 2021. Section 10 of the Outer Space Act 1986 carried the obligation to indemnify the United Kingdom government against damage claims arising out of space activities subject to any limit placed on the liability ceiling as per section 10(1). This is now repeated under section 36 of the Space Industry Act. Section 34(2) imposes a no-fault liability scheme whereby proof of negligence or intention is not required. The effect is that strict liability is imposed on operators should any uninvolved individuals suffer any injury as a result of an operator's space activities. This development serves to supplement the Liability Convention[366] which renders state parties liable to compensate other state parties on the basis of damage resulting from their space activities to the territories of other states[367] but does not provide for any compensatory mechanism as regards citizens of the state liable. Indeed, nationals of the liable state are expressly excluded by Article VII (a) with foreign nationals affected within that state's territory excluded by VII (b) should they be involved with the space activities in question. Further, the structuring of the Space Industry Act on liability – specifically, the requirement under section 36(1)(a) for a licencee to indemnify the government for claims arising from space activities – is reflective of the international regime on liability which recognises only inter-state liability. The practical impart of this is, that should a private actor launch a space object from within the United Kingdom which causes damage to another state as per the requirements of Article II of the Liability Convention, compensation paid by the United Kingdom government thereunder would be effectively underwritten by the licencee who would be required to reimburse the latter. It is important to note that there are likely to be significant developments as regards the liability limit under section 36 which looks set to be capped under Regulations made under section 34(5) pending the outcome of the recent

365 C50, see Cassley's case, [2015] EWHC 722.

366 N102.

367 *Ibid*, Article II.

government consultation Orbital Liabilities, Insurance, Charging and Space Sustainability.[368]

Some areas of strict liability in tort law – part of the English Law of Obligations – arise from the common law rather than as a creation of Parliament. This is to say, that in addition to legislated measures, strict liability can arise from judicial decisions in individual cases which serve as precedent[369] but, as mentioned, strict liability can also be legislated for. In addition to securing compliance with the Liability Convention and providing for compensation to be paid for damage suffered by United Kingdom nationals, it is justified here in the interests of public safety and legal certainty.

In the domestic realm, the use of strict liability as a tool to ensure high standards is nothing new.[370] It seems fair that those carrying out dangerous activities that have the potential to do a vast amount of harm to be held to as high a standard as those providing food deemed fit for human consumption.[371] As noted, the measures also bring the level of protection offered to citizens of the United Kingdom in line with that offered to citizens of the rest of the world under the Liability Convention[372] should they be so affected by the United Kingdom's space activities.

As set out, no-fault liability in this sense does not mean no-fault liability as regards the whole world. Under section 34(3), the rules do not apply to 'individuals of a prescribed description, taking part in, or otherwise engaged in connection with, the spaceflight activities'. In addition to mirroring the Liability Convention, this appears to be based on the legal maxim *'volenti non fit injuria'* – that a voluntary assumption of risk by the claimant will relieve a potential tortfeasor of their liability. Individuals as defined by section 34(3) should in theory and principle still be able to claim against operators under the 'fault-based' regime, that is under the existing common law tort and delictual principles of negligence.

Section 34(2) is tempered with reference to Regulation 220 of the Space Industry Regulations which states that operator licences must specify limits on the amount of operator's liability for injury or damage and other third-party liability. This arrangement has been met with ambivalence by some in

368 N19.

369 See *Rylands v Fletcher* (1868) LR 3 HL 330.

370 See *Callow v Tillstone* (1900) 64 JP 823 322.

371 *Ibid.*

372 N102.

the industry. For instance, Skyrora, in their written evidence to the House of Commons Select Committee on Science and Technology,[373] stated that:

> Whilst industry is encouraged by the fact that an operator licence must specify a limit on the amount of the operator's liability limit, the limit is determined on a case-by-case basis. However, the normal position in most space faring nations is to specify a cap, with governments then taking on any additional risk. If this approach is not replicated in the United Kingdom, it may stall industry before it has a chance to properly start.

This is indeed the position in the United States;[374] Russia, on the other hand does not take this approach. Instead, the state is liable itself for liability for damage caused within its own territory, going over and above the requirements of the Liability Convention, but reserves the right to pursue private actors who may have caused the said damage in order to recoup losses arising.[375] The situation in Ukraine is vague on this matter,[376] as is the case in Kazakhstan.[377] Other national legislatures that are silent on this matter include Norway,[378] and the position in Sweden is in some regards similar to Russia in respect of the state reserving the right to pursue private actors as regards disbursements arising from 'space activities' in cases of liability via international treaty obligations.[379] The French position, however, appears to be one of 'absolute' liability on the part of operators for any damage caused[380] but there is also the possibility of state guarantees if the operator insures themselves to the appropriate limit.[381] Like other states in Europe, the Netherlands follows the approach of requiring compulsory insurance for operators[382] but Austria takes an interesting path whereby the state may cover costs for damage caused

373 Science, Innovation and Technology Committee, 'UK Space Strategy and UK satellite infrastructure, reviewing the licensing regime for launch', Written Evidence Submitted by Skyrora, (SPA0064), 6, <committees.parliament.uk/writtenevidence/37269/pdf/> accessed 14 October.

374 14 CFR (US) 440.19(a).

375 Russian Law on Space Activities, Federal Law No. 5663–1[2], Article 30.

376 Irmgrad Marboe, *National Space Law,* in Frans Von Der Dunk, Fabio Tronchetti, *Handbook of Space Law,* (2017 Edward Elgar), 149.

377 *Ibid* 151.

378 *Ibid* 152.

379 *Ibid* 154.

380 French Space Operations Act, 2008, Article 13.

381 N382, 159.

382 *Ibid*, 164.

should the space activity be considered to be 'in the public interest'.[383] Elsewhere, South Korea provides for a cap on the amount of compensation to be guaranteed by the state[384] but this is by no means a universal practice.

The desire to see a fixed statutory cap on liability within the Space Industry Act has also been advocated by other prominent voices within industry such as Lockheed Martin[385] who claim that the absence of such a cap represents a challenge to competitiveness. This was echoed in the initial consultations conducted around the time of the Space Industry Act with respondents desiring a limit on liabilities to avoid losing a competitive edge.[386] The responses were nuanced, with some respondents desiring limitations based on the types of mission whilst others desired a case-by case approach to liability based on a 'Maximum Possible Loss approach as is used in the US and Australia'.[387] Whilst there may be some merit to the claims that unlimited liability reduces competitiveness, an equally valid consideration is the extent to which the UK taxpayer should have to subsidise the consequences of any disaster the operator is responsible for. Some operators went so far as to propose that their liabilities towards third parties should also be limited. It is hard to see how either of these approaches could be completely justified save for the matter of obtaining third-party liability insurance – some respondents to the consultation stated that this type of cover is unavailable on an 'unlimited liability' basis and others raised legitimate points regarding the overall cost of insurance generally and how this could be potentially prohibitive.[388] This tension represents a fine balancing act – the absence of a cap or perceived lack of transparency may dissuade some would-be operators from setting up business in the United

383 *Ibid*, 165.

384 *Ibid*, 170.

385 Written Evidence Submitted by Lockheed Martin UK to the House of Commons Select Committee on Science and Technology (SPA0050), <https://committees.parliament.uk/writtenevidence/37239/pdf/> accessed 14 October 2024.

386 Department for Business, Energy and Industrial Strategy, Department for Transport, United Kingdom Civil Aviation Authority, United Kingdom Space Agency, Call For Evidence: Space Industry Act 2018 – Government Response, 28 May 2019, 5 <https://assets.publishing.service.gov.uk/media/5ce81980ed915d247cd802f1/Government_Response_to_Call_for_Evidence_-_Spaceflight_liabilities_-_Final_190528.pdf> Accessed 14 October 2024.

387 *Ibid*, 5, – the following footnote was added re the definition of MPL: 'MPL is an approach that would seek to calculate the amount of potential third-party liability claims that an Operator could incur in a realistically probable scenario. The US definition is 'The MPL is a dollar value assessment of government and third-party properties at risk of damage from launch-related activities or conduct."

388 *Ibid*, 6.

Kingdom. On the other hand, if the amount of an operator's liability is to be determined on a case-by-case basis, is this not a fairer approach than simply imposing a single cap for all operators regardless of their size or the extent of their ambitions? The United States has such a system, albeit quite a complex one as a result of the 1988 amendment to the Commercial Space Launch Act.[389] Individual liability caps are calculated with reference to 'Maximum Probable Loss' on the submission of required information to the Secretary of Transportation.[390] Some operators stated that insurance would be higher for 'untested' vehicles and at least one reported that, in their opinion, it may not be possible to obtain insurance for the first spaceflight from the United Kingdom or otherwise be prohibitively expensive. It may be proportionate for a cap on liabilities to be imposed in the early stages of the United Kingdom space industry with this being liable to change as the cost of insurance comes down following what will hopefully be a series of safe and successful space activities. It should be noted that at the time of writing there is an ongoing consultation on liabilities which could very well see a legislative shift in the provisions relating to maximum ceilings of liability such as the ones discussed here.

On the topic of liability for negligent acts more broadly, it is important to note the supplementary provisions that were brought about by the Space Industry Regulations 2021 in this area. As Regulation 219 states, where an operator is grossly negligent or guilty of wilful misconduct as regards their obligations under the Act they become automatically exempt from any limit on liability. The wording of this Regulation is deserving of some attention here – and will also be explored later in this work. 'Gross' negligence at common law is a criminal term of art and one that has no formulaic definition as such. The Act itself defines gross negligence as:

a. the person or body is in breach of a duty of care owed under the law of negligence, and
b. the conduct constituting that breach falls far below what can reasonably be expected of the person or body in the circumstances.[391]

The key term here is 'far below' which has the effect of divorcing this species of negligence from that under the common law, and would, it is to be assumed, be determined at a criminal trial to a higher standard of proof as opposed to a

---

389 51 USC Ch. 509 §50914.

390 *Ibid*, 50914, 5(C), 2(C). For further details including a concise overview of the United States regime, see Frans von der Dunk, 'Billion-dollar questions? Legal aspects of commercial space activities', June 2018, *Uniform Law Review*, Vol 23, 2, 418–446, esp. chapter IV.

391 Space Industry Act 2018 s 37(5).

civil one requiring less of an evidential burden. The bar for proving 'wilful misconduct', however, may be significantly lower and likewise suggests a civil – as opposed to a criminal – character. Instances in which limitations on liability will be lifted, therefore, are likely to come only after determinations made by the criminal courts. It is interesting to reflect that civil negligence – as opposed to gross negligence as determined by the criminal law – could potentially result in the same amount of damage being caused yet not, in theory, be subject to the cap on liability being lifted.

Relatedly, under section 35 the Secretary of State is granted the 'power or duty' to indemnify an operator for 'injury or damage' if the 'liability amount' exceeds the 'insurance amount' – the amount the operator has been insured for in respect of the 'spaceflight activities' in question. Whether this is likely to act as an incentive for lower insurance premiums is to be seen – perhaps the state serving as a guarantor in this regard may do just this. On the other hand, it is questionable whether this method represents the most equitable means of supporting space activities given that, in effect, the UK taxpayer would ultimately provide an indemnity.

At this stage, it is worth reminding ourselves what 'space activity' is defined as within the Act. Section 1(4) states that a 'space activity' means:

> launching or procuring the launch or the return to earth of a space object or of an aircraft carrying a space object ... operating a space object, or any activity in outer space ... 'suborbital activity' means launching, procuring the launch of, operating or procuring the return to earth of ... a craft to which subsection (5) applies, or an aircraft carrying such a craft, but does not include space activity.

The liability provisions within the Act apply to both suborbital and orbital endeavours as they are both classified as 'spaceflight activities' although the precise level of liability for these different activities is yet to be determined.

Subsections 5 and 6 state that:

> (5) This subsection applies to—
> a. a rocket or other craft that is capable of operating above the stratosphere;
> b. a balloon that is capable of reaching the stratosphere carrying crew or passengers.
>
> (6) Space activities and suborbital activities are referred to in this Act as 'spaceflight activities'.

Whilst initially straightforward, questions remain as to the precise definition of 'procuring' in this sense as previously discussed – no guidance is given in the Interpretation section as to what this means although accordingly it is classified as 'spaceflight activities'. Moreover, the sections regarding 'range control' services appear to divorce range control from spaceflight activities themselves which begs the question as to what status they have as regards liability. Would range control services themselves come within the definition of 'procuring' the launch or return to earth of a space object as per section 35 or are such services exempt from liability provisions? In this sense clarification is certainly needed as regards which services are and are not covered by the liability provisions. The government response that was published in the wake of the call for evidence on liabilities, insurance and charging further states that range control activities '... are 'associated activities'. Therefore the Space Industry Act does not appear to impose strict liability under section 34 on persons operating spaceports or providers of range control services or require them to indemnify the Government for claims brought against it.[392] However, under section 34(4)(c) an operator is entitled to claim back damages caused whereby a 'person other than the operator is liable in respect of ... injury or damage' as set out in section 34(2). On this basis, those conducting range control or other 'associated activities' could be indirectly bound by strict liability. Such matters will surely be detailed within any contractual arrangements between operators and the providers of such services.

Given that ineffective range control services could seemingly lead to considerable damage, it is not easy to fathom the rationale for why such services are not held more directly accountable. This is unless one takes into account the principles of the Liability Convention which centres on space activities (involving space objects) rather than an act more associated with the support of such activities. Range control would appear to be an activity which could lead to the kind of damage envisaged by the Convention. As is stated in Article II, 'a launching state shall be absolutely liable to pay compensation for damage caused by its space object on the surface of the Earth or to aircraft in flight'. Range control would appear to be integral to efforts made to avoid a space object causing damage to the surface of the earth or even aircraft by its very definition. Under the Act, they are distinct from spaceflight activities, being referred to variously as 'services for spaceflight activities' as opposed to being an integral part of them. Interestingly, the government consultation response determined that the activities of the operator are more likely to cause damage

392 N127.

but at the same time these aspects of the operation could be arguably said to be indivisible in terms of the practical consequences. The motive is likely to be for legal certainty and clarity as was stated:

> there may be multiple parties involved in a spaceflight activity and by making the operator of a spacecraft liable, this provides third parties sustaining injury and damage with clarity regarding who they can bring a claim against without needing to prove fault.[393]

Other than section 35, there does not seem to be the provision made in the Act for the Secretary of State to claim back any monies rendered over and above the insured amount save for cases of gross negligence or wilful misconduct. This would appear to be a high threshold for the government to overcome should such a situation arise. Why 'gross' negligence? As mentioned, 'gross negligence' in a legal sense in England and Wales is a criminal matter which would need to be proved beyond reasonable doubt should such a claim need to be sustained. 'Gross negligence' itself has no statutory definition and is usually a question for a jury to determine in a criminal matter. As Lord Hewart stated in the case of *R v Bateman*:

> In explaining to juries the test which they should apply to determine whether the negligence, in the particular case, amounted or did not amount to a crime, judges have used many epithets, such as 'culpable,' 'criminal,' 'gross,' 'wicked,' 'clear,' 'complete.' But, whatever epithet be used and whether an epithet be used or not, in order to establish criminal liability the facts must be such that, in the opinion of the jury, the negligence of the accused went beyond a mere matter of compensation between subjects and showed such disregard for the life and safety of others as to amount to a crime against the State and conduct deserving punishment.[394]

393 The United Kingdom Space Agency, Department for Transport, Department for Business, Energy and Industrial Strategy, The United Kingdom Civil Aviation Authority, 'Unlocking Commercial Spaceflight for the UK consultation on draft insurance and liabilities requirements to implement the Space Industry Act', 2020, 18, <https://assets.publishing.service.gov.uk/media/5f8e8bbfe90e0727c3edba6b/unlocking-commercial-spaceflight-for-the-uk-consultation-on-draft-insurance-and-liabilities-requirements-to-implement-the-space-industry-act.pdf#:~:text=This%20consultation%20document%20describes%20and%20explains%20what%20we,and%20guidance%20and%20sets%20out%20our%20key%20questions,> accessed 14 October 2024.

394 *R. v Bateman (Percy)*, (1927) 19 Cr. App. R. 8 [11–12].

'Wilful misconduct', on the other hand, is not a specific form of criminal liability and if it is to be viewed in the way of contracts for carriage of goods, may only need be proven on a balance of probabilities as opposed to beyond reasonable doubt.[395] 'Wilful misconduct' is clearly discrete from 'ordinary' negligence, yet it likely has to be proven to the same standard. What both 'wilful misconduct' and 'gross negligence' have in common, therefore, appears to be some element of intention or mindfulness usually associated with the criminal law. This does appear to give operators a convenient defence in these circumstances. Should a significant amount of damage arise out of an operator's spaceflight activities as a result of the operator's negligence, in the absence of a criminal conviction or evidence of 'wilfulness', the government may be precluded from claiming any money back in spite of the operator's fault. Whether this is a satisfactory means of ensuring compliance is yet to be seen. It appears confusing that 'gross negligence' and 'wilful misconduct' are treated in the same section of the Act as almost interchangeable when they are potentially anything but, both appearing to require different standards of proof. The extent to which the liability regime is built upon following the present consultation remains to be seen. Essentially, the provisions are likely to remain similar so long as they give effect to international liabilities arising from the Liability Convention.

There are other significant dimensions to the Space Industry Act, such as those relating to enforcement and monitoring and the various Schedules. The Act also creates a range of new criminal and civil offences in relation to spacecraft and ensures that the criminal law applies to spacecraft themselves. Section 51 sets out that criminal law applies to offences on board spacecraft and carrier aircraft in respect of both acts and omissions. Schedule 4 also sets out a range of new criminal offences in relation to spacecraft themselves, such as hijacking,[396] destroying, damaging or endangering safety of spacecraft[397] and the carrying of certain dangerous articles.[398] Some of these areas will be discussed later in this work when attention turns to aspects of safety and enforcement. More will also be written specifically as regards the Act's requirement for an Assessment of Environmental Effects to be submitted under the chapter on sustainability.

In spite of the inevitable questions arising, the Space Industry Act 2018 truly marked a giant leap for UK space law, taking it from the merely perfunctory

395 See for example *Datec Electronic Holdings Ltd v United Parcels Service Ltd* [2007] UKHL 23, [2007] 1 W.L.R. 1325.

396 Schedule 4 (1).

397 Schedule 4 (2).

398 Schedule 4 (5).

into the actual Space Age proper. As has been written, there are some aspects of the Act which may not be as strong as may be desirable, but the 2021 Regulations that followed provided a welcome and significant level of detail and expansion. As a concluding thought, it is of interest to note the possibility that the 2018 Act and 1986 Act could, at some stage, become merged into one single 'framework for space activities'.[399] In the interests of consolidation and for the avoidance of unwieldiness, this could be a welcome development. This should not be done at the overall expense of addressing some of the more pressing concerns within the legislation, and neither at the expense of observing some of the comparative evidence from other jurisdictions to this end.

3 The Space Industry Regulations 2021

The Space Industry Regulations 2021 build significantly upon their parent Act, presenting an even larger expansion into unchartered territory for UK space legislation. There are almost 300 regulations along with 8 schedules, most of which seek to flesh-out the provisions of the preceding Space Industry Act 2018 marking a considerable expansion on both the latter and the Outer Space Act 1986.

The Regulations can be said to be of broadly 3 types: Regulations directly connected with spaceflight activities; Regulations indirectly connected; and Regulations peripherally concerned with spaceflight activities. Those directly connected are those regarding launches and spaceflight activities – rules relating to space objects, their occupants and their launches. Regulations of the second type include risk assessment matters and licensing whilst those of the third type are concerned with more peripheral – though in some cases no less important – matters. These would be Parts 11, 14, 15, 16 and 17 on Security, Monitoring and Enforcement, Civil Sanctions, Occurrence Reporting and Miscellaneous provisions respectively.

Part 3 gives further guidance on the grant of licences, including the eligibility criteria for licencees and places mandatory requirements on spaceport licencees to appoint certain individuals in specific roles, namely an accountable

399 The United Kingdom Government, Department for Science,Innovation and Technology, 'Space Regulatory Review 2024; A targeted review of space regulations', Research Paper Number 2024/007, May 2024, 35, <https://assets.publishing.service.gov.uk/media/6644d26fb7249a4c6e9d3597/space_regulatory_review_2024.pdf> accessed 4 October 2024.

manager, a safety manager and security manager[400] and makes it a criminal offence punishable by up to two years in prison to fail to inform the Regulator of any changes to the status of such individuals in the event of death or termination of employment for whatever reason. Chapter 3 provides rules on the procedure for applying for licences and how such applications will be considered by the Regulator.

Part 4 lays down rules relating to the determination of risk 'to persons who are not crew or spaceflight participants'.[401] Regulation 26(1)(c) sets out the requirement that an applicant for a spaceflight operator licence must provide an estimation 'numerically of the risk of death or serious injury arising from the hazards mentioned in sub-paragraph (a) to persons who are not human occupants'. The hazards referred to are 'hazards that could, whether or not the launch vehicle malfunctions – (i) arise from, or cause a major accident during, the proposed spaceflight activities, or (ii) arise from the launch vehicle, or any part of it, during the proposed spaceflight activities'. A ground safety analysis must also be undertaken under this part.[402]

Regulation 28 lays down 'steps to be taken for each identified hazard'. These are to 'identify the conditions under which it could occur … identify what could cause it or contribute to it … assess the likelihood of it arising … assess its foreseeable consequences … evaluate the risk of a major accident … define any appropriate measures to take to prevent a major accident from occurring, and mitigate the consequences if a major accident does occur'.[403]

Chapter 3 stipulates requirements for risk assessments which must be undertaken under the regulations and Regulation 33 states what information needs to be passed on to the Regulator regarding such risk assessments. Whilst the right to inspection is reserved elsewhere in the rules, the overall ethos of risk assessment according to the Regulator is in line with the principle that 'those that create the risks are best placed to manage those risks'.[404]

Part 5 on the grant of a spaceport licence puts forward 'prescribed criteria for horizontal spaceports' requiring them to be located at an aerodrome which is 'either certified or CAA licenced and NASP directed'. 'NASP directed' is defined as 'an aerodrome which is subject to the direction of the Secretary of State under sections 12, 13, 13A, 14 and 15 of the Aviation Security Act 1982(a).

400 R7.

401 Chapter 2.

402 R27.

403 R28(1)(a)–(f).

404 As echoed elsewhere within other regulatory bodies where safety is a key concern. See, for example, the Health and Safety Executive, 'Our role as a regulator', <https://www.hse.gov.uk/enforce/our-role-as-regulator.htm> accessed 14 October 2024.

For the sake of completeness, 'NASP' stands for 'National Aviation Safety Plan' which is the standard adopted by the United Kingdom CAA in respect of assuring safety across the spectrum of aviation activities, including the design of aircraft, the training of maintenance engineers and the safety of aerodromes generally. It is designed to implement the International Civil Aviation Organization's Global Aviation Safety Plan in addition to the United Kingdom's own safety protocols.[405]

Regulation 38 requires applicants to perform a 'siting assessment'. Such assessments must culminate in a 'numerical estimate of the annualised risk of death or serious injury to members of the public posed by the spaceflight activities proposed'[406] and that this level of risk 'must be acceptable to the Regulator'.[407] How the Regulator will determine what is and is not an acceptable level of risk is not commented upon within the regulations. The aforementioned 'members of the public' are defined under Chapter 3 – essentially those who are not working in connection with the space activities underway or with the spaceport generally in numerous capacities or otherwise haven't put themselves 'voluntarily in close proximity to a source of danger at a spaceport'.[408]

Interestingly, members of the armed forces and employees of the emergency services are also not classified as 'members of the public' under Regulation 40. However, for launch and return operators, the guidance states that, when submitting a Safety Case which identifies 'major accident hazards',[409] potentially affected persons 'could include the Operator's own staff; persons in the vicinity of the launch site (spaceport); and persons in nearby habitations or under the flight trajectory.' Although it is encouraging to see this at least in the form of guidance, it would be preferable for such matters to be brought within actual legislation.

Part 6 concerns Range Control Services, and begins by laying down certain requirements for the holder of range control licences which are similar in

---

405 The United Kingdom Civil Aviation Authority, 'The CAA Safety Plan- our approach to protecting UK citizens and the general public from aviation risk' < https://www.caa.co.uk/safety-initiatives/how-we-regulate/safety-plan/the-caa-safety-plan/#:~:text=Our%20Safety%20Plan%20sets%20out%20at%20a%20high,not%20introduce%20risks%20that%20are%20unacceptable%20to%20us> accessed 14 October 2024.

406 R38(2)(c).

407 R38(3).

408 R39 and 40.

409 Defined under Regulation 2 as: 'an accident arising out of or in the course of spaceflight activities or preparation for spaceflight activities that is highly likely to:
(a) cause death or serious injury to, or.
(b) destroy or seriously damage the property of,
persons who are not human occupants of the launch vehicle.'

scope to requirements in respect of licences generally elsewhere in the regulations but include specific conditions such as technical capacities in respect of tracking and range surveillance.[410] Chapter 3 lays down the requirement for licencees under this part to enter into agreements with 'relevant authorities' regarding the predicted range for the space activity. Specifically the 'relevant authorities' are the relevant air navigation service providing for aircraft flying within the designated range, authorities concerned with managing the territorial waters should these fall within the designated range and the United Kingdom Hydrographic Office.[411] The regulations then specify rules for the identification of specific ranges and for particular hazard areas[412] with Chapter 5 laying down 'notification requirements' whereby particular persons – emergency services, local authorities and owners/occupiers of land within the designated range in addition to the Regulator should be notified if this comes within the licencee's range control services. Regulation 50 stipulates the precise form in which these notifications should take place.

Part 7 applies to 'Training, qualifications and medical fitness' of those directly engaged in spaceflight activities for the purposes of space activities ensuring that those who participate in such activities are both qualified to do so and medically fit. Under Regulation 60 it is stated that training records, the training manual and records of various other associated records should be kept for at least 2 years. This seems unusual when considering that the limitation period for most personal injury claims is 3 years- and potentially longer – as per the Limitation Act 1980.[413] Criteria are also laid down regarding the appointment of the Training Manager and the contents of the Training Manual and Training Program also specified later. Requirements for medical fitness including those relating to disability is covered under Chapter 5.

Part 8 refers to 'Safety of Operators' spaceflight activities' with Regulation 79 placing a specific safety duty on spaceflight operators, specifically that they must carry out such activities 'in accordance with the current safety case by preventing a major accident from occurring and mitigating the consequences of such an accident if it does occur' in addition to 'securing the

410 R42 (e) (I)–(II).

411 R44. The United Kingdom Hydrographic Office is an agency of the UK Ministry of Defence whose role within government is to collect and analyse data relating to the seabed on a range of matters, from those of defence interest through to transport considerations and matters relating to climate change. The UK Hydrographic Office, 'Our Role in Government', <https://www.admiralty.co.uk/government> accessed 9 April 2024.

412 R46 and R47.

413 1980 c. 58.

safety of a human occupant' if relevant 'in accordance with the current risk assessment'.[414] Various other rules relating to safety are detailed throughout the sizeable Part, including the requirement that 'flight termination personnel' should be appointed should the particular flight not have an 'autonomous flight safety system'.[415] Specific rules relating to the fitness for purpose of any such autonomous system are notably absent. Chapter 5 provides extra safety requirements in respect of flights involving 'Human Occupants' including determining the number of crew members, emergency equipment and atmospheric conditions.[416] They also lay down detailed rules about the responsibilities and authority of respective crew members and obligations to each other.[417] Regulation 121 goes so far as to require spaceflight participants to remain seated with belts fastened at all times other than when express permission is granted.[418] Chapter 6 provides a list of 'offences and penalties' in connection with failures to act under these regulations ranging from a 'failure to carry out flight safely' to the 'failure of a spaceflight participant to remain at station'.[419]

Part 9 builds on previous regulations made in respect of cosmic radiation[420] and details various provisions relating to acceptable levels of exposure. In contrast to the 2-year requirement for retaining various records relating to training and medical fitness, Regulation 147 requires that records relating to radiation exposure be kept until either the crew member's 75th birthday or the 30th anniversary of any such exposure to cosmic radiation, whichever is later.[421]

Part 10 relates to Spaceport safety and, like Part 8, lists various rules and requirements including the placement of a specific overarching duty on the spaceport licencee to act safety with respect to its activities worded in an almost identical way to that for spaceflight operators.[422] Other more specific requirements are also laid down including rules relating to the storage of hazardous materials under Regulation 158 and Chapter 8 requiring that an emergency response plan be in place at the spaceport. Regulation 167 makes specific provision regarding powers for firefighters at spaceports.

414 R79 (2)(a) and (b).
415 R89.
416 R111, 112 and 113.
417 R116 and 117.
418 R121.
419 R127 and 132.
420 S.I. 2017/1075.
421 R147(3)(a)–(b).
422 R152.

Whilst all these efforts are commendable, it is always useful to reflect upon whether the rules appear to work in practice. In respect of safety matters at spaceports, it is worth considering the recent experience of the unsuccessful Virgin Orbit launch as described in written evidence given to the House of Commons Select Committee on Science and Technology by Newton Launch Systems[423] as regards blast safety zones. Given the relative absence of meaningful launch experience from the United Kingdom itself, it is worth quoting the material aspects of the evidence in full:

> At any point after fuelling, there is a risk of the launch vehicle exploding resulting in fragments of the rocket (and burning fuel) being spread over a wide area. In practice, a low CEC from such an event is achieved by defining a blast safety zone around the launch vehicle, within which non-essential personnel are not permitted once the launch vehicle is fuelled. The radius of the zone is dependent on the size of the vehicle, expressed in equivalent TNT, and the availability of shelter, e.g. buildings. As a rough approximation for bi-propellant rockets, the equivalent TNT is 20% of the propellant mass (fuel and oxidiser), so for the Virgin Orbit launcher with a propellant mass in excess of 20 tonnes, the equivalent TNT will be at least 4 tonnes. FAA guidance defines the radius of the safety zone in terms of the Hazard Fragmentation Distance (HFD) ... there should have been no occupied building within 374 m of the vehicle from the point of propellant loading to take-off. The corresponding distance for outdoor spectators or non-essential employees is 747 m ... Video evidence from the January 2023 Virgin Orbit launch shows significant numbers of people, including members of the public, in close proximity to the aircraft and its fully-fuelled rocket as it taxied to the runway – for example, photographs published by the Guardian newspaper [3] showing spectators well within this radius crowded around the site's perimeter fence. Although the risk of the rocket exploding while on the ground is quite low, if the FAA recommendations had been applied, CEC would clearly have been greater than 10–3 in this case, i.e. had the rocket exploded, people would have been killed.[424]

423 UK space strategy and UK satellite infrastructure: reviewing the licencing regime for launch, Written Evidence Submitted by Newton Launch Systems, (SPA0107), 2–3, <committees.parliament.uk/writtenevidence/119106/pdf> accessed 14 October 2024.

424 *Ibid*, 1–2.

The rules in the Space Industry Regulations on 'safety clear zones' can be found in Regulation 36 which states that an applicants' safety case must:

a. identify that a safety clear zone is required,
b. define the area that will comprise the safety clear zone,
c. stipulate the times that the safety clear zone will be in place,
d. set out the measures the applicant will take to ensure that a safety clear zone is put in place and is monitored, and
e. set out the arrangements the applicant will have in place to ensure that no person, other than a person permitted to be present under regulation 157(3)(d), is inside a safety clear zone.

This is subject to Regulation 37 which states:

1. An applicant must, unless paragraph (2) applies, show that it will be able to put in place an appropriate safety clear zone to ensure that the risk to any person from blast overpressure, fragmentation debris, thermal radiation or toxic release will be as low as reasonably practicable during any hazardous pre-flight and post-flight operations.
2. Paragraph (1) does not apply if the safety case demonstrates that a safety clear zone will not be required for the hazardous pre-flight or post-flight operations.

The legal requirements for calculating a safety clear zone are not specified. The guidance from the FAA referred to in the submission from Newton Launch Systems on this matter gives a 5-step method of calculating a minimum safety clear zone[425] which should be within the ability of UK operators to follow. Accordingly, it would be wise for the Regulator to formally prescribe the following of this document or, even more desirable, to transpose these steps into legislation or otherwise incorporate them by reference. Conversely, it could be argued on basic principles of tort law that any failure to follow a reasonable method in calculating a safety clear zone would likely be held to be negligence on the part of the operator. As the oft-cited passage from Lord Atkin in the famous case of *Donoghue v Stevenson* goes:

> You must take reasonable care to avoid acts or omissions which you can reasonably foresee would be likely to injure your neighbour. Who, then, in law, is my neighbour? The answer seems to be – persons who are so closely and directly affected by my act that I ought reasonably to have

425 US Department of Transportation, Federal Aviation Administration, Guide 437.53-1, <https://www.faa.gov/about/office_org/headquarters_offices/ast/regulations/media/Guide-Cal-of-Safety-Clear-Zones.pdf> accessed 14 October 2024.

> them in contemplation as being so affected when I am directing my mind to the acts or omissions which are called in question.[426]

Any spectators in this instance would likely come within the definition of 'neighbour' and, in the event of catastrophe, be so closely and directly affected by the omission of calculating a safety clear zone in a reasonable manner and, therefore, the relevant operator would be likely to be held liable for any injury or death in any case. The purpose of the law cannot be to merely provide compensation when it could also have a preventative dimension – if operators were required by law to follow a certain process when calculating a safety zone and the legally mandated calculation averted injury or death in a certain instance this would be a far preferable outcome.

Part 11 is concerned with security functions which must be in place at spaceports. Uniquely, specific provision is made for instances involving the storage of technology and data from the United States but no other nation is mentioned.[427] This is likely due to the UK-US Technology Safeguards Agreement[428] which was entered into around the time of the Space Industry Act's inception, explicitly allowing for United States companies to safely and securely participate in spaceflight activities from within the United Kingdom.[429] Section 25 states that the Regulator can provide assistance in such matters as required but can choose to recover any associated cost for such assistance under section 25(7). The associated guidance document states that 'appropriate and proportionate' levels of security should be employed as regards space activities.[430] Whilst this expression could be regarded as derivative, the importance of security matters at launch facilities is underscored with reference to the United Kingdom's international obligations since: 'Launch technology, in particular, could be misused for destructive purposes, including the delivery of weapons

426 *Donoghue v Stevenson*, 1932 SC (HL) 31, 44 (Atkin LJ).

427 R192–202.

428 N92.

429 The United Kingdom Foreign, Commonwealth and Development Office, 'International Treaty; UK-US Technology Safeguards Agreement for Spaceflight Activities: Understanding the TSA', <https://www.gov.uk/government/publications/ukusa-agreement-in-the-form-of-an-exchange-of-notes-between-the-united-kingdom-and-the-united-states-of-america-on-technology-safeguards-associated/uk-us-technology-safeguards-agreement-tsa-for-spaceflight-activities-understanding-the-tsa> accessed 14 October 2024.

430 The United Kingdom Civil Aviation Authority, Guidance on Security Matters,13, <https://assets.publishing.service.gov.uk/government/uploads/system/uploads/attachment_data/file/904451/guidance-on-security-matters-for-applicants-and-licensees.pdf> accessed 14 October 2024.

of mass destruction'.[431] Three instruments are referred to by way of example including UN Security Council Resolution 1540[432] regarding non-proliferation of weapons of mass destruction. Of particular relevance is point 2 of the Resolution which requires that:

> … all States, in accordance with their national procedures, shall adopt and enforce appropriate effective laws which prohibit any non-State actor to manufacture, acquire, possess, develop, transport, transfer or use nuclear, chemical or biological weapons and their means of delivery.[433]

Concerning this part of the Resolution it is clear why the Space Industry Act legislated for security measures by way of compliance. In a less sinister sense, what is proportionate may also depend on the type of payload being launched or the site itself, chiefly whether it is classified as 'Critical National Infrastructure' – CNI – or an 'Operator of Essential Services' – OES. CNI in the guidance is referred to as:

> those critical elements of infrastructure (namely assets, facilities, systems, networks or processes and the essential workers that operate and facilitate them), the loss or compromise of which could result in: (a) major detrimental impact on the availability, integrity or delivery of essential services – including those services whose integrity, if compromised, could result in significant loss of life or casualties – taking into account significant economic or social impacts; and/or, (b) significant impact on national security, national defence, or the functioning of the state.[434]

This is replicated in the Regulations almost word for word under Regulation 191. Whether or not a site is to be designated as such is determined by the Secretary of State in consultation with the Centre for Protection of National Infrastructure (CPNI).[435] Determining whether or not a site or payload is categorised as OES may be defined in the same way[436] under the Network and Information Systems Regulations 2018,[437] specifically Regulation 8(1), which lists the factors that may be important in identifying any such service:

431 *Ibid.*
432 N120.
433 *Ibid.*
434 N436, 15.
435 R191 (1).
436 R191 (1)(b).
437 SI 2018 No. 506.

1. the number of users relying on the service provided by the person;
2. the degree of dependency of the other relevant sectors on the service provided by that person;
3. the likely impact of incidents on the essential service provided by that person, in terms of its degree and duration, on economic and societal activities or public safety;
4. the market share of the essential service provided by that person;
5. the geographical area that may be affected if an incident impacts on the service provided by that person;
6. the importance of the provision of the service by that person for maintaining a sufficient level of that service, taking into account the availability of alternative means of essential service provision;
7. the likely consequences for national security if an incident impacts on the service provided by that person; and
h. any other factor the competent authority considers appropriate to have regard to, in order to arrive at a conclusion under this paragraph.'

However, the guidance points out that applicants or licencees are not required by the regulations to conform with the standards laid out for Critical National Infrastructure (CNI), but that they should liaise with the UK Space Agency CNI Team or the CPNI directly should any potential threats be identified.[438]

The Regulations require that Spaceport licencees, Launch Operator licencees and Range Control licencees appoint dedicated security managers under Regulations 7, 9 and 11 respectively. Orbital operators and return operators on the other hand, may require a licence if it is deemed that issues of national security may arise as a result of their operations. Under Regulation 170, the security manager is responsible for drafting an appropriate security program. Applicants are encouraged to work with the Regulator on these matters and also with the CPNI.[439]

Regarding the aforementioned use of technology from countries other than the United Kingdom, in particular, the United States, there is a requirement that:

> If an applicant for a launch operator licence wishes to conduct any spaceflight activity involving both US technology and either a non-US launch vehicle or foreign spacecraft, the Regulator must be informed of the nationality of any person who has contributed money, equipment,

438 N436, 15.
439 *Ibid*, 13.

> technology or personnel to the production or acquisition of any essential and integral part of the non-US launch vehicle at the application stage.[440]

There are a raft of measures within the regulations as regards the use of US technology. This arises, at least in part, from the previously mentioned UK-US Technology Safeguards Agreement for Spaceflight Activities.[441] One aim of the agreement is to ensure the safe export of materials which could be used in the creation of weapons of mass destruction as per the counter-proliferation frameworks previously mentioned.[442] The advantages of such a partnership are clear given the gulf of technological advancement between the United Kingdom and the United States in this area. The United Kingdom could benefit greatly from US assistance. Further, the opportunities for United States companies to utilise polar-synchronous orbits from launch platforms such as SaxaVord in Shetland could also be a useful incentive for outward investment.

The agreement itself goes somewhat deeper than may be gleaned at first blush. Article III (1)(a) of the Safeguards Agreement for Spaceflight Activities states that 'Her Majesty's Government shall … not permit the launch from the United Kingdom of Great Britain and Northern Ireland of Foreign Spacecraft or Foreign Launch Vehicles (i) owned or controlled by countries that, at the time of launch, are subject to United Nations Security Council sanctions or have governments determined by either of the Parties to have repeatedly

440 *Ibid*, 14. The definition of 'Foreign Spacecraft' within the UK USA Technology Safeguards Agreement means 'any payloads, spacecraft, groups of spacecraft, spacecraft systems or subsystems, spacecraft components (including satellites, groups of satellites, satellite systems or subsystems, and/or satellite components), and/or orbital transfer motors authorized for export to the United Kingdom of Great Britain and Northern Ireland by a government other than the Government of the United States of America, or produced as part of a declared European Space Agency program, for launch on U.S. or Foreign Launch Vehicles from U.K. Spaceports.' USA No 1. (2020) 'Agreement in the form of an Exchange of Notes between the Government of the United Kingdom of Great Britain and Northern Ireland and the Government of the United States of America on Technology Safeguards associated with United States Participation in Space Launches from the United Kingdom', Washington, 16 June 2020, <https://assets.publishing.service.gov.uk/media/5f886c5b8fa8f504267c453b/CS_UK_USA_1.2020_USA_Techno_Safeguards_Space_Launches.pdf> accessed 13 September 2024. The distinction between 'non-US' and 'foreign spacecraft' is thus drawn between spacecraft authorised for export by to the UK other than by the United States Government or pursuant to any European Space Agency agreement.

441 N92.

442 See also the website of the Missile Technology Control Regime, <https://mtcr.info/> accessed 14 October 2024.

provided support for acts of international terrorism; or (ii) identified through consultation and mutual determination of the Parties.'

Therefore the United States, under this agreement could potentially veto launches or space activities from within the United Kingdom in partnership with a country which the United States unilaterally deems to have 'repeatedly provided support for acts of international terrorism', apparently without any need for an objective or agreed justification. The agreement also contains many other provisions relating to launch sites, launch equipment and repatriation of US technology following launches.

It is important to note that not all the security measures thus detailed will be applicable to every operator, in particular, horizontal spaceports that share aerodromes directed under the National Aviation Security Programme (NASP) as per Regulation 35 will be excluded from some measures within this part. As outlined in the guidance, the NASP is comprised of relevant United Kingdom and EU Legislation, with Regulation (EC) No 300/2008[443] setting out the basic standards required at aerodromes within EU Member States. Although EU Law, this instrument is classed as retained under the European Union (Withdrawal Agreement) Act 2020[444] and still applies. There are certain exceptions for space sites which are situated at NASP directed aerodromes. For example, under Regulation 170 a space site security program must provide controls over prohibited articles but this does not apply if the site is a NASP directed one under Regulation 176 (6), presumably to avoid unnecessary duplication with logic dictating that the security program already in place will already cover these matters.

On closer reading of the Regulations, it is apparent that there are two categories of prohibited article – Regulation 176(4) sets out 'prohibited articles for individuals other than spaceflight participants' and lists a number of items that could be expected – guns, stun devices, explosives and suchlike. Regulation 176(5) sets out prohibited articles for 'spaceflight participants' which includes all of the articles mentioned in the previous subsection along with '(b) any tools capable of being used either to cause injury or to threaten the safety of launch vehicles or carrier aircraft, and (c) any objects capable of being used to cause injury.' The fact that this Regulation does not extend to NASP directed aerodromes could be regarded as a potentially dangerous loophole. Whilst aviation security is very strict as regards passengers travelling via commercial

443 REGULATION (EC) No 300/2008 OF THE EUROPEAN PARLIAMENT AND OF THE COUNCIL of 11 March 2008 on common rules in the field of civil aviation security and repealing Regulation (EC) No 2320/2002.

444 C.1.

air traffic, is this level of strictness proportionate to the use of experimental aircraft or spacecraft by fee-paying participants? It could be naïve to assume that the same level of security could apply to both fields of activity, particularly where there is a higher level of risk associated with space activities.

Other aspects of security include the approval of suppliers of goods to space sites under Regulation 179. Under this provision, suppliers are mandated to provide certain details about what they are bringing into the space site, much in common with procedures for aerodromes. The logic is to prevent prohibited articles from being introduced. The published guidance suggests that the CAA's CAP (Civil Aviation Publication) 1260, 'Guidance for Airport Operators Designating Known Suppliers of Airport Supplies'[445] be used as regards suppliers of spaceports. Regarding the actual definition of 'in-flight supplies', this is likely to be informed by EU Regulation No 185/2010[446] on basic standards in aviation security. Chapter 8 of the Regulation is dedicated to supplies and, regarding 'regulated suppliers', states:

> 'regulated supplier of in-flight supplies' means a supplier whose procedures meet common security rules and standards sufficient to allow delivery of in-flight supplies directly to aircraft.[447]

Similar to the previous point on prohibited articles, whether or not 'regulated for aircraft' should be the same standard as 'regulated for spacecraft' is certainly worthy of academic and legislative enquiry to ensure the law is as effective as possible. Moreover, as stated under paragraph 8.1.3.1, 'The approval of a regulated supplier shall be site specific'. In this sense, then, if an aerodrome were the co-location of a spaceport – either vertical or horizontal – a supplier under the Regulation could potentially supply both aircraft and spacecraft without necessarily being suitable to supply spacecraft, unless the authorization granted by the site specifically excludes this. Whether, as a matter of fact, there may be any practical or significant difference between supplying aircraft and supplying spacecraft is beyond the technical expertise of the author but, given that the Regulation predates the recent expansion of domestic space law it would be desirable for it to be reviewed at a supra-national level.

---

445 The United Kingdom Civil Aviation Authority, 'Guidance for Airport Operators Designating Known Suppliers of Airport Supplies', CAP 1260, <https://www.caa.co.uk/publication/download/15044> accessed 17 October 2024.

446 COMMISSION REGULATION (EU) No 185/2010 of 4 March 2010 laying down detailed measures for the implementation of the common basic standards on aviation security.

447 N451, 8.0.2.

Other important matters pertaining to security include the need for details to be provided regarding the nationality of those contributing to licenced activities when the applicant is seeking a licence which would involve launches of both non-US and US or foreign spacecraft. For the sake of clarity, 'foreign spacecraft' is given the same meaning as that in the UK-US Technology Safeguards Agreement under Regulation 168. This in turn, means:

> any payloads, spacecraft, groups of spacecraft, spacecraft systems or subsystems, spacecraft components (including satellites, groups of satellites, satellite systems or subsystems, and/or satellite components), and/or orbital transfer motors authorized for export to the United Kingdom of Great Britain and Northern Ireland by a government other than the Government of the United States of America, or produced as part of a declared European Space Agency program, for launch on U.S. or Foreign Launch Vehicles from U.K. Spaceports.[448]

Therefore, 'foreign' in this context means a broad range of equipment and articles associated with space activities which are not authorised for export to the United Kingdom by either the United States or under a European Space Agency program but apparently excludes launch of any such component by United Kingdom launch vehicles.

Regulation 202 states that applicants for launch activities must disclose to the Regulator the nationality of those who have 'contributed money, equipment, technology or personnel to the production or acquisition of any essential and integral part of … 'a non-United States vehicle as defined, a foreign spacecraft being launched or the launch business itself'. Regulation 202(2) states that the same applies to spaceport licencees.

There are extensive controls regarding the security payloads and launch vehicles admitted to space sites under Regulation 178 which, for reasons of confidentiality as regards certain technologies, seeks to strike a balance between security on one hand and privacy on the other. Under Regulation 178 (1)(c) a spaceflight operator must 'obtain a signed declaration from a manufacturer of payloads and launch vehicles and a person responsible for transporting payloads and launch vehicles from their place of manufacture to the spaceport or other place from which the launch is to take place or takes place confirming that all reasonable steps have been taken to ensure the security of payloads and launch vehicles'. Reading this in conjunction with the guidance, this was

448 N92, Article II (3).

specifically included for situations '[w]here space site operators are not able, for reasons related to proprietary technology and sensitivity, to screen a payload or launch vehicle ... before it enters the restricted or controlled area'.[449] Under Regulation 178 (1)(d) a spaceflight operator must 'retain the final authority to allow any payloads and launch vehicles to enter the restricted area'. Given the importance of ensuring that dangerous payloads – or launch vehicles – are not sent into orbit and the potential for national security concerns to arise, it would be desirable for more precision to be employed within the regulations as to exactly which circumstances of 'proprietary technology' or 'sensitivity' should indeed deprive an operator of the right to inspect or observe such payloads, especially given the fact that the ultimate responsibility shifts to them for allowing the payload into restricted areas. Whilst it is not desirable to unnecessarily add to existing administrative burdens, it is certainly more undesirable for potentially dangerous or detrimental payloads to be launched under the guise of such a term as 'proprietary technology'. In addition to the relevant operator, it is submitted that the CAA should have some responsibility for deeming certain payloads to be exempt from screening in addition to the requirement for signed declarations to be submitted.

In respect of 'restricted' or 'controlled' areas, Regulation 174 lists the requirements for areas that *must* be designated as controlled areas by the Secretary of State following a licencee's mandated proposal. These are chiefly concerned with vehicle assembly but also mission management and range control where necessary.[450] Under Regulation 174 (3) there is also a mandatory requirement for the Secretary of State to designate a controlled area where US technology is being used in the area and the area is being used for launch activities. The licencee is responsible for ensuring that the restricted area is clearly identified and appropriately protected by specialist personnel or electronic means.[451] However, there is an exemption for emergency services when attending an emergency at a space site under Regulation 175.

A further important provision regarding security controls comes under Regulation 181 on hazardous material. Where hazardous material – which includes propellants whether solid or liquid, radioactive substances and anything else defined as such under the Planning (Hazardous Substances) Act 1990[452] – is stored at a space site or spaceport there are additional obligations on a licencee to ensure that they ensure that there are means for detecting unauthorised

449 N436, 20.
450 R174 (2).
451 R174 (4).
452 C10.

access to the materials and, further, that they take into account any 'statutory or contractual prohibitions, restrictions or conditions which apply to the material'.[453] Whilst it is clear that security conditions must be imposed in such circumstances and that a licencee should be put on notice as regards adherence to existing statutory provisions, it is possibly rare for a Regulator to remind a private individual to observe 'contractual prohibitions' in such a context. Presumably, the contractual prohibitions referred to are contractual warranties relating to correct storage of propellants, shelf life or any other action – or inaction – on the part of the licencee which could result in the materials becoming unstable.

'Security' under the provisions also extends to cybersecurity, and there are certain rules which must be observed for this also. Chapter 3 of the Regulations requires that licencees put 'cyber security strategies' in place for 'network and information' systems[454] and the guidance directs licencees to a number of 'best practice' sources including the CAA's CAP1753 policy.[455] On a similar note, the licencee is also reminded about its obligations under the Data Protection Act 2018[456] and the General Data Protection Regulation:[457] 'Where personal data related to spaceflight operations, for example flight crew rosters, customer information or employee information is held on a system'.[458] Under Regulation 186 there is a duty to report a notifiable cybersecurity incident to the CAA. A 'notifiable incident' is one that subject to other qualifying provisions 'may have a significant impact on future essential services provided by the licencee'.[459] An operator, therefore, may also be under a duty to anticipate which of its services may, in future, be regarded as 'essential' should a cybersecurity incident take place. As outlined, this can be assessed with regards to the criteria listed under the Network and Information Systems Regulations 2018,[460] Regulation 8(1).

453 R181(3)(a).

454 R185 (1).

455 The United Kingdom Civil Aviation Authority, 'CAP1753: CAA Cyber Security Oversight Process for Aviation', <https://www.caa.co.uk/publication/download/17492> accessed 17 October 2024.

456 C12.

457 Regulation (EU) 2016/679 on the protection of natural persons with regard to the processing of personal data and on the free movement of such data, and repealing Directive 95/46/EC (Data Protection Directive).

458 N315, para 3.80,

459 R186(2)(b).

460 SI 2018 No. 506.

National security vetting must also be carried out in respect of certain individuals under Regulation 187, namely the security manager, software and hardware engineers involved with network and information systems and those holding 'administrator rights for information management systems and critical supplies used by, or made available to, space sites'.[461] As Regulation 187(3) states, this does not apply to spaceports located at NASP directed aerodromes. In addition to vetting, there are also training requirements for security staff under Regulation 188 and all staff working at a space site must have 'appropriate general security awareness training before being granted unescorted access to the site'.[462] An interesting discrepancy is disclosed by Regulation 189(1) on the keeping of training records in respect of 'training and qualifications which indicate that an individual has the appropriate training and necessary qualifications for the security related functions that the individual has been engaged to perform'.[463] It is stated that 'A licencee must keep the records ... for as long as an individual is engaged to carry out security functions at the space site.' This should be contrasted with the specification under Regulation 60 relating to the training of spaceflight participants where there is only a requirement that records be kept for a period of 2 years. As previously stated, this would not seem to be a sensible choice of timeframe since the Limitation Act 1980 specifies a limitation period for personal injury cases of 3 years,[464] hence, such documents may not be available for evidential purposes. Whilst the necessity of keeping security records for an indefinite period is clear, so too is keeping training records at least for the duration of any material limitation period. It would be disingenuous to say that the 2-year requirement under Regulation 60 is an exercise in reducing the administrative burden for the licencee when there are other requirements relating to the same within the Act which, in fact, require similar documents to be kept for potentially longer periods of time.

On a broader note, Regulation 191 potentially requires licencees to exercise higher standards as regards security measures if the space site is determined by the Secretary of State in consultation with the Centre for Protection of National Infrastructure to be part of 'critical national infrastructure' or that spaceflight activities carried out there are 'essential services'.[465] An interesting point arising is the process by which spaceflight activities carried out are to be determined by the Secretary of State to be an 'essential service'. Is it

461 R187 (2).
462 R188(3)(a).
463 R189 (2).
464 N419, S11(4).
465 R191 (1).

incumbent upon the CAA to notify the Secretary of State if it feels that a given licence application discloses such a case or is it the responsibility of the licencee to notify the Secretary of State themselves? This point is left unanswered although it is to be assumed that activities relating to satellite and communications systems would fall within this definition.

In keeping with the bilateral agreement regarding the use of US technology[466] and the associated legal provisions, there is an entire Chapter within the Regulations aimed at safeguarding US technology. It grants further extensive rights over segregated areas[467] to which access must not be granted without US Government authorisation[468] and the person granted authority must be escorted unless this requirement has otherwise been waived.[469] Regulation 194 also creates a criminal offence of allowing unauthorised access to US technology with a maximum penalty of 2 years imprisonment and a fine.[470]

In common with other bodies exercising considerable control over dangerous activities,[471] authorised individuals can, under Section 24 of the Act, create byelaws on a range of matters. This is limited if section 63 of the Airports Act 1986[472] applies as per the guidance. If so, the licencee is required to consult the individual responsible for any existing byelaws made pursuant to that section. As would be expected, the usual rules regarding the creation of byelaws must be followed – they must be made publicly available for inspection, for example, prior to official promulgation. Schedule 3 of the Airports Act 1986 applies also to spaceports and sets out the formal requirements for the creation of byelaws in this context.

Not all of the Security Regulations apply to horizontal spaceports provided they are located at CAA licenced or EASA (European Union Aviation Safety Agency)[473] certified aerodromes and NASP directed. These are Regulation 172

466 N92.

467 R192.

468 R193 (a).

469 R193 (b).

470 R194 (4).

471 The Airports Authority and Railway providers for example.

472 C. 31.

473 Such aerodromes are those falling within Regulation (EU) 2018/1139 of the European Parliament and of the Council of 4 July 2018 on common rules in the field of civil aviation and establishing a European Union Aviation Safety Agency, and amending Regulations (EC) No 2111/2005, (EC) No 1008/2008, (EU) No 996/2010, (EU) No 376/2014 and Directives 2014/30/EU and 2014/53/EU of the European Parliament and of the Council, and repealing Regulations (EC) No 552/2004 and (EC) No 216/2008 of the European Parliament and of the Council and Council Regulation (EEC) No 3922/91. This, in turn, is based on Annex 14 to the Convention on International Civil Aviation.

on sufficient security measures regarding access control, Regulation 176 on Security Controls for prohibited articles as previously outlined, Regulation 177 on Security Controls for supplies, Regulation 180 on Surveillance of Space Sites, Regulation 182 on Protection of Carrier Aircraft, Launch Vehicle or Payload: Pre-Integration, Regulation 183 on the same Post Integration and Regulation 187 on National Security Vetting Procedures. Therefore, there will be two sets of regulations whereby a space site is hosted at such an aerodrome. Moreover, the question is left open as to the situation regarding a vertical spaceport at a NASP directed aerodrome – would this be subject to both sets of regulations too? Paragraph 4.5 of the guidance on security matters for applicants and licencees[474] states that 'Vertical spaceports and all other space sites outside of the boundaries of a horizontal spaceport, where security measures are required, will only be subject to monitoring and enforcement under the Space Industry Regulations.' which suggests that both horizontal and vertical spaceports are in fact exempt from the security regulations outlined if they are located at a NASP directed aerodrome.

In respect of the most appropriate security measures to adopt at spaceports, through the guidance, licencees are directed to various 'soft' sources for models of practice. They are also provided with recommended instruction within the guidance document itself, such as the 'Secure by Design' approach[475] and 'Layered Security (defence in depth)' approach.[476] They are likewise directed to the CPNI extranet for further recommendations. In addition to this, licencees are also advised to adopt a range of standards and codes for their security measures, including the 'Manual Forced Entry Attack Standard' and others as provided by the British Standards Organisation.[477] Where no guidance for a specific security matter exists, licencees are advised to adopt 'an approach derived from existing codes or standards for similar equipment, in applications with similar security significance, should be adopted. The codes and standards adopted for aviation security would be the most relevant: further information on these may be obtained from the Regulator.'[478] It is likely that the most relevant codes and standards from the aviation field will be those in place at NASP directed aerodromes given the fact that a number of security regulations, as has been written, do not apply at such facilities since a separate

474 N436.
475 *Ibid*, 30
476 *Ibid.*
477 *Ibid*, 31.
478 *Ibid.*

regime applies there. Licencees are also advised to adopt a 'Security Management System'. As stated:

> A Security Management System enables a licencee to identify and address security risks, threats, gaps and weaknesses in a consistent and proactive way. In short, a Security Management System provides the necessary organisational structure, accountabilities, policies and procedures to ensure effective security oversight.[479]

This is not a licence requirement as such, but licencees are directed to a number of CAA documents which give guidance on how to implement one.[480]

Overall, the security measures required by the legislation are tight. It must be noted that some of the security exemptions granted to horizontal spaceports provided that they are operating within NASP directed aerodromes seem like a blanket approach to the issue of security, particularly when, as a fledgling space-faring nation, we do not presently know what the security parameters pertaining to what may, in some cases, amount to experimental aircraft may be. Although there may be separate checks for 'prohibited articles' as regards spaceflight participants ahead of any given mission, does this mean that general entry to the space site should only be set at the same standard as a commercial airport? Under Regulation 176, 'prohibited articles' for spaceflight participants are the same sort prohibited in respect of travelers on all commercial jet traffic[481] in addition to:

> (b) any tools capable of being used either to cause injury or to threaten the safety of launch vehicles or carrier aircraft, and (c) any objects capable of being used to cause injury.[482]

The phrasing of this section imports a degree of intent or 'deliberateness' as regards the use of a prohibited article – 'capable of being used'. What it does not cater for is items which may inadvertently interfere with flight safety, such as, for example, any finely granulated substance which could cause problems in low gravity conditions should it be permitted to escape or any other item which could cause damage in such circumstances without the need for intent on the part of the user. Whether this is strictly a matter of 'security' is debatable but

479 *Ibid* para A.7.
480 Specifically CAP 1223, CAP 1273, CAP 1224, CAP 1297, CAP 1997.
481 R176 (4) (a).
482 R176 (5).

the broader implications should be considered. Furthermore, NASP directed aerodromes, for reasons that should be obvious, do not have any rules relating to products or items which are potentially dangerous in low-gravity scenarios.

Part 12 issues provisions on 'informed consent' for spaceflight participants and largely repeats the provisions of the Space Industry Act 2018 in respect of mental capacity. Chapter 3 contains the details the consent form must include whilst Chapter 4 specifies that adequate information about the flight should be given to the human occupant at least 24 hours before the consent form is signed.[483] The author's previous article[484] on the informed consent provisions of the Space Industry Act 2018 was tendered in evidence during the consultation period on the draft regulations and was heeded.[485] The original draft regulations specified that such information should be given to the participant at least 12 hours before the form is signed. It was submitted that, due to the case law from the medical experience on informed consent in the United Kingdom this may not be enough time since the information given is likely to be highly technical and would require significant examination.[486]

As outlined previously, Part 13 on Liabilities and indemnities importantly expands upon section 34(3)(a) by providing a list of 'prescribed individuals' who are henceforth removed from the no-fault liability regime established by virtue of that section. Essentially – and not surprisingly – these individuals are the same as those not classified as 'Members of the Public' under Regulation 40. Regulation 219 provides, however, that liability could still ensue in cases of 'gross negligence ... wilful misconduct ... (or) noncompliance (with) licence conditions (or) the Act /regulations'.[487] The limit on liability must be specified on the licence under Regulation 220 the amount of which, under paragraph 2, will be, somewhat nebulously, 'determined by the Regulator having regard to, in particular, the spaceflight activities which the Operator applicant proposes to carry out'. Pursuant to the provisions of the Space Industry Act 2018, Regulation 221 liberates the Secretary of State from their duty to indemnify under section 35(5)(b) in the circumstances listed under Regulation 219.

The remainder of the Regulations are concerned with matters relating to monitoring and enforcement including the power of inspectors[488] and the

483 R209.

484 Alex Simmonds, 'The UK Perspective on Informed Consent in Commercial Space Travel', (2020), 45, Air and Space Law, Issue 4, 367.

485 N399, 5.355–5.357. Also confirmed in an email to the author from the United Kingdom Space Agency.

486 N363.

487 R219(a)–(b).

488 R239.

sharing of information between the Regulator and other bodies.[489] Part 15 specifies rules relating to Civil sanctions in respect of activities and Part 16 refers to Occurrence Reporting. Such matters will be addressed later within this work.[490]

The schedules provide further useful expansion on many of the principles and parts within the regulations, such as information the safety case must include,[491] training and qualification,[492] information which must be included in a health record[493] and the information which must be included in a spaceport manual.[494]

The Regulations branch into many areas which have parallels in existing legislation, particularly as regards safety, reporting requirements and the storage of hazardous materials for instance. Provisions regarding range control and hazard/warning zones also have interesting implications for matters such as environmental health. An interesting comparison could be made with other private sector actors in respect of dangerous activities; controlled demolition may be the most pertinent parallel.

In specific respect of human spaceflight, the guidance document apparently purports to incorporate by reference several other 'soft' instruments from outside the United Kingdom. As stated in paragraph 7.12 in the 'Guidance for Launch Operator and Return Operator Licence Applicants and Licencees':[495]

> The Regulations do not define any set standard or acceptability requirements concerning the levels of risk that crew members and spaceflight participants may be exposed to and there is no other UK legislation that sets out standards and medical criteria for human occupants of spacecraft. To assist applicants, the following information and recommendations from the US may be of use:

- FAA-AST Recommended Practices for Human Space Flight Occupant Safety A compilation of practices that the Federal Aviation Administration (FAA) Office of Commercial Space Transportation (AST) recommends for commercial human spaceflight occupant safety.

489 Chapter 4.
490 See Chapter 5 on Enforcement.
491 Schedule 1.
492 Schedule 3.
493 Schedule 6.
494 Schedule 8.
495 N368, 77.

- NASA Space Flight Human System Standards NASA Standard 3001. The two Standard documents are used by NASA for its professional astronaut cadre and establish requirements for providing a healthy and safe environment for crew members during all phases of spaceflight.
- NASA Human Integration Design Handbook A companion document to NASA Standard 3001, this serves as a compendium of human spaceflight history, lessons learned and design information for a wide variety of disciplines and provides background information on the rationale for human system design standards including natural and induced environments.

These documents themselves are extremely detailed. The FAA-AST Recommended Practices for Human Space Flight Occupant Safety[496] contains various recommendations pertaining to the design of human spaceflight systems ranging from the regulation of the atmosphere of the interior of any such vehicle[497] through to waste management processes.[498] Recommended emergency systems are also outlined comprehensively.[499]

Of particular interest are principles of risk management in respect of flights involving human occupants. Instructively, the FAA-AST Recommended Practices state that:

> This document does not aim to achieve a single level of risk for commercial human space flight systems. Because of the wide variety of commercial human space flight activities that are likely to take place in the future, with differing destinations, purposes, and architectures, different risk levels may be appropriate in different situations. In addition, establishing a single level of risk may inadvertently limit innovation. Collectively, however, the application of these recommended practices will ensure that occupant safety is considered throughout the life cycle of a space flight system, and that occupants are not exposed to avoidable risks.[500]

This appears to be a sensible approach overall.

NASA Standard 3001 Volume 2A compliments this whereas the NASA Human Integration Design Handbook is incredibly detailed at over 1300 pages.

496 Federal Aviation Administration, Recommended Practices for Human Space Flight Occupant Safety, Version 1.0 August 27 2014, <https://www.faa.gov/media/71481> accessed 14 October 2024.

497 *Ibid*, 9.

498 *Ibid*, 10.

499 *Ibid*, 16.

500 *Ibid*, 2.

Further consideration will be given to the potential influence of these sources later in this work.

Regulation 26 provides for Flight Safety Analysis to be carried out in which they must:

> (a) identify the major hazards that could, whether or not the launch vehicle malfunctions- (i) arise from, or cause a major accident during the proposed spaceflight activities or (ii) arise from the launch vehicle or any part of it during the proposed spaceflight activities.

Regulation 28 must then be observed in respect of each hazard identified and, under Regulation 26(c), the applicant must also:

> estimate numerically the risk of death or serious injury arising from the identified hazards 'referred to in paragraph 18(2) of Schedule 1. These are (a) the locations of individuals who could be harmed by any of the identified hazards; (b) the applicant's own and each proposed range control service provider's capabilities in—(i) tracking; (ii) telemetry; (iii) communications; (c) how any flight safety system will be activated if its activation is necessary; (d) how the applicant will coordinate and communicate with air traffic control service providers, meteorological information providers and emergency services; (e) any legal requirements relevant to the applicant's proposed use of airspace; (f) information available about any known space object with which there is a risk of the launch vehicle colliding.

The further matters referred to under 18(2) are that the applicant must also consider '(a) blast overpressure; (b) fragmentation debris; (c) thermal radiation; (d) toxic release; (e) major accident hazards arising from—(i) any discarded part of the launch vehicle and any object, including any payload, released or separated from the launch vehicle; (ii) collision with a space object; (iii) meteorological or environmental conditions; (iv) the use of a carrier aircraft, if applicable; (v) re-entry of the launch vehicle, or any part of it, from orbit, if applicable'.

A 'ground safety analysis' must also be carried under Regulation 27(1) if the applicant is seeking a launch operator licence to identify 'major accident hazards that could arise-(a) during, or cause a major accident during, preparations for the launch from the time when the launch vehicle or its components arrive at the spaceport or other place from which the launch is to take place, or

(b) from the launch vehicle, or any part of it, or from a payload, upon or after landing, whether or not the launch vehicle malfunctions.

Safety cases must also be provided as a condition of launch operator or return operator licences under Regulation 29 which must contain the information required by virtue of Schedule 1, notionally, the important details about the flight – the vehicle, what it will be carrying and the launch site.[501] The provision of a safety case is not unique to the space industry. The Offshore Installations (Offshore Safety Directive) (Safety Case etc.) Regulations 2015,[502] for instance, require that operators in the oil industry provide safety cases for certain activities. This was also a requirement for railway operators[503] but such a requirement was superseded by a 'safety certificate' regime. The history of the safety case technique was also outlined in the CAA's Space Launch and Orbit Group Launch Session Meeting, March 2023, where it was pointed out that this approach has been taken since at least as far back as the 1960's when licensing hazardous activities. Several unfortunate and high-profile disaster incidents were referenced as providing a justification for this, namely the Windscale fire, the Piper Alpha disaster and Grenfell Tower.[504] Safety cases have been described as "A structured argument, supported by a body of evidence that provides a compelling, comprehensible and valid case that a system is safe for a given application in a given environment'.[505] 'Soft' requirements for the safety case have been further set out by the Civil Aviation's Space Launch and Orbit Group Launch Session:[506]

> The safety case needs 'to tell a story' – it should deliver a safety narrative
> - It provides evidence to support safety-related decisions
> - It needs to set out arguments and reasoning for safety-related decisions
> - It needs to draw conclusions

There should be an ongoing process of continuous improvement.

501 Schedule 1(2).

502 SI 2015 No. 398.

503 See the Railways (Safety Case) Regulations 2000/2688.

504 N327.

505 The Ministry of Defence, Defence Standard 00–56 Part 1, Safety Management Requirements for Defence Systems, Part 1: Requirements, 28 February 2017, 26, <https://s3-eu-west-1.amazonaws.com/s3.spanglefish.com/s/22631/documents/safety-specifications/def-stan-00-056-pt1-iss7-28feb17.pdf> accessed 14 October 2024.

506 The United Kingdom Civil Aviation Authority, Space Launch and Orbit Group, Launch Session, March 2023, 16, <https://www.caa.co.uk/media/xm4budqo/march-2023-launch.pdf> accessed 16 October 2024.

The Safety Case should be regularly reviewed and updated as more knowledge and data is accrued.

It will remain to be seen how effective this regime is in practice.

Schedule 1(2) requires information to be provided about 'the applicant's organisation and management structure'. Regulation 33 only seems to require the submission of a risk assessment to the Regulator for spaceflight activities which involve 'human occupants'.

Part 5 on Spaceport Licences is similar to Part 4 regarding Spaceflight Operator Licences. A 'safety case' is similarly required under Regulation 36 which should include a description of the aerodrome concerned along with the surrounding area should the proposed spaceport be a horizontal one. Regulation 36(4)(d) requires a plan of spaceport to be submitted which contains the associated infrastructure and storage facilities including those for hazardous waste. The location of any 'proposed static engine or other test areas' is also required.[507]

Under Regulation 35, horizontal spaceports must be CAA licenced and Certified under sections 12, 13, 13A, 14 and 15 of the Aviation Security Act 1982.[508] Curiously, there is no specific mention of vertical spaceports in the Regulations. Other legislation/documents deemed relevant to the operation of spaceports includes, on the basis of the published guidance, CAP 168: Licensing of Aerodromes from the CAA[509] which is applicable to horizontal spaceports only and consists exclusively of rules and guidance which could theoretically apply to any airport facility with no specific mention of space operations or vertical launch. Additionally, the Control of Major Accident Hazards Regulations 2015[510] particularly as regards hazardous chemicals and explosive materials is also deemed relevant in addition to the controversial Civil Contingencies Act 2004[511] along with regulations made pursuant to it pertaining to emergency responses. Other relevant legislation includes the EU Regulation on

---

507 Safety provisions relating to static testing areas should be regarded as prescient given the recent incident at SaxaVord spaceport where a rocket exploded during tests carried out by Rocket Factory Augsburg, see BBC News, 'Rocket engine explodes during test at Sheltand spaceport', 19 August 2024, <https://www.bbc.co.uk/news/articles/cy54wqzzokvo#:~:text=A%20rocket%20engine%20has%20exploded%20during%20a> accessed 1 October 2024.

508 C. 36.

509 The United Kingdom Civil Aviation Authority, CAP 168, 'Licensing of Aerodromes', 14 January 2022 <https://www.caa.co.uk/our-work/publications/documents/content/cap-168/> accessed 14 October 2023.

510 SI 2015 No. 483.

511 N349.

classification, labelling and packaging[512] in respect of hazardous substances kept at spaceports in addition to the Explosives Regulations 2014.[513] As the guidance points out, there are also potential dangers relating to the storage and/or contamination of propellants if the spaceport operator is responsible for such matters. In such an instance, Article 220(2) of the Air Navigation Order 2016[514] is stated to be of particular relevance. Interestingly, this article specifies that:

> an aviation fuel installation manager must not cause or permit any fuel to be dispensed from the installation to an aircraft unless satisfied as the result of sampling that the fuel is fit for use in aircraft.

This is significant as there is no requirement within the space industry legislation for operators to appoint a specific 'aviation fuel installation manager' unless this role is to be subsumed within the duties of one of the other required appointees. Given the apparent safety-critical nature of this task it would be wise for this role to be further highlighted within the regulations themselves, with operators being directed to provide for this role where propellant storage comes within their remit. Whilst the guidance states that extensive measures must be adopted, the regulations themselves do not go as far in respect of individuals who would be appointed to undertake such responsibilities.[515]

A horizontal spaceport must also be located at a CAA licenced aerodrome[516] with the option to apply for such a licence if necessary.[517] This does not appear to be a requirement for sites intended only for vertical launches.[518] This may be because there is presently no authoritative literature regarding vertical launch facilities this being a relatively novel development for Europe in general and the United Kingdom in particular, at least as far as non-military usage is concerned. Any dereliction could likely be cured by referring to further standards from overseas which may be relevant to vertical spaceports which an applicant could be directed towards.

512 Regulation (EC) No 1272/2008.

513 SI 2014 No. 1638.

514 N302.

515 R160.

516 The United Kingdom Civil Aviation Authority, Guidance for spaceport licence applicants and spaceport licencees, CAP2212, 5 <https://www.caa.co.uk/publication/download/18913> accessed 14 October 2024.

517 *Ibid.*

518 *Ibid.*

The guidance further states that:

> If you're applying to host horizontal launches, you must also include a description of the aerodrome and plans of the aerodrome showing relevant infrastructure.[519]

Once more, the absence of a requirement of the same in respect of vertical launches seems unusual, unless such a requirement is satisfied elsewhere in the licensing application. It should be hoped that such information would be forthcoming from a prospective applicant.

Regulation 37 requires that the applicant be able to demonstrate that it can put in place an 'appropriate safety clear zone to ensure that the risk to any person from blast overpressure, fragmentation debris, thermal radiation or toxic release will be as low as reasonably practicable during any hazardous pre-flight and post-flight operations'. It should be noted that the above does not apply if the safety case shows that a safety clear zone will not be required.

Part 6 on 'Range Control Licences' requires the applicant to prove that it is up to the task of identifying appropriate ranges or tracking the flight and return of a space object. Regulation 46 requires that the licencee identifies the appropriate range and a determination of the object's flightpath subject to environmental expectancies. Regulation 46(e)(i) and (i) require that such considerations must also encompass populated areas close to the expected trajectory of the vehicle. Areas where the launch vehicle or space object could come down are also expected to be identified and reported to the Regulator. Hazard areas under Regulation 47 must also be identified and can also be nominated as'. Such zones could legally exclude 'persons or things' posing a hazard or which would be exposed to hazards should they be permitted to remain within the zone for the duration of the flight. As a limitation on the exercise of this power a time limit must also be stipulated for the lifetime of the exclusion zone.

The licensing application appears thorough and detailed and, to ensure compliance, Regulation 19 requires that an applicant also submit to inspections. Under Regulation 15 it is not necessary for the operators of carrier aircraft to hold operator licences should the aircraft be used to transport a space object from one site to another, presumably since this is a step away from 'space activities'.

519 *Ibid*, 16.

Should an applicant be refused, the Space Industry Act 2018 lays down an appeals process[520] as do the Space Industry Appeals Regulations 2021.[521] These will be addressed later.

3.1 *'Members of the Public'*

Regulations 39 and 40 exclude certain classes of people from this definition. These include human occupants of spacecraft and those 'taking part in spaceflight activities' along with those in attendance at spaceports by invitation of the licencee. Employees of the Regulator or those acting on the Regulator's behalf are not classed as members of the public and neither are emergency services employees, members of the armed forces or other categories of public servant including those of health and safety authorities. Neither are people who place themselves voluntarily in close proximity to danger at a spaceport. This is only insofar as falling within the ambit of 'public safety' under section 10(a) of the Space Industry Act regarding spaceport licences. The term is used interchangeably elsewhere on a more limited basis, for example, Schedule 3(1) of the Regulations state that members of the public can be permitted to enter certain restricted areas in limited circumstances.

The effect of this is somewhat controversial. Whilst an operator will be expected to operate in a way that minimises risk or danger, this duty does not extend to a very wide class of people as borne out by the Regulations. In addition to those set out, the regulations also include a very wide class of 'compliance authority personnel', encompassing CAA employees and Air Traffic Controllers.[522] There is, of course, the common law doctrine of *'volenti non fit injuria'* whereby a person who voluntarily assumes a risk is taken to suffer the consequences alone and, in some cases, have no recourse against a tortfeasor.[523] There are also domestic instruments such as the Law Reform (Contributory Negligence) Act 1945[524] which renders compensation for tortious acts liable to reduction in the light of negligence on part of the claimant.

It seems draconian to exclude a wide ambit of individuals from a given public safety duty, especially when this could include those other than fee-paying space tourists who, it could be argued, are placing themselves in a position of risk on a completely voluntary basis. In the middle of this class there are flight crew and police officers whom it could be argued assume some degree of risk

520 Section 60, Schedule 10.

521 N168.

522 R40.

523 See *Sayers v Harlow UDC* [1958] 1 WLR 623.

524 C. 28.

as per their chosen occupations. At the other end of the spectrum, though, are employees of the CAA who may have been requested by management to attend a spaceport, along with other associated personnel. For such individuals, the questions arise in respect of section 2(2) of the Health and Safety at Work Act 1974[525] regarding an employer's duty to provide a safe working environment. Is there any tension between, on one hand, a legal provision which blanketly excludes a range of individuals from a public safety duty – at least partially in respect of available recourse – and another which states that it is an employer's duty to provide a safe working environment?

Where such individuals are not directly employed at the spaceport or otherwise by the operator but are instead sent there by their employer, could this have the effect of triggering section 100(1) and (2) of the Employment Rights Act 1996?[526] Under these provisions, an employee who is dismissed for refusing to work in a 'dangerous' environment can claim unfair dismissal. This is qualified by the expression 'serious and imminent' danger. Could it be argued that *prima facie*, working in an environment where there is no duty as regards public safety is inherently dangerous? It is at least possible, given the nature of some of the activities conducted. Section 44 of the same Act likewise protects an employee from suffering a detriment because of refusing to work in such circumstances.

Some examples of what have been held to be dangerous circumstances include *Edwards & Others v The Secretary of State for Justice*[527] where dangerous driving conditions on a prison officer's commute brought about by snow and ice was held to be a serious and imminent danger. Certain activities at spaceports are likely to be at least commensurate with this threshold.

3.2 *Notification Requirements*

Under Regulation 49 certain entities falling within a designated range under Regulation 46 such as local authorities, property owners, lessees, occupiers or other persons deemed relevant must be given notification of any spaceflight activities 'not longer than 4 weeks prior'. Notifications must contain information relating to the activities so that those in receipt of the notice can avoid exposure to associated hazards or avoid presenting them. Regulation 51(2)(C) states that notifications must 'be issued in a manner which is reasonably necessary to alert the individuals referred to in paragraph (3) to the operator's spaceflight activities'.

---

525 N370.

526 C. 18.

527 Appeal No. UKEAT/0123/14/DM.

Paragraph 3 of Regulation 49 specifies two types of individual:

a. an individual whose regular place of work is situated on any part of the land falling within the designated range, and
b. any individual who might enter or traverse any part of the land falling within the designated range in exercise of a legal right, entitlement or privilege including, but not limited to, an easement or a public right of way.

Individuals under paragraph (b) would include walkers, mountaineers and tourists from across the United Kingdom and potentially further afield. In Scotland, the Land Reform (Scotland) Act 2003[528] provides that 'everyone' has the right to 'be on land' and has 'the right to cross land' for recreational purposes with section 6(d) excluding land which is subject to any exclusions under enactment which would also include the Regulations.

4 The Spaceflight Activities (Investigation of Spaceflight Accidents) Regulations 2021

Another key piece of legislation in the United Kingdom's domestic space law program is the Spaceflight Activities (Investigation of Spaceflight Accidents) Regulations 2021,[529] the first regulations of their kind.

They are engaged following an 'accident' arising out of an 'operator's spaceflight activities'. The Regulations[530] define these as 'authorised by an operator licence' and include, numerously, the launching of a launch vehicle, launching of a carrier aircraft addition to 'operating the launch vehicle or a carrier aircraft' as an end to carrying spaceflight participants, payloads, carrying out suborbital activities and orbital activities insofar as they are necessary to complete any of the aforementioned. It also covers the return to earth of a relevant vehicle and, also, the operation of any vehicle landing in the United Kingdom which had not previously been licenced to the operator.[531] Regarding the temporal parameters of the 'operation of a launch vehicle' there are key differences as to the definition dependent upon whether the launch vehicle does or does not contain a 'human occupant'. Where a human occupant is involved, 'operation' is classified as 'the time a human occupant boards the launch vehicle with the intention of being carried on it during the proposed spaceflight activity

528 ASP 2.
529 SI 2021 No. 792.
530 R3.
531 R3(c)(I–IV).

until such time as all human occupants have disembarked'.[532] Where there is no 'human occupant', operation is classified as being between 'the time the launch vehicle is ready to move with the purpose of flight until such time as it comes to rest at the end of the flight and the propulsion system is shut down'.

Per Regulation 3, an investigation is to be carried out by the Space Accident Investigation Authority (SAIA) nominated by the Secretary of State under Regulation 5. Under Regulation 5(2), the authority must 'operate independently of the UK Space Agency … the Civil Aviation Authority … and any other person … whose interests conflict, or might conflict, with the responsibilities given to SAIA under these Regulations, or … who might influence its objectivity'. The United Kingdom Government website confirmed on 29th July 2021 that the Secretary of State for Transport had nominated the Air Accidents Investigation Branch to fulfil this role.[533]

The Secretary of State is also responsible for ensuring that the authority has the resources needed for any investigations[534] and there does not seem to be any requirement for indemnification on the part of the operator for this as such – this may be to avoid any such conflict of interest arising and avoid any unnecessary complications as regards potential influence of proceedings on the part of the operator.

A 'Safety Investigation' is defined under Regulation 4 as a 'process conducted by SAIA for the purposes of spaceflight accident prevention' and is taken to include 'the gathering and analysis of information', the 'drawing of conclusions' which includes determining causes/contributing factors. It can also include the issuance of 'safety recommendations' derived from such investigations.

Under Regulation 14 Investigations are mandatory in some instances should an incident such as that outlined below occur:

> 'serious spaceflight accident' means—
>
> a. a spaceflight accident occurring in the course of the operation of a launch vehicle in which an individual is fatally or seriously injured, or

532 R3(a), this echoes the relevant parts of the Warsaw Convention 1929. (Convention for the Unification of Certain Rules relating to International Carriage by Air (Warsaw Convention) (as amended at the Hague, 1955, and by Protocol No. 4 of Montreal, 1975); 137 LNTS 11; USTS 876; UKTS 1933 No. 11; ATS 1963 No. 18.).

533 United Kingdom Government, Air Accidents Investigation Branch, 'Air Accidents Investigation Branch appointed as Space Accident Investigation Authority for the United Kingdom', 29 July 2021, <'https://www.gov.uk/government/news/air-accidents-investigation-branch-appointed-as-space-accident-investigation-authority-for-the-united-kingdom> accessed 14 October 2024.

534 R5(3).

> b. a spaceflight accident occurring during the course of spaceflight activities where there was a high probability that such injury would occur, as a result of that accident;
>
> 'spaceflight accident' means an accident—
> a. arising out of, or in the course of, spaceflight activities, and
> b. occurring—
> 3. in or over the United Kingdom, or
> 4. elsewhere, if any of the circumstances referred to in regulation 16 apply.

The Chief Inspector – appointed under Regulation 6(2) – must, under Regulation 14, 'cause a safety investigation to be conducted in accordance with (the) Regulations where a serious spaceflight accident occurs in or over the United Kingdom'.

Under Regulation 3 a 'serious injury' is defined as:

> an injury which is sustained by an individual in a spaceflight accident which involves—
> e. hospitalisation for more than 48 hours, commencing within 7 days beginning with the day after the day on which the injury was received;
> f. lacerations which cause severe haemorrhage, nerve, muscle or tendon damage;
> g. injury to any internal organ;
> h. second or third degree burns, or any burns affecting more than 5 per cent of the body surface; [or]
> i. exposure to infectious substances or harmful radiation, which has been verified by a medical doctor.

This has been taken at least partially from Chapter 1 of Annex 13 of the Chicago Convention on Civil Aviation or the source common to both legislative bodies at the drafting stage.[535] A fatal 'injury' means 'a person sustaining an injury in a spaceflight accident which results in that person's death within 30 days of the date of the accident'.

Whilst an investigation is mandatory for such incidents, there is also a discretionary power to investigate 'spaceflight accidents' generally under Regulation 15 where the accident 'occurs in or over the United Kingdom', and 'the

535 N109, Annex 13, Chapter 1 – 'Definitions'.

Chief Inspector expects to draw safety lessons for spaceflight activities from the safety investigation'. It is likely that this discretionary power will be invoked more often than not in the infancy of the United Kingdom's space program in order to make future operations as safe as possible although the Regulations themselves do not stipulate whether the Secretary of State could refuse an allocation of resources in such instances if it regarded something as unworthy of investigation. Under Chapter 8 'reasonable expenses' can be claimed from a licencee including the 'reasonable costs' of 'recovering property, transporting it from the site of the spaceflight accident to a hangar or any other facility which is being used by SAIA for the purposes of a safety investigation and storing the property in that hangar or facility ... destroying or disposing of property where SAIA has to make arrangements for such destruction or disposal in accordance with regulation 27 ... overtime, travel or subsistence claims made by staff of SAIA in connection with a safety investigation.'[536]

Interestingly, Regulation 28(4) states that: 'The reasonable costs referred to in this regulation will be recoverable from a licencee as a debt due to the Secretary of State.' In keeping with other related legislative provisions in this area[537] this could be said to amount to a de facto duty to indemnify the Secretary of State for costs arising out of an investigation.

It is important to note that the Regulations give power to the Chief Inspector to begin safety investigations in places other than the United Kingdom in certain limited circumstances and 'if practicable'[538] and if the United Kingdom is the state 'from which the launch vehicle was launched'[539] or which has 'jurisdiction over the organisation responsible for the design of the launch vehicle'[540]/ 'jurisdiction over the organisation responsible for the manufacture or final assembly of the launch vehicle, or of any component parts of the launch vehicle'[541]/ 'jurisdiction over the organisation responsible for the maintenance of the launch vehicle, or any component parts of the launch vehicle',[542] 'in which the spaceflight operator's principal place of business is located'.[543] This seems to grant quite extensive powers and could even be said to be a controversial exercise of extra-territoriality, but it appears conditional upon Regulation 16(c) which states that this power can be exercised where 'an

536 R28.
537 See Outer Space Act 1986 s10(4A) (7).
538 R16.
539 R16 (b)(I).
540 R16 (b)(II).
541 R16 (b)(III).
542 R16 (b)(IV).
543 16 (b)(V).

investigation is not conducted by another state, or the United Kingdom has been requested by another state to assist with an investigation carried out on behalf of that state.' As stated in the guidance:

> Currently, there are no international conventions relating to the investigation of spaceflight accidents, so any UK accredited representative does not have any rights in relation to an investigation.[544]

This is an important point, and at first it may seem unusual that no international instruments cover such scenarios but, thankfully, there have not yet been any significant *international* spaceflight accidents unlike air transport generally. This does not mean that the present situation is satisfactory. The point was also identified as part of the 2024 Space Regulatory Review, with the powers to investigate accidents outside of the United Kingdom being identified as 'insufficient' in certain circumstances.[545] Responsibility for this may not lie entirely with the United Kingdom legislature. The international community should be minded to consider an agreement in this area much like Annex 13 to the Convention on International Civil Aviation[546] on Aircraft Accident and Incident Investigation.[547] Chapter 5 concerns accidents or incidents in the territories of both contracting and non-contracting states, in addition to those occurring outside of any state's territory. Where a contracting state is 'the state of occurrence', they are responsible for the initial institution of any investigatory processes but may delegate responsibility either wholly or partly to another state 'by mutual agreement and consent'.[548] As regards non-contracting states, the recommendation is that 'the State of Registry or, failing that, the State of the operator, the State of Design or the State of Manufacture should endeavour to institute and conduct an investigation in cooperation with the State of Occurrence but, failing such cooperation, should itself conduct an investigation with such information as is available.'[549] Similar rules exist for accidents or

544 The United Kingdom Civil Aviation Authority, Guidance on the Investigation of Spaceflight Accidents, para 4.10, <https://www.caa.co.uk/publication/download/18927> accessed 17 October 2024.

545 N405.

546 N109.

547 International Civil Aviation Organisation, International Standards and Recommended Practices, Annex 13 to the Convention on International Civil Aviation, Aircraft Accident and Incident Investigation, <http://www.airsafe.com/downloads/icao-annex-13.pdf> accessed 15 October 2024.

548 *Ibid*, Chapter 5.1.

549 *Ibid*, Chapter 5.2.

incidents occurring outside any state's territory with the contracting state able to delegate investigations by mutual consent as in Chapter 5.1 and under section 5.3.1 'States nearest the scene of an accident in international waters shall provide such assistance as they are able and shall, likewise, respond to requests by the State of Registry'. At this juncture, it would be a reasonable enquiry to consider whether or not the Convention automatically covers spaceflight accidents but all references to 'Accident' under Chapter 1 on definitions refer exclusively to 'aircraft'. This appears to leave the door open for accidents involving 'carrier aircraft' as set out in the UK space legislation. The definition of 'aircraft' under Chapter 1 is:

> Any machine that can derive support in the atmosphere from the reactions of the air other than the reactions of the air against the earth's surface.

This definition would certainly apply to carrier aircraft such as Virgin's 'Cosmic Girl' and others like it. For the sake of certainty between space-faring and non-space-faring nations it would be a relatively simple exercise to adopt these parts of the Convention for aircraft accidents and thus, in the unfortunate event of such an investigation being needed, avoid any confusion or inefficiency against the backdrop of what would be a time-sensitive matter. At the very least it should be decided whether an accident involving a carrier aircraft would be covered by the Chicago Convention. Given that the Convention appears to be concerned more with respect to the category of vehicle than the type of operation it is involved in, it would seem logical to conclude that they are.

The powers conferred upon Chief Inspectors and their subordinates are extensive. Under Chapter 7, they have the power to call and examine witnesses by means of a served summons[550] and the witnesses are entitled to call upon legal representation for such instances[551] which, by definition, move such investigations into the scope of a legal or quasi-legal enquiry requiring observance of the rules of natural justice and procedural fairness although it is important to note that a determination of blame or liability is not the purpose. As per Regulation 11(1) 'The sole objective of a safety investigation which is undertaken pursuant to these Regulations is the prevention of spaceflight accidents' and 'must be independent of and separate from any judicial or administrative proceedings to apportion blame or liability'. It should be

550 R25(2).
551 R25(4).

considered that any evidence taken in the manner outlined in Regulation 25 could potentially be admissible in judicial proceedings in accordance with Regulation 32(8) if a Court makes a determination under Regulation 31(3) to apply for disclosure of such information. This is subject to the information not '(disclosing) the identity of any person involved with the spaceflight accident or (damaging) the international relations of the United Kingdom and … that the benefits of disclosing that information outweigh the adverse domestic and international consequences that disclosure of that information might have on the safety investigation to which the information relates or any future safety investigation'.[552] Such a determination must be made by either the High Court or the Scottish Court of Session.[553] It is important, therefore, that licencees are aware of the potential legal consequences of giving evidence in such matters.

Following the conclusion of the investigation there is a requirement under Regulation 32 for a report to be written by the investigator in charge and published as soon as possible. The report must be in writing and state that it is not seeking to apportion blame or liability and only publish sensitive information insofar as is necessary for the purposes of the report[554] and 'may' contain safety recommendations. It is interesting to note that such recommendations do not necessarily have to be drawn from an active investigation into a domestic spaceflight accident. Under Regulation 35, a safety recommendation where the SAIA considers that 'preventative action must be taken promptly to enhance the safety of spaceflight activities'can be given 'at any time on the basis of … studies or other information about the safety of spaceflight activities, or … analysis of a series of safety investigations'. This appears to put the SAIA under an almost continuous duty to keep safety under review by way of monitoring the academic literature in addition to live investigations in other jurisdictions. As previously mentioned, in the absence of any international agreement as to the sharing of this kind of information, this task may prove more troublesome than should be necessary given the potential importance of such information to all space-faring nations. The importance of this must be balanced against factors such as unauthorised disclosure of sensitive data and commercial confidentiality, particularly as regards technological development, a theme previously encountered.

Importantly, under Regulation 35(4), it is stated that 'The safety recommendation does not create a presumption of blame or liability for the spaceflight accident', asserting the independence of such an investigation, pre-emptively

552 R31 (3)(a)–(b).
553 R31(4).
554 R32 (2).

declining any cause of action per se and presumably also to remove some of the associated 'sting'.

Under Regulation 36, the person to whom any of the SAIA safety recommendation is addressed must acknowledge receipt and either take action to implement the recommendation, explain the reason for any delay in acting or give reasons for not implementing the recommendation.[555] The SAIA then have the duty to respond to the addressee by either stating whether they consider the action taken is sufficient or recording their reasons for disagreeing with the decision to take no action.[556]

Although there are no statutory penalties for failure to follow an SAIA recommendation – though it could be evidence of common law negligence in the context of a relevant tort or delict action – the Regulations create a number of statutory offences that licencees must be wary of. Largely they correlate with duties of licencees set out in Part 3 of the Regulations. For example, failure to notify the Chief Inspector of a spaceflight accident is an offence punishable by a fine and up to 51 weeks imprisonment on indictment.[557] These are also the potential consequences for a number of other matters, such as a failure to preserve evidence,[558] a failure to protect sensitive safety information[559] and the failure to provide information on persons and dangerous goods on board a launch vehicle following a spaceflight accident.[560] Regarding the definition of 'dangerous goods', the Regulations stipulate that this is defined as 'any article or substance which is identified as such in the 2021–2022 English language edition of the Technical Instructions for the Safe Transport of Dangerous Goods by Air, approved and published by decision of the Council of the International Civil Aviation Organisation.'[561] What is less clear is the definition of 'accident' which could be a source of some concern. Whilst definitions of 'spaceflight accident' and 'serious spaceflight accident' appear, there is no technical definition of what an 'accident' consists of. There is likewise no definition under Regulation 270 in the Space Industry Regulations regarding occurrence reporting. It is to be assumed that *de minimis* principles would come into play regarding trivial incidents. Stroud's Judicial dictionary states that 'The essential characteristics of an accident are that it is an event which was neither expected nor intended

555 R36 (1)(b).
556 R36 (2).
557 R37, 45.
558 R40.
559 R41.
560 R43.
561 R8 (4).

and which causes hurt or loss'.[562] Ordinary occurrences such as snowstorms would not be classified as accidents[563] but as an 'Act of God', which according to Stroud, is an accident on the basis of ordinary language as shown by the case of *Makin v London & North Eastern Railway*.[564] A more instructive source could be taken once again from Annex 13 of the Chicago Convention[565] which defines an accident as 'An occurrence associated with the operation of an aircraft which takes place between the time any person boards the aircraft with the intention of flight until such time as all such persons have disembarked' in which there is either death or serious injury as per limb (a) – for our purposes immaterial here since this would plainly be covered elsewhere in the regulations – but limb (b) of the definition could prove very helpful. It states that the following would be considered an accident during the time that a passenger is on board:

> (the) aircraft sustains damage or structural failure which … adversely affects the structural strength, performance or flight characteristics of the aircraft, and would normally require major repair or replacement of the affected component … except for engine failure or damage, when the damage is limited to the engine, its cowlings or accessories; or for damage limited to propellers, wing tips, antennas, tires, brakes, fairings, small dents or puncture holes in the aircraft skin.[566]

A modification of this wording would be appropriate for the UK legislative regime although the provisions relating to a passenger being on board would not be relevant for flights without human occupants, likely to be the majority of flights for the foreseeable future.

So far, the only incident requiring engagement of the regulations has been the Virgin Orbit flight of January 2023. It was decided that both the Federal Aviation Administration and SAIA would investigate this incident,[567] with the involvement of the FAA necessary as the operation also required an FAA licence under US law being a company based in the United States. On the 3rd

---

562 Daniel Greenberg (ed), Stroud's Judicial Dictionary, 11th Edition, *Definition of 'Accident'*.

563 *Fenwick v Schmalz* (1867–68) L.R. 3 C.P. 313.

564 [1943] K.B. 467.

565 N109.

566 N109, Chapter 1, 'Accident'.

567 The United Kingdom Government, Air Accidents Investigation Branch, 'SAIA and FAA to jointly oversee Virgin Orbit investigation', 13 January 2023, <https://www.gov.uk/government/news/saia-and-faa-to-jointly-oversee-virgin-orbit-investigation> accessed 15 October 2024.

of October 2024, a statement was released by the Air Accidents Investigation Branch on the Virgin Orbit LauncherOne failure.[568] Within the statement, the engagement of the US/UK Technology Safeguards Agreement was noted, specifically, Article VIII (3) on Launch Anomalies or Failure[569] and the agreement between the parties to 'provide ... information necessary to determine the cause'[570] thereof. It is evident from the statement that data relevant to the investigation was not disclosed to the SAIA from US Authorities until later in proceedings owing to the contents of a US Technical Assistance Agreement (TSA) which was only approved after the launch had taken place.[571] Investigators from the SAIA visited facilities linked to the incident in the United States in March 2023, but information disclosed during the visit was 'limited by export controls in that it did not reflect the most current information on the state of the investigation'.[572] Whilst the importance of maintaining compliance with export controls should not be understated, the added inconvenience caused to the investigation along with the initial delays associated with the TSA were clearly not conducive to an efficient and effective process. This appears particularly acute when considering that the operator filed for bankruptcy on 4 April which led to it withdrawing its support for the SAIA's participation owing to the associated complications.[573] If certain matters had been resolved earlier in the timeframe, any impact on the investigation from the operator's bankruptcy could have been avoided. These problems were noted by the bodies involved, it being stated therein that 'The SAIA is currently working with the UK Department for Transport, the UK CAA and relevant US agencies to improve the flow of information to the SAIA should there be a future launch failure involving a US vehicle in or over the UK'.[574]

In any event, it was found that the cause of the launch failure was a displaced fuel filter which led to significant engine overheating, in turn leading to further system failures.[575] Importantly in the context of this work, it was

568 The United Kingdom Civil Aviation Authority, Air Accidents Investigation Branch, 'Statement on an investigation into why launch vehicle LauncherOne did not reach orbit following its launch from Cornwall Spaceport on 9 January 2023', 3 October 2024, <https://assets.publishing.service.gov.uk/media/66feaae73b919067bb482bed/Boeing_747-400__modified__LauncherOne_Spaceflight.pdf> accessed 15 October 2024.

569 N92.

570 N574, 2.

571 Ibid, 3.

572 Ibid.

573 Ibid.

574 Ibid, 5.

575 Ibid, 4.

stated that, on the basis of the operators' report as submitted, the UK licensing framework did not contribute to the failure. The SAIA also upheld the CAA's finding that the operator 'had taken all reasonable steps to reduce the risks to as low as reasonably practicable (ALARP) and that the residual risks were acceptable'.[576]

The failure of LauncherOne also prompted a 'Lessons Learned' report to be issued from the United Kingdom Space Agency[577] on the 14th December 2023. Besides a review of existing space legislation which, presumably, manifested itself in the shape of the 2024 Space Regulatory Review,[578] clearer guidance, more familiarisation with the launch processes of other international partners along with updated decision-making protocols were also put forward as areas for specific focus.[579]

5 The Space Industry (Appeals) Regulations 2021[580]

In the 2024 Space Regulatory Review, it was stated that 'officials identified that the SIA Appeals process is potentially difficult to manage, and we are looking to streamline the process'.[581] There have, at the time of writing, been no public appeals that the author is aware of under the Space Industry Act. Whether or not it is 'difficult to manage' in practice is yet to be seen. Given that the primary legislation concerned is one of licensing, in general, such regimes give rise to a number of public law rights against decision makers as stated at the outset of this work. Whilst a cumbersome procedure is to be avoided, there is certainly a need for a somewhat extensive and overarching framework so as not to abrogate rights and ensure a fair hearing of disputes. This need is particularly acute where an individual's livelihood is dependent upon obtaining – or continuing to hold – a licence to carry out certain activities. Therefore, in line with conceptions of procedural fairness and natural justice, the Space Industry legislation, in some cases, gives an applicant the option of appealing decisions under Schedule 1, Part 2, paragraphs 2–4 of the Space Industry Act which must

576 Ibid 4–5.

577 The United Kingdom Space Agency, '(First) Pathfinder Launch Lessons Learned report, 14 December 2013, <https://www.gov.uk/government/publications/uk-pathfinder-launch-lessons-learned-report/pathfinder-launch-lessons-learned-report-html> accessed 15 October 2024.

578 N405.

579 N583.

580 SI 2021 No. 816.

581 N405, 35.

be read in conjunction with the Space Industry Appeals Regulations 2021 and the Space Industry Regulations 2021. The Appeals Regulations themselves are similar to other instruments regarding appellate functions in respect of licensing, the National Lottery (Imposition of Penalties and Revocation of Licences) Procedure Regulations 1999[582] sets out a similar regime.

The first two areas open to appeal are for refusals to grant licences and decisions in connection with licences.[583]

Appeals against refusals to grant licences – or in connection with them – lie against a panel. Under Part 2, panel members will be senior officials[584] from the 'UK Space Agency and government departments'.[585] An appeals panel hearing a decision 'must consist of three or more members, including, where possible, a representative from UKSA'[586] but in circumstances where 3 panel members are not available there is the discretion for a hearing to proceed with just 2 members[587] with the chair of the panel retaining a second vote.[588]

In the case of a licence application under the Space Industry Act, the other party will be the Regulator – the CAA – and in the case of an application for the same under Section 4 of the Outer Space Act 1986, the Secretary of State.[589] The meaning of 'in connection with' in this context covers grounds such as appeals against licence conditions an applicant may not agree with,[590] refusals to renew licences,[591] suspensions,[592] revocations,[593] matters regarding variations of licence terms[594] and refusal to allow the transfer of a licence.[595]

Where things become more convoluted are with Section 4 on appeals against 'other decisions'. This refers to '... any other decisions of the Regulator under this Act, or under regulations made under this Act, that are prescribed ... any other decisions of the Secretary of State under the Outer Space Act 1986 that are prescribed.'[596] Such 'prescribed' grounds are set out under Regulation 7

582 SI 1999 No. 137
583 Space Industry Act 2018 Schedule 10, Part 2, Section 2–3.
584 R3 (3) (a)–(b).
585 *Ibid* R3 (2).
586 *Ibid* R4 (2).
587 *Ibid* R4 (6).
588 *Ibid* R4 (7).
589 Space Industry Act 2018 Schedule 10, Part 2, Section 2.
590 *Ibid* s3(1)(a).
591 *Ibid* s3(1)(b).
592 *Ibid* s3(1)(e).
593 *Ibid* s3(1)(f).
594 *Ibid* s3(1)(b).
595 *Ibid* s3(1)(d).
596 *Ibid* s4(1) (a)–(b).

of the Space Industry Appeals Regulations and refer to decisions made relating to various aspects of a licencee's business such as the approval of training managers,[597] required revisions to safety cases and risk assessments[598] along with other matters under the regulations.

Similarly to Part 2 sections 2 and 3 of the Space Industry Act regarding appeals against refusals to grant licences/in connection with licences, appeals under section 4 can only be brought by 'prescribed persons'.[599] 'Prescribed persons' are listed under Regulation 7(2) and consist of licencees/licence applicants[600] and those whom 'prohibition' and 'stop' notices have been served under the Space Industry Regulations.[601]

As would be expected there are time limits to comply with[602] and the Regulations provide extensive rules on the format of the appeals themselves. These include the procedure to be followed,[603] the service of documents[604] and the way in which hearings should be conducted.[605] It is worthy of note that under Regulation 19(1), it is stated that 'If there is an oral hearing of the appeal, the hearing must take place in private.' Whilst this may be understandable for reasons of convenience, given the possible quasi-judicial nature of the process as set-out in the Appeals Regulations, it seems extreme to cast this as a mandatory requirement rather than introducing an element of discretion, particularly since there may be elements of public interest at stake.

For 'prescribed persons' there are numerous 'prescribed grounds' on which an appeal can be made. However, if an individual does not fall into the category of a 'prescribed person' or the nature of their dispute does not fall within the 'prescribed grounds' as outlined above, they have no direct means of recourse under these regulations. Given that the Space Industry Act and accompanying Regulations were established as a licensing regime it makes sense that only those subject to its licensing measures should be able to bring proceedings under it. The guidance document appears to contradict the regulations in an important respect at paragraph 1.18 whereby it is stated that 'an appeal against a refusal to grant a medical certificate may be brought against the approved

597 R7(1)(a)–(b).

598 *Ibid* 7(1)(d)–(f).

599 Space Industry Act 2018, Part 2, Section 4(2).

600 R7(2) (a)–(e).

601 *Ibid* (f)–(g).

602 *Ibid* R8(1) – Application for permission to appeal must be within 14 days unless there are 'exceptional circumstances' under 8 (2).

603 *Ibid* R13.

604 *Ibid* R16.

605 See Part 4 generally.

aeromedical examiner responsible'.[606] This, by the guidance's own measure, would not be a cause of action. The flowchart given at paragraph 3.2 states this uncontrovertibly whereby if the question 'Does the decision that you want to appeal fall under either paragraphs 2, 3 or 4 of Schedule 10 (of the Space Industry Act 2018)?'[607] is answered in the negative, the answer that follows is 'You cannot appeal the decision'. An appeal against an aeromedical examiner's decision is not one of the prescribed grounds under paragraphs 2, 3 or 4 of Schedule 10 and nor – on the assumption that such an individual wishing to launch such an appeal would be likely to be a member of spaceflight/flight personnel or a paying customer – would they be regarded as a 'prescribed person' being neither a licence holder, transferee or the applicant for a licence.[608] This may not be as clear as it first seems. Paragraph 6(1) of Schedule 10 states that 'Where a person appeals to a panel and there is no appealable decision, the panel may not accept the appeal.' The use of the term 'may' grants an element of discretion by which the panel could, theoretically, hear decisions which would not on a strict reading of the regulations, be 'appealable' ones. This present situation is to an extent desirable for reasons discussed elsewhere in this work – particularly as regards the discussion regarding mental capacity and informed consent[609] – but that is only insofar as it appears that there may be some avenue of redress under the regulations for those other than licencees, operators and applicants on a strict reading of the rules. What would be much more desirable would be either for a separate set of Regulations to be drafted which would establish pathways for appealing decisions not covered by the present Regulations or, at the very least, some guidance on how such matters could be resolved, even if this extends only to signposting private avenues of appeal against, for example, aeromedical examiners. Whilst it is conceded that candidates for spaceflight crews and associated personnel are more likely to be familiar with the procedures for appealing the decision of an aeromedical examiner[610] it is not as likely to be the case for paying customers or other

606 The United Kingdom Civil Aviation Authority, 'Guidance on Appealing Decisions made Under the Space Industry Act 2018 and the Outer Space Act 1986', 5, <https://assets.publishing.service.gov.uk/government/uploads/system/uploads/attachment_data/file/904910/guidance-on-appealing-decisions-made-under-the-space-industry-act-2018.pdf> accessed 15 October 2024.

607 *Ibid*, 11.

608 Per Schedule 10 (3)(2) and (2)–(3).

609 See chapters 8.

610 Being 'grounded' for medical reasons is a not-uncommon occurrence in the space-faring community, see, for example the experiences of Mercury Astronaut and later Apollo Soyuz Docking module pilot - Deke Slayton, America's first person in space aboard

potential spaceflight participants with little or no experience of the industry. It is important that such individuals are given a legitimate means of redress, particularly given the likely technical nature of such appeals. There could also be significant contractual issues to navigate should an aeromedical examiner's decision lead to a possible cancellation of a spaceflight participant's arrangement with an operator or licencee. This eventuality does not seem to be provided for within the scope of the existing legislation. This could be due to the fact that the 2018 Act and accompanying Regulations are to be viewed as laying the foundations for private spaceflight operators to set out their stalls, but moving beyond this it is important that some consideration be given to how best to administer fee structures in contractual relationships between customers and operators. It would seem to be unjust for an entire purchase price to be forfeited if a spaceflight participant is refused a seat on the grounds of an aeromedical examiner's decision. It is perhaps more desirable that initial payments in such circumstances are to be taken on a deposit-only basis so that, in the event of an adverse decision, less financial loss ensues. Commercial considerations aside, it could also be the case that failing to provide an avenue for redress could be discriminatory to those with disability related concerns.

Whilst there may be a desire for 'streamlining',[611] as can be shown, appeals under the Space Industry Act could be wide ranging and diverse. They could be brought by numerous classes of appellants, and in respect of numerous significant rights. Not providing a comprehensive appeals framework in such instances could give rise to challenges on human rights grounds amongst other avenues. Refinement, as opposed to partial repeal, would be the more sensible suggestion until the existing system has been adequately tested.

6 The Air Navigation (Amendment) Order 2021

For the sake of completeness, the Air Navigation Amendment Order of 2021[612] adds to the body of UK space law. Amending the seminal Air Navigation Order 2016,[613] it requires that those operating unmanned aircraft systems (UAS) must

---

Freedom 7, later Commander of Apollo 14 and fifth person to walk on the Moon, Alan Shepard, and Ken Mattingly who was grounded prior to the unsuccessful Apollo 13 mission, the latter incident being portrayed in the 1995 movie, *'Apollo 13'* with Mattingly played by Gary Sinise.

611 N587.

612 SI 2021 No. 879.

613 N302.

not fly – or permit the flying – of the UAS over or near space sites[614] without permission from the relevant operator.[615] A 'protected space site' under the article has the definition in section 3(2) of the Space Industry Act 2018 – 'a site from which spacecraft or carrier aircraft are launched or (as the case may be) are to be launched' or 'a site at which controlled and planned landings of spacecraft take place or (as the case may be) are to take place' and, additionally, 'an installation at sea, at which controlled and planned landings of spacecraft take place or are to take place, which can be moved from place to place without major dismantling or modification'. The requirement for permission does not apply to certified aerodromes, government aerodromes or national licenced aerodromes under this article which have restrictions in place regarding such matters under other enactments. Importantly, the Order also amends Article 96 of the 2016 Order regarding rockets to fully exclude those licenced under the 2018 Act. The 2016 Order defines rockets as either 'large rockets' – defined as 'a rocket of which the total impulse of the motor or combination of motors is more than 10,240 Newton-seconds'[616] – or 'small rockets' which means rockets 'of which the total impulse of the motor or combination of motors exceeds 160 Newton-seconds'[617] (to put both of these numbers in context, the Saturn V Moon Rocket stood at 35,000,000 Newton-seconds[618]). A crucial amendment to the use of 'large rockets' which was made by the 2021 order was the requirement as regards the person operating the rocket to provide a safety case and demonstrate that they have adequate insurance to cover the launch activities before the CAA can grant permission for such usage.[619] The overall effect, therefore, of the Air Navigation Order 2021 on UK space law, is to exclude certain categories of rocket from within the ambit of the Air Navigation Order 2016 and to provide clarity as regards the definition of the term 'rocket' which is to be welcomed.

Regrettably, the legal requirements for launches under the Air Navigation Order 2016 are not as stringent as those for launches under the Space Industry Act 2018. This is particularly acute as regards environmental considerations. In sharp contrast to the requirements of the Space Industry Act 2018, a rocket launched under a 'permission' granted under the Air Navigation Order 2016 is

614 Article 5 (3).

615 *Ibid.*

616 N302, Schedule 1.

617 *Ibid*, Article 96 (1)(b).

618 Richard Hollingham, BBC.com, 'Apollo in 50 numbers: The rocket', 26 June 2019, <https://www.bbc.com/future/article/20190626-apollo-in-50-numbers-the-rocket> accessed 15 October 2024.

619 N469, Article 5(4)(e).

not subject to any – or any equivalent – assessment of environmental effects. The proposed SaxaVord launch from the Shetland Islands[620] is one such example of this, as will be discussed in more depth later. Whilst it may be unreasonable to hold operators of smaller rockets to as high a standard as other classes of operators, the intent of Parliament to regulate the space industry must not be circumvented, and a proportionate linkage between these two disparate regimes should be considered.

6.1 *The Law Relating to the Use of Airspace*

Whilst setting out the applicable law as regards activities carried out under the new regime, the local rules relating to airspace usage should be addressed. As and when a 'space activity' is under way, a NOTAM – or 'Notice to Airmen' – could be required. NOTAM's have their basis in Annex 15 of the Chicago Convention on Civil Aviation, itself stemming from Article 28 of the same. The recent experience with Virgin Orbit saw the issuance of NOTAMs (and 'NOTMARS' – 'Notice to Mariners') in respect of their launching activity from Spaceport Cornwall[621] which would then result in 'temporary airspace closures' by association if deemed necessary by the CAA.[622] The latter are responsible for carrying out an assessment of the airspace pursuant to Article 2 of Regulation (EC) No 549/2004[623] ahead of making any such determination in line with the UK Airspace Management Policy.[624] The responsibility for issuing such notifications under UK space law falls on the provider of range control services under Section 6(d) of the Space Industry Act 2018. For the Virgin Orbit launch such notices were issued to a wide range of stakeholders which were codified via a Memorandum of Understanding (or 'Letter of Authority' or 'LOA')[625] and,

620 SaxaVord UK Spaceport, 'SaxaVord and Hylmpulse announce launch plans', SaxaVord website, November 15 2023, <https://saxavord.com/saxavord-and-hyimpulse-announce-launch-plans/> accessed 15 October 2024.

621 Virgin Orbit (and multiple authors), 'Assessment of Environmental Effects Virgin Orbit LLC LauncherOne Operations from Spaceport Cornwall, Cornwall Airport Newquay, United Kingdom, July 2022, 3–13, para 3.1.37–3.1.38 <https://consultations.caa.co.uk/corporate-communications/aee-consultation-virgin-orbit-spaceport-cornwall/user_uploads/virgin-orbit-spaceport-cornwall-aee--13jul22--1.pdf> accessed 15 October 2024.

622 See chapter 4.6.

623 Regulation (EC) No 549/2004 of the European Parliament and of the Council of 10 March 2004 laying down the framework for the creation of the single European sky (the framework Regulation).

624 The United Kingdom Civil Aviation Authority Safety and Airspace Regulation Group, CAP740, UK Airspace Management Policy, <https://www.caa.co.uk/publication/download/12498> accessed 15 October 2024.

625 N627, 1.4.7.

apparently, 'subject to any additional requirements that may apply per UK space launch regulations'.[626] As regards this statement, there are no – or no significant – regulations in the corpus of UK space law so it is unclear what exactly was being referred to here. It is interesting to note that calculations as to 'hazard areas' have their legal basis under section 5 of the Space Industry Act and are again the responsibility of those providing range control services.

Those notified by Virgin Orbit in the course of this exercise – 'affected UK agencies', included the CAA, the Ministry of Defence, the United Kingdom Meteorological Office in addition to the airspace authorities of various countries affected, in this instance, Ireland, France, Spain and Portugal.[627] This is in addition to entering into LOAs with Coastguard authorities for this kind of launch[628] who must also be notified of 'SHAs' – 'Ship Hazard Areas' – as estimated on the basis of the operator's own calculations.[629] In the case of the Virgin Orbit launch, these were calculated as being the 'drop point' – that is, where the rocket was 'dropped' from the carrier aircraft – Cosmic Girl – following the end of the Captive Carry Flight Path in addition to the 'Stage 1 and Fairings Re-Entry' area over the Atlantic Ocean.[630] In addition to 'Ship Hazard Areas' there are also 'Aircraft Hazard Areas' which must be calculated and communicated also.[631] For the Virgin Orbit launch, these areas were the same as the Ship Hazard Areas given the nature of the mission, that is, a launch from a carrier aircraft. The logic behind designating such areas was to ensure that no aircraft or ships are operating in the vicinity where the rocket – in this case 'LauncherOne' – would be dropped to avoid potential damage.[632] Such areas included areas where the stages of the rocket were due to fall post-ignition under the calculated flight plan.[633] All such details would be included in the mandated NOTAMs/NOTMARS.[634]

Given that the responsibility for formulating NOTAMs/NOTMARS appears to fall squarely on the operator it may be that further legislation or guidance is provided specifically for space operators given the unique nature of such

626 *Ibid*, 3.1.37.

627 *Ibid* para 1.4.7. Regarding the airspace management in general for the Virgin Orbit launch, see 3.13–3.18 in the report.

628 *Ibid* para 3.1.48.

629 *Ibid* para 3.1.49.

630 *Ibid*, 3–15.

631 *Ibid*.

632 Para 3.1.56.

633 Para 3.1.57.

634 *Ibid*.

ventures. The main guidance document in respect of these matters is hosted on the CAA's website.[635]

It is also useful to note that airspace changes were consulted on far in advance of any activities by SaxaVord, who opened discussions with stakeholders for this purpose at least as far back as April 2023,[636] and applied for an airspace change with the CAA as far back as 2018.[637] Furthermore, paragraph 18(2) of Schedule 1 of the Space Industry Regulations 2021 stipulates that a Flight Safety Analysis under Regulation 26(3) must take into consideration 'any legal requirements relevant to the applicant's proposed use of airspace'. The implication of this requirement may be that such engagement with the CAA is to take place a significant amount of time ahead of any space or launch activity, and at the very least during the planning stage. Further, it appears incumbent upon the provider of range control services, albeit 'where the licencee's range control services consist of or include monitoring the designated range',[638] to enter into a written agreement with 'the appropriate air navigation service provider for aircraft flying in the volume of airspace within the designated range'.[639] Given that licences can be applied for in lieu of having contracted range control services, it is possible that delays could ensue should such matters be left solely within the preserve of range control providers should they not be contracted until later in the planning stages.

---

635 The United Kingdom Civil Aviation Authority, 'CAP1616 Airspace change: Guidance on the regulatory process for changing the notified airspace design and planned and permanent redistribution of air traffic, and on providing airspace. information' <https://publicapps.caa.co.uk/modalapplication.aspx?appid=11&mode=detail&id=8127> accessed 15 October 2024.

636 SaxaVord UK Spaceport, 'SaxaVord Spaceport Permanent Airspace Reservation', 12 June 2023, <https://airspacechange.caa.co.uk/PublicProposalArea?pID=92> accessed 16 September 2024.

637 See DAP 1916 'Statement of Need', submitted by Shetland Space Centre Limited in respect of application ACP-2017-79, 30 June 2018, The United Kingdom Civil Aviation Authority, Airspace Change, <https://airspacechange.caa.co.uk/PublicProposalArea?pID=92> accessed 16 September 2024.

638 N173, R43(1).

639 *Ibid*, R44(a).

CHAPTER 5

Enforcement

It is important to note that once a licence has been granted the licencee will be under various duties to comply with the terms and conditions of that licence. Failure to comply can result in prosecution and, in some cases, imprisonment. The associated guidance document states that these duties comprise 3 broad areas:

> providing information to the Regulator, to enable the Regulator to fulfil its international obligations to supervise space activities under its jurisdiction … keeping records of, and in relation to, licenced activities … (and) reporting occurrences.[640]

As the guidance points out, there are also 'specific ongoing duties and responsibilities related to each licence type'.[641]

Before looking deeper into the legislation, it is important to understand what, in law, is meant by a 'duty'. In the case of duties arising under domestic space industry legislation, such duties are known as 'statutory duties' – that is, derived from statute, as opposed to 'common law duties' – those derived from case decisions such as duties of care arising within the common law tort of negligence. With this in mind, it is important to consider that the Space Industry Act – and associated Regulations – has not been the subject of any judicial rulings as regards duties under it owing to the relative infancy of both the law and the industry it seeks to guide. Therefore, we have no judicial guidance as to how the statutory duties imposed will be interpreted and cannot definitively state whether or not a court will find a licencee in breach of a statutory duty on the basis of the rules. However, there are a number of cases decided under similar statutory regimes in relation to duties in respect of record keeping and reporting which may be instructive.

640 The United Kingdom Civil Aviation Authority, 'Guidance on duties for all licencees under the Space Industry Act 2018 including monitoring and enforcement by the Regulator', para 3.1, <https://www.caa.co.uk/publication/download/18935> accessed 15 October 2024.

641 *Ibid.*

 | DOI:10.1163/9789004732551_006

As Oliver LJ stated: 'it is not necessary, in construing a statutory expression, to take leave of one's common sense'.[642] Therefore, a court will not expect compliance to be executed in a fashion that could be regarded as absurd – pure literal compliance is not what is being sought in giving effect to such provisions. A vivid example of this can be seen from the case of *Banque de l'Indochine et de Suez SA v Euroseas Group Finance Co Ltd* and others[643] which concerned the presentation of cheques in a company's name which were subsequently dishonoured. The registered name of the company in question was 'Euroseas Group Finance Company Limited' but the printed name on the cheques was 'per pro Euroseas Group Finance Co Ltd'. The cheques were dishonoured by the plaintiff on the basis that 'Co' did not satisfy the requirements of the Companies Act 1948 under section 108 (1) (c) which stated that cheques and other bills should bear the company name in 'legible characters' and, thus, under section 108 (4) (b) the officer of the company would be liable to a fine. This was rejected by the Court. Although strictly speaking the full name of the company had not been used, as a matter of common knowledge 'Co' was used interchangeably with 'company' and the same went for other terms such as 'Ltd'. In line with this, it is important to note that '… A statutory duty is regarded as discharged where more is done than the duty requires. This is in accordance with the maxim *omne majus continet in se minus* (the greater includes the less)'.[644]

Compliance with such duties under the space industry legislation are monitored by the Regulator under section 26 of the Space Industry Act. Under Regulation 237 the Regulator has the power to appoint an inspector by way of ensuring licencees are acting in compliance with any conditions or, otherwise, not in a way that compromises public safety and national security.[645] Powers granted to inspectors can be very extensive, with Regulation 241 conferring power of entry to spaceports, space sites or a variety of other premises connected with a licencee or regulated person's business under the provisions.[646] This power naturally extends to the inspection of any vehicle – meaning 'any vehicle involved in spaceflight activities' including carrier aircraft as well as spacecraft[647] – but goes much further under Regulation 241(4) whereby the inspector has the power to inspect any document or record permitted under

642 *Exxon Corpn v Exxon Insurance Consultants International Ltd* [1982] Ch 119 at 144, [1981] 3 All ER 241 at 249.

643 [1981] 3 All ER 198.

644 Professor David Feldman, Diggory Bailey, Luke Norbury, *Bennion, Bailey and Norbury on Statutory Interpretation*, 8th Edition Supplement, November 2022, 325.

645 Space Industry Act 2018 s26 (2).

646 R241 (1)–(2).

647 R241 (3), (4)(a).

the Regulations in addition to the power to examine material intended for use in the manufacture of any vehicle or any such servicing equipment.[648] The powers can also extend to inspecting 'the training and assessment of persons for a specified role'[649] – meaning those under Regulation 56(1) which covers key personnel ranging from the launch director through to flight crew and remote pilots.[650] As extensive as these provisions may seem, they are undercut by Regulation 241(f) which gives the inspector extremely broad powers, permitting him/her 'to carry out any examination, inspection or test necessary to discharge the inspector's duties', which essentially appears to give inspectors free reign to examine anything they wish as long as it could be broadly classified as a reasonable extension of their remit. It is also important to note that inspectors have power of entry 'at any reasonable time'[651] but no specific guidance is given as to how this is to be interpreted. Further, as stated in Regulation 241(5), '[t]he power to enter any premises or vehicle under this regulation includes the power to be on the premises or vehicle during testing, training, demonstration flights, and commercial flights.' In addition to having extensive powers in their own right, inspectors can also bring other approved individuals with them in the course of their duties under Regulation 242 including representatives of a health and safety authority and even a police officer should the inspector feel that there may be issues of obstruction.[652]

During the inspection, an inspector can take samples of any substance found within or in the vicinity of the relevant premises in addition to possession of materials and equipment designated for the purpose of manufacturing vehicles[653] and also direct that any such vehicle – or other article/substance designated for inspection – is to remain 'undisturbed for as long as reasonably necessary for the purposes of any inspection, examination or test'.[654] It is also worth noting that the inspector has the power to 'cause any article or substance found in any premises or vehicle ... to be dismantled ... be the subject of any demonstration showing how the article or substance functions ... to be deactivated or otherwise rendered safe for handling ... (or) to have any other process applied to it'.[655] There are also extensive powers of inspection over information and documents under Regulation 244 which can extend to

648 R241 (4) (b)–(d).
649 R241 (4) (e).
650 See R56 (1) (a)–(f).
651 R241 (1) (a).
652 R242 (a).
653 R243 (2)–(3).
654 R243 (4).
655 R245 (6).

taking possession of documents or any electronic equipment that holds any such information as may be of interest to the inspector.[656]

There then follows the initial provisions of 'enforcement'. Following any such inspection, should it be decided that there has been a contravention – past or present – of any licence conditions or any provision of the Space Industry Act 2018 or its associated regulations,[657] the first of what amounts to a 3-stage enforcement procedure can begin. Firstly, a 'contravention notice' is issued setting out what the contravention is deemed to be in the opinion of the inspector and specify a reasonable timeframe within which the contravention should be remedied.[658] It can also 'include directions as to the measures to be taken to remedy the contravention identified in the notice'. If, on expiration of the set timeframe, the contravention has not been addressed, there is somewhat of an escalation of matters whereby the inspector 'may' serve a 'warning notice' stating that, should the remedial action specified previously not be taken within another specified 'reasonable' timeframe, then the Regulator or Secretary of State have the option of suspending/revoking or varying any licence granted, giving a direction or serving a 'prohibition notice'.[659]

Should the remedial action still not be taken following the expiration of the allotted time in the warning notice, then, theoretically, a prohibition notice can be issued under Regulation 249 which would compel the licencee or other relevant person to stop the specified activity unless remedial action is taken[660] either immediately or within a timeframe specified in the notice.[661] On a closer reading of Regulation 249, it appears that such a prohibition notice can only be granted if the inspector believes that the person in receipt of the warning notice:

1. is carrying on activities which involve a risk to public safety or the national security of the United Kingdom, or
2. is likely to carry on activities which involve a risk to public safety or the national security of the United Kingdom.[662]

Therefore, a prohibition notice does not seem likely unless any given contravention of the Act, associated regulations or licence terms are likely to be a risk to public safety or national security. Theoretically a licencee could be in breach of one of the Act's provisions, be in receipt of a contravention notice

656 R244 (2), (6).
657 R247 (1) (a)–(b).
658 R247 (2)–(4).
659 R248.
660 R249 (2)–(3).
661 R249 (5).
662 R249 (d)(I)–(II).

followed by a warning notice, not take any remedial action at the conclusion of the specified timeframe and face no consequences whatsoever should the contravention not be deemed to have crossed this threshold. Such matters will be filtered out at the 'warning notice' stage whereby the Regulator has power under Regulation 248 (3)(a) and Section 15 of the Space Industry Act to 'revoke, vary or suspend' a licence. In particular, Section 15 (4) gives power to revoke or vary licences where conditions have not been complied with[663] or, importantly, where 'the licencee has failed to comply with, or to secure compliance with, obligations imposed under or by virtue of any enactment.'[664] Therefore, there is a split of enforcement responsibilities between the Regulator, the Secretary of State and the inspector with the Regulator having very broad powers under section 15 of the Space Industry Act. Under section 15, as stated, a licence could be revoked for failure to comply with 'any enactment' which, possibly, could mean any legislation whatsoever including provisions applicable to commercial air traffic and general health and safety matters giving operators more to consider where inspections are concerned. Putting these considerable powers regarding prohibition notices exclusively within the hands of any inspector should hopefully preserve independence in decision making and largely avoid political or commercial pressures. It is important to note that, as previously discussed, there is a right to appeal any such decision and under Regulation 250 a prohibition notice must bring this fact to the recipient's attention.

Regarding the statutory monitoring and enforcement regime more generally it is instructive to observe the practical domain in which it operates. For every licence granted under the Space Industry Act by the CAA there is a corresponding 'Oversight and Monitoring Plan'.[665] The exception to this is the 'licence' granted to Hylmpulse Technologies GmbH under Article 6 and 269 of the Air Navigation Order 2016[666] for the SaxaVord launch site. This is interesting since the 'licence' in question is not a 'licence' as such. It is instead considered an 'Air Navigation Order Large Rocket Permission' and is therefore exempt from the monitoring and oversight requirements as prescribed under the Space Industry Act 2018. Whilst this may seem like a minor detail, the fact that the 'permission' is not, in the statutory 'space law' sense, regarded as a

663 Space Industry Act 2018 s15(4)(a).

664 *Ibid* s15 (4)(b).

665 The United Kingdom Civil Aviation Authority, Licences Granted Under the Space Industry Act 2018, <https://www.caa.co.uk/space/about-the-space-team/licences-granted-and-registers-of-space-objects/> accessed 15 October 2024.

666 The United Kingdom Civil Aviation Authority, Air Navigation Order 2016, ANO Large Rocket Permission granted for HyImpulse Technologies GmBh, ORS10 2023–001, <https://www.caa.co.uk/publication/download/20588> accessed 15 October 2024.

'licence', there could be implications for the rights of applicants under it. As was established earlier, the grant of licences and, more pointedly, revocation or unilateral forms of amendment of licences, can attract rules of natural justice in a public law sense, particularly where such an action on the part of a local authority, regulator or other relevant body has an adverse impact upon the licencee or applicant's livelihood.[667] The Air Navigation Order 2016 does, however, prescribe certain rules regarding 'permission'. Article 269 provides that a certificate of permission must be in writing and may even be granted subject to conditions and subject to the CAA's discretion as arises under Article 253.[668]

The powers the Regulator has as regards 'permissions' under Article 253 are extensive. Permission can be provisionally suspended pending what appears to be an open-ended form of inquiry[669] and the Regulator can subsequently revoke or amend the permission 'on sufficient ground being shown to its satisfaction'[670] and the holder of the document containing the written permission must henceforth forfeit it within a reasonable time.[671] Further, the breach of a 'condition' within any given permission – in the absence of any contrary provision – renders the written permission invalid.[672] Unlike provisions made for foreign registered aircraft under Articles 250 and 252, there is, apparently, no freestanding statutory avenue for the making of representations in the case of the revocation or amendment of a large rocket permission under the 2016 Order or, for that matter, the Space Industry Regulations.[673] Appeals against decisions of the CAA in connection with licences and a number of other matters appear to be dealt with separately under the Civil Aviation Authority Regulations 1991,[674] specifically Regulation 6. Under Regulation 6(3)(a) it is stated that decisions relating to the refusal (or variation of) 'a certificate, licence, approval, (or) authorisation' can be the subject of a request for review by the applicant within 14 days. It is unclear whether or not this would strictly include 'permissions' for large rockets since the functions listed under Regulation 6 (1) – that is, the functions that can be the subject of a 'request to review' do not include this explicitly – the closest analogous function could be said to be paragraph (h), on 'validation of any certificate or licence'. On the basis of

667 See Chapter 3.1–3.2.
668 Article 269 (a)–(c).
669 Article 253(1).
670 *Ibid*, para 2.
671 *Ibid*, para 3.
672 *Ibid*, para 4.
673 See Article 255 (4) of the Air Navigation Order 2016 for provisions relating to foreign aircraft.
674 SI 1991 No. 1672.

open-textured interpretation or by taking a 'purposive' approach, a decision relating to a granted large rocket permission could be said to come within paragraph (h) as being a 'certificate' or, perhaps, a 'licence' on the basis of common law definitions. Paragraph 2 of Regulation 6 also refers to decisions to 'grant', 'vary' or 'revoke' an authorisation. It is also interesting to note the wording on the CAA website as regards appeals, which states that:

> where a CAA official has advised you of a refusal to issue or a proposal to vary, suspend or revoke ... any other type of licence, certificate, authorisation or approval issued by the CAA ... You are entitled to have the decision or proposal reviewed.[675]

As outlined, paragraph (h) is not as broad as the information on the website, not including 'authorisation' or 'approval', although it should be pointed out that 'approval or authorization of persons' appears under paragraph (i). Whether this extends to 'legal persons' in the context of granting permissions is not clear but could be assumed.

Whilst this could simply be the result of an overly technical or semantic analysis of the rules, it does seem that some clarification is in order for these rockets, particularly due to the fact that vertical launches from SaxaVord look likely to be commonplace owing to its geographical location – ideal for sought after polar-synchronous orbits – and the apparent political and commercial will surrounding the venture. Moreover, the fact that such 'permissions' fall outside of the requirement for an Oversight and Monitoring Plan may not be germane to legitimate questions of safety. The large rocket in question under the permission granted to HyImpulse Technologies GmbH[676] is stated to be a 'large suborbital sounding rocket'[677] which is expected to use paraffin and liquid oxygen as a propellant.[678] Given the extensive considerations relative to other aspects of the launch such as airspace closure[679] it seems illogical not to

675 The United Kingdom Civil Aviation Authority, 'Appeal a decision the CAA has made affecting your organisation' <https://www.caa.co.uk/our-work/make-a-report-or-complaint/challenge-a-caa-decision/appeal-a-decision-the-caa-has-made-affecting-your-organisation/> accessed 15 October 2024.

676 HIT/ANO/SR75ROCKET, see N672.

677 *Ibid*, 2.

678 HyImpulse Rocket Flight from SaxaVord Spaceport (Shetland) ACP-2021-058 Assessment Meeting, 30.09.2022.

679 The United Kingdom Civil Aviation Authority, Hylmpulse Sounding Rocket Launch from SaxaVord Spaceport – Shetland, Airspace Change Proposal documentation, <https://airspacechange.caa.co.uk/PublicProposalArea?pID=402> accessed 15 October 2024.

subject the launch to other relevant monitoring protocols on the basis of what appears to be a technical classification. It must be made clear that such rocket permissions granted under the Air Navigation Order 2016 are conditional on a safety case being provided showing that 'risks to public safety and property are as low as reasonably practicable' and that adequate insurance arrangements 'in respect of those risks for each proposed launch' are in place.[680] Furthermore, the 'level of risk to public safety and to property' must be acceptable to the CAA.[681] As previously stated, the fact that a rocket could fall into a much less stringent category of regulation based on a slight difference in its projected ceiling could be problematic, and consideration ought to be given to an intermediate category of regulation.

By contrast, the operation and associated ventures regarding Virgin Orbit were the subject of Oversight and Monitoring Plans given their inclusion within the Space Industry Act regime. There are various requirements under the plan – or 'OMP' as it is referred to – which are termed 'Notifications'. These Notifications must be submitted to the Regulator or consequences may ensue for the operator under the Regulations. The particular notifications required under the OMP in respect of the Spaceport Licence included a request for a copy of the revised safety case, a copy of the cyber security strategy post annual review and a copy of the emergency response test plan.[682] There were also some general 'health warnings' provided to the operator reminding it of its responsibilities elsewhere in the Regulations, in particular the requirement to keep the Regulator informed of any material changes on pain of criminal conviction and expectations regarding occurrence reporting as detailed. Pertinently, there was a stipulation that information must be provided on a yearly basis regarding the progress made on the operator's move towards carbon neutrality,[683] a matter notably absent from the 'permission' granted in respect of the Hylmpulse Large Rocket under the 2016 Air Navigation Order and regrettable as per the importance of matters of sustainability both in a legislative and real-world context. This apparent loophole becomes even more acute when the notification requirements stipulated within the Oversight and Monitoring Plan for the Launch Licence – arguably a more analogous instrument – are more extensive as regards the environment. Paragraph 4.6 of the OMP stipulates that:

---

680 N302, Article 96 (9)(a) (I–II).

681 *Ibid*, Article 96(9)(b).

682 The United Kingdom Civil Aviation Authority, Oversight and Monitoring Plan v.1.0 for Cornwall Airport Limited, 2, <https://www.caa.co.uk/publication/download/20109> accessed 15 October 2024.

683 *Ibid*, 3.

> The Licencee must provide the following information, by way of annual report to the Regulator, no later than 31 January (or other date agreed in writing by the Regulator) each year the Licence is in force … calculation of greenhouse gas emissions, including the greenhouse gas emissions for all in-scope launch activities for the preceding calendar year, and the reduction in tonnes of greenhouse gas emissions arising from the purchase of the credits by the Licencee.[684]

This is supplemented by evidential requirements regarding the purchasing of carbon offset credits.[685]

The environmental regime as regards the launching of small/large rockets is not *prima facie* evident. That Parliament wished to purposefully exclude such matters from a requirement to submit an Assessment of Environmental Effects does not sit well with the volume of environmental regulation in other industrial contexts. The 2021 Air Navigation Amendment Order did not insert any environmental requirements into the regulations regarding large rockets in spite of providing that a safety case was required along with a demonstration of adequate insurance provisions. There were also calls to change the current definition of 'large rocket' within the 2016 Air Navigation Order from Higher Education establishments in the 2024 Regulatory Review, to which the government responded by stating that it would give the public safety impacts its due consideration.[686]

It is also interesting to note that the ongoing holding of a current flight permit from the Federal Aviation Authority was a notification requirement under the Launch OMP in addition to an Office of Commercial Space Transportation licence from the same.[687] This is a positive step in the interest of avoiding duplication and excessive administrative burdens.

In assisting the United Kingdom in its international obligations under the Registration Convention,[688] the OMP also required that, within 10 days of a launch, a 'post launch information form' must be submitted to the Regulator which contains 'final orbital parameters of all space objects' so that the Regulator can:

684 The United Kingdom Civil Aviation Authority, Oversight and Monitoring Plan v.1.0 for Virgin Orbit LLC in relation to its Spaceflight Operator Licence, 4, <https://www.caa.co.uk/publication/download/20113> accessed 15 October 2024.

685 *Ibid*, 5.

686 N405, 35.

687 *Ibid*, 3.

688 N126.

> register details of the launch as required under section 61 of the Act; and register any objects arising from the Launch which achieve orbit on either the UK Registry of Outer Space Objects and with the United Nations Office for Outer Space Affairs (UNOOSA), or on the UK Supplementary Registry of Outer Space Objects.[689]

The monitoring and enforcement mechanisms under the new space legislation are comprehensive and largely praiseworthy. They appear to cater well to the intended ambitions of ensuring public safety whilst also affording operators the opportunity of appealing any decisions deemed adverse to their interests. As repeatedly mentioned, the fact that many rocket-based activities will fall outside of the monitoring and enforcement regime may well prove to be a considerable oversight, and a proportionate intermediate category of regulation should be considered in the interests of sustainability, public safety and parity.

---

689 N690, 3–4.

CHAPTER 6

Other Relevant Standards

As has been adhered to at various stages throughout this work, the influence of other standards/rules existing elsewhere than in the domestic legislative framework will have some bearing on the operation of space sites and activities within the United Kingdom. At its most extreme level, such standards and rules are likely to permeate the common law by becoming an accepted trade custom, commercial practice or standard of reasonable behaviour across the space industry. Various sources of such rules and standards will be discussed in this chapter, but it is firstly important to examine the extent to which such rules and standards could be said to have legal force. Regarding the common law in relation to contractual matters, Parke B stated in the case of *Hutton v Warren, Clark*:[690]

> It has long been settled, that, in commercial transactions, extrinsic evidence of custom and usage is admissible to annex incidents to written contracts, in matters with respect to which they are silent.[691]

As will be seen, the influence of external rules and standards within the space industry is likely to form a considerable body of evidence as regards expectations between contracting parties and licencees at various levels. It is likely that external rules and standards will be equally – if not more – influential in laws of tort and delict. This is with particular reference to the case of *Bolam v Friern Hospital Management Committee*[692] and the eponymous 'Bolam' test. The test essentially means that it will be a defence in a claim for negligence for a professional individual to prove that they were acting in accordance with a reasonable body of professional opinion.[693] The fact that the United Kingdom space industry is in its infancy means that reasonably prudent operators and applicants should be seeking to ensure that they are carrying out their activities in line with such a 'reasonable body of professional opinion' or, at the very least, an established and reputable procedure used to good effect elsewhere in the world. This could come in the forms of written legislation, codes of

690 150 E.R. 517 (Ex).
691 *Ibid.* 521 (Parke B).
692 [1957] 1 WLR 582 (EWHC).
693 *Ibid*, 586, (McNair J).

 | DOI:10.1163/9789004732551_007

practice or international standards. Such sources of guidance should be used with the aim of replicating safe practice rather than a decision based on cost-effectiveness alone.

Starting with the published guidance documents, it was outlined in the Guidance for Launch Operator and Return Operator Licence Applicants And Licencees'[694] that some of the standards employed by the United States in respect of human occupant safety could be 'of use' to UK operators, namely the FAA-AST Recommended Practices for Human Space Flight Occupant Safety, NASA Space Flight Human System Standards NASA Standard 3001 and the NASA Human Integration Design Handbook.[695] Whilst following this guidance is clearly not mandatory, it is evident that operators will likely adopt procedures such as these on a voluntary basis. For example, Virgin Orbit recently stated that in respect of handling its payloads at the space site prior to launch, that it would 'follow a tailored version of US Air Force Space Command Manual 91–710'.[696] The manual contains a significant amount of detail regarding the movement of materials around space sites and would appear to be especially useful given that the United Kingdom is, at this stage, unlikely to have legislated for such matters given the relative lack of experience. The operator is also to be praised for being proactive in seeking out such rules by way of guidance in circumstances where no such rules exist domestically. Such latitude should not give way to a 'cherry picking' exercise as regards rules and standards – particularly when it comes to important matters of safety. As regards the adoption of standards from overseas jurisdictions it would be desirable if such standards could be drawn from an 'approved' list provided by the CAA to avoid either of these possibilities.

There will also be the requirement to observe regulations relevant to a range of other matters outside the terrestrial environment and those regarding air quality. Where operations extend over the sea or otherwise involve the marine environment, associated rules will require observance. Within the United Kingdom this will include the Marine Works (Environmental Impact Assessment) Regulations 2007[697] and, in an international forum, the Conven tion for the Protection of the Marine Environment of the North East Atlantic.[698] As demonstrated by the Virgin Orbit experience, regulatory requirements

694 N368, 77.

695 *Ibid.*

696 N627, para 3.1.23.

697 SI 2007 No. 1518.

698 The Convention for the Protection of the Marine Environment of the North-East Atlantic (COSPAR) 22 September 1992.

of other jurisdictions will need to be observed as a matter of course where a space activity takes place over various territories. According to the Assessment of Environmental Effects submitted by Virgin Orbit, relevant rules from other jurisdictions included the Irish Wildlife Act and the Portuguese Decree-Law No. 140/99 on biodiversity protection[699] owing to the intended flightpath. Moreover, as per the situation regarding their launch licence generally, the Federal Aviation Administration may have been required to launch its own consultations based on Virgin Orbit's activities as the body responsible for granting the licence. This type of duplication may be the sort of problem that future inter-state agreements can address.

On a related note, under the Space Industry Regulations 2021, Regulation 101 requires that

> If necessary to ensure that an Operator's spaceflight activities are carried out safely or to secure compliance with the international obligations of the United Kingdom, the spaceflight Operator must after a launch vehicle has reached a stable orbit … take reasonable steps to … avoid the launch vehicle interfering with the space activities of other persons in the peaceful exploration and use of outer space.

According to the website of the CAA, the Department for Transport has made the decision that a Launch Collision Analysis will need to be carried out owing to increased orbital debris and to ensure that there is no collision or interference with space activities of other persons as per Regulation 101. Operators will therefore have to 'enter a sharing agreement with US Space Command' to facilitate such analyses.[700] As a result of this, the CAA will refer to US law from Title 14 of the US Code of Federal Regulations 'Notice of Proposed Rule Making' in addition to adopting the approach of US Space Command regarding separation distances when assessing risks. Moreover, to satisfy Regulation 101, a licencee or applicant will have to demonstrate that they have arrangements in place with US Space Command who will carry out Launch Collision Analyses for them.

699 N627, para 5.4.29.

700 The United Kingdom Civil Aviation Authority, 'Launch Collision Avoidance Analysis', <https://www.caa.co.uk/space/resources/launch-collision-avoidance-analysis-lcola/> accessed 15 October 2024.

Regarding orbital operator licences there appeared to be additional requirements laid down in the first edition of the guidance document[701] in respect of international standards which must be followed as part of the licence conditions under section 5. It is stated under section 5.2 that 'Applicants should use the list of Best Practice Standards in Annex A of this document to aid in the compilation of applicable standards to their activities'. This consists of 9 pages of standards ranging from those of the European Cooperation for Space Standardization on Spacecraft[702] and the International Organization for Standardization.[703] It should be noted that the 2nd edition of the guidance published on May 31 2024[704] does not refer to any such documents. Instead, it states that orbital operator licence applicants should 'set out where (their) operation meets international standards and guidelines on spacecraft and launch vehicle design, qualification, operation and disposal, testing and ground segment and mission operations.'[705] It is questionable whether this new absence of any specific standards is to be welcomed. On the one hand, it would be fair to assume that operators, if not the manufacturers themselves, would have knowledge of such standards. Further, it can also be assumed that such individuals are likely to understand which set of guidance supports their unique operational requirements. On the other hand, this could lead to more diffuse practices and fragmentation of approach. Regardless of whether they are contained in any of the Civil Aviation Authorities guidance documents their legal effect is likely to be the same. It has been written in the context of the United Nations Convention on the Law of the Sea that ISO standards can be reviewed by the UNCLOS tribunal under Part XV[706] with the example of the Chagos Arbitration[707] given

701 The United Kingdom Civil Aviation Authority, Guidance for Orbital Operator Applicants and Licencees, 1st Edition, <https://assets.publishing.service.gov.uk/media/5f203132d3bf7f1b0e2440d3/guidance-for-orbital-operator-licence-applicants-and-licensees.pdf> accessed 15 October 2024.

702 For example, ECSS Q70C Rev.1 on Materials, Mechanical Parts and Processes, and ECSS-E-ST-20C on Electrical and Optical Engineering – Electrical and Electronic.

703 For example, ISO 14302:2002 on Space systems – Electromagnetic compatibility requirements and ISO 14303:2002 on Space systems – Launch-vehicle-to-spacecraft interfaces.

704 The UK Civil Aviation Authority, 'Guidance for Orbital Operator Licence Applicants and Licencees', 2nd edition, 31 May 2024, <https://www.caa.co.uk/publication/download/18909> accessed 15 October 2024.

705 *Ibid*, 20.

706 Makoto Seta, The contribution of the International Organization for Standardization to ocean governance, July 2019, Review of European, Comparative, and International Environmental Law.

707 *The Chagos Marine Protected Area Arbitration* (Mauritius v United Kingdom) (Award) (18 March 2015) (PCA Case No 2011-03) ICGJ 486, para 316.

that UNCLOS tribunals could indeed decide disputes relating to 'the contravention of specified international rules and standards'. It appears, then, that such standards are potentially justiciable internationally to some extent and possibly *de facto* legally binding on operators for specific licences under the Regulations.

Although not strictly speaking a 'standard', it is important to note that, whilst not specified in the legislative provisions, the interpretation of licences issued under the Space Industry Act look to be subject to the Interpretation Act 1978[708] as indicated by paragraph 2.3 of the Spaceflight Operator Licence granted to Virgin Orbit[709] which states that the Act applies to the licence as it does to an Act of Parliament. This looks to be a sensible move as the Interpretation Act clarifies the position on a number of widely encountered and prescribed matters such as 'time of day',[710] 'distance'[711] and questions on postal matters.[712] Reference to the Act appears in the Spaceport Licence for Spaceport Cornwall too[713] although, curiously, not within the permission granted to SaxaVord for the launch of a large suborbital sounding rocket.[714] Whether this owes to the fact that 'large rockets' and other launching activities are handled under the Air Navigation Order 2016 is unclear and calls into question why the Act would be explicitly stressed to cover some licences and not others. Regardless of this disparity a legitimate argument could certainly be raised in respect of it applying to all licences by implication in the absence of any valid objection.

Very worthy of note is the significant influence of the space law of other jurisdictions in respect of ventures requiring licence(s) from that jurisdiction in addition to the same in the United Kingdom under the Space Industry Act. As has been mentioned, the Virgin Orbit launch from Spaceport Cornwall was licenced under both the Space Industry Act and by the FAA due to being

708 C.30.

709 The United Kingdom Civil Aviation Authority, Space Industry Act, Spaceflight Operator Licence for the Launch of the Carrier Aircraft Cosmic Girl and Launch of the Launch Vehicle Type LauncherOne, 20 December 2022, Licence ref: SR-APP-001002, 3, <https://www.caa.co.uk/publication/download/20111> accessed 15 October 2024.

710 S9.

711 S8.

712 S7.

713 The UK Civil Aviation Authority, Spaceport Licence: Cornwall Airport Limited, ORS10 2022–001, para 2.3 <https://www.caa.co.uk/our-work/publications/documents/content/ors10-2022-001/> accessed 23 November 2023.

714 N518. This may be due to the permission deriving from an 'Order' as opposed to an Act of Parliament or Regulation but it is a curious omission, nonetheless.

registered in the United States.[715] Under the terms of the licence granted to Virgin Orbit, paragraph 6.3 stated – as one of its 'General Conditions', that:

> The Licencee must inform the Regulator in writing as soon as reasonably practicable if the Federal Aviation Administration suspends, varies or revokes any of the authorisations it has issued in relation to the Licenced Activities and referred to in condition 3.1.6.

Therefore, an infringement of any of the terms of the FAA issued licence with respect to US space law could result in consequences to the operator in terms of their UK licence. Although this will not be of consequence to all operators/applicants it could affect a significant number of them, particularly as seeing as launches and space activities involving US technology have been specifically legislated for, presumably as a result of forecasts suggesting that this may be a common occurrence. As discussed earlier, further obligations for licencees could arise from the terms of the UK-USA Technology Safeguards Agreement[716] should this be the case.

In order to make the licensing process more efficient, it would be prudent to suggest that the Regulator seek to establish, via the relevant Secretary of State or Government Department, a joint-licensing regime between the United States and United Kingdom to avoid unnecessary duplication as well as cost. On another note, it may be that, should a significant number of launches or space activities be conducted by 'dual registered' licencees, any practice undertaken or standards adopted by those operators so as to satisfy the requirements of an FAA licence could potentially be adopted by other operators as models of best practice.

---

715 Code of Federal Regulations (US) § Title 14 413.3(c)(1).

716 N92, see Chapter 4.4 for an outline of how this agreement impacted upon the investigation of the failed Virgin Orbit launch.

CHAPTER 7

Commercial Spaceflight and Its Human Dimensions

A distinctive mark of the Space Industry Regulations 2021 and the 2018 Act is that they legislate specifically – and broadly – on the matter of human spaceflight. An extremely novel and unchartered area, the legal implications are far-reaching.

Individuals involved in such human spaceflight range from the 'pilot in command', 'flight crew' and 'remote pilot'[717] through to 'spaceflight participants'.[718] Under Part 7 there are requirements for training, qualification and medical fitness in respect of such 'spaceflight participants' and Part 9 makes provision to mitigate cosmic radiation exposure. Part 12 is dedicated to 'informed consent' provisions in respect of spaceflight participants.

Regarding personnel involved with the spaceflight processes more generally, Regulation 56 gives life to section 18(4)(b) of the Space Industry Act 2018 in defining the following 'specified roles': the launch director,[719] the flight termination personnel,[720] the flight crew and remote pilots,[721] the suborbital aircraft engineer,[722] the range operations manager[723] and the range safety manager.[724] Associated competence criteria for these specified roles can be found within Part 1 of Schedule 3 with certain expectations for flight personnel including the licences which must be held by those who would be in direct control of spacecraft. Pilots of suborbital craft are required to hold a commercial pilot's licence with instrument rating or an equivalent ICAO compliant licence and also be qualified in respect of turbo-jet aircraft. There is also provision made for where the launch vehicle is a balloon[725] where it is stipulated that the pilot must hold a balloon-specific licence granted by the CAA or an equivalent ICAO

717 Space Industry Act 2018, s4.
718 *Ibid.*
719 (a).
720 (b).
721 (c).
722 (d).
723 (e).
724 (f).
725 Ss3.

 | DOI:10.1163/9789004732551_008

licence. 'Rockoons' have themselves been used at least as far back as 1955[726] for small-scale scientific launches and could be used in modern times for launching microsatellites.[727] This could also be advantageous in respect of mitigating any adverse environmental impacts.[728] There is no treatment of 'Rockoons' in the governing EU legislation[729] but there are rules relating to the launch of high-altitude balloons generally including the notice periods required for launch of 'medium-heavy' balloons.[730]

Schedule 3[731] requires that 'An MFC (Member of Flight Crew) must be able to demonstrate the MFC's ability to withstand the mental and physical stresses of spaceflight including disorientation, illusory effects, rapid acceleration, microgravity, noise and vibration, in sufficient condition to be able to operate the launch vehicle throughout all phases of flight safely and competently'.

It is further stated that '(2) Whether the MFC satisfies the criteria in sub-paragraph (1) must be tested in a centrifuge device or an aircraft, or in a combination of the two, that is able to replicate the effects on the human body of the forces of acceleration, the rate of change of those forces and their duration, in conditions equivalent to the periods of the flight when those forces are most acute'[732] and that '[a]n MFC must have previous experience as a member of the flight crew or as a remote pilot in a launch vehicle or aircraft that exposed the MFC—(a) to a workload which is equivalent to that expected of an MFC or a remote pilot undertaking the spaceflight activities, and (b) to effects on the body of rapid onset and diminution of acceleration at least equivalent to those which would be experienced during a typical flight of the spaceflight Operator's launch vehicle.'[733]

726 Eugene M. Emme, *Aeronautics and Astronautics Chronology, 1955–1957*, online at <https://history.nasa.gov/Timeline/1955-57.html> accessed 7 October 2021.

727 Michael Hepfler, Tom Coyne, 'Successful 'rockoon' launch makes space more accessible to microsatellites', Purdue University School of Industrial Engineering, <https://engineering.purdue.edu/IE/news/2019/hepfer-leo-rocket-launch.> accessed 15 October 2024.

728 Marti Sarigul-Klijn, Nesrin Sarigul-Klijn, *'Flight Mechanics of Manned Sub-Orbital Reusable Launch Vehicles with Recommendations for Launch and Recovery'* (Spacefuture.com, January 2003) <http://www.spacefuture.com/archive/flight_mechanics_of_manned_sub-orbital_reusable_launch_vehicles_with_recommendations_for_launch_and_recovery.shtml> accessed 7 October 2021.

729 Regulation (EU) No 923/2012 of 26 September 2012 retained under the European Union (Withdrawal) Act 2018.

730 See rule 1.1 and rule 5.1.1.

731 s17.

732 s18.

733 s20.

Regulation 58 provides that individuals in the specified roles outlined must be both medically fit and competent to discharge the duties their role requires of them. Underscoring the commitment to a high level of training Chapter 2 of the Regulations solely provides for the 'training manager' who is appointed under Regulation 61 which also delineates the scope of this role and the expectations. This is supported by Chapters 3 and 4 which concern the 'Training Manual' and 'Training Program'. Under Regulation 70, regular 'Competence Assessments' must be undertaken by the training manager.

Medical fitness is catered for under Chapter 5 in Part 7. Regulation 72 holds that valid medical certificates are required of flight crew and other roles and that they must have been issued by an 'approved aeromedical examiner'.[734] Furthermore, the level of fitness of the crew at the time of the flight must reflect that in the certificate and that no crew should have '... suffered a decrease in fitness due to illness or injury since the date of issue of their medical certificate which might affect their ability to—(i) withstand the physical and mental rigours of spaceflight; (ii) perform safety-critical functions reliably during the spaceflight activities; (iii) carry out any emergency procedures which may be required during the spaceflight activities, including the evacuation of the launch vehicle'. Moreover: 'no person takes part in spaceflight activities, either as a crew member or a spaceflight participant, if that person is not medically fit to fly'.

Regulation 75 allows for spaceflight participants with a disability or reduced mobility to fly if certified fit under Regulation 73(1) and if they would not present a danger to the flight itself.

The 1980 Limitation Act lays down a limitation period for personal injury claim of 3 years from the date that the individual knew a claim could be made. A 2-year retention period for documents that may be relevant for evidential purposes in the event of such a claim does not appear to take account of this.

Part 8, the longest part of the regulations, provides for 'safety' in respect of spaceflight activities. Under Chapter 2 there is a duty placed on spaceflight operators to ensure that 'spaceflight activities are carried out safely'. This is defined under Regulation 79(2) as conducting such activities 'in accordance with the current safety case by ... (i) preventing a major accident from occurring, and (ii) mitigating the consequences of such an accident if it does occur and ... (b) by securing the safety of a human occupant'.

Chapter 3 stipulates regular reviews of the safety case are required to ensure that it is up to date in line with the parameters and scope of the proposed

734 R73(1).

activities.[735] Further, under Regulation 83, the operator is required to comply with Regulations 84–104 as regards managing the risk of such activities including enhanced expectations in respect of space flight with human occupants.[736] Regulation 84 requires that the operator's resources can cover the actual proposed activities whilst Chapter 4 lays down the requirements of specific roles concerned with safety[737] such as the accountable manager,[738] the launch director[739] and in certain cases, flight termination personnel.[740] Section 5 covers aspects of the launch itself including both the preparation and the launch vehicle itself[741] along with meteorological considerations[742] and dangerous.[743] The vehicle and equipment used must not be used unless they 'do not conform with (certain) technical requirements'.[744]

Under Regulation 99 there are 12 conditions which must be fulfilled for spaceflight to occur. These include requirements that the vehicle,[745] spaceport[746] along with the designated range[747] are fit for purpose. Furthermore, there is the requirement that the 'relevant emergency services have confirmed that they are on stand-by'[748] and there must have been a rehearsal.[749] Under Regulations 100 and 101 there is a duty to monitor the flight and terminate if required.

Regulation 101(1)(c)(i) requires that the operator ensures that the spaceflight is carried out 'in compliance with the international obligations of the United Kingdom' and, that 'the spaceflight operator must after a launch vehicle has reached a stable orbit … take reasonable steps to … avoid the launch vehicle interfering with the space activities of other persons in the peaceful exploration and use of outer space'. There is also the obligation under section 101(1)(c)(iii) to '… prevent contamination of outer space arising from the launch vehicle in orbit or adverse changes in the environment of the earth from that vehicle

735 R80(2).
736 R83(2).
737 R86.
738 R87.
739 R88.
740 R89.
741 R91/93.
742 R97.
743 R98.
744 See R93(2)(b)(1).
745 R99(2)(a).
746 R99(2)(b).
747 R99(2)(c).
748 R99(2)(e).
749 R99(2)(d).

in orbit' and provisions for the disposal of launch vehicles are laid down under s101(3) in a proportionate manner.

Under Section 7, information relating to the space activity must be considered and retained. Under Regulation 102 certain personal details of the human occupants along with the payload of a given space flight must be retained for a period of 3 years – as noted, the same period of time that a personal injury claim can be brought within.[750] Other data includes the correspondence the Regulator engages in with the spaceflight operator 'before launch and during the operator's spaceflight activities'.[751]

Regulation 103(4) states once again that the 3 year retention period applies here too, excluding the information recorded on the flight recorder where the 'launch vehicle has not been involved in a spaceflight accident arising from or in the course of the operator's spaceflight activities'and, further, '[w]here no spaceflight accident arose from or in the course of the operator's spaceflight activities, information recorded by the launch vehicle's flight recorder must only be retained until the completion of those activities.' These provisions seem mandatory by the use of the term 'must'- this is unusual as such recordings could presumably exonerate an operator in the event of a claim being brought for personal injury. Perhaps this provision is related to issues of data protection but, even so, this is a curious use of phrase in this context and further exploration is advised. Relatedly, the term 'Accident' under section 20(3) of the Space Industry Act 2018 includes 'any fortuitous or unexpected event by which the safety of any spacecraft or person is threatened'. Moreover, under the Spaceflight Activities (Investigation of Spaceflight Accidents) Regulations 2021[752] the footnote to Regulation 2 states that 'The definition of 'accident' in section 20(3) (investigation of accidents) of the 2018 Act is wide and includes unexpected events which threaten the safety of any spacecraft or person, whether or not any person is injured or the spacecraft is damaged.' The grey area here could be problematic.

A comprehensive emergency response plan is required under Regulation 104 along with the stipulation that such a plan must be tested every 3 years,[753] the results – and any consequential revisions – of such testing being communicated to the Regulator.[754]

750 N419, s11(4)(b).
751 R103 (2)(b).
752 N535.
753 R104(3).
754 R104(4).

'Additional Safety requirements for launch vehicles with human occupants' are given under Chapter 5. Under Regulation 105: '(2) A pilot in command, pilot or a remote pilot carries out the flight safely by carrying it out—(a) in accordance with the current safety case by—(i) preventing a major accident from occurring, or (ii) mitigating the consequences of such an accident if it does occur, and (b) in accordance with the current risk assessment, by securing the safety of a human occupant.'. The spaceflight operator further must ensure that the crew are aware of their responsibilities for spaceflight activities and have the requisite information to carry out the flight safely.[755]

Where human occupants are involved, there are, predictably, extra conditions laid down under section 3 such as adequate life support systems[756] and associated redundancies in the event of depressurization.[757] There must also be provisions made in respect of ice-build up on the exterior of the craft,[758] facilities for smoke detection[759] along with 'a system capable of restraining any member of the crew or any spaceflight participant in their seat when necessary to ensure that the flight is carried out safely'.

General aviation law provides that the pilot in command 'must take all necessary measures so as to minimise the consequences on the flight of disruptive passenger behaviour'[760] and section 52(1) of the Space Industry Act states that sections 94 and 95 of the Civil Aviation Act 1982[761] could apply to spacecraft by regulation. Section 94(2) of the Civil Aviation Act provides that:

> If the commander of an aircraft in flight, wherever that aircraft may be, has reasonable grounds to believe in respect of any person on board the aircraft—
>
> a. that the person in question has done or is about to do any act on the aircraft while it is in flight which jeopardises or may jeopardise—
>   1. the safety of the aircraft or of persons or property on board the aircraft, or
>   2. good order and discipline on board the aircraft, or
>
> that the person in question has done on the aircraft while in flight any act which in the opinion of the commander is a serious offence under any law in force in the country in which the aircraft is

755 R106.
756 R109(a).
757 R109 (b).
758 R109 (c).
759 R109 (d).
760 N479, Annex v, Article 3(g).
761 N1.

registered, not being a law of a political nature or based on racial or religious discrimination, then, subject to subsection (4) below, the commander may take with respect to that person such reasonable measures, including restraint of his person, as may be necessary—

3. to protect the safety of the aircraft or of persons or property on board the aircraft; or
4. to maintain good order and discipline on board the aircraft …

The application of the Civil Aviation Act to pilots of launch vehicles and spacecraft is not mentioned within the Act. Given that the Space Industry Act does not apply to 'aircraft' other than 'carrier aircraft', the necessary implication is that they do not automatically apply here. It is likewise not clear whether Regulation (EU) 2018/1139 applies. The potential confusion that could arise here as regards pilots' duties could be problematic. Further, the term 'flight' is defined under section 105 of the Civil Aviation Act as '… a journey by air beginning when the aircraft in question takes off and ending when it next lands' which appears to largely exclude spaceflight. The Space Industry Act regulates 'space activities … suborbital activities (and) associated activities'[762] with 'space activity' defined under section 1(4) as 'launching or procuring the launch or the return to earth of a space object or of an aircraft carrying a space object … operating a space object' or 'any activity in outer space'.[763] There is also the pre sent contrast between 'launch vehicles' and 'carrier aircraft' under Regulation 2 of the Space Industry Regulations and 'spaceflight activities'is designated as a discrete sphere of activities to flight.

There must be a safe number of crew selected under Regulation 110 in keeping with the vehicle's capacity and mission profile along with 'any medical needs of a human occupant'.[764] Actual crew numbers are not specified, leaving a variable standard here dependent on other factors at play as set out by the other provisions within Regulation 110.

Regulation 111 requires that the spaceflight operator ensures 'that instruments, systems and equipment within the launch vehicle are readily operable and accessible from the station where … (a) any pilot in command who needs to use them is seated, and (b) another member of the flight crew who needs to use them is seated'. It would be assumed that user interfaces associated with spacecraft would be within the preserve of the manufacturer who, in turn, may draw on guidance from other sources when making such design choices.

762 S1(1)(a)–(c).
763 (a)–(c).
764 R110 (g).

Paragraph 7.12 of the Guidance for Launch Operator and Return Operator Licence Applicants and Licencees[765] provides links to a number of documents in respect of medical criteria and other standards for human occupants. The most useful source presented in the guidance for such matters is likely to be the NASA Human Integration Design Handbook[766] which gives comprehensive details on how the design of spacecraft used by NASA has accommodated human occupants whilst also providing a rationale. It is also interesting to note that Annex V, Article 2 (c)(iii) of Regulation (EU) 2018/1139[767] requires that 'instruments and equipment as specified in point 5 required for the execution of that flight are installed in the aircraft and are operative, unless waived by the applicable MEL (Minimum Equipment List) or equivalent document'. The equivalent document in this case may be the aforementioned NASA standards or other analogous rules.

Emergency equipment and an emergency evacuation procedure are deemed the responsibility of the spaceflight operator under Regulation 112. The procedure itself and the location of any emergency equipment must also be made known to the crew and any human occupants by the spaceflight operator:[768] 'immediately before the flight, each human occupant is provided with information about how to use the emergency equipment and means of emergency evacuation and that such information is available on board the launch vehicle'.[769]

The 'specific obligations of pilot in command, flight crew or remote pilot' are detailed under section 4. Under Regulation 114 the pilot in command or remote pilot is required to '(a) perform an inspection of the launch vehicle and its systems and equipment to the extent that it is practicable to do so, and (b) consult any of the spaceflight operator's written records relating to the fitness, condition and preparation of the launch vehicle, in so far as necessary to ensure the flight is carried out safely'. Similarly, Regulation 115 provides for the pilot to 'carry out flight safely'. Regulation 115(1) stipulates that the pilot/remote pilot 'must give commands, make appropriate decisions and take appropriate actions during the flight of that vehicle which are necessary to ensure that the flight is carried out safely'. Regulation 115(2) obligates the pilot in command to report that any orders

765 N257.

766 National Aeronautics and Space Administration, *Human Integration Design Handbook* (NASA/SP-2010-3407/REV1), June 5 2014, <https://www.nasa.gov/wp-content/uploads/2015/03/human_integration_design_handbook_revision_1.pdf?emrc=f08f8a> accessed 17 September 2024.

767 N479.

768 R112 (2)(a).

769 R112 (2)(b).

inconsistent with the regulations or the Space Industry Act 2018 to the Regulator and spaceflight operator.

One important question here is whether pilots of spacecraft, as potentially opposed to carrier aircraft, will also be bound to follow the EU Regulation on rules relating to civil aviation[770] which apply to aircraft. Duties under this Regulation are much more extensive than those contained in the Space Industry Regulations – explicit instruction here would be welcome.

Obligations of other individuals, namely spaceflight participants, the launch director, safety manager and crew are covered under Regulations 117, 118 and 119 '... during periods of flight when the effects on the human body of the forces due to acceleration and their duration are most acute'.[771] Spaceflight participants are obligated under Section 5 to remain at their station at material times during the flight on pain of criminal conviction under Chapter 6. Under Regulation 132 the offence of failure of a spaceflight participant to remain at their station could be a fine and/or two years imprisonment on indictment.

Annex V of Regulation (EU) 2018/1139[772] regarding common rules in civil aviation is more expansive than the Space Industry Regulations regarding the responsibilities of commercial pilots. One contrast lies in section 2(g) regarding fuel – 'the amount of fuel/energy for propulsion and consumables on board must be sufficient to ensure that the intended flight can be completed safely, taking into account the meteorological conditions, any element affecting the performance of the aircraft and any delays that are expected in flight. In addition, a fuel/energy reserve must be carried to provide for contingencies. Procedures for in-flight fuel/energy management must be established when relevant.' The Space Industry Regulations are silent on this matter but Schedule 1 of the Space Industry Act states that 'requirements regarding the assembling, integration and fuelling of spacecraft or carrier aircraft, mating of spacecraft or carrier aircraft to their payloads and fuelling of payloads' may be part of a licence condition.[773]

Part 12 on 'Informed Consent' is another aspect of the Space Industry Regulations that impacts 'human occupants' under Regulation 2(1) meaning crew members or spaceflight participants.

Regulation 206 (1)–(2) appears to suggest that both 'space tourists' and crew need to give informed consent before embarking on spaceflight activities. This raises interesting questions from an employment law perspective – requiring

770 N479.
771 R117(b), 118(b) and 119(b).
772 N479.
773 Schedule 1(1)(b).

employees to give informed consent in the course of their employment is not apparently a common practice. This Regulation appears to be a direct legal transplant from the United States regime, in particular, the US Commercial Space Launch Act.[774] The practice of using legal transplants in this area could be problematic as per the amount of information to be given to spaceflight participants generally owing to differences between the two legal cultures.[775] Such an approach should be used cautiously. In the case law, *Cassley v. GMP Securities Europe Ltd*[776] appears to be the only reported authority. In this case a waiver that was issued in the course of employment was commented upon by the High Court as being potentially invalid under the Unfair Contract Terms Act 1977 as 'an attempt to exclude liability for death or personal injury'.[777] This would also seem to apply to independent contractors. This aspect of the Regulations will be commented upon in more detail when the informed consent provisions themselves are considered.

Regulation 205 states that a person must be at least 18 years of age[778] to give valid consent and also have capacity as per the definition given in the Mental Capacity Act 2005 or the equivalent in Scotland or Northern Ireland.[779] Interestingly, the definition of 'adult' under the Adults with Incapacity (Scotland) Act 2000[780] is someone of 16 years of age[781] and, likewise[782] with the Mental Capacity Act (Northern Ireland) 2016.[783] Otherwise, the definitions of capacity are similar across all three instruments on the matter. Whether this is likely to prevent any practical difficulties will remain to be seen in years to come, but it is possible that there could be a discrepancy arising between two of the United Kingdom jurisdictions on this point.

There is an attempt to stave off the impact of cosmic radiation on the crew of both launch vehicles and carrier aircraft under Part 9. Prior to the 2021 Regulations, specific regulations in this area were made in 2019[784] under Civil Avia-

774 N211.

775 See Alex Simmonds, 'The UK Perspective on Informed Consent in Commercial Space Travel', (2020), 45, Air and Space Law, Issue 4, 367

776 [2015] EWHC 722.

777 *Ibid*, para 292.

778 R205.

779 R205(2).

780 Adults with Incapacity (Scotland) Act 2000, asp 4, (Scot).

781 S6(1).

782 S1(1).

783 C.18.

784 The Air Navigation (Cosmic Radiation: Protection of Air Crew and Space Crew and Consequential Amendments) order 2019 No. 1115.

tion Act 1982.[785] Spaceflight operators are hence not to expose such individuals to any dose of cosmic radiation exceeding '6mSv[786] in a calendar year unless the individual is a classified crew member'. 6mSv per year is a standard contained in European Council Directive 2013/59/EURATOM.'[787] Classified Workers' are explained with reference to Article 40 – 'category A' and 'category B' workers with the former 'liable to receive an effective dose greater than 6 mSv per year …'.[788] Article 52(1)(a) provides that spacecraft crew specifically can be subjected to 'Specially Authorised Exposure' should certain conditions be met.[789] Whether any material considerations are necessary as regards 'tourists' who may not be exposed to such levels – is not apparent. Such details may arise in the context of information given as part of the informed consent process.

Part 10 refers to 'Spaceport Safety' and is drafted in a similar manner to the proceeding parts on safety issues – as before there is a safety duty and a safety case is required under Regulation 152. Part 6 deals with the storage of hazardous materials[790] matters relating to propellants 'etc'[791] and the location of 'static engine test areas' should these be located at the spaceport itself.[792] Regulation 165 requires an emergency response plan and Regulation 166 specifies that 'firefighting personnel, facilities and equipment' are to be provided.[793] Such firefighters are given a significant degree of operational autonomy under Regulation 167 which enables them to take pre-emptive action should they suspect that fire may break out[794] and in such an event do what is 'reasonably necessary' to curtail its effect.[795] Anybody obstructing such actions could be fined or sentenced to two years in prison under Regulation 167(4).

Part 13 on 'Liabilities and Indemnities' is another important aspect of the Regulations. Regulation 218 defines the 'prescribed' individuals under section 34(3)(a) of the Space Industry Act 2018, excluding them entirely from the

---

785 N186.

786 Radioactivity.eu.com, 'MilliSievert; A unit for low doses of radioactivity', <https://radioactivity.eu.com/articles/questions_of_doses/millisievert> accessed 4 October 2021.

787 COUNCIL DIRECTIVE 2013/59/EURATOM of 5 December 2013 laying down basic safety standards for protection against the dangers arising from exposure to ionising radiation, and repealing Directives 89/618/Euratom, 90/641/Euratom, 96/29/Euratom, 97/43/Euratom and 2003/122/Euratom.

788 *Ibid* Article 40(1)(a).

789 Article 52(3).

790 R158.

791 R160.

792 R161.

793 R166(1).

794 R167(1)(a)–(c).

795 *Ibid.*

'no-fault' liability regime which is established under section 34(2) of the Act. Such individuals are essentially those who situate themselves at the Spaceport as a matter of choice rather than those who are injured or damaged by the Space Activities tangentially, that is members of the public as discussed previously. Regulation 219 sets out exceptions to the no-fault basis of liability, effectively where the damage arises through gross negligence/wilful misconduct or non-compliance with the Law.[796] Regulation 220 stipulates that the operator must seek to assign a limit to their liability subject to the approval of the Regulator[797] however, in keeping with the overall intention of the Regulations, the limit will not apply if the operator has been grossly negligent or acted otherwise unlawfully or in non-compliance with the Regulations or Act.[798] Moreover, in such instances, the Secretary of State is not obliged to indemnify the operator.[799]

1 Knowledge Is Empowerment: Informed Consent and the United Kingdom Space Industry Regime

A particularly unique dimension of the new rules is informed consent. It incorporates for 'human occupants' and 'space flight participants'. Nowhere else in UK legislation is this provided for so expansively for 'leisure' activities, leaving arrangements under the Space Industry Act as *sui generis*, particularly in an employment context.[800] Informed consent in this context is the acknowledgment by a spaceflight participant or human occupant of the risks involved in certain space activities. It represents the first legislative measure in the United Kingdom to establish that, should certain measures be satisfied, an individual can effectively consent to their own serious injury or even death. Within the

796 R219(a)–(b).

797 R220(2).

798 R220(3).

799 R221.

800 The Medicines for Human Use (Clinical Trials) Regulations 2004, SI 1031 provides for informed consent in respect of participants in drug trials, and The Veterinary Medicines Regulations 2013 SI 2033 provides for informed consent to be given by an owner of an animal in certain veterinary procedures, and various other instruments make mention of informed consent. There is no corresponding legislation as detailed as the new Space Industry provisions and none which make the giving of informed consent mandatory as a requirement to undertake a profession or engage in a dangerous leisure activity.

criminal law it is well established that consent to grievous bodily harm and death is no consent at all.[801]

Informed Consent was introduced under section 17 of the Space Industry Act 2018 and was later expanded upon under Part 12 of the Space Industry Regulations. The provisions appear capable of applying to personnel employed by the operator for the purpose of flying and operating spacecraft as stated within Regulation 209:

> 210. At least 24 hours, but not more than one month, before a human occupant signs a consent form, the spaceflight operator must give that human occupant—
> a. the details of the current risk assessment for the operator's spaceflight activities in an easily understandable form,
> b. information in writing about the availability of emergency services in the event of an accident or medical emergency, and
> c. where that human occupant is a crew member or a launch vehicle task specialist, the information relating to exposure to cosmic radiation which is referred to in regulation 140(1).

As indicated under 210 (c), additional information is to be given to crew members or launch vehicle task specialists on cosmic radiation exposure but it is not clear whether this is in addition to the other information which is to be furnished to all human occupants. If this information is in addition to – which it strongly seems to be – this is a further distinctive feature of the space industry regime – it is a very rare situation whereby employees are required to give informed consent as regards the dangerous nature of their own occupations, at least insofar as being mandated by statute.

Regarding the need for informed consent, it is important to be cognisant of the risks that spaceflight can entail. The most obvious risks associated with the ignition of large volumes of propellant are not the only risks that must be considered in this context. The FAA undertook a study into the risks and potential dangers, some of the additional risks were listed as:

> … high decibel noise, loss of pressure, high G-forces (sustained acceleration), high or low temperature, high radiation levels, physical impact trauma, exposure to toxic chemicals, and adverse composition of the

801 See *R v Brown* [1994] 1 AC 212 (HoL).

> cabin atmosphere'[802] This was in addition to 'psychological response hazards' which include 'claustrophobia, excitement, agitation, fear, motion sickness, vertigo or loss of bearing or balance, and rapid pulse or increased blood pressure.[803]

In addition to known hazards, as Title 14 of the United States Code of Federal Regulations states, there are also 'hazards unknown'.[804]

As stated, this particular regime of informed consent could be regarded as *sui generis* within English law. Regarding the interpretation of the terms within, it is necessary to look towards the case law and, in particular, the medical context from which most of the jurisprudence arises. The leading decision in this area is *Montgomery v. Lanarkshire Health Board*, wherein the Court effectively consolidated a number of judicial statements by way of setting out the position in medical law:[805]

> The correct position, in relation to the risks of injury involved in treatment, can now be seen to be substantially that adopted in Sidaway by Lord Scarman, and by Lord Woolf MR in Pearce, subject to the refinement made by the High Court of Australia in Rogers v Whitaker, which we have discussed at paras 77–73. An adult person of sound mind is entitled to decide which, if any, of the available forms of treatment to undergo, and her consent must be obtained before treatment interfering with her bodily integrity is undertaken.
>
> The doctor is therefore under a duty to take reasonable care to ensure that the patient is aware of any material risks involved in any recommended treatment ... The test of materiality is whether, in the circumstances of the particular case, a reasonable person in the patient's position would be likely to attach significance to the risk, or the doctor is or should reasonably be aware that the particular patient would be likely to attach significance to it.

802 G. Nield et al., 'Informed Consent in Commercial Space Transportation Safety', Federal Aviation Administration doc IAC-13-D5. 1.4, <https://www.faa.gov/sites/faa.gov/files/space/additional_information/international_affairs/Informed_Consent_paper_IAC_Sept_2013_FAAfinal.pdf> accessed 12 May 2020.

803 *Ibid.*

804 CFR (U.S.) Title 14 Part 460, at 45 (2).

805 *Montgomery v Lanarkshire Health Board* [2015] A.C. 1430, [2015] UKSC 11, para 87.

By way of consolidation this statement incorporates by reference several judicial statements in this area, firstly the statement of Lord Scarman from *Sidaway*:[806]

> I think that English law must recognise a duty of the doctor to warn his patient of risk inherent in the treatment which he is proposing: and especially so, if the treatment be surgery. The critical limitation is that the duty is confined to material risk. The test of materiality is whether in the circumstances of the particular case the court is satisfied that a reasonable person in the patient's position would be likely to attach significance to the risk.

Then Lord Woolf in *Pearce*:[807]

> if there is a significant risk which would affect the judgment of a reasonable patient, then in the normal course it is the responsibility of a doctor to inform the patient of that significant risk, if the information is needed so that the patient can determine for him or herself as to what course he or she should adopt.

And finally, *Rogers v Whittaker*, an Australian authority regarding the matter of 'material risk':[808]

> a risk is material if, in the circumstances of the particular case, a reasonable person in the patient's position, if warned of the risk, would be likely to attach significance to it or if the medical practitioner is or should reasonably be aware that the particular patient, if warned of the risk, would be likely to attach significance to it.

In the case of *Diamond v Royal Devon and Exeter NHS Foundation Trust*[809] the Court decided upon a 'rationality test' by way of establishing whether or not a patient would have consented to a medical procedure if a very small risk were

---

806 *Sidaway v. Board of Governors of the Bethlem Royal Hospital* [1985] A.C. 871, [1985] UKHL 1, [13] (Scarman LJ).

807 *Pearce v. United Bristol Healthcare NHS Trust* [1999] PIQR 53, [59] (Woolf LJ) (EWCA).

808 *Rogers v. Whitaker* (1992) 175 CLR (Aus) 479, 490.

809 [2019] P.I.Q.R. 12.

known – in this case, the risk factor was 1 in a thousand.[810] This was by way of clarifying the meaning of a 'reasonable person in the patient's position'.

Regarding what is meant by a 'material risk' in this sense, the Supreme Court clarified this in *Montgomery*:[811]

> … it follows from this approach that the assessment of whether a risk is material cannot be reduced to percentages. The significance of a given risk is likely to reflect a variety of factors besides its magnitude: for example, the nature of the risk, the effect which its occurrence would have on the life of the patient, the importance to the patient of the benefits sought to be achieved by the treatment, the alternatives available, and the risks involved in those alternatives. The assessment is therefore fact-sensitive, and sensitive also to the characteristics of the patient.

As previously established, the informed consent regime under UK space industry rules appears to be directed at both employees (or agents) of the operator in addition to potential 'space tourists'. The attention of both must be drawn to 'material risks' regarding any relevant space flight activity under section 17 of the Space Industry Act.

The concept of 'material risks' – and the common law surrounding it – introduces a level of subjectiveness for a number of reasons.

Firstly, there is a significant argument to say that the risks of spaceflight must be obvious to anybody giving it the slightest thought – the most anticipated being death arising from catastrophic failure of the propellant system. It is worth noting that this risk is not exactly remote as was shown by a joint study between the Federal Aviation Administration, the Aerospace Corporation and the NASA Armstrong Flight Research Centre concluded that fatal consequences could be 'expected' for initial suborbital flights.[812]

Second, what is the 'standard' in these circumstances? Would a space tourist be judged by the standard of a 'reasonable space tourist' and the pilot be judged by the standard of a 'reasonable spacecraft pilot', or will the blanket provision of a 'reasonable spaceflight participant' prevail? This approach would seem problematic given the expected differences in knowledge between a

810 *Ibid.*, para. 83.

811 N647, para. 89.

812 R. Siebold, R. Young & N. Demidovich, 'Safety of Spaceflight Participants Aboard Suborbital Reusable Launch Vehicles – Background Research, NTRS/NASA', 2019, <https://ntrs.nasa.gov/api/citations/20190025274/downloads/20190025274.pdf> Accessed 15 October 2024.

fee-paying tourist and professional pilot in this context. A related point is that all those attracted to space travel, be it in a professional or touristic capacity, could be less risk averse than the average individual. By extension this would go against the very fabric of the accepted definition of the 'reasonable person' within the law of the United Kingdom. As was stated in the case of *Muir v Glasgow Corporation*:[813]

> Some persons are by nature unduly timorous and imagine every path beset with lions. Others, of more robust temperament, fail to foresee or nonchalantly disregard even the most obvious dangers. The reasonable man is presumed to be free both from over-apprehension and from over-confidence, but there is a sense in which the standard of care of the reasonable man involves in its application a subjective element.

It is the 'subjective' element that Lord Macmillan refers to that must be considered carefully in respect of the informed consent provisions under the UK space industry regime.[814]

Could it be argued with any credibility that such individuals – having either carved out a career in this field or having been drawn to space for a long time – would be overly concerned about motion sickness or a 4% chance of suffering with anxiety? In the case of space tourists, would the fact that these individuals have voluntarily placed themselves in a position of potentially grave danger have any bearing on the judge's assessment of their characteristics as regards the consent given? Could the fact that one has, by boarding a dangerous aircraft with the expectation of being propelled many more thousands of feet above the earth's surface than would otherwise be reasonable, effectively mean that, on voluntary acceptance of this greater risk, the individual has automatically consented to every smaller risk involved in such an activity?

In addition to looking at the consent process from the spaceflight participants perspective, it is important to consider it from the perspective of the operator. It is imperative that there is no attempt to misrepresent the levels of risk involved on their part or engage in any high-pressure sales tactics – in addition to being bad commercial practice, this too could vitiate the consent given. As was stated by Lord Donaldson, MR in the case of *Re T*:[815]

---

813 1943 SC(HL) 3 (MacMillan LJ).

814 The evidence of Thomas Cheney submitted to Parliament is of particular interest here where he writes of 'go fever'<https://publications.parliament.uk/pa/cm201719/cmpublic/space/memo/sib01.htm> accessed 15 October 2024.

815 *Re T (Adult)* [1992] 4 All ER 649, 113 (EWCA).

> A special problem may arise if at the time the decision is made the patient has been subjected to the influence of some third party …

A sensible measure to take may be for independent information on the risks involved to be provided by the CAA to all prospective space tourists in addition to the risk assessment and other documents which must be provided by the operator. This would at least ensure some degree of objectivity in respect of informing the consent process. Regarding any unscrupulous commercial practices that could arise, the Misrepresentation Act 1967[816] offers a cause of action for certain matters as does the common law although it shouldn't be forgotten that such avenues would be of scant consolation and even less use to the deceased.

It is helpful at this stage to consider the practice of the United States. An interesting contribution came from Jeff Greason, founder of XCOR Aerospace who stated that a rather blunt approach should be adopted, advocating statements such as 'You have a 1 in 14 chance of dying on this flight'[817] and, further, that videos should be shown to such individuals showing disasters and mishaps involving rockets.[818] More macabre, perhaps was the idea of Greg Maryniak, Executive Director of the X-Prize Foundation who suggested that potential spaceflight participants be advised to draft a will prior to take-off.[819] As extreme as this may sound, it would certainly make an impression.

Like other 'extreme' activities, the reason why spaceflight holds such a significant amount of attraction could also be because of the risks involved. Walker has pointed out that this may indeed induce the consumer to overlook the magnitude of the risk in question.[820]

Another subjective element of this conundrum is the ability to truly comprehend any information given by means of establishing informed consent. The written evidence of Thomas Cheney correctly questions whether 'the highly technical nature of spaceflight, particularly in these early, experimental phases, can be distilled in a way the average layperson can truly understand …'[821]

816 C7.

817 Melanie Walker, Suborbital Space Tourism Flights: An Overview of Some Regulatory Issues at the Interface of Air and Space Law, 33 J Space L 375, 384 (2007).

818 *Ibid.*

819 *Ibid.*

820 *Ibid.*

821 N820.

The most logical place to look to see how this has operated in practice is the medical field. As Lord Templeman in the seminal case of *Sidaway* stated:[822]

> ... the duty of the Doctor ... is to provide the patient with information which will enable the patient to make a balanced judgment if the patient chooses to make a balanced judgment. A patient may make an unbalanced judgment because he is deprived of adequate information. A patient may also make an unbalanced judgment if he is provided with too much information and is made aware of possibilities which he is not capable of assessing because of his lack of medical training, his prejudices or his personality.

The statement of Lord Templeman is instructive for a number of reasons. Related to the previous discussion on those who may have a more 'risk taking' personality, they could be said to make an 'unbalanced judgment' based on their 'prejudices' or 'personality' as stated here. The operator should, therefore, regard it as being incumbent upon it to make the strongest possible impression on the potential space flight participant regarding the inherent risks, perhaps in the ways discussed in the United States. On the other hand, the Regulator could assume responsibility to some degree and ensure that the risks have been communicated in the strongest possible terms.

Regarding the statement of Cheney on technical information, it is clear from Lord Templeman's statement that, whilst it is important to provide those concerned with sufficient information so that they can legitimately give informed consent, too much information of a highly technical nature could render the validity of consent in such circumstances questionable.

This was relayed in no uncertain terms in the case of *Montgomery*:

> The doctor's duty is not therefore fulfilled by bombarding the patient with technical information which she cannot reasonably be expected to grasp, let alone by routinely demanding her signature on a consent form.[823]

An interesting point here is that this does not seem to mirror the position in the United States. Tracy Knutson has effectively advised that the more information the potential occupant is appraised of, the better:

---

822 N812, para 13 (Templeman LJ).

823 N811, para 90.

> warnings and contractual exculpation documents for this developing adventure activity will need a detailed and descriptive section titled 'Inherent Risks' and/or 'You Need to Understand These Issues' followed by a list of industry concerns or 'realisms.' ... where it is clear that one of the primary hazards or risks associated with this young industry is that there are no accepted standards guiding the industry regarding critical concerns like the physical condition of the SFP, what gear the SFP should be required to wear, what safety equipment should be in the vehicle, what is required in a safety briefing, what type of vehicle is capable of routinely traveling to suborbital space, or even what specific categories of aircraft or specific instrument ratings a pilot must have, SFPs should be appraised of this dearth of standardized knowledge, awareness and response.[824]

And, to a more blunt and extreme degree, that:

> The space operators should tell you everything.[825]

The case of *Chester v Afshar*[826] further complicates matters in this regard if informed consent is to be administered in the same way in the space industry as is done in the medical context. In this case, although a failure to warn of a 1–2% risk of complications that could give rise to serious brain damage would not have stopped the patient consenting to the treatment in question, the patient stated that, although they would have ultimately consented, they would have initially taken more time to consider this information and come to a decision and, consequentially, would have had the surgery at a later date. On basic tort principles, the chain of causation was therefore intact and, 'but for' the failure to advise of the risk, the surgery would have taken place on a different date and the damage very likely would not have arisen.

Where would this reasoning leave an operator? On one hand, bombarding a customer with too much technical information can lead to vitiating consent but on the other the failure to warn of a very small risk can have the same consequences – or at least leave the door open for future claims based on the chain of causation being intact. Would the consequences be the same legally if a customer – or their estate – could mount an argument that they would not have boarded an unsuccessful flight if they had information relating to the

824 Tracey Knutson, *What Is Informed Consent for Space-Flight Participants in the Soon-to-Launch Space Tourism Industry*, 33 J Space L 105 at 114 (2007).

825 *Ibid.*

826 [2004] UKHL 41, (Lords Bingham and Hoffman dissenting).

smallest of risks to consider? It may be that the best overall advice to operators is to give as much information as possible but also give the information to the occupant at the earliest possible opportunity – in the case of the regulations, this would be one month before the actual flight.[827]

It is also submitted that instruction could be taken from guidelines within the medical profession when refining informed consent under the space industry regime, in particular, the General Medical Council's guidelines from 2008.[828] These state requirements such as the disclosure of all material risks made on the basis of un-biased, preferably independent information. The 'independence' factor here is one that could certainly be developed vis-à-vis the CAA in its present role and it may be preferable that such information in an accessible form comes from the CAA as opposed to the operators themselves who would provide important supplementary information.

The issue of 'unknown risks' is an interesting one from the operator's perspective. Whilst the US Federal Code, as mentioned, provides that a spaceflight participant be given information regarding such risks, the reasoning in the United Kingdom may fall under the European Union Product Liability Directive 1985 as regards the state of scientific and technical knowledge.[829] As was stated in the case of *Commission v UK*, an Article 7 defence may arise under the Directive whereby:

> ... the producer of a defective product must prove that the objective state of scientific and technical knowledge, including the most advanced level of such knowledge, at the time when the product in question was put into circulation was not such as to enable the existence of the defect to be discovered. Further, in order for the relevant scientific and technical knowledge to be successfully pleaded as against the producer, that knowledge must have been accessible at the time when the product in question was put into circulation.[830]

Whether or not an 'unknown risk' could be said to be part of the body of scientific and technical knowledge at any given time is a considerable

827 R209(2).

828 The General Medical Council, *'Consent: Patients and Doctors Making Decisions Together'*, (2008),<https://www.gmc-uk.org/static/documents/content/Consent_-_English_0617.pdf>, accessed 15 October 2024.

829 85/374/EEC.

830 Commission of the European Communities v. United Kingdom of Great Britain and Northern Ireland. [1997] EUECJ C-300/95 (29 May 1997) para. 29.

philosophical conundrum in its own right. What is clear is that, in order to avail themselves of any kind of defence as regards a failure to disclose what could be regarded as a material risk of human spaceflight, operators must ensure that they keep abreast of all such relevant scientific information, most of which is likely to be held at the behest of NASA and the European Space Agency though a significant amount of data should also be available in the scientific literature, particularly that produced by specialist institutions.[831] The extent to which the entire body of data available from these bodies would be of use to operators is certainly questionable. Data from orbital space shuttle flights and lunar excursions, for example, would be of little use to a commercial enterprise operating suborbital flights. The hazardous nature of space ventures will be clearly documented within the literature, particularly as regards spaceflight disasters such as *Challenger* and *Columbia*. At the other end of this spectrum, the NASA Human Integration Design Handbook sets out a number of injuries that could arise in the course of spaceflight in addition to ways in which these could be avoided. For example, injuries to eyesight that could arise from exposure to non-ionizing radiation,[832] injuries to 'ears, sinuses or teeth with cavities or fillings' arising from changes in barometric pressure,[833] and injuries arising from the acceleration environments arising in the course of spaceflight[834] The medical law context in the United Kingdom takes the 'reasonable awareness' approach when judging whether or not a medical practitioner has a duty to warn,[835] and it would not be unreasonable to assume that an operator has an awareness of the type of factors listed above. A selective appraisal of literature of this nature should indeed be within their purview.

The federal law of the United States is a strong source of instruction as regards the practice of informed consent as set out in statute regarding spaceflight. Under Title 14 of the Code of Federal Regulations:[836]

> An operator must inform each space flight participant in writing about the risks of the launch and reentry, including the safety record of the launch or reentry vehicle type. An operator must present this information

831 Embry-Riddle Aeronautical University, for example.

832 N772, 560.

833 *Ibid*, 339.

834 *Ibid*, 398.

835 *Duce v. Worcestershire Acute Hospitals NHS Trust* [2018] P.I.Q.R. P18, 43.

836 § 460.45 (2).

in a manner that can be readily understood by a space flight participant with no specialized education or training, and must disclose in writing –

1. For each mission, each known hazard and risk that could result in a serious injury,
2. death, disability, or total or partial loss of physical and mental function;
3. That there are hazards that are not known; and
4. That participation in space flight may result in death, serious injury, or total or partial loss of physical or mental function.

Information regarding the safety records of the vehicles involved is also required to be presented along with figures regarding the number of casualties that have been incurred on any flights in addition to the number of flights the vehicle has undertaken with people on board in addition to any catastrophic failures.[837] Opportunities to seek further information must be allowed and requests may be made for additional information on accidents or incidents arising.[838] A potential spaceflight participant must also be allowed to 'ask questions orally to acquire a better understanding of the hazards and risks of the mission'.[839]

The consent form itself should also:

1. Identify the specific launch vehicle the consent covers;
2. State that the space flight participant understands the risk, and his or her presence on board the launch vehicle is voluntary; and
3. Be signed and dated by the space flight participant.[840]

It would be unwise to undertake a full legal transplant of the US regime – or even a mirroring of their practices – as has already been established, giving too much information under English medical law could lead to vitiating consent through bombardment. If such information is, as is likely, of a technical nature relating to space flight accidents and any 'corrective action' taken because of such accidents is disclosed, this could add to the inherent complexity and hence vitiate consent. The caveat of being allowed to ask specific questions may also not be enough to offset liability on the part of the operator. In the case of *Rodney Crossman v. St George's Healthcare NHS Trust*[841] the High Court decided that an absence of questions asked by a patient did not 'absolve the

---

837 *Ibid.*, (c) (2).
838 *Ibid.*, (d) (2) & (3).
839 *Ibid.*, (f).
840 *Ibid.*
841 [2016] EWHC 287.

hospital of its responsibility for the mistake and does not break the chain of causation that flows from it'.[842]

It has also been stated that:

> It is questionable, however, whether an SFP would know what kinds of questions to ask. For example, an SFP is likely to make general inquiries related to quantity of accidents. The SFP may not have enough information to make more specific inquiries. For example, an SFP may not think to pose questions that would distinguish between quantity of accidents that occurred in the air or on the ground.[843]

Other interpretations of space flight activities in the context of the informed consent rules is that of space flight being akin to a 'dangerous sport'. As stated by Swinton Thomas, L.J.:

> Many sports, such as motor racing, rafting, mountaineering, rock climbing and many others have innate dangers. That is part of their appeal.[844]

In the motor-racing related case of *Wattleworth v Goodwood*,[845] Goodwood Road Racing Company were the occupier of a racing circuit where the claimant's husband had been fatally injured as the participant in a motor race after colliding with a crash barrier. It was held that Goodwood had discharged their duty of care under the Occupiers Liability Act 1957[846] since they had sought expert advice on the crash barriers installed. Should an absence of informed consent not be successfully established, it is likely that the Occupiers Liability Act 1957 could be invoked against spaceport operators in England and the alternative legislation in other jurisdictions. In England and Northern Ireland, other remedies in tort law may be sought as regards duties of care with similar actions being raised in Scotland under the law of delict.

Analogous cases have arisen in England including *Poppleton v. Trustees of the Portsmouth Youth Activities Committee*[847] which involved a claimant who was injured when falling from a climbing wall at the defendant's premises. May, LJ stated:

842 *Ibid.*, at para. 32.
843 N823, 384.
844 *Stratton v. Hughes*, unreported, 17 Mar. 1998.
845 [2004] P.I.Q.R. P24.
846 C.31.
847 [2009] P.I.Q.R. P1.

> Adults who choose to engage in physical activities which obviously give rise to a degree of unavoidable risk may find that they have no means of recompense if the risk materializes so that they are injured.[848]

In this case, the risk of injury was held to be 'plainly obvious' and the defendants were absolved from liability.

A similar case that draws parallels with the proposed informed consent regime is that of *Maylin v. Dacorum Sports Trust (t/a XC Sportspace)*[849] whereby the claimant, having signed a disclaimer prior to use of the defendant's climbing facilities, suffered an injury. The disclaimer form included a statement from the British Mountain Council which stated that:

> The British Mountain Council recognises that climbing and mountaineering are activities with a danger of personal injury or death. Participants in these activities should be aware of and accept these risks and be responsible for their own actions …

A series of questions followed which participants were required to assent to:

> Do you understand that failure to exercise due care could result in your injury or death?
> Do you have any questions regarding the application and Conditions of Use or Rules?
> Do you agree to abide by the Rules of the climbing centre?[850]

In giving judgment, McKenna J stated,

> There being, in my judgment, inherent and obvious risks in the activity which Miss Maylin was embarked upon, the law, as May LJ makes clear in Poppleton, does not require the Defendant to train, supervise or warn and again, as is made clear in Poppleton, it makes no difference that the Defendant charged Miss Maylin to use the bouldering wall and, as it seems to me, that the claim fails on that ground. As to the amount of warnings displayed throughout the site: there were at least two notices warning users of the bouldering wall that matting did not make it any safer and at least one notice that spelt out that broken or sprained limbs

848 *Ibid*, para 1.
849 [2017] EWHC 378 (QB).
850 *Ibid*, paras 9–10.

> are common. These were located on both sides of the entrance to the bouldering area and were there to be seen, whether or not the Claimant in fact read them. The mere fact that the Defendant could have done more by perhaps having a receptionist spell out the risks verbally or by handing out a photocopy of the notice warning of the risks and that the mat did not make it any safer is nothing to the point if the steps which were taken were themselves sufficient, as I find they were.[851]

Where the judge's reasoning differs from that which would be necessary under the space industry regime is that there is a requirement to train, at least some, participants. Other than this it would seem that in the majority of cases where ample warning is given to the general threat of danger – as opposed to specific examples that could arise – ultimately, liability can be avoided by the defendant.

In support of this, is the case of *Tomlinson v Congleton Borough Council*.[852] This case was decided along similar principles though not in the context of dangerous sports as such, but in the context of a failure to observe warning signs. The case involved a young man who, ignoring warning signs at an artificial lake, dived into the water and was rendered tetraplegic. In finding for the defendant council, Lord Hoffman pronounced that:

> The fact that such people take no notice of warnings cannot create a duty to take other steps to protect them.[853]

No consideration of the case law in these areas would be complete without at least some contemplation of *Watson v British Boxing Board of Control*[854] in which the national boxing authorities were held in breach of their duty of care to the boxer Michael Watson who suffered a serious brain injury owing to insufficient medical services in close proximity to the boxing ring. The Board was held to be under a duty to make rules ensuring that personal injuries would be treated effectively and, therefore, they were liable for the injuries to Watson. Significantly, Lord Phillips MR cited the case of *Perrett v Collins*[855] which concerned an aircraft inspector's duty of care to those who may fly an aircraft he was responsible for inspecting.

851 *Ibid*, para 29 (Mckenna J).

852 [2004] 1 A.C. 46.

853 *Ibid* at para 46.

854 [2001] 2 W.L.R.1256.

855 [1998] 2 Lloyds Rep 255.

On the basis of the foregoing, operators, should they wish to avoid liability for injuries to human occupant, would be advised to ensure adequate warning is given, perhaps even above and beyond any details provided in the consent form.

As will be visited later in this chapter, there are also contractual issues regarding informed consent which should be examined whereby death or personal injury are caused through negligence. Section 2(1) of the Unfair Contract Terms Act 1977[856] excludes liability for either on a 'business to business' basis whereas on a 'consumer' basis, the Consumer Rights Act 2015 provides that:

'A term which has the object or effect of excluding or limiting the trader's liability in the event of the death of or personal injury' may be regarded as unfair.[857] Interestingly it is provided under section 65(1) that '[a] trader cannot by a term of a consumer contract or by a consumer notice exclude or restrict liability for death or personal injury resulting from negligence' which is followed with:

> Where a term of a consumer contract, or a consumer notice, purports to exclude or restrict a trader's liability for negligence, a person is not to be taken to have voluntarily accepted any risk merely because the person agreed to or knew about the term or notice.[858]

A 'consumer notice' under section 61 is a notice that:

> ... relates to rights or obligations as between a trader and a consumer, or ... purports to exclude or restrict a trader's liability to a consumer'[859] which 'includes an announcement, whether or not in writing, and any other communication or purported communication.[860]

It is certainly arguable that the Consumer Rights Act may have the effect of defeating any defence based on informed consent – under the Act, it is not a defence to say that a person voluntarily assumed a risk on the basis of knowledge of a term or notice. A human occupant who contracts on a fee-paying basis – or their estate – could, therefore, point to these provisions and claim that even though the damage was 'consented' to, the term is unfair and the

856 N371.
857 Sch. 2(1).
858 s65(2).
859 S61(4)(a)–(b).
860 S64(8).

notice the consumer was placed upon – as to probable death or injury – should have no effect on a finding of liability.

It is to be assumed as a matter of public policy that informed consent in any context should not mean informed consent to injury caused by negligence but, given the inherent novelty of space activities, it would be unsurprising to see such an argument mounted by way of divergence from accepted principles in medical law. More specifically, it may be more difficult to prove negligence when a spaceflight itself could be regarded as inherently 'experimental' which may make the establishment of the appropriate standard of care to be exercised in such circumstances inherently challenging.[861] Regardless of the challenges presented, should a finding of negligence be made, any argument based on consent would in all probability fail as a matter of both law and policy.

There are other implied terms in consumer contracts as to negligence related matters[862] including provisions as to the imbalance of power between parties rights and obligations as per Council Directive 93/13 on Unfair Terms in Consumer Contracts[863] reflected in Schedule 2 of the Consumer Rights Act 2015 which could also come into play regarding information asymmetry which could be said to arise under such arrangements, particularly if can be shown that such information cannot be readily understood by lay individuals. Whilst it would be unwise to speculate upon all possible permutations that could arise in a contractual sense, issues of information asymmetry highlight the need for the involvement of the CAA as an impartial arbiter of information in these matters.

The regime also provides that employees – or their estates – cannot claim compensation without proof of negligence if they have provided consent to the risks involved.[864] This appears to be a very unusual requirement – informed consent in the context of risks to health and safety is by no means a common practice and, at the time of writing, the space industry laws are the only legislative provisions which direct this practice within the employment context. Flying an experimental air or spacecraft, whilst inherently dangerous, is not the only dangerous occupation in existence – various examples abound in both private and public sectors, yet none – with the possible exception of the Armed Forces – are required by statute to give informed consent to their

861 The current approach is to incrementally develop the law in respect of which situations lead to a duty of care arising, see Robinson v Chief Constable of West Yorkshire Police [2018] UKSC 4.

862 See s13 of the Supply of Goods and Services Act 1982 – 'the supplier will carry out the service with reasonable care and skill'.

863 Directive 93/13/EEC of 5 Apr. 1993.

864 Regulation 218 (1)(c).

employer on the basis of the dangerous nature of a task they are required to perform in the course of their employment. Whilst the justification for such a regime in the context of fee-paying passengers makes sense – and also in the context of scientific personnel – it is harder to see the rationale for requiring informed consent in respect of an employee such as a pilot or flight engineer who would surely be presumed to have knowledge of the risks by occupational virtue. Whether or not this was born of a desire for insulation by way of ensuring that all individuals involved have knowledge of the inherent risks is not clear, but because this is such a unique dimension of the space industry regime it is worthy of additional consideration.

The dearth of legislation requiring informed consent possibly accounts for the fact that there is very little case law on informed consent in the employment setting. Of that which there is, the result is positive for employees. In the case of *Cassley v. GMP Securities Europe LLP*[865] it was held that the employer's duty of care was not abrogated by a waiver where an employee was killed in a plane crash. Interestingly, the document was unsigned but the presiding judge stated that in any case 'it would have been invalid under the Unfair Contract Terms Act 1977 as an attempt to exclude liability for death or personal injury'[866] which is an area previously covered within this work. The case was appealed but this point was not commented upon by the Court of Appeal.

Within the Space Industry Regulations, section 34(2) of the Space Industry Act on strict liability does not apply to individuals who have 'entered into a reciprocal waiver of liability with a licencee'. However, the explanatory note sets out that such individuals can 'still claim for injury or damage under the common law'. Be this as it may, this enactment appears contrary to the Unfair Contract Terms Act 1977. Cross-waivers of liability are not uncommon in respect of domestic space legislation[867] and, given the absence of an analogous informed consent regime or liability waiver regime elsewhere in UK legislation, its existence within the space industry rules may be a result of a legal transplant, and, therefore, in danger of being rejected.[868]

Another argument could be that, in the context of the Space Industry Act, the relevant provisions of the Unfair Contract Terms Act could be said to be

865 N371.
866 *Ibid*, para 292.
867 See N365. the United States and Australian rules also provide for this.
868 See Otto Khan Freund, 'On uses and misuses of Comparative Law' (1974) Modern Law Review 37.

impliedly repealed[869] in light of the subsequent Act. As was stated in the case of *Dean and Chapter of Ely v Bliss* by Lord Langdale, MR:[870]

> … it appears to me to be a sufficient answer to the objection to say, that if two inconsistent Acts be passed at different times, the last is to be obeyed, and if obedience cannot be observed without derogating from the first, it is the first which must give way.

There is no express language in the Space Industry Act which seeks to displace any provisions in the Unfair Contract Terms Act but this needn't be the case, as was stated in *Re Williams*:[871]

> Now, it is clear that the provisions of an earlier Act may be revoked or abrogated in particular cases by a subsequent Act, either from the express language used being addressed to that particular point, or from implication or inference from the language used.

The tests at common law would appear to suggest that, when read together, the provision on waivers under the Space Industry Act could indeed be taken to supersede anything under the Unfair Contract Terms Act or even the Consumer Rights Act 2015. As was stated in *Churchwardens and overseers of West Ham v Fourth City Mutual Building Society* by Smith J:[872]

> The test of whether there has been a repeal by implication by subsequent legislation is this: are the provisions of a later Act so inconsistent with, or repugnant to, the provisions of an earlier act that the two cannot stand together?

And by Laws J in the influential case of *Thoburn*:[873]

> If Parliament has enacted successive statutes which on the true construction of each of them make irreducibly inconsistent provisions, the earlier statute is impliedly repealed by the later.

869 Thanks to my colleague, Dr Tarik Olcay, of the University of Dundee for his helpful guidance in respect of this.

870 (1842) 49 ER 700.

871 (1887) 36 Ch D 573(Ch D).

872 [1892] 1 QB 654 (EWHC).

873 *Thoburn v Sunderland City Council* [2002] All ER (D) 223 (Feb) at para [37], (Laws LJ), (EWHC).

On one argument, the relevant words of the Space Industry Act are clearly 'repugnant' to the Unfair Contract Terms Act in that the Space Industry Act – and subsequent regulations – clearly provide for an avoidance of liability in respect of personal injury or death in a contractual context. Therefore, the relevant provisions of the Unfair Contract Terms Act could be said not to apply here. There is, however, a general presumption against implied repeal in circumstances such as this. Laws LJ stated in *O'Byrne v. Secretary of State for Environment, Transport and the Regions*:[874]

> … the contradiction asserted must be inescapable; so that where … an implied repeal is said to be based on the construction of the later statute, that construction must be shown to be the only rational interpretation which is available.

This bar seems capable of being surpassed as 'the only rational interpretation'. This seems even more likely when the rule relating to general and specific provisions is considered, namely that general provisions in a previous Act – the Unfair Contract Terms Act in this case – can be supplanted by more specific provisions in a later one – the Space Industry Act. As the Earl of Selbourne stated in *Seward v 'Vera Cruz'*;:[875]

> Now, if anything be certain it is this, that where there are general words in a later Act capable of reasonable and sensible application without extending them to subjects specially dealt with by earlier legislation, you are not to hold that earlier and special legislation indirectly repealed, altered or derogated from merely by force of such general words, without any indication of a particular intent to do so.

This could mean that, in the absence of specific words in the Space Industry Act 2018 which expressly call for the repeal of parts of earlier statutes – or which state they are not to apply in spheres of activity covered by it – there is no such repeal.

There could also be an argument to suggest that the sheer 'weight' of the Unfair Contract Terms Act 1977 makes it incapable of being supplanted[876] but this would seem tenuous.

---

874 *O'Byrne v. Secretary of State for Environment, Transport and the Regions* [2001] EWCA Civ 499, [2002] H.L.R. 30 (Laws LJ).

875 (1884) 10 App Cas 59 (EWCA).

876 See Richards Respondent and Richards Appellant [1984] A.C. 174 (HoL).

In conclusion, based on what is known about the limited extent of implied repeal – and in accordance with the demonstrable treatment of such matters from the case of *Cassley*,[877] it would appear that the Unfair Contract Terms Act could impact contractual matters based on informed consent.

A further possible unintended consequence of giving a large amount of information out to participants is that trade secrets could be inadvertently disclosed, particularly as regards aspects of engineering should information regarding rectification of design flaws following accidents be part of this. Should this sort of information be disclosed to flight personnel in the course of their employment, the case of *Faccanda Chicken v Fowler*[878] along with numerous dimensions of data protection and export controls law[879] could be engaged.

The question of informed consent under the UK space industry regime is interesting for a number of reasons. There is a wide variety of risks and hazards, both physical and psychological, which are associated with spaceflight. These even extend to hazards and risks yet unknown. It may be that questions of informed consent under the space industry regime are never ventilated in court but, given the inherent risks, it is likely, if not inevitable should crewed flights become a regular occurrence. During the consultation period for the Space Industry Regulations 2021, the author submitted a published article as evidence which considered many of the issues previously raised here. Specifically, it concerned the question of timing as regards the dispensation of information to a spaceflight participant as part of the informed consent process. The draft regulations proposed that 12 hours was enough time for a participant to consider the relevant information and give valid consent. The author proposed, on the basis of the research outlined here – in particular the position within medical law – whereby consent can be vitiated if it can be shown that there has been 'bombardment' of information as per the judgment in *Montgomery*[880] that spaceflight participants should be given more time to consider the risks. The regulations were ultimately redrafted and Regulation 209 (2) reads that 'At least 24 hours, but not more than one month, before a human occupant signs a consent form, the spaceflight Operator must give that individual … (the relevant information)'. It was confirmed by the United Kingdom Space Agency that the author's research in this area had contributed to

877 N809.

878 [1986] 3 W.L.R. 288 (EWCA).

879 See N462–463, N578.

880 N811, para 90.

the decision to change the law in this respect.[881] This arguably does not go far enough for some of the reasons stated – and for those that follow.

There is also the question of why trained professionals in this context – either as the operator's agent or employee – should have to sign consent forms. Ultimately, as discussed, the consequence would be that they are excluded from claiming compensation on a strict liability basis as per section 34(2) of the Space Industry Act. Whilst one can see the logic in this as regards fee-paying customers, it does not seem particularly fair as regards the operator's staff. As has been alluded to, signing up in knowledge of the fact that one may be called upon to make the ultimate sacrifice is not something that is ordinarily part of employment contracts for professions and jobs that involve a high degree of risk outside of the armed forces. Considering the principles of implied repeal it seems that it was indeed the intention of Parliament that such terms allowed under the Space Industry Act would not be rendered unfair under the Unfair Contract Terms Act and this appears to be the required legal practice. It is worth repeating that nothing prevents such individuals pursuing a claim for negligence at common law.

The informed consent process is likely due to occur a significant amount of time after any given contract for space tourism purposes has been entered into. Should there be any issues with the consent process – such as those discussed later – the contractual timing could be an issue. It is even possible that, should an individual have already paid a significant amount of money, they may be very reluctant to bail on such plans at the consent stage. Could a novel argument also be mounted to suggest that such compulsion brought on by something resembling a 'sunken cost' syndrome could, in and of its own right, vitiate consent? This can be linked to Thomas Cheney's writings on 'go fever'.[882] If not an area deemed worthy of hard legal rules, the Regulator is at least encouraged to provide guidance on the charging regime in light of such possibilities come the material time.

Other problems that could arise could be a separate form of 'space law informed consent', discrete from the medical law regime, regarding space activities as akin to a dangerous sport as previously explored. If so, it would be judicially prudent to ensure that the medical law provisions do not borrow too heavily from the space law provisions and vice versa so as to avoid confusion and misapplication given the largely different contexts. The extent to which law on matters such as occupier's liability and cases such as *Congleton, Maylin*

881 Email in authors possession from the United Kingdom Space Agency, received 9 March 2021.

882 N820.

and *Poppleton* are influential as regards warning notices in this context will be interesting too, and it is likely that the space law informed consent regime could be aligned with that relating to professional sports[883] although it is important to note the interesting overlaps with the criminal law here. The general rule in criminal law is that consent cannot be given to serious bodily injury in certain contexts[884] but there are exceptions to this for sporting injuries – up to and including death – incurred within the rules of the game.[885] The overarching justification as such is one of public policy. Engaging in sporting activities is a desirable public good; where such an injury has been implicitly consented to in such circumstances, there will be no criminal liability unless the defendant's standard of behaviour is so egregious that it would warrant prosecution.[886] In respect of injuries incurred within the rules of a sporting activity, the reasoning is echoed within the Space Industry Act itself in respect of nuisance and trespass. Section 34 states that '[n]o liability arises in trespass or nuisance in respect of spaceflight activities carried out in compliance, or substantially in compliance, with the requirements and conditions imposed by or under this Act.' Should the question of consent in the sense of the criminal law ever be tested in the context of injury to human occupants it will be interesting to see if the qualification in Section 34 is used as a basis for determining whether or not an operator can be held to have acted 'criminally'. The evidential value of documentation assented to by human occupants in respect of consenting to injury sustained in the course of spaceflight will, of course, be significant but its value as any kind of blanket immunity is questionable.

Given the inherent risks as outlined, it is likely that insurance may be sought by fee-paying 'tourists' but one only has to look at the experience of the Apollo astronauts in this regard to see that this could be problematic – life insurance for them proved to be impossible to obtain.[887]

More domestic legislatures are creating rules in respect of space tourism as a smaller faction of national space infrastructure. Professor Frans von der Dunk has written that:

883 Ben Livings, 'A Different Ball Game – Why the Nature of Consent in Contact Sports Undermines a Unitary Approach' JCL 71 (534).

884 See *R v Brown* [1993] UKHL 19, a famous case on the topic of injury sustained in the course of consensual sado-masochistic activities.

885 R v Barnes [2004] EWCA Crim 3246. See also R v Coney (1882) 8 Q.B.D. 534, [539–540] (Lord Justice Cave), [549] (Lord Justice Stephen).

886 *Ibid.*

887 See Dave Scott & Alexei Leonov, *Two Sides of the Moon*, 345, (Bedford Square Books, London 2004).

> such national legislation threatens to preclude any uniform interpretation and application of the terms of the Liability Convention. Gaps and overlaps in terms of scope may appear, threatening the consistency and uniformity of the application of the international liability regime as a whole, and thereby its effective operation.[888]

Based on the layers of common law and myriad rules that could apply even at the UK level, there is a significant possibility of fragmentation in respect of informed consent. As such flights are becoming more commonplace globally speaking[889] it is perhaps sensible to call for a new international agreement on these matters, similar to the 1929 Warsaw Convention[890] and, when the time comes, a possible cap on liabilities under section 34(5) of the Space Industry Act could potentially aid the provision of affordable insurance policies. It would also be desirable to maintain, as much as possible, an entitlement to the strict liability regime within the spirit of the initial international instruments.

Until now, this chapter has considered the position with informed consent without prejudice to issues of capacity. This facet of the process reveals some interesting discussion points. The consent form – as previously discussed – requires that a 'human occupant' 'must be at least 18 years of age'.[891] Moreover, an individual must have the required mental capacity. As Regulation 205(2)(a) states, 'if the launch vehicle is to be launched from England or Wales, a human occupant must have capacity within the meaning of the Mental Capacity Act 2005(a) to understand the risks involved in the Operator's spaceflight activities and the meaning of signifying their consent to take part in those activities'. There are 5 principles laid down by section 1 of the Mental Capacity Act 2005[892] which help in guiding this process:

---

888 Frans Von der Dunk, 'The 1972 Liability Convention: Enhancing Adherence and Effective Application' (1998). Space, Cyber, and Telecommunications Law Program Faculty Publications 371, <https://digitalcommons.unl.edu/spacelaw/50.> accessed 25 November 2023.

889 See the recent activities of Virgin Orbit in the United States: Tom Acres, 'Virgin Galactic's first space tourism flight launches today – here's what you need to know', Sky News, 10 August 2023, <https://news.sky.com/story/amp/virgin-galactics-first-space-tourism-flight-launches-today-heres-what-you-need-to-know-12936619> accessed 25 November 2023. As a matter of public record there have been numerous flights since, see the website of Virgin Galactic for details, <https://www.virgingalactic.com/> accessed 25 November 2023.

890 N538.

891 R205(1).

892 C9.

> … (2)A person must be assumed to have capacity unless it is established that he lacks capacity. (3) A person is not to be treated as unable to make a decision unless all practicable steps to help him to do so have been taken without success. (4) A person is not to be treated as unable to make a decision merely because he makes an unwise decision. (5) An act done, or decision made, under this Act for or on behalf of a person who lacks capacity must be done, or made, in his best interests. (6) Before the act is done, or the decision is made, regard must be had to whether the purpose for which it is needed can be as effectively achieved in a way that is less restrictive of the person's rights and freedom of action.

As regards decision making itself, an 'inability to make decisions' is dealt with under Section 3:

> A person is not to be regarded as unable to understand the information relevant to a decision if he is able to understand an explanation of it given to him in a way that is appropriate to his circumstances (using simple language, visual aids or any other means). (3) The fact that a person is able to retain the information relevant to a decision for a short period only does not prevent him from being regarded as able to make the decision. (4) The information relevant to a decision includes information about the reasonably foreseeable consequences of—(a) deciding one way or another, or (b) failing to make the decision.

The Regulations also make clear that the same must be made with reference to instruments in Scotland and Northern Ireland as regards questions of mental capacity and spaceflight in those jurisdictions.[893] In Scotland, the primary instrument is the Adults with Incapacity (Scotland) Act 2000[894] which is similar in scope to the Mental Capacity Act albeit – possibly significantly in this context – an 'adult' is defined as 'a person who has attained the age of 16 years'[895] yet the Space Industry Regulations state that a human occupant must be at least 18 years old.[896] It is likely that, since the Regulations make no prescription regarding the legal status of an 18 year old, that is, they do not specify that this indicates 'adulthood' or attempt to override this definition in any of

893 R205(1)(b)–(c).
894 N786.
895 *Ibid*, s1(6).
896 R205 (1).

the jurisdictions, it would be held as 'non-discriminatory' under section 13(2) of the Equality Act 2010[897] which states that:

> If the protected characteristic is age, A does not discriminate against B if A can show A's treatment of B to be a proportionate means of achieving a legitimate aim.

It may be argued that the legitimate aim being sought is at least twofold – ensuring that the individual is mature enough to understand the risks involved whilst, perhaps, also ensuring that the individual is physically strong enough to withstand the rigours of spaceflight. The age restriction, therefore, could be seen as a proportionate means of achieving this aim. Whilst this is a mere educated guess at the logic behind such matters, the decision could also have been made on the basis that 18 is the age of adulthood across the majority of jurisdictions covered by the Space Industry Act, and, therefore, this makes by far the most sense.

In respect of the general principles involved as stated, the Northern Irish rules are similarly phrased. Section 1(4) of the Mental Capacity Act (Northern Ireland) 2016[898] states that

> The person is not to be treated as unable to make a decision for himself or herself about the matter unless all practicable help and support to enable the person to make a decision about the matter have been given without success.

Across the relevant jurisdictions, the concept of 'unwise decisions' frequently emerges. Under the Northern Irish rules it states that

> The person is not to be treated as unable to make a decision for himself or herself about the matter merely because the person makes an unwise decision.[899]

The relevance of 'unwise decisions' in the context of UK space legislation will be revisited in due course.

897 2010 c5.
898 Acts of the Northern Ireland Assembly 2016 c18.
899 *Ibid* s1(5).

Concerning the expression 'unable to make a decision', the Northern Irish rules state that a person is to be regarded as unable to make a decision for themselves if the person:

> (a) is not able to understand the information relevant to the decision; (b) is not able to retain that information for the time required to make the decision; (c) is not able to appreciate the relevance of that information and to use and weigh that information as part of the process of making the decision; or (d) is not able to communicate his or her decision (whether by talking, using sign language or any other means); and references to enabling or helping a person to make a decision about a matter are to be read accordingly.

The legislation in this regard is framed in the same way across the relevant jurisdictions save for the provision about age in Scotland. The shared ethos of these enactments is to give as much effect to individual autonomy as possible and could certainly play an important role in respect of assessing the capacity of a 'human occupant' under the more recent space legislation which is largely silent on this matter, particularly where informed consent is concerned. The first edition of the 'Guidance for launch operator and return operator applicants and licencees'[900] stated that:

> A human occupant must have the mental capacity to understand the risks involved in the spaceflight activities carried out by the spaceflight operator and the meaning of signifying his or her consent to take part in these activities. A prospective human occupant who lacks capacity may not be able to properly comprehend the hazards and risks of the spaceflight activities and therefore may not be able to give informed consent to take part in them.[901]

Paragraph 9.12 goes a step further by stating that:

> An underlying principle of mental capacity law is that an individual is presumed to have capacity, unless it is established that they do not.

900 N257.

901 *Ibid*, para 9.11.

And, further and importantly that:

> It is therefore the responsibility of the spaceflight operator to establish whether an individual lacks capacity; the operator is recommended to obtain his own legal advice on the matter.

The guidance then signposts applicants and licencees to the relevant law, in particular, the basic provisions in England and Scotland and the relevant guidance documents for both of these jurisdictions.[902] Interestingly – and perhaps incorrectly – there was no reference to the Northern Irish Mental Capacity Act as has been discussed here and it is even stated that:

> In Northern Ireland, the test for determining whether an individual has capacity to understand the risks involved in an operator's spaceflight activities, and the meaning of signifying consent to those activities, is determined by the common law of Northern Ireland.[903]

This is echoed to a lesser extent in the Regulations themselves:

> (c) if the launch vehicle is to be launched from Northern Ireland, a human occupant must have capacity in accordance with the law of Northern Ireland to understand the risks involved in the operator's spaceflight activities and the meaning of signifying their consent to take part in those activities.[904]

The omission of any specific reference to the Northern Irish Mental Capacity Act is curious, as is the reference to any such matters regarding capacity and informed consent being resolved with reference to the common law of Northern Ireland. As will be demonstrated here – and as has been demonstrated previously – the common law of all of the relevant jurisdictions is likely to play an extremely important role in determining these kinds of questions alongside the provisions of national legislation on these matters.

As the original guidance went on to say: 'The Regulator expects a spaceflight operator to consider using elements of their training programme and medical assessments to identify any persons that potentially lack capacity'.[905]

Importantly, it was stated further that:

902 *Ibid*, para 9.13.
903 *Ibid.*
904 R205(2)(c).
905 N257, para 9.14.

> the Regulator expects a spaceflight operator to carry out a formal assessment of a person's capacity to understand the risks and meaning of giving consent referred to in paragraph 10.11 if, during training or a medical assessment, the individual … exhibits an inability to make decisions or understand or retain information relevant to that understanding and giving consent (or) shows a sustained inability to comprehend or follow instructions'.[906] A similar position is adopted in the new guidance.[907]

There may be some problems with this approach, particularly if it is undertaken at the post-contractual stage as seems to be implied here. Further still, operators will be under an obligation to ensure that they are cogent of the relevant practice of the various adjudicating authorities on issues of capacity in addition to the overall international thrust as regards disability rights so as to avoid serious transgressions of equality law. This has to be balanced, of course, against the fact that under section 18 of the Space Industry Act, an operator can find themselves convicted of a criminal offence if they allow an 'unqualified' individual to take part in space activities.

It is of great interest to observe that the most recently published guidance on these matters has less detail on the law as it relates to mental capacity. There is no reference to any of the Acts or guidance from the General Medical Council as was contained in the first edition,[908] although the general thrust of the document is similar.

In respect of when a relevant medical assessment might take place, there is no specific rule on this, but Chapter 5 of the Regulations provides for medical fitness overall. Regulation 72(2)(a) provides that:

> 'medical examinations and medical assessments' are to be carried out by an 'approved aeromedical examiner.'

An 'approved aeromedical examiner' is defined under section 5 as someone who

> (a) is qualified and holds a valid licence to practise medicine from the General Medical Council, (b) has qualifications in aviation or space medicine, and (c) has been approved by the CAA for the purposes of carrying

906 *Ibid.*

907 N368.

908 N368, 83–84.

> out medical assessments or medical examinations for the purposes of these Regulations.

The latter is reassuring in this context as it is to be assumed that a medical examination 'for the purposes of these regulations' would have regard to mental capacity in respect of its relevance to the question of informed consent – there is no specific requirement for this but a 'medical assessment' under the regulations means investigating an individual's medical history in addition to medical examinations and tests. A medical certificate or confirmation of the fact that the individual is medically fit to fly can only be issued if such an examination has been carried out.[909] Crucially, it is important to add, a disability will not necessarily be a bar to participation in spaceflight activities. Regulation 75 provides that:

> If a spaceflight participant with a disability or reduced mobility has been certified as being fit to fly under regulation 73(1), the spaceflight operator may make arrangements for that participant to take part in a spaceflight if—(a) doing so would not compromise the safety of the flight; (b) the presence of an individual with that disability or reduced mobility would not impede or obstruct any member of the crew or spaceflight participant in carrying out their functions during the course of the flight, including executing emergency procedures or leaving the launch vehicle.[910]

The statutory definition of 'disability' comes from The Equality Act 2010 which states:

> A person (P) has a disability if—(a) P has a physical or mental impairment, and (b) the impairment has a substantial and long-term adverse effect on P's ability to carry out normal day-to-day activities.[911]

This definition certainly does not necessarily preclude an individual from being able to give informed consent and nor should it, and the position taken under Regulation 75 should be applauded. One question at this stage – which is hopefully answered by Regulation 72(2)(c) on the qualifications of the aero-medical examiner, is whether or not a certification of fitness to fly is the same as fitness to give informed consent. It is worth noting that, per the guidance and

---

909 R73(2).
910 R75 (a)–(b).
911 S6(1).

Regulation 61(3)(a), some of the responsibility for determining capacity may fall on the Training Manager who must ensure that 'the licencee complies with the requirements in these Regulations in relation to the qualification, training and medical fitness of individuals performing specified roles and spaceflight participants'. Furthermore, under section 63(1)(a) the Training Manager is required to organise and manage 'such instructors and medical staff, facilities and equipment as are sufficient and appropriate to comply with the licencee's obligations under this Part' in addition to 'administering any informed consent process required by Part 12'.[912] It seems that the Training Manager will have responsibility for ensuring that any individual wishing to participate in space activities gives consent and, moreover, that such consent is valid. The gateway to this is surely the initial determination of capacity which is not specifically provided for or given a timeframe. As will be addressed later, consideration of these specific matters will be needed at some stage to ensure that the right of autonomy is balanced effectively with the requirement to protect the vulnerable. More exploration is required of the proposed extent of medical screening undertaken in the case of potential human occupants. The ICAO rules, as discussed, check mental capacity to some degree, but this is for pilots rather than passengers – as is well-known, air travelers require no such assessments. It is encouraging to note that the updated guidance contains significantly more detail as regards medical fitness. In particular, it goes above and beyond the previous guidance by stating that medical fitness of crew and spaceflight participants can be assessed 'immediately prior to flight'.[913]

In respect of how mental capacity may be assessed by an aeromedical examiner, it may be instructive to observe what is listed in the Manual of Civil Aviation Medicine[914] as regards the licensing requirements for pilots:

> The applicant shall have no established medical history or clinical diagnosis of: (a) an organic mental disorder; (b) a mental or behavioural disorder due to use of psychoactive substances; this includes dependence syndrome induced by alcohol or other psychoactive substances; (c) schizophrenia or a schizotypal or delusional disorder; (d) a mood (affective) disorder; (e) a neurotic, stress-related or somatoform disorder; (f) a behavioural syndrome associated with physiological disturbances or physical

912 R63(1)(g).

913 N364, 83.

914 The International Civil Aviation Organisation, 'Manual of Civil Aviation Medicine', Annex 1, Requirements of Mental Fitness, Chapter 9.1.3, (Third Edition 2012, Quebec) <https://www.icao.int/publications/documents/8984_cons_en.pdf> Accessed: 16 October 2024.

> factors; (g) a disorder of adult personality or behaviour, particularly if manifested by repeated overt acts; (h) mental retardation (sic); (i) a disorder of psychological development; (j) a behavioural or emotional disor der, with onset in childhood or adolescence; or (k) a mental disorder not otherwise specified; such as might render the applicant unable to safely exercise the privileges of the licence applied for or held.

In terms of UK legislation, the Air Navigation Order 2016 lists the following as 'disqualifying conditions':

> (a) any alcohol or drug abuse, addiction or misuse; (b) any neurological condition; (c) any functional disability; (d) any surgery or medical treatment; (e) any collapse, fainting or loss of consciousness.[915]

This paints a very broad picture of what could potentially lead to a finding of mental incapacity – should such criteria be applied to all 'human occupants' and not just pilots and other relevant personnel, the operator may find themselves at risk of pursuing an outdated 'status-based' or 'functional' approach in respect of determining an individual's fitness to fly or capacity for understanding the risks involved in order to give consent. It is also important to ensure that aeromedical examiners are truly qualified as regards the assessment of mental capacity as a discreet medical area. EU Regulation 2018/1139[916] on common rules in the field of Civil Aviation states that, regarding an aeromedical examiner's qualifications:

> An aero-medical examiner must: (a) be qualified and licenced in the practice of medicine; (b) have received training in aviation medicine and regular refresher training in aviation medicine to ensure that assessment standards are maintained up to date; and (c) have acquired practical knowledge and experience with regard to the conditions in which pilots carry out their duties.[917]

In a general sense, it could be reasonably expected that an individual qualified and licenced in the practice of medicine would be qualified to assess mental capacity. It is not clear whether this is reconcilable with an assessment of whether human occupants – in the sense of fee-paying passengers or

915 Article 163.

916 N479.

917 Annex VIII, Article 6.1.

'space tourists' – necessarily understand the risks associated with space flight or, more particularly, whether they possess the requisite mental capacity to understand these risks.

It would be desirable to see a requirement enacted by which an aeromedical examiner would be obliged to assess this specific attribute in the context of an overall medical examination which should take place at as early a juncture as possible. Leaving such an assessment until significantly later in the process could lead to potential contractual liability. By the time a medical assessment is undertaken, a binding contract between the human occupant and operator for a space journey may well have already been concluded. What will be the situation if the aeromedical examiner makes an adverse decision at this stage? If such an adverse decision was based on disability this may be open to challenge under the Equality Act and if it was made on the basis of insufficient mental capacity as regards the ability to give valid informed consent there is the possibility that the decision could be challenged on the basis of it being overly paternalistic as per the main thrust of the mental capacity instruments across all concerned jurisdictions in addition to the emerging international picture.

The Mental Capacity Act 2005 for England and Wales, seeks to protect the autonomy of individuals in respect of individual decision-making processes and is also an attempt to steer the law away from what could be regarded as a traditional paternalism.[918] The starting point of the Act is a presumption that the individual has capacity. This has been referred to in the case law of the England and Wales Court of Protection as a 'cardinal principle' of the legislation,[919] 'every bit as important as the presumption of innocence in a criminal trial.'[920]

A unique dimension of UK space law, specifically the question at hand – that of giving informed consent to potential risks which may be of a complex and technical – but no less dangerous – nature, is that the individual concerned is giving consent to a highly unorthodox procedure.[921] Could the wish to board a potentially dangerous and experimental aircraft and be fired into space be evidence of mental imbalance or an absence of capacity? The Mental Capacity Act states that 'A person is not to be treated as unable to make a decision merely because he makes an unwise decision.'[922] This is supported in

918 Catriona Mackenzie and Wendy Rogers, 'Autonomy, vulnerability and capacity: a philosophical appraisal of the Mental Capacity Act', Int. J.L.C. 2013, 9(1), 37–52, 37.

919 *London Borough of Tower Hamlets v PB (by his litigation friend, the official solicitor)* [2020] EWCOP 34, para 6, (Hayden, J).

920 *Ibid.*

921 This could be said to be akin to the famous 'Catch 22' paradox in Joseph Heller's eponymous novel – 'because war is dangerous it is sane behaviour to avoid war' etc.

922 s1(4).

the statutory guidance which states that unwise decisions themselves do not justify a judicial finding of incapacity.[923]

A look at some of the case law in this area is likewise instructive. It has been stated in the Court of Protection that:

> Even where an individual fails to give appropriate weight to features of a decision that professionals might consider to be determinative, this will not in itself justify a conclusion that P lacks capacity. Smoking, for example, is demonstrably injurious to health and potentially a risk to life. Objectively, these facts would logically indicate that nobody should smoke. Nonetheless, many still do.[924]

Furthermore, Macfarlane L.J. in the Court of Appeal stated:

> there is a space between an unwise decision and one which an individual does not have the mental capacity to take … it is important to respect that space, and to ensure that it is preserved, for it is within that space that an individual's autonomy operates.[925]

This indicates the importance now lent to freedom of choice – including the ability to choose to undertake courses of action which could be deemed unwise. This, of course, in the context of the UK space law regime, must be balanced against the requirement under the Space Industry Act and Regulations that an individual must have understood the risks involved in spaceflight in order to give valid consent. If – owing to a lack of mental capacity – such risks are not understood, a restriction must be placed on the individual's autonomy. Such a limitation on the face of things may seem justified – and, indeed, will be if capacity has been assessed appropriately and by an appropriately qualified individual.

The case law discloses many instances involving the question of whether a decision maker had adequate capacity. Correctly – and in line with the thrust of the legislation – incapacity is not judged purely on the basis of a diagnosis in such matters. In one case, it was held that an individual with Prader-Willi

---

923 Department for Constitutional Affairs, 'Mental Capacity Act Code of Practice', Issued by the Lord Chancellor on 23 April 2007 in accordance with sections 42 and 43 of the Act, 24, <https://assets.publishing.service.gov.uk/media/5f6cc6138fa8f541f67632295/Mental-capacity-act-code-of-practice.pdf> accessed 16 October 2024.

924 N926, para 14, (Hayden, J).

925 *PC v City of York* [2013] EWCA Civ 478, [2014] 2 W.L.R. 1, para 54 (Macfarlane LJ).

Syndrome and an IQ of 57 did not automatically lack capacity.[926] Another applicant was described as:

> ... having ADHD, foetal alcohol spectrum disorder as well as specific difficulties with cognition and speech and language. Her expressive language is quite good but her receptive and processing skills are only those of a child aged 7 to 9. She does not have a learning disability; it is Dr Rippon's view that her IQ would be in the 80s and thus properly described as low average but well above that which would justify the diagnosis of a learning disability.[927]

In this case she was judged to have the capacity for both consensual sexual relations and internet usage.[928]

A key point in respect of informed consent and how this interacts with the Mental Capacity Act regards weighing 'information relevant to the decision'.[929] This has been the subject of judicial interpretation as regards the use of social media in situations whereby the individual's capacity is in question. The following formulation by Cobb J is instructive as regards a position that could be adopted as regards the informed consent process (as a whole, rather than just in respect of those whose mental capacity may be in doubt as discussed later).

Cobb J opined that the relevant information would be, in the potentially hazardous usage of the internet:

> (i) Information and images (including videos) which you share on the internet or through social media could be shared more widely, including with people you don't know, without you knowing or being able to stop it ... (iii) If you place material or images (including videos) on social media sites which are rude or offensive, or share those images, other people might be upset or offended ... (iv) Some people you meet or communicate with ('talk to') online, who you don't otherwise know, may not be who they say they are ... (v) Some people you meet or communicate with ('talk to') on the internet or through social media, who you don't otherwise know, may pose a risk to you ... [or] (vi) If you look at or share

926 *FX v A Local Authority* [2017] EWCOP 36.

927 *Liverpool City Council v CMW (By her litigation friend, the Official Solicitor)* Case No: 13699739, Court of Protection, para 10.

928 *Ibid*, para 23.

929 s3(1).

> extremely rude or offensive images, messages or videos online you may get into trouble with the police.[930]

Whilst risks arising in the context of social media and the internet are of a largely different order to those associated with spaceflight it is still a complex and demanding area. Other potentially more analogous cases have been decided upon – in one case, the applicant was held not to be able to make decisions about foreign travel[931] whereas in another case, in spite of a psychiatrist's report which came to a different conclusion, the Court decided that valid informed consent could be given by an elderly woman with dementia as regards going on a cruise.[932] It is possible then, that in the context of 'fitness to fly' and capacity to give informed consent, that an aeromedical examiner's report could also be subject to an adverse ruling should a court be of the opinion that an individual is indeed capable of giving validly informed consent in spite of some form of mental incapacity.

Operators would be wise to consider the approach outlined by Cobb J when determining the form of the information to be given or at least use a similar template. Moreover, the form of the information should necessarily be available to all potential spaceflight participants as outlined earlier. As will be discussed, in line with preservation of autonomy and the spirit of the various legislative instruments in this area, it is important to establish a minimum ceiling of information which is available to all those to whom it is relevant, rather than to single certain individuals out for scaffolding – something in itself that could potentially be considered discriminatory. In simple terms, this would be the process whereby individuals considered to have particular disabilities in respect of mental capacity would be given information in a different format to those not deemed to have the same disabilities. Effectively, one 'class' of individual would be receiving differentiated treatment, and such an approach could be deemed overly paternalistic and out with the aim of the relevant legislation and overall policy objectives.

As has been repeated, it is the context of spaceflight which makes this problem an interesting one. It would seem from the case law of the Court of Protection that the instruments pertaining to capacity will be interpreted as far as possible in the spirit of maximizing individual autonomy. Individuals who, on the face of things, may have had issues with mental capacity have been

930 *Re A (An Adult)* [2019] Fam. 586, [2019] 3 W.L.R. 59, para 28 (Cobb J).

931 *Greenwich RLBC v EOA* [2021] EWCOP 20, para 49.

932 *Cardiff County Council v Peggy Elizabeth Ross (by her litigation friend the Official Solicitor)*, Case No. 12063905, para 8.

held to be able to consent to and engage in areas which are potentially hazardous. Spaceflight is an inherently risky area and, as has already been written, the technical complexity of the risks involved- a point that has been tacitly acknowledged by the United Kingdom Space Agency—means that individuals should be given as much assistance as possible as regards comprehending such risks. Paternalistic views of what may or may not be in an individual's 'best interests' are certainly not the way in which the courts are deciding matters, particularly as regards what could be referred to as 'unwise decisions'.

It was very pertinently stated in a 2007 case that:

> A great judge once said, 'all life is an experiment,' adding that 'every year if not every day we have to wager our salvation upon some prophecy based upon imperfect knowledge' (see Holmes J in Abrams v United States (1919) 250 US 616 at pages 624, 630). The fact is that all life involves risk, and the young, the elderly and the vulnerable, are exposed to additional risks and to risks they are less well equipped than others to cope with ... The emphasis must be on sensible risk appraisal, not striving to avoid all risk, whatever the price, but instead seeking a proper balance and being willing to tolerate manageable or acceptable risks as the price appropriately to be paid in order to achieve some other good – in particular to achieve the vital good of the elderly or vulnerable person's happiness. What good is it making someone safer if it merely makes them miserable?[933]

It is likely that a significant number of individuals will see participating in space activities as being something that would 'achieve happiness' in the way outlined above, and operators may find that they are treading a fine line in respect of potential discrimination under section 29 of the Equality Act 2010 if they unjustifiably – even if well-meaningly – refuse an individual a service on the basis of mental capacity. There is also the converse scenario, where an individual who may have issues with capacity gives consent and then either suffers an injury or dies in the space activity they have consented to. Legal action may come as regards the consent given on the grounds that consent could not have been validly given owing to an absence of capacity or on the basis that the individual was not well-informed enough within the context of their disability. This is where section 3(2) of the Mental Capacity Act is relevant. Information at the consent stage should be 'given to him in a way that is appropriate to his

933 *Local Authority X v MM* [2007] EWHC 2003, [2009] 1 F.L.R. 443, (Munby J), para 20.

circumstances (using simple language, visual aids or any other means)'. Such a practice is designed to enable or empower an individual in respect of their decision making and is in line with the direction of travel as far as International Law is concerned. Article 3 of The Convention on the Rights of Persons with Disabilities[934] has 8 guiding principles of which Principle 1 – 'individual autonomy including the freedom to make one's own choices' – and Principle 3 – 'full and effective participation and inclusion in society' – are important in this context. The Convention has been described as marking a positive change in respect of furthering the legal rights of disabled individuals, in particular, the aspects of empowerment that it brings.[935]

Particularly relevant to this discussion is Article 30 (5) under which 'states parties to the Convention 'shall take appropriate measures ... to ensure that persons with disabilities have access to services from those involved in the organization of recreational, tourism, leisure and sporting activities.'

Underscoring the broader commitment towards equal recognition for disabled persons is Article 12(2) – (3): 'States Parties shall recognize that persons with disabilities enjoy legal capacity on an equal basis with others in all aspects of life' and 'States Parties shall take appropriate measures to provide access by persons with disabilities to the support they may require in exercising their legal capacity'.

As has been written though: 'It is important to distinguish the concept of 'legal capacity' from 'mental capacity'. Legal capacity is a concept contained within the broad heading of equal recognition before the law. It has been defined as the right to be recognised as a person before the law and therefore to have one's decisions legally recognised ... In contrast, mental capacity is used to refer to a combination of cognitive ability, impairment and a person's extent of understanding of the consequences of their actions.'[936]

Operators would be well-advised to heed this important distinction which is borne out in the United Nations General Comment on Article 12: 'Legal capacity and mental capacity are distinct concepts. Legal capacity is the ability to hold rights and duties ... Mental capacity refers to the decision-making skills of a person, which naturally vary from one person to another and may

934 Convention on the Rights of Persons with Disabilities, Treaty Series vol. 2515, December 2006 <https://treaties.un.org/doc/Publication/CTC/Ch_IV_15.pdf>, Accessed 03 October 2022.

935 Cliona de Bhailis and Eilionoir Flynn, 'Recognising legal capacity: commentary and analysis of Article 12 CRPD', Int. J.L.C. 2017, 13(1), 6–21.

936 *Ibid*, 9–10.

be different for a given person depending on many factors, including environmental and social factors.'[937]

As outlined earlier, the different jurisdictions served by the Space Industry Act and its Regulations are required to assess mental capacity on the basis of their own enactments regarding it. Whilst the anomalous treatment of Northern Ireland is certainly a cause for concern in respect of the space industry rules, the fragmentation that could arise owing to the devolved administrations relying on their own legislation and their interpretations of the Convention has been held to be an area of concern by the Committee on the Rights of Persons with Disabilities who described the situation in their 2017 report as:

> The insufficient incorporation and uneven implementation of the Convention across all policy areas and levels within all regions, devolved governments and territories under its jurisdiction and/or control.[938]

This is a legitimate concern as the Convention itself has been considered for direct implementation into Scots law which could lead to disparity of treatment.[939] This sort of fragmentation is not unforeseeable given that the current overall approach in the United Kingdom is out of step in many respects with the international momentum. The approach taken thus far is what can be described as 'functional'. As the Law Commission found, 'the assessor asks whether an individual is able, at the time when a particular decision has to be made, to understand its nature and effects'.[940] The United Nations Committee on the Rights of Persons with Disabilities have stated that 'any test amounts to indirect discrimination when it disproportionately affects people with cognitive disabilities'[941] and the General Comment stated 'In order to fully recognize 'universal legal capacity' … States must abolish denials of legal capacity that are discriminatory on the basis of disability in purpose or effect … functional tests of mental capacity or outcome-based approaches that lead to denial of legal

937 United Nations Committee on the Rights of Persons with Disabilities Eleventh session 30 March–11 April 2014 Item 10 of the provisional agenda General comments and days of general discussion, General comment on Article 12: Equal recognition before the Law, <https://digitallibrary.un.org/record/779679> accessed 16 October 2024.

938 *Ibid.*

939 Alliance Scotland, 'Incorporating the United Nations Convention on the Rights of Disabled People in Scotland' November 2020 <https://www.alliance-scotland.org.uk/wp-content/uploads/2020/11/ALLIANCE-Inclusion-Scotland-CRPD-Incorporation-in-Scotland-Main-Report-Nov-2020.pdf> accessed 16 October 2024.

940 The Law Commission, 'Mental Incapacity' (1995) Law Com No 231, 28 February, 33.

941 N944, 10.

capacity violate article 12 if they are discriminatory or if they disproportionately affect the right of persons with disabilities to equality before the law.'[942]

Whilst this is correct and clearly well-meaning, at the risk of being potentially discriminatory, legislative care must still be taken to ensure that people are protected from bad marketing practices and high-pressure sales in such matters in addition to the general need to ensure flight safety. Of course, the legal 'personhood' dispensed under the Convention is not to be regarded as absolute under any circumstance[943] – it is tempered by Article 2 which states:

> 'Reasonable accommodation' means necessary and appropriate modification and adjustments not imposing a disproportionate or undue burden, where needed in a particular case, to ensure to persons with disabilities the enjoyment or exercise on an equal basis with others of all human rights and fundamental freedoms.

This provision should be read in conjunction with the similar provisions of the Equality Act 2010 section 20(3)–(5) regarding the duty to take reasonable steps to avoid disadvantages to individuals as a result of policy, criterions or practices and to eradicate obstructive physical features and provide auxiliary aids where possible – this seems to go further than merely doing that which does not impose a 'disproportionate burden' as the Convention sets out.

In the context of disability more generally, alterations to physical features of buildings and the like to enable access was considered within the Convention, with Article 2 promoting principles of 'Universal Design':

> 'Universal design' means the design of products, environments, programmes and services to be usable by all people, to the greatest extent possible, without the need for adaptation or specialized design. 'Universal design' shall not exclude assistive devices for particular groups of persons with disabilities where this is needed.

In theory this provision applies to spacecraft manufacturers, whom, it is submitted, should attempt to accommodate all people where possible. It must be born in mind that there will be certain engineering parameters that must be observed, the weight of any given spacecraft being the most obvious one – this will have an impact on many design aspects and also fuel consumption /

942 N944, para 12.

943 See *Latimer v AEC* [1953] AC 643 and *Watts v Hertfordshire CC* [1954] 1 WLR 835 for a Common Law illustration of more general matters in a Tort Law context.

efficiency as regards environmental obligations. It is also fundamental to note on this point that Schedule 2(2) states in no uncertain terms that modifications to certain transport is not always necessary. This point will be addressed in more detail later.

Regardless of the 'reasonable adjustments' which could be made at any stage of the human occupant's journey, what approach could be taken to avoid discrimination on the part of operators? As referred to previously, a 'functional' approach could be taken to assessment, but this is not very well regarded in respect of the Convention. As Paragraph 15 of the General Comment stated:

> The functional approach attempts to assess mental capacity and deny legal capacity accordingly. It is often based on whether a person can understand the nature and consequences of a decision and/or whether he or she can use or weigh the relevant information. This approach is flawed for two key reasons: (a) it is discriminatorily applied to people with disabilities; and (b) it presumes to be able to accurately assess the inner-workings of the human mind and, when the person does not pass the assessment, it then denies him or her a core human right—the right to equal recognition before the law.[944]

Nevertheless, protection must be given for the reasons previously stated to avoid any exploitation. With this in mind, it may be worth considering a different approach whereas an increased level of help in respect of these decisions is offered to all potential human occupants, not just those who may have issues of mental capacity, which would appear to be in line with the General Comment. As has been written:

> … if an individual is having difficulty making a decision or communicating a decision, the answer is not to deny legal capacity to the individual, it is instead to provide access to support for the exercise of legal capacity–which will vary greatly depending on the individual and the specific situation. This is a groundbreaking distinction that the GC has explicitly made and has the potential to be revolutionary in legal capacity law, leading to a system that respects the right of all individuals to decision-making support, regardless of disability or decision-making ability.[945]

944 N944, para 12.

945 Anna Arstein-Kerslake & Eilionóir Flynn (2016) 'The General Comment on Article 12 of the Convention on the Rights of Persons with Disabilities: a roadmap for equality before the law', The International Journal of Human Rights, 20:4, 471, 475.

Whilst the CRPD is not directly enforceable, the European Convention on Human Rights is. Articles 14 – prohibition on discrimination – and 8 – right to respect for private and family life – have proven to be particularly important as regards disability discrimination.[946] Important decisions which may be analogous to the space industry include *Botta v Italy*,[947] whereby a finding of discrimination was made on the basis that there were no facilities available by which the applicant could go into the sea and *Zehnalova and Zehnal v Czech Republic*[948] in which the applicants successfully challenged the absence of access facilities at public buildings which sounded in a finding of discrimination. If space is to be regarded as for everybody it must be open to everybody on a non-discriminatory basis. Like other regimes there are qualifications with human rights law and, arguably, no human right can be said to be truly unfettered or absolute. In the case of *Senteges v the Netherlands*[949] a failure on the part of the state to fit the applicant with a prosthetic robotic arm was held to be non-discriminatory as this would have been consistent with the rights and entitlements of citizens in the Netherlands to medical treatment generally.

In the decision of *Glor v Switzerland*[950] the Court read Articles 8 and 14 and decided that psychological and physical integrity formed part of the right to private life in Article 8. In respect of this decision and regarding the flow of traffic overall in respect of disability discrimination and the European Court of Human Rights, it has been written that decisions are made more on the basis of:

> whether similarly placed people or situations are treated differently – thus whether the law is making distinctions (and whether this is justified) – to considering whether the effect of the law is discriminatory. This provides a more comprehensive guarantee of nondiscrimination in that it encompasses not only direct discrimination but also discrimination that is indirect or covert.[951]

There are practical implications here for operators as regards the informed consent process and human occupants with issues of mental capacity. There

946 However, see the case of *Glor v Switzerland* (Application no. 13444/04) where the ECHR explicitly referred to the CRPD.

947 *Botta v Italy* 21439/93, [1998] ECHR 12, [1996] ECHR 83.

948 *Zehnalová and Zehnal v Czech Republic* (38621/97) May 2002.

949 *Senteges v. The Netherlands* (2002) 27677/02.

950 N953.

951 Jill Stavert, 'Glor v Switzerland: article 14 ECHR, disability and non-discrimination', Edin. L.R. 2010, 14(1), 141.

are effectively 3 approaches that could be taken as regards such individuals. The first would be to take a status-based approach and not allow anybody who falls into a certain category of mental incapacity – or those with any mental capacity issues at all – to participate in space flight activities. For the reasons outlined previously, this would probably be unlawful. The second would be to offer those with mental capacity issues more information – or information in a different form – as regards the consent process, effectively a pure functional approach. As mentioned, this too could be problematic owing to the discrepancy which would arise between those with capacity issues and those without – it could also potentially be interpreted as an additional 'test' which would not be imposed on others. Moreover, it is possible that an inverse claim could be made by those without capacity issues set out on the basis that those without capacity issues are deprived of information or information in a clearer format. Operators are advised, considering the forgoing, to ensure that a high level of support is offered to all whom informed consent is required on a universal basis. Whether or not specific legislation is required to facilitate this is questionable but at the very least some comprehensive guidance needs to be published over and above that presently available.

Whilst the actual form of the information to be given as regards the consent process is important and, as discussed, legislated for to a comprehensive degree, the actual timing of any assessment as to mental capacity – and, potentially, the obtaining of consent itself in light of the forgoing – also needs to be considered, as does the situation whereby an individual may be judged to lack mental capacity at the post-contract stage.

Section 7(1)–(2) of the Mental Capacity Act state that:

> If necessary goods or services are supplied to a person who lacks capacity to contract for the supply, he must pay a reasonable price for them.

And, importantly that:

> 'Necessary' means suitable to a person's condition in life and to his actual requirements at the time when the goods or services are supplied.

'Capacity' in this context was taken by Stephen Jourdan Q.C. in the case of *Fehily v Atkinson*[952] to mean: 'the capacity to absorb, retain, understand, process

952 *Fehily v Atkinson* [2017] Bus. L.R. 695, [2016] EWHC 3069 (Ch), para 102 (Jourdan J).

and weigh information about the key features and effects of the contract, and the alternatives to it, if explained in broad terms and simple language'.

Moreover, Baroness Hale stated in *Dunhill v Burgin*[953] that, in such cases, 'capacity is to be judged in relation to the decision or activity in question and not globally.'

This should alarm operators since, as previously established, the guidance for launch and return operators refers to assessments for capacity being undertaken at the training stage or should it come to the attention of certain individuals that the potential human occupant has trouble making decisions.[954] Any such instances would presumably arise after the initial contract has been formulated which, if it then transpires the individual lacks capacity, could lead to complications – the individual could bring an action for breach of contract should they not be permitted to participate in the activities they initially signed up for. A finding of frustration of contract could be made out if the finding of incapacity could be said to be a 'frustrating event'. As was stated by Master Dagnall in *Bank of New York Mellon (International) Ltd v Cine-UK Ltd*,[955] quoting from the second edition of Treitel on frustration and force majeure:[956]

> The general rule is that the question whether the contract is discharged is to be determined by reference to the time of the occurrence of the allegedly frustrating event. The contract will be discharged if at that time a reasonable person would have taken the view that the event would lead to a sufficiently serious interference with performance to bring about discharge. It is not necessary to wait and see whether such interference actually takes place or would have taken place if attempts to perform had not been abandoned; indeed, the contract will be discharged even though subsequent events show that there would have been no such interference.[957]

As regards a determination by a training manager or aeromedical examiner regarding the mental capacity of an individual to either give valid consent or safely participate in space activities, the timing of the determination would be ahead of the performance of the contract and, further, it would be a reasonable

953 *Dunhill v Burgin* [2014] UKSC 18, [2014] 1 W.L.R. 933, 452 (Hale LJ).

954 N257/N368.

955 [2021] EWHC 1013 (QB) (Dagnall, J).

956 Sir Guenter Treitel was Vinerian Professor of Contract Law at Oxford University, and an eminent authority on English Contract Law), Guenter Treitel QC, *Frustration and Force Majeure (2nd Edition)*, Sweet and Maxwell, 2004.

957 *Ibid*, para 196.

argument to say that the presence of a non-consenting individual aboard a spaceflight – or the presence of an individual who potentially poses a danger to others on board – makes the contract one which could be regarded as 'radically different'.

Going a step further, the Court of Appeal wrote at length on the peculiarities of frustration in the case of *The Sea Angel*:[958]

> Among the factors which have to be considered are the terms of the contract itself, its matrix or context, the parties' knowledge, expectations, assumptions and contemplations, in particular as to risk, as at the time of contract, at any rate so far as these can be ascribed mutually and objectively, and then the nature of the supervening event, and the parties' reasonable and objectively ascertainable calculations as to the possibilities of future performance in the new circumstances.

As directed, allocation of risk in such contracts is a key factor and is in line with the modern approach as regards frustration. If parties have allocated any involved risks and this allocation is seen as covering the arising event in the eyes of the court, they will be reluctant to make a ruling that the contract has been frustrated. This is in line with basic principles of freedom of contract. It is very likely that, in order to circumvent any particular difficulties as regards findings of unfitness – or a finding that the proposed human occupant is unable to give valid consent owing to mental capacity issues – that any contract between the operator and customer will state that the risk will fall on the customer. As regards the legality of such a move – which could potentially result in a finding of discrimination – an operator tempted to allocate the risk as such would be well advised to view any such clause as a very onerous one indeed, particularly if the result would be total forfeiture of the purchase price. In such a case, they would be minded to follow the words of Lord Denning:

> Some clauses which I have seen would need to be printed in red ink on the face of the document with a red hand pointing to it before the notice could be held to be sufficient.[959]

If such matters had not been brought to the express attention of the paying customer and a claim for breach was made, operators should be mindful of the fact that the court could determine that the contract is a 'severable' one

958 *The Sea Angel*, [2007] EWCA Civ 547, [2007] 2 Lloyd's Rep. 517, para 111.

959 *Spurling v Bradshaw* [1956] EWCA Civ 3, [1956] 1 W.L.R. 461.

as opposed to an 'entire agreement'. Following the well-established authority of *Cutter v Powell*[960] and looking at the nature of the transaction as a whole it could be determined that the contract was intended to be severable in the minds of the parties since there would always be a risk that an individual might fail some of the training elements and that any training component could be deemed 'severable' from the flight itself. Considering these risks, operators are thus advised to consider the contractual structure for any privately paying individuals, perhaps managing fee payments on a 'deposit' and opposed to a 'whole sum' basis to avoid potential litigation. Alternatively, a satisfactory medical examination including a finding of capacity could be regarded as a 'condition precedent' for any such transaction. Applicants may be less inclined to bring an action for a loss of a deposit should it be a significantly smaller percentage of what will likely be a much higher figure as regards an actual spaceflight.

In the absence of a finding of frustration or actionable breach, the question of contractual capacity must be considered. If there is an adverse finding of mental incapacity, what would the determination be about the entire contract be it entered into on a whole-sum, deposit only basis or severable agreement? If an individual lacked capacity at the time they entered into the contract would this not render the contract void in any case? There are essentially two prongs in answer to this question. The first is the transaction itself and the second is the question of the subject matter. Individuals who lack capacity are generally said to be liable to pay for goods and services contracted for[961] and an individual contracting for 'necessaries'– under the rule in *Imperial Loan Co v Stone*,[962] will be generally bound to pay for them if they did not understand the nature of the transaction and the other party was aware that this was the case. It is important to note that 'knowledge' on the part of the vendor can be 'constructive' knowledge[963] and, importantly, that the requirement for absolute knowledge on the part of the vendor does not apply in Scotland[964] which could lead to issues of disparity.

An interesting question arises in respect of such transactions – in the absence of sharp practice – or constructive knowledge – on the part of the operator – that is, in circumstances where they could not be reasonably said

960 *Cutter v Powell* 101 ER 573 (KB).

961 *Rhodes, Re* (1890) L.R. 44 Ch. D. 94.

962 [1892] 1 Q.B. 599- note that other jurisdictions have expanded the rule to include assessments as to 'fairness' – see *Archer v Cutler* [1980] 1 NZLR 386.

963 Per Baroness Hale in *Dunhill v Burgin* [2014] UKSC 18, para 25 as confirmed by the High Court in *Josife v Summertrot Holdings* [2014] EWHC 996 (Ch).

964 *Loudon v Elder's*, 1923 CB.

to have knowledge of a customer's lack of capacity at the time of the transaction – could it not be argued that no customer can be taken to fully understand the nature of the transaction until they are fully appraised of the information they need to understand prior to the signing of the consent form and that such information has been presented to them in a form that they can understand? It follows that it would be desirable for a 'pre-informed consent informed consent' procedure to be followed at the initial contractual stage for such matters, that is, the customer should see the information they would see – or as close an approximation as possible – for the informed consent procedure prior to entering into any agreement. As per Regulations 209 and 210, the information given as part of the informed consent procedure is to be given no more than a month from the launch itself. It is likely that the initial contract will be entered into earlier than this. Of course, this still leaves open the question of at what stage of the process is mental capacity to be determined. Operators should – as a minimum – insist on a range of screening questions at the pre-contractual stage that all potential human occupants should undertake and then use these as a platform from which to initiate any further enquiries as to whether a given individual has capacity. Thereafter, any medical assessments should be scheduled for as early a time as possible. Regardless of the format, the operator should seek evidence of due diligence in these regards.

The second question that arises is the subject matter of the contract – is 'spaceflight' to be regarded as a 'necessary'? 'Necessary' in section 7(1) of the Mental Capacity Act shares the same definition as it does at common law.[965] Whether something is to be regarded as a 'necessary' is determined as a question of fact in each case.[966] 'Spaceflight' has, naturally, not been considered in this respect yet but examples of what have been held to be 'necessaries' in past cases include '11 fancy waistcoats',[967] a racing bicycle,[968] hiring horses[969] and flying lessons.[970] The rule is that what is necessary depends on 'a person's condition' in life and is context dependent – it is certainly possible that a journey into space could be seen to be a 'necessary' in this context.

Another dimension to consider as regards transactions with individuals who may lack capacity is Regulation 3 of the Consumer Protection from Unfair

965 *Aster Healthcare Ltd v Shafi (The Estate of)* [2014] EWCA Civ 1350, [2016] 2 All E.R. 316.

966 *Ryder v Wombwell* (1868) L.R. 3 Ex. 90

967 *Nash v Inman* [1908] 2 K.B. 1. (EWCA).

968 *Clyde Cycle Co v Hargreaves* (1898) 78 L.T. 296.

969 *Hart v Prater* (1837) 1 Jur. 623.

970 *Hamilton v Bennett* (1930) 94 J.P.N. 136.

Trading Regulations 2008[971] whereby it is deemed to be an unfair commercial practice whereby

> (3) A commercial practice is unfair if
> a. it contravenes the requirements of professional diligence; and
> b. it materially distorts or is likely to materially distort the economic behaviour of the average consumer with regard to the product.

And:
'professional diligence' is regarded as

> the standard of special skill and care which a trader may reasonably be expected to exercise towards consumers which is commensurate with either—
> a. honest market practice in the trader's field of activity, or
> b. the general principle of good faith in the trader's field of activity.[972]

These provisions should be read in conjunction with Regulation 2(5) which states that:

> In determining the effect of a commercial practice on the average consumer—
> c. where a clearly identifiable group of consumers is particularly vulnerable to the practice or the underlying product because of their mental or physical infirmity, age or credulity in a way which the trader could reasonably be expected to foresee, and
> d. where the practice is likely to materially distort the economic behaviour only of that group, a reference to the average consumer shall be read as referring to the average member of that group.

A potential cause of action could arise under these provisions then in respect of individuals who may lack mental capacity in some form if the operator has not exercised due diligence or has misled customers as to the likelihood of them being able to participate in a spaceflight should no screening measures have been conducted.

In respect of a claim for disability discrimination, such a cause of action could be founded under the Equality Act 2010. An operator in this context

---

971 2008 No. 1277.
972 *Ibid*, R2.

would be defined as a 'Service Provider' under section 29. Section 13(1) states that 'A person (A) discriminates against another (B) if, because of a protected characteristic, A treats B less favourably than A treats or would treat others.' A defence would arise for operators under section 15(1)(b) – if discriminatory treatment can be shown to be 'a proportionate means of achieving a legitimate aim' which on the basis of the previous discussion, could be successfully mounted, the 'proportionate means' in question being the denial of an expected spaceflight and the 'legitimate aim' could be the objective of mission safety or the need to promote consumer protection and avoid unfair trading practices. Regulation 75 concerns issues of disability and incorporates this – if a disabled person has been certified as 'fit to fly', then they may do so providing that:

> (a) doing so would not compromise the safety of the flight … and … (b) the presence of an individual with that disability or reduced mobility would not impede or obstruct any member of the crew or spaceflight participant in carrying out their functions during the course of the flight, including executing emergency procedures or leaving the launch vehicle.

It is submitted that an amendment could be made here regarding mental capacity since this has not been catered for. As previously discussed, fitness to fly might not necessarily mean fitness to give informed consent.

A further interesting point is the duty to make reasonable adjustments which arises under section 20 of the Equality Act 2010. Under section 20(4) it is stated that 'where a physical feature puts a disabled person at a substantial disadvantage in relation to a relevant matter in comparison with persons who are not disabled, to take such steps as it is reasonable to have to take to avoid the disadvantage.' The 'reasonableness' of such adjustments is subject to an objective test with any reasons for not making such adjustments being open to enquiry.[973] It follows that, in the interests of public safety, a court may be sympathetic to the complex engineering needs particular to space travel and consider any 'good faith' measures as regards air and spacecraft design in favour of the operator.

Though not specific to spaceflight, section 3(10) of Schedule 2 states that there is no duty to make adjustments for services of 'transporting people by land, air or water'. There are four points here. Firstly, 'space' is not specifically mentioned. Secondly 'air' transport is mentioned. Thirdly is spaceflight

973 *Royal Bank of Scotland Group Plc v Allen* [2009] EWCA Civ 1213, (2010) 112 B.M.L.R. 30.

not covered, at least to a degree by 'air' transport? Fourthly, would 'space' be covered by virtue of a purposive approach to statutory interpretation here? A possible fifth question is whether 'transport' in the sense of getting from 'a to b' could be regarded in the same light as a 'pleasure voyage' as is anticipated here. Given the somewhat tertiary nature of travel for pleasure in the context of forms of transport that could be regarded as a vital public good, it is at least questionable as to whether the Act covers it specifically.

There has only been one judicially significant case involving this area of the law, *Paulley v FirstGroup Plc*[974] in which it was considered by the Supreme Court that not strictly enforcing a policy regarding priority seats for disabled individuals was a breach of the Equality Act.

Regarding the meaning of 'adjustment' in this context, Schedule 2(2) expands on this: 'It is never reasonable for A to have to take a step which would – (a) involve the alteration or removal of a physical feature of a vehicle used in providing the service; (b) affect whether vehicles are provided; (c) affect what vehicles are provided; (d) affect what happens in the vehicle while someone is travelling in it.' As strongly worded as this is, operators would be advised to consider the position under section 20(5) on provision of auxiliary aids[975] and take reasonable steps to introduce these where appropriate.

Regarding auxiliary aids, this may cause some issues in the specific context of spaceflight as previously outlined, since any increase in weight will result in an increased need for fuel and should probably be considered at the design stage of any craft specified for this purpose. Justification would still have to be given under the Equality Act Statutory Code of Practice an increased financial cost cannot justify such an omission in the absence of good reasons.[976] Coupled with the fuel considerations other safety factors would have to be considered as regards loose objects floating within the cabin in low gravity conditions. The Code of Practice also expands on what would be considered a 'legitimate aim' in the context of section 15 of the Act, with paragraph 5.33 confirming that 'ensuring the health and safety of those using the service provider's service or others, provided risks are clearly specified' and 'ensuring the wellbeing or dignity of those using the service' are the overarching priorities

974 [2017] UKSC 4, [2017] 2 All E.R. 1.

975 For definitions of 'auxiliary aids' see paragraph 7.47 of the Equality Act Statutory Code of Practice, Equality and Human Rights Commission, 'Equality Act Statutory Code of Practice', <https://www.equalityhumanrights.com/sites/default/files/servicescode_0.pdf> accessed 16 October 2024.

976 *Ibid*, para 5.33.

Relatedly, an operator would not be obligated to drastically alter the nature of any services rendered to accommodate a disability. In *Edwards v Flamingo Land*[977] it was held that a restaurant did not have to provide takeaway services to a similar end. Although decided under the Disability Discrimination Act 1995[978] it is likely that the same result would come about under the 2010 Act.

Not all disabled individuals will suffer from physical disabilities and, therefore, physical adjustments may not be an issue in some instances. It is very important to note that reasonable adjustments will need to be considered in respect of the obtaining of informed consent whilst, at the same time, honouring the principle of autonomous decision making as enshrined in the mental capacity legislation and associated international instruments. Careful consideration must be given to the way in which information in this regard is presented to all relevant individuals whether they present with a disability or not, in addition to ensuring that there is not an excessive amount of stratification as regards the methods and that no specific group of individuals is subject to more stringent testing than the other for the reasons of parity envisaged in the international instruments.

Informed consent in the context of the UK space industry regime has the potential to be a problematic legal area. It also has the potential to be even more difficult to manage when questions of mental capacity arise. The legislative objective should be to firstly ensure safety and restrain any potentially exploitative business practices whilst at the same time ensuring that individual autonomy is protected. The Law Commission's Consultation Paper on Capacity[979] described various approaches to assessment – 'status', 'outcome' and 'functional' with the 'functional' approach being held the most desirable[980] – a status-based approach has the most potential to lead to unfair results – individuals should not be excluded on the basis of a simple 'paper diagnosis' or 'computer says no' approach. In the functional approach, 'the assessor asks whether an individual is able, at the time when a particular decision has to be made, to understand its nature and effects'[981] and aeromedical examiners should be mindful of this whilst also being cognizant of the opposition posed in the international fora as discussed.

Although the Space Industry Appeals Regulations, being chiefly concerned with licensing matters, do not give any avenue for challenging mental capacity

977 [2013] EWCA Civ 801, [2013] Eq. L.R. 888.
978 C50.
979 N947.
980 *Ibid*, 33.
981 *Ibid*.

decisions, the published guidance states that appeals can be made against aeromedical examiners' decisions[982] as would be expected. As previously noted, in the absence of any contrary information, aeromedical examiners do not necessarily appear to be qualified in respect of determining mental capacity or to understand information relevant to informed consent. As was also discussed, a Court, using the Mental Capacity Act, ruled against a psychiatrists' report which stated that, in their opinion, consent couldn't be given.[983] In theory, this could happen with respect to an aeromedical examiner's decision – or even that of the operator, hence the need for further guidance on this matter. As pointed out, waiting, as the guidance suggests, for evidence of mental incapacity to arise in the course of a training program or other related activity may not be the best course of action if the contract has already been concluded. The most desirable situation would be to make the completion of a customer contract contingent upon a full independent capacity assessment as a condition precedent. This would serve to protect the vulnerable and the operator against potential costly and unnecessary litigation in addition to reducing the likelihood of discrimination. Without introducing a 'status' approach through the backdoor, one further consideration would be the establishment of a minimum level of mental capacity as regards informed consent.

As regards the informed consent process generally, the 24-hour period for consideration of relevant information under Regulation 209 should be changed to at least 48 hours so as to give all individuals a greater chance of understanding the risks. This would also have the effect of providing a common standard for all individuals rather than simply stating that disabled individuals have extra time which, as has been discussed, could be viewed as discriminatory considering the common international trends.

The question of timing and duress more broadly has been discussed in the context of surgery. As surmised below, the closer to the date of the event consent is obtained, the more likely it is that an individual will feel compelled to undertake the activity:

> Most patients will have firmly decided to proceed before attending for surgery. However, a minority may develop doubts upon learning about the procedure in more detail, during the consent process. If these doubts arise on the day of surgery the patient may feel under duress to proceed, as all the arrangements have been made. Therefore it would be wiser to obtain informed consent at the time of listing in clinic, when the risks

982 N612, 5.

983 N939, para 8.

> and benefits are often explained. The patient will feel under less pressure to proceed, and hence will not be acting under duress.[984]

Regarding consumer contracts in the context of space tourism in the United Kingdom, the idea of 'go fever' ought to be examined in the context of the doctrine of undue influence.[985] There is no set definition of what undue influence means, but essentially it is a form of relief in circumstances whereby the will of the more powerful party to a transaction has overborne that of the weaker party in a sense that could be regarded as unconscionable though not necessarily fraudulent. Throughout the discussion on informed consent a common theme was the inherent informational asymmetry between a fee-paying customer and an operator, as regards the technical information that will necessarily be furnished as part of the consent process. It was postulated that the imbalance could, in certain circumstances, lead to a vitiating of consent via 'bombardment'. The imbalance is borne from the relationship between the fee-paying space tourist and the operator which, in the context of dispensing information relevant to the spaceflight activities, will involve a unique position of trust. The customer will largely be at the mercy of the operator in respect of the accuracy of information given as regards the spaceflight activities, particularly the information relating to the levels of potential risk. The operator, in this context it is to be assumed will also be responsible for the direction of the associated marketing materials and promotional literature. The positions of the two parties, then, could well come within the parameters of the equitable doctrine of undue influence.

Regarding the precise definition of undue influence, it has been written that:

> As no court has ever attempted to define fraud so no court has ever attempted to define undue influence, which includes one of its many varieties. The undue influence which courts of equity endeavour to defeat is the undue influence of one person over another; not the influence of enthusiasm on the enthusiast who is carried away by it, unless indeed such enthusiasm is itself the result of external undue influence.[986]

---

984 Owen Anderson, Mike Wearne, 'Informed consent for elective surgery – what is best practice?' J R Soc Med. 2007 Feb, 100(2), 97.

985 Although in English Law, Undue Influence is an 'equitable' doctrine, it is also a ground for challenge under Scots Law, see the case of *Gray v Binneyv (1879) 7 R 332*. Thank you to my student, Katia Sher, for assisting me with this.

986 *Allcard v. Skinner*, 36 Ch.D. 145, 182–183 (Lindley LJ).

This was echoed by Lord Scarman in the important case of *National Westminster Bank Plc v Morgan*:[987]

> There is no precisely defined law setting limits to the equitable jurisdiction of a court to relieve against undue influence. This is the world of doctrine, not of neat and tidy rules. The courts of equity have developed a body of learning enabling relief to be granted where the law has to treat the transaction as unimpeachable unless it can be held to have been procured by undue influence. It is the unimpeachability at law of a disadvantageous transaction which is the starting point from which the court advances to consider whether the transaction is the product merely of one's own folly or of the undue influence exercised by another. A court in the exercise of this equitable jurisdiction is a court of conscience. Definition is a poor instrument when used to determine whether a transaction is or is not unconscionable: this is a question which depends upon the particular facts of the case.

In the opinion of Lord Scarman, Parliament's legislative interventions in respect of statutory implied terms in consumer contracts as evidenced by such enactments as the Consumer Credit Act 1974 and the Supply of Goods and Services Act 1982 were enough of an interference with the English ideal of freedom of contract on the part of Parliament to the extent that the courts should not, in the wake of such measures, 'assume the burden of formulating further restrictions'.[988]

Whilst this may be so as regards many consumer contracts, the space industry regime could prove to be a special case given the novelty and stakes involved. As Thomas Cheney pointed out in his evidence to Parliament[989] in respect of the Space Industry Act 2018, some fee-paying spaceflight participants, for whom a journey to space has been a life-long ambition, may be so determined to see these ambitions realised that the informed consent procedure becomes nothing more than a box-ticking exercise of the most vacuous nature. Whilst aggressive marketing strategies and issues of misrepresentation are certainly by no means unique to the space tourism industry, the novel aspect of 'go fever' in this particular context which involves high levels of danger and the transfer of large sums of money is worthy of consideration from a contractual standpoint.

---

987 [1985] A.C. 686, 709 (HoL) (Scarman LJ).

988 *Ibid*, 708.

989 See the evidence of Thomas Cheney submitted to Parliament N820.

Crucially, the enthusiasm associated with 'go fever' should it have been fostered and endeared by the operator, could come within the scope of undue influence in line with the previously mentioned statement in *Allcard v Skinner*,[990] chiefly that 'The undue influence which courts of equity endeavour to defeat is the undue influence of one person over another; not the influence of enthusiasm on the enthusiast who is carried away by it, unless indeed such enthusiasm is itself the result of external undue influence.' On this measure, it would be a question of fact as to whether or not the enthusiasm was fostered by the operator to the extent that the customers will was overpowered or whether such enthusiasm was already present.

Rather than discussing undue influence as a blanket term, it is important to distinguish the different types of undue influence – actual and presumed – and consider how each may apply in this context. Actual undue influence is closely related to the doctrine of duress, and the requirements were laid out succinctly in the case of *Bank of Credit and Commerce International SA v Aboody*[991] by Slade LJ:

> [W]e think that a person relying on a plea of actual undue influence must show that (a) the other party to the transaction (or someone who induced the transaction for his own benefit) had the capacity to influence the complainant; (b) the influence was exercised; (c) its exercise was undue; (d) its exercise brought about the transaction.[992]

This can arise from non-disclosure of material information or misrepresentation and does not necessarily have to be the sole basis for the claimant entering the transaction complained of nor is a finding that the claimant would have entered into the transaction in any case a bar to a claim for undue influence.[993] It is also possible for actual undue influence to arise during a one-off transaction as opposed to an ongoing commercial relationship which would appear to bring the kind of transactions likely to arise in our context within the doctrine.[994]

The other type of undue influence is 'presumed' undue influence, whereby a rebuttable presumption in respect of a particular relationship between the parties arises and the burden shifts to the defendant to prove that no such

990 *Ibid.*

991 [1990] 1 Q.B. 923.

992 *Ibid*, 967.

993 See *UCB Corporate Services Ltd v Williams* [2002] EWCA Civ 555; [2002] 3 F.C.R. 448.

994 See *Holyoake v Candy* [2017] EWHC 3397 (Ch),[405] (Nugee J).

influence was a factor. Examples of relationships to which this presumption applies are parent/guardian and child,[995] doctor and patient[996] and solicitor and client.[997] Given the exploration of the theme of informed consent and the valid analogy between the medical law regime and the likely manifestations of this practice under the space law regime, it is at least tenable that the relationship between customer and space operator could be viewed in law as similar to that of doctor and patient, particularly given the issues of information asymmetry previously discussed.

In keeping with the discussion on bombarding a customer with too much information potentially vitiating consent, the operator could potentially find themselves in a bind should they choose not to disclose a high volume of information in a bid to avoid this bombardment as, on one reading, this could also be seen as a material omission and, therefore, open the operator's position to a claim for actual undue influence should such information be so regarded. For this reason alone, the legislator should reconsider existing timeframes under Regulation 209(2) to firstly, attempt to ensure the information is as fully understood as possible in order to facilitate true consent, and secondly, allow for as high a volume of information as reasonably necessary to be disclosed so that operators do not run the risk of falling foul of undue influence in the actual sense by means of non-disclosure.

As previously called for regarding the informed consent regime, more involvement on the part of the CAA in an independent advisory capacity would be highly desirable as regards information pertaining to the transactions discussed. In addition to insulating a customer from potentially misleading or aggressive marketing strategies as regards information given at the consent stage, this would equally be in the operator's interest given that the provision of effective independent advice in delicate transactions can serve to negate the presumption of undue influence[998] although it is important to note that this is by no means guaranteed.

Whilst the foregoing has been largely concerned with the effect of the strict liability regime in the domestic context, attention should also be given to overarching international instruments and whether the United Kingdom's approach is consistent with them. As should be apparent, at least some of an operator's activity involving human passengers will, by definition, involve travelling below the stratosphere as defined by the Space Industry Act 2018. One

995 *Bainbrigge v Browne* (1881) 18 Ch. D. 188.
996 *Mitchell v Homfray* (1881) 8 Q.B.D. 587 (EWCA).
997 *Markham v Karsten* [2007] EWHC 1509 (Ch).
998 *Coles v Reynolds* [2020] EWHC 2151 (Ch), [2021] 1 P. & C.R. DG8.

further possible development in respect of space activities more generally is the possibility of hypersonic A-to-B travel. With this in mind, it is interesting to consider certain provisions of the Warsaw Convention of 1929 on the Unification of Certain Rules Relating to International Carriage by Air.[999] In particular, Article 17 on 'Death and Injury of Passengers' states:

> The carrier is liable for damage sustained in case of death or bodily injury of a passenger upon condition only that the accident which caused the death or injury took place on board the aircraft or in the course of any of the operations of embarking or disembarking.

As can be seen, there is no exemption for passengers from what is a strict liability regime of compensation in this instance. The only qualification is that the individual claiming the compensation was aboard an aircraft at the time the accident happened. There are two crucial questions regarding interpretation at this juncture. Firstly, to what extent can those covered by the informed consent rules in the United Kingdom be considered 'passengers'? Clearly not all of them, as has been found – crew members and other personnel may be required to sign a consent form. Secondly, to what degree can the kind of vehicle covered by the United Kingdom's space industry regime be considered an 'aircraft'? Vehicles covered by the rules will clearly spend a degree of time traveling through airspace. Not all of them could be considered 'aircraft'. However, when the prospect of hypersonic A-to-B travel is raised, could this not in some way be regarded as an aircraft? At least when it is travelling beneath the stratosphere or other relevant demarcation? As has already been written, other jurisdictions have informed consent regimes – the United States being the one most influential on the UK enactment and regulations. It is at least possible that further jurisdictions will follow a similar path.

Will this lead to the creation of a class of disenfranchised legal 'pseudo-passengers' in the event of accidents involving craft undertaking A-to-B travel? Whilst 'pleasure seekers' could be said to fall outside the definition of 'passengers', the original framers of the Warsaw Convention could not have intended its disapplication to a swathe of individuals solely on the basis that the 'aircraft' they were travelling on did not exclusively travel through the air. At the risk of sounding facetious, all aircraft spend some of their time on the ground and the Convention does not specify that it applies to only those in flight.

999 N538.

As previously called for and regardless of the merits of the Convention or any ambiguity, given the proliferation of domestic and commercial space industries worldwide coupled with the fact that human beings now regularly participate in space tourism activities, it is perhaps the time for a true international consensus to emerge on this matter. Given the famed international disagreements about such matters as the demarcation of airspace and outer space, attracting the agreements of all parties could prove a difficult task, particularly where such boundaries may be fixed domestically for policy reasons pertaining to national security or some other significant reason. Regardless of the probable difficulties, endeavours should be made so as to attempt to set out a uniformed approach and cover any possible gaps in the international order.

CHAPTER 8

Aspects of United Kingdom Telecommunications Law Relevant to Space Activities

The UK 2024 Space Regulatory Review described the electromagnetic spectrum as 'the lifeblood of space capabilities' and alluded to possible reform of this area to 'ensure equitable allocation and use' of 'frequencies in orbit, beyond orbit and around the moon' in addition to securing the United Kingdom's national interests and enabling competition.[1000] By way of completeness, the UK experience in respect of telecommunications law will be addressed here, at least insofar as it relates narrowly to what could be considered space activities. It is important to stress that this chapter does not represent a comprehensive analysis of UK telecommunications law, but seeks to address any aspects of it that overlap with any licenced activities under the Outer Space Act 1986 and Space Industry Act 2018. In addition, this chapter will seek to give an overview of the role of the United Kingdom in the formation of international telecommunications agreements insofar as they relate to the uses of outer space. A broader discussion of the rules pertaining to purely terrestrial activities is beyond the scope of this work.

The reality of satellite communication was predicted by the novelist Arthur C. Clarke in 1940's as being an efficient communication method in addition to avoiding problems with terrestrial transmissions.[1001] The post-war era of technological advancement and interest in the exploration of space soon led to discussions at the United Nations on such matters, culminating in General Assembly Resolution 1721 on equitable global access to satellite communications.[1002] The United States followed its own vision on such matters, proposing and creating COMSAT but reservations were expressed over this model by a number of states including the United Kingdom,[1003] particularly – but not limited to – the desire of the framers for privatisation and fears of what a United States monopoly would lead to as regards charging for access.[1004]

1000 N405, 17.
1001 N8, 283.
1002 (XVI) December 20, 1961.
1003 Francis Lyall, *Law and Space Telecommunications*, Dartmouth, 1989, 79. 'COMSAT' – 'Communications Satellite Corporation'.
1004 *Ibid,* 285–286.

 | DOI:10.1163/9789004732551_009

Pursuant to Resolution 1721,[1005] the Interim INTELSAT Agreement was entered into regarding satellite communications.[1006] Prior to its inception, matters relating to satellite communications were the preserve of individual states, often with private organisations prevailing over such matters.[1007] INTELSAT represented a departure from such practices. Known as the first Intergovernmental Satellite Organisation (ISO), there were 6 other signatories besides the United Kingdom. At the time, the United Kingdom was an early leader in matters of international communication due to its part-ownership of transatlantic cables and related investments.[1008] It was later an important financial contributor under the subsequent Special Agreement[1009] providing 8.4 percent of revenues based on its share of telecommunications traffic.[1010] Such funding was used to establish the early system infrastructure of this new venture.[1011] In 1971, arrangements were cemented and INTELSAT was formed.[1012] It is worthy of note that, whilst not frequently cited alongside the central space law treaties, the INTELSAT Agreement explicitly referred to the Outer Space Treaty in the preamble, considering specifically Article I, 'that outer space shall be used for the benefit and in the interests of all countries'.[1013] The United Kingdom is also a current member of the International Telecommunications Satellite Organisation which was established by

1005 N1009.

1006 Agreement establishing Interim Arrangements for a Global Commercial Communications Satellite System and Special Agreement, Washington, 20 August 1964; 514 UNTS 25; TIAS 5646; 15 UST 1705; 1966 UKTS 12; 3 ILM 805 (1964).

1007 For a detailed overview of the historical and commercial background of the creation of INTELSAT, see Patricia K McCormack, 'Intelsat: Pre and Post Private Equity Ownership' in Patricia McCormack, Murray J. Mechanick (eds), *The Transformation of Intergovernmental Satellite Organisations: Policy and Legal Perspectives*, Brill Niijhoff, 2013, 89: 'At the time of INTELSAT's creation, the prevailing economic rationale held that natural monopolies in the provision of public utilities were the most efficient. In virtually every country in the world, providers of telephony and telegraph services were either private monopolies, crown corporations, or, most commonly, government Ministries of Post, Telegraph and Telephone. This historical structure, in accord with the natural monopoly argument that contended it was more economically efficient to construct a single satellite network connecting different countries rather than building several competing satellite systems'.

1008 N1010, 75.

1009 See chapter 1.

1010 *Ibid.*

1011 *Ibid.*

1012 Agreement relating to the International Telecommunications Satellite Organization 'INTELSAT', Washington 20 August 1971; 1220 UNTS 21; TIAS 7532; 23 UST 3813; UKTS 1973 No. 80; Cmnd. 4799; ATS 1973 No. 6; 10 ILM 909 (1971).

1013 *Ibid*, 23.

the INTELSAT arrangements of 2000.[1014] The United Kingdom was also a founding member of EUTELSAT[1015] and an initial signatory to INMARSAT[1016] in 1976 regarding maritime satellite communications, even serving as the headquarters of the organisation.[1017] It was later expanded to include mobile and air communications.[1018] Like other international telecommunications bodies, INMARSAT was privatised and is presently a UK company.[1019] It is of interest to note that, while privatised, through the United Kingdom as the 'flag state' it is still under obligations arising from international public law for safety of life at sea.[1020]

At this juncture, it is pertinent to reflect on a fundamental divergence between the United Kingdom and the international order of space telecommunications. In the mid-1980's the United Kingdom and United States withdrew from UNESCO because of perceived overreaching in respect of international space broadcasting regulation.[1021] A report commissioned by several UNESCO members – which became known as the 'MacBride Report' – called for closer international oversight of state broadcasting in the interests of 'the 'democratisation' of communications, the strengthening of national media and the lessening of dependence on international news sources'.[1022] The United Kingdom and the United States subsequently resigned from UNESCO over what they perceived as unacceptable infringements in the implementation of the MacBride Report on the freedom of the press and information.[1023] This was followed by a refusal to assent to the 1982 Direct Broadcasting Principles in the UN General Assembly.[1024] Although not frequently cited alongside the 5 space

---

1014 Agreement relating to the International Telecommunications Satellite Organisation, 2001 UK Misc. 4, Cm 5092.

1015 Agreement on the Constitution of a Provisional European Telecommunications Satellite Organisation, Paris, 13 May 1977; UKTS 1990 No. 15; Cm. 956; Cmnd. 9069; *Space Law – Basic Legal Documents*, C.II.1.

1016 Convention on the International Maritime Satellite Organization (INMARSAT), London 3 September 1976; 1143 UNTS 105; TIAS 9605; 31 UST 1; UKTS 1979 No. 94; Cmnd. 6822; ATS 1979 No. 10; 15 ILM 1052 (1976).

1017 Headquarters Agreement between the Government of the United Kingdom of Great Britain and Northern Ireland and the International Maritime Satellite Organisation, London, 15 February 1980; 1203 UNTS 131; 1980 UKTS 44, Cmnd. 7917.

1018 INMARSAT Assembly, Sixth (Extraordinary) Session, January 1989. International Maritime Satellite Organization: Amendments to the Convention and Operating Agreement.

1019 N8, 300.

1020 *Ibid*, 301.

1021 N8, 330–331.

1022 *Ibid*, 330.

1023 *Ibid*, 331.

1024 N139.

treaties, the Direct Broadcasting Principles purport to apply to space activities. As Article 4 of the principles state: 'Activities in the field of international direct television broadcasting by satellite should be conducted in accordance with international law, including the Charter of the United Nations, the Treaty on Principles Governing the Activities of States in the Exploration and Use of Outer Space, including the Moon and Other Celestial Bodies, of 27 January 1967, the relevant provisions of the International Telecommunication Convention and its Radio Regulations and of international instruments relating to friendly relations and cooperation among States and to human rights'. Notwithstanding any political pressures from its international partners, the United Kingdom's rejection of the resolution could be indicative of where it views the boundary of its international obligations to lie as regards any future initiatives of this kind.

This development coincided with the United Kingdom's planned orbiting of two satellites in pursuance of its ambitions in direct broadcasting.[1025] One of these satellites was developed by Unisat, itself a creation of British Telecom, at the material time the United Kingdom's sole telephone operator,[1026] and both were to be launched by Ariane.[1027] There were also contemporaneous ambitions for further satellite launch and construction[1028] and the United Kingdom has maintained and developed its satellite ambitions consistently since. As of 2022, the United Kingdom's satellite infrastructure was the largest contributor to its space economy, with direct-to-home broadcasting making up to 45% of its income and contributing around £110 billion to the economy in general.[1029] It has also been estimated that, as of 2024, the United Kingdom is second only to the United States in terms of the number of registered orbiting satellites.[1030] The United Kingdom presently has a significant share of the Low Earth Orbit radio spectrum following the launch of 6 satellites by OneWeb in French Guiana.[1031] OneWeb later filed for Chapter 11 bankruptcy in the United States but was

---

1025 INTERIM REPORT REALITIES AND TENDENCIES IN EUROPEAN TELEVISION: PERSPECTIVES AND OPTIONS (Report from the Commission to the European Parliament), 127, para 80.
COM/1983/0229 final.

1026 *Ibid*, 127, para 81.

1027 *Ibid*, 127, para 82.

1028 *Ibid*, 127, para 87.

1029 House of Commons Science and Technology Committee, 'UK Space Strategy and Satellite Infrastructure; Second Report of session 2022–2023' HC 100, 4 November 2022, 10, <https://committees.parliament.uk/publications/31490/documents/176763/default/> accessed 17 June 2024.

1030 N405, 12–13.

1031 *Ibid*, 11.

subsequently purchased in part by the United Kingdom government[1032] who are now one of several shareholders following a merger with Eutelsat.[1033]

The United Kingdom deviates from a number of other jurisdictions domestically insofar as its national space legislation is largely silent on telecommunications matters such as spectrum allocation and management.[1034] Matters of spectrum management are handled by Ofcom – the UK office of communications[1035] to whom applicants for orbital operator licences are required to submit details of intended spectrum usage.[1036] In addition to powers to limit the number of licences issued regarding the use of the electro-magnetic spectrum generally[1037] Ofcom also has responsibility for regulating satellite broadcasts in accordance with broadcast licences granted[1038] and ensuring that any such broadcasts are compliant with regulations of the International Telecommunications Union[1039] (ITU). Examples of where Ofcom set out parameters for spectrum usage in accordance with ITU Regulations and the ITU Broadcasting Regional Agreement 1984[1040] can be observed within its Interface Requirements[1041] which were, themselves, the United Kingdom government's means of expanding upon the implementation of EU Directive 2014/53.[1042] The influence

1032 *Ibid.*

1033 Eutelsat Group press release, 'EUTELSAT AND ONEWEB COMBINATION HERALDS NEW ERA IN SPACE CONNECTIVITY AS WORLD'S FIRST GEO-LEO OPERATOR', 28 September 2023, <https://www.eutelsat.com/en/news/press.html#/pressreleases/eutelsat-and-oneweb-combination-heralds-new-era-in-space-connectivity-as-worlds-first-geo-leo-operator-3276261> accessed 17 June 2024.

1034 See The United Kingdom Civil Aviation Authority, 'SRG2229 Radio Frequency / Spectrum Question Set', 1 November 2021, <https://www.caa.co.uk/publication/download/21873> accessed 14 June 2024. This is a set of questions regarding radio frequencies of satellites which is to accompany applications for orbital operator licences.

1035 The Communications Act 2003, s3 (2)(a) and the Wireless Telegraphy Act 2006, s1(1). Ofcom is the UK's national administration for telecommunications matters designated as such by section 22 of the Communications Act 2003, pursuant to Article 6 (1) of the ITU Constitution.

1036 N18.

1037 See The Wireless Telegraphy (Limitation of Number of Licences) (Amendment) Order 2006, SI 2006 2786, Regulation 164.

1038 The Wireless Telegraphy Act 2006, s9A (2).

1039 *Ibid,* Section 8B (3)–(4), Schedule 2(6)(12).

1040 Final Acts of the Regional Administrative Conference for the Planning of VHF Sound Broadcasting (Region 1 and Part of Region 3) Geneva, 1984.

1041 Ofcom, 'UK Interface Requirement 2022', January 2018, <https://www.ofcom.org.uk/siteassets/resources/documents/spectrum/interface-requirements/ir_2022.pdf> accessed 17 June 2024.

1042 Directive 2014/53/EU of the European Parliament and of the Council of 16 April 2014 on the harmonisation of the laws of the Member States relating to the making available on the market of radio equipment and repealing Directive 1999/5/EC.

of EU law in respect of its telecommunications rules can be observed in other areas[1043] but it does not seem to substantially alter the core of the United Kingdom's regime, which has Ofcom at its heart as a 'primary space regulator'[1044] alongside the CAA. It is further responsible for licensing satellite earth stations under Parts 1 and 2 of the Wireless Telegraphy Act 2006, which 'can be on the ground or on aircraft or ships'.[1045] The licences granted by Ofcom in respect of satellite earth stations[1046] are for 'Permanent Earth Stations' (PES),[1047] 'Transportable Earth Stations' (TES),[1048] 'Earth Station Network'(ESN),[1049] 'Non-Geostationary Earth Stations' (Non-Geo),[1050] 'Non-Fixed Satellite Earth Stations' (Non-FSS),[1051] Receive-Only Earth Stations (ROES) and GNSS Repeaters.[1052]

1043 See, for example, SI 1997 2930, The Telecommunications (Licensing) Regulations 1997, s2.

1044 N405 26.

1045 Ofcom, 'Space Spectrum Strategy', 10 November 2022, 7, <https://www.ofcom.org.uk/siteassets/resources/documents/consultations/category-2-6-weeks/233841-space-spectrum-strategy/associated-documents/statement-space-spectrum-strategy.pdf> accessed 9 June 2024.

1046 Ofcom, 'Apply for a satellite earth station licence', 30 October 2023 < https://www.ofcom.org.uk/spectrum/space-and-satellites/earth-stations> accessed 19 June 2024.

1047 Defined by Ofcom as 'a satellite earth station operating from a permanent, specified location for the purpose of providing wireless telegraphy links with one or more geostationary satellites in certain frequency bands allocated to the fixed-satellite service. A PES is typically used to provide telephony and data backhaul, broadcast feeder links, private corporate networks and satellite telecommand and control.' (N1053).

1048 Defined by Ofcom as 'a satellite earth station operating from a specified location to a satellite in the fixed satellite service. TES operations are commonly associated with the broadcasting industry, where they are used to provide outside broadcast links either back to a studio or directly to a broadcasting satellite. Installations range from small fly-away terminals to large vehicles.' (N1053).

1049 An Earth Station Network Licence is defined by Ofcom as covering 'any number of earth station terminals operating in a network where traffic is routed via satellite to and from a hub or gateway earth station. Applications include residential and business broadband; point of sale communications; private corporate networks; and remote monitoring for the utilities industries.' (N1053).

1050 Defined by Ofcom as 'A non-geostationary earth station is a satellite earth station operating from a permanent, specified location for the purpose of providing wireless telegraphy links with one or more non-geostationary satellites in certain frequency bands allocated to the fixed-satellite service. They are used typically to provide backhaul for direct-to-consumer broadband services, broadband services to businesses and Internet of Things.' (N1053).

1051 Defined by Ofcom as 'A Non-Fixed Satellite Earth Station is a satellite earth station operating from a permanent, specified location for the purpose of providing wireless telegraphy links with one or more satellites in certain frequency bands not allocated to the fixed-satellite service. They are used typically for satellite telemetry and telecommand, as well as for backhauling data associated with the observation of the Earth and its weather.' (N1053).

1052 GNSS repeater equipment is defined by Ofcom as equipment that 'consists of an external antenna for the reception of the GNSS signal; an amplifier (with a restricted

Compliance with various dimensions of the ITU Radio Regulations[1053] is a required licence condition for almost all these operations,[1054] and this largely relates to the apparatus to be used under the auspices of the licence granted. PES licencees must comply with Article 21.14 regarding the elevation of their antennas, and Articles 21.8–21.15 regarding, *inter alia*, their power limits. Compliance is also ordered with Articles 5.503 and 5.35A regarding frequency allocation along with observation of ITU Recommendation ITU – RS.465[1055] on reference radiation patterns or ITU Recommendation ITU – RS.580-6[1056] on radiation diagrams where appropriate depending on the date the antenna in question was installed.[1057] Where the intended operations require international coordination with other governments or departments with Ofcom as per Article 9, Article 4.4 is engaged which prohibits Ofcom from assigning a frequency to a licencee unless such an assignment is conditional on that the licencee does not cause 'harmful interference' to other stations operating under ITU rules. 'Harmful interference' is defined within the Radio Regulations as: 'interference which endangers the functioning of a radionavigation service or of other safety services or seriously degrades, obstructs, or repeatedly interrupts a radiocommunication service operating in accordance with Radio Regulations'.[1058] The same Radio Regulations are incorporated as licence conditions for TES licences,[1059] Non-GEO licences[1060] and

maximum gain), connected via cabling to a second antenna inside a building. This re-radiates the GNSS signals inside a building allowing, within a limited distance of that transmit antenna, the continued operation of GNSS receivers.' (N1053).

1053 The International Telecommunications Union, Radio Regulations Articles, Edition of 2020, <https://www.itu.int/en/publications/ITU-R/Pages/publications.aspx?parent =R-REG-RR-2020&media=electronic> accessed 19 June 2024.

1054 The following information is taken from the various licence templates as published on the Ofcom site 'Apply for a satellite earth station licence' 30 October 2023 <https://www .ofcom.org.uk/spectrum/space-and-satellites/earth-stations> accessed 19 June 2024.

1055 The International Telecommunications Union, Recommendation S.465-6 (01/2010), Approved in 2010-01-23, <https://www.itu.int/rec/R-REC-S.465-6-201001-I/en> accessed 19 June 2024.

1056 The International Telecommunications Union, Recommendation ITU-R S.580-6, (01/2004), Approved in 2004–01–06, <https://www.itu.int/rec/R-REC-S.580-6-200401 -I/en> accessed 19 June 2024.

1057 Ofcom, Permanent Earth Station Licence Template, 3, <https://www-bau.ofcom.org.uk /siteassets/resources/documents/manage-your-licence/satellite-earth-stations/templa tes/permanent-earth-station-licence-template.pdf?v=328908> accessed 19 June 2024.

1058 N1060, Article 1.169

1059 Licence template issued by Ofcom pursuant to the Wireless Telegraphy Act 2006 for Transportable Earth Station Licences, <https://www-bau.ofcom.org.uk/siteassets/res ources/documents/manage-your-licence/satellite-earth-stations/templates/trans portable-earth-station-licence-template.pdf?v=328907> accessed 19 June 2024.

1060 Licence template issued by Ofcom pursuant to the Wireless Telegraphy Act 2006 for Non-Geostationary Earth Stations, <https://www-bau.ofcom.org.uk/siteassets

Non-FSS licences.[1061] Being of a markedly different operational character, ESN licences do not appear to require compliance with quite the specific ITU rules as PES and TES licences in respect of apparatus, but there are additional specific conditions, including those for the protection of radio astronomy and other geostationary satellites and earth stations,[1062] and observance of Articles 21–22 of the Radio Regulations is still a requirement where necessary.[1063] No specific ITU rules are incorporated into grants for recognised spectrum access as regards ROES,[1064] and GNSS Repeater licences,[1065] presumably since they are not broadcasting operations and therefore fall outside of international regulation (although GNSS Repeater Licences are issued subject to Article 4.4 of the Radio Regulations on non-interference). With the exception of ROES spectrum grants, all permissions are subject to the provisions of the EU Radio Equipment Directive.[1066] Compliance with interface requirements is also necessary in some cases[1067] in addition to further licensing requirements under the Broadcasting Act 1990.[1068] Licences for satellite operations[1069] are also subject to Ofcom's general licensing requirements under the Wireless Telegraphy Act.[1070] As a basic condition, all licencees are also bound to follow the

/resources/documents/manage-your-licence/satellite-earth-stations/templates/non-geostationary-earth-station-licence-template.pdf?v=328909> accessed 19 June 2024.

1061 Licence template issued by Ofcom pursuant to the Wireless Telegraphy Act 2006 for Non-Fixed Satellite Earth Stations, <https://www.ofcom.org.uk/siteassets/resources/documents/manage-your-licence/satellite-earth-stations/templates/non-fixed-satellite-earth-station-licence-template.pdf?v=328910> accessed 19 June 2024.

1062 Licence template issued by Ofcom pursuant to the Wireless Telegraphy Act 2006 for Earth Station Networks, para 3.5–3.8, <https://www.ofcom.org.uk/siteassets/resources/documents/manage-your-licence/satellite-earth-stations/templates/esn-licence-template.pdf?v=328754> accessed 19 June 2024.

1063 *Ibid*, 3.7(p), 3.8(q).

1064 Notification of RECOGNISED SPECTRUM ACCESS (RSA) grant by the Office of Communications ('Ofcom') under section 18 of the Wireless Telegraphy Act 2006 ('the Act') template issued by Ofcom, <https://www.ofcom.org.uk/spectrum/space-and-satellites/rsa-earth-stations> accessed 19 June 2024.

1065 Licence template issued by Ofcom pursuant to the Wireless Telegraphy Act 2006 for GNSS Repeater licences <https://www.ofcom.org.uk/siteassets/resources/documents/manage-your-licence/satellite-earth-stations/templates/gnss-repeater-licence-template.pdf?v=328912> accessed 19 June 2024.

1066 N1049.

1067 See, for example, UK Interface Requirement (IR) 2089 for Global Navigation Satellite Systems Repeaters.

1068 This is a requirement for certain PES licences.

1069 above 10Watts E.I.R.P. transmit power.

1070 Ofcom, 'Booklet OfW 597 Wireless Telegraphy Licence Conditions', 20 January 2023, <https://www.ofcom.org.uk/siteassets/resources/documents/spectrum/emf/emf-glc-licence-conditions-booklet.pdf?v=325992> accessed 20 June 2024.

International Commission on Non-Ionizing Radiation Protection Guidelines on Limiting Exposure to Electro-Magnetic Fields[1071] when using the spectrum for matters of public health protection. Ofcom sets out separate guidance on its enforcement role as regards electro-magnetic fields in a separate document.[1072]

PES, Non-FSS and Non-Geo licences are all considered 'site' or 'shell' licences for earth stations. This is defined by Ofcom as meaning that 'the licence can incorporate any number of earth stations that are located within 500 metres of a nominated centre point for the licence'[1073] and similar rules apply to ROES licences.[1074]

In addition to issuing licences, Ofcom has enforcement powers and can give notices under section 9A of the Wireless Telegraphy Act 2006 and failure to surrender a revoked licence can have criminal consequences.[1075] Schedule 1 of the Act prescribes the rules on revocation of licences and sets out the necessary procedures while Schedule 3 details the 'fixed penalty' regime under the Act. A 'fixed penalty' notice has the same meaning and legal effect as fixed penalties elsewhere within the jurisdiction. As Schedule 3(2)(3) states: "fixed penalty notice' means a notice offering the opportunity of the discharge of any liability to conviction of the offence to which the notice relates by payment of a fixed penalty in accordance with this Schedule'. It is of interest to observe that fixed penalty notices are not an enforcement tool under either the Space Industry Act or subsequent Regulations, and it is not immediately clear as to why this method has not been included. One suggestion may be that, since fixed penalty notices are typically used for less serious offences,[1076] they may not be commensurate with the gravity of likely offences under the Space Industry legislation where the scale of harm could be much greater. The fixed

1071 ICNIRP Guidelines For Limiting Exposure to Electromagnetic Fields (100 KHZ TO 300 GHZ) Health Phys 118(5): 483–524, 2020, <https://www.icnirp.org/cms/upload/publications/ICNIRPrfgdl2020.pdf> accessed 20 June 2024.

1072 Ofcom, 'Guidance on EMF Compliance and Enforcement' 18 May 2021 <https://www.ofcom.org.uk/siteassets/resources/documents/spectrum/emf/guidance-emf-compliance-enforcement.pdf?v=326016> accessed 20 June 2024.

1073 N1053.

1074 *Ibid.*

1075 N1045, s11.

1076 Some examples are minor traffic offences- see Part 3 of the Road Traffic Offenders Act 1998 and incorrect disposal of certain waste products per the Environmental Protection Act 1990 s33(1)(a) – s.33ZA where a penalty of £150 – £400 can be levied in some circumstances. Fixed penalty notices also played a significant role during the Coronavirus Pandemic to enforce restrictions, see the (since repealed) Health Protection (Coronavirus, Restrictions) (Self-Isolation) (England) Regulations 2020/1045, reg. 4.

penalty notice method referred to under the Wireless Telegraphy Act could also impact those undertaking licenced activities under the Space Industry Act. Section 9A of the Wireless Telegraphy Act gives Ofcom the power to issue fixed penalty notices to 'satellite uplinkers'. A satellite uplinker is defined within the Act as 'a person who operates satellite uplink apparatus', and 'satellite uplink apparatus' is defined as 'wireless telegraphy apparatus, the purpose of which is to emit, to one or more satellites, energy to which section 116(2) applies'.[1077] The 'energy' referred to is set out as 'electromagnetic energy of a frequency not exceeding 3,000 gigahertz that (a) serves for conveying messages, sound or visual images (whether or not the messages, sound or images are actually received by anyone), or for operating or controlling machinery or apparatus; or (b) is used in connection with determining position, bearing or distance, or for gaining information as to the presence, absence, position or motion of an object or of a class of objects'.[1078] Given that a satellite is, by definition, a 'space object' for the purpose of the Space Industry Act 2018, operation of a satellite should fall within the definition of 'space activities'. It should be noted, as outlined in Regulation 2(1), operation of a satellite could at least be partially covered by the further definition of 'spaceflight activities'. These are defined as, besides launching a launch vehicle or carrier aircraft, '(i) to carry a spaceflight participant, (ii) to carry a payload until its release or separation from the launch vehicle, (iii) to carry out suborbital activities, or (iv) to return to earth and complete its flight, including orbital activities only in so far as they are necessary to complete such an assignment;'. The activities of carrying a payload until separation or returning a space object could fall within section 116(2) as regards the transmission of any associated telemetry data for the operation of a space object whilst in orbit, which could include payload separation. Moving past the separation phase, the role of a satellite is to orbit a celestial body in the performance of its designated functions. Regulation 101(1) places additional duties on an operator as regards a launch vehicle that has reached a stable orbit, which include monitoring its trajectory and orbital parameters, in addition to taking 'reasonable steps to—(i) avoid the launch vehicle interfering with the space activities of other persons in the peaceful exploration and use of outer space, (ii) limit or prevent major accident hazards to the health, safety and property of persons arising from the launch vehicle in orbit, and (iii) prevent contamination of outer space arising from the launch vehicle in orbit or adverse changes in the environment of the earth from that vehicle in orbit, and (d) take any other action necessary to carry out the operator's

1077 N1045, s115(1).

1078 N1045, s116(2).

spaceflight activities safely'. Notable by its absence here, is any reference to a satellite itself, the Regulation focusing exclusively on 'launch vehicles'. Clearly, a satellite in orbit could cause similar problems to those the regulation is seeking to prevent. A 'launch vehicle' is defined within the Regulations as '(a) a craft to which section 1(5) applies and the component parts of that craft, or(b) a space object(14) which is a vehicle and the component parts of that vehicle that is used for the purpose of the proposed spaceflight activities or the operator's spaceflight activities, as applicable, but does not include a payload carried by the launch vehicle'.[1079] Crucially, then, a satellite itself is effectively reduced to a mere 'payload' within the regulations, to which the duties under Regulation 101(1) do not apply.

In spite of the fact that the Space Industry Act and Regulations do not make extensive provision for satellite operation beyond orbital insertion and a degree of monitoring thereafter, the regulatory spheres of Ofcom and the CAA come into contact whenever an orbital operator licence is applied for under the Space Industry Act 2018. As part of this process, the applicant is required to answer Ofcom's 'Radio Frequency/Spectrum Question Set',[1080] requiring information on the orbital location along with the details of any relevant ground facilities. A separate 'technical question set' is also required, where detailed information about the proposed operation covering launch to orbit and disposal is required.[1081] Of particular interest is that orbital operator licences, unlike many other licence types, do not require a safety case to be prepared unless there are exceptional circumstances.[1082] Whilst the regulator has been keen to impose the duties under Regulation 101(1) upon operators of launch vehicles whilst in orbit, it seems peculiar that licences for orbital operations outside this definition do not generally have to provide a safety case given that the practical consequences and possible harm arising from both seem very similar. It may be that answers given in the technical question set are comprehensive enough to satisfy the regulator as regards aspects of safety, but it appears unusual that there is no law or regulation that directly

1079 N173, R2(1).

1080 The United Kingdom Civil Aviation Authority, 'Radio Frequency/Radio Question Set', November 2021, <https://www.caa.co.uk/publication/download/21873> accessed 26 September 2024.

1081 The United Kingdom Civil Aviation Authority, 'Technical Question Set', v2, 16 February 2024, <https://www.caa.co.uk/publication/download/19252> accessed 26 September 2024.

1082 The United Kingdom Civil Aviation Authority, 'Guidance for Orbital Operator Licence Applicants and Licencees', 2024 2nd edition, <https://www.caa.co.uk/publication/download/18909> accessed 26 September 2024.

mandates the safe operation of a satellite in the guise of Regulation 101(1). The guidance does though, remind licencees of their occurrence reporting duties – including occurrences of collision involving the space object- under the Space Industry Act 2018[1083] and that they are hence liable to the enforcement provisions of the Act. It also sets out that orbital operator licencees are responsible for obtaining adequate insurance cover and registering their space object as would be expected.[1084]

There is, therefore, some overlap between the Space Industry Act and Regulations with the telecommunications rules, specifically, the role of Ofcom in respect of frequency usage. There also appears to be a soft void between the two regimes into which actual satellite operations fall, however. The word 'satellite' cannot be found in any piece of space legislation in the United Kingdom, and only appears by virtue of open textured interpretation of terms such as 'payload', 'orbital operations', and, to some extent, 'space object'. The Space Industry Act and Regulations are very much designed, it appears, with launch infrastructure and operations in mind, without considering in much detail the ramifications of orbital activities such as those involving satellites. Clearly, matters relating to the 'flight' of such an object whilst in orbit should come within space specific legislation rather than that of Ofcom. That is, unless, there is an argument to say that controlling a space object in orbit via radiocommunications falls within Ofcom's remit by virtue of its medium. This does not seem satisfactory, and it is submitted that more robust provisions should be established in respect of conducting responsible satellite operations in orbit rather than leaving them on the periphery.

Ofcom is further responsible for 'administering UK satellite filings to the ITU',[1085] navigating these through directions from the Secretary of State in addition to ITU treaty rules, the ITU Constitution and Radio Regulations.[1086]

As mentioned, Ofcom also represents the United Kingdom at ITU discussions where it can enter into international agreements on its behalf and make decisions that ultimately bind it although there is constant supervision of Ofcom by the United Kingdom government and its officials often attend meetings alongside their representatives.[1087] UK policy, in this area, although

---

1083 *Ibid*, 25.

1084 *Ibid*, 27–28.

1085 Ofcom, 'Satellite filings; Satellite filing submissions', 17 January 2024, <https://www.ofcom.org.uk/spectrum/space-and-satellites/satellite-filings> accessed 16 October 2024.

1086 Ofcom, 'Space Spectrum Strategy- Consultation', 15 March 2022, 62 <https://www-bau.ofcom.org.uk/siteassets/resources/documents/consultations/category-2-6-weeks/233841-space-spectrum-strategy/associated-documents/secondary-documents/consultation-space-spectrum-refresh.pdf?v=327607> accessed 17 June 2024.

1087 Department for Culture, Media and Sport, 'The UK Spectrum Strategy; Delivering the best value from spectrum in the UK', 10 March 2014, para 4.13 <https://assets.publishing

proposed on the international stage by Ofcom, is ultimately agreed by the government beforehand[1088] and Ofcom also takes views from stakeholders such as satellite operators and those from the science community through its International Frequency Planning Working Groups.[1089] Ofcom further plays an important role in representing the United Kingdom at the World Radio Conferences.[1090] The body also maintains a presence in the defence realm in respect of radio frequency usage as regards the United Kingdom's 'Identification of Friend or Foe' and 'Secondary Surveillance Radar' faculties.[1091]

Further to the 2024 regulatory review referred to at the outset of this work,[1092] Ofcom will almost certainly be at the forefront of any such policy and regulatory discussions regarding spectrum and frequency usage in relation to space activities. Moreover, in tandem with the United Kingdom's new space legislation, the body is considering authorisations of radio use onboard rockets in addition to range control spectrum requirements which could also see Ofcom assume larger relevance in the context of the United Kingdom's regulatory launch infrastructure.[1093] It is also worth noting that Ofcom considers its existing powers sufficient to accommodate any spectrum requirements associated with other domestic space activities.[1094]

On this note, there are some legal issues that could be resolved in respect of Ofcom's practices. In 2016, the BBC, in response to Ofcom's Spectrum Strategy consultation, stated that the proliferation of 'paper satellites' and their associated filings renders the submission of complaints in respect of spectrum interference very difficult.[1095] They stated further, that the 'biggest problem for a user suffering interference is that the file name and notifying administration is often very different from the country of registration and name of the

---

.service.gov.uk/government/uploads/system/uploads/attachment_data/file/287994/UK_Spectrum_Strategy_FINAL.pdf> accessed 17 June 2024.

1088 *Ibid.*

1089 *Ibid*, 10.

1090 Ofcom, 'Space Spectrum Strategy Statement', 10 November 2022, para 1.10.

1091 The Ministry of Defence, The United Kingdom Civil Aviation Authority, Safety and Airspace Regulation, CAP761 'Operation of IFF/SSR interrogators in the UK: Planning principles and procedures' 4 January 2019, 12, <https://www.caa.co.uk/publication/download/13116> accessed 17 June 2024.

1092 N405, 17.

1093 Ofcom, 'Space Launch UK', 16 March 2023, <https://www.ofcom.org.uk/spectrum/space-and-satellites/space-launch-uk> accessed 19 June 2024.

1094 *Ibid.*

1095 BBC, 'BBC Response to Ofcom's Space Spectrum Strategy' 10 May 2016, 5–6, <https://www.ofcom.org.uk/siteassets/resources/documents/consultations/uncategorised/7813-space-spectrum-strategy/responses/bbc.pdf?v=212879> accessed 16 October 2024.

satellite operator. It is therefore difficult to ascertain which regulatory body has responsibility.' However, an uncompromising battle against 'paper satellites' has not been universally embraced. In their evidence to Ofcom's 2022 consultation on Space Spectrum strategy, O3b Ltd, a Medium Earth Orbit Satellite Operator (now owned and operated by SES[1096]), stated that it would be contrary to the ideals of innovation and growth to employ a blanket recognition of infant satellite filings as 'paper satellites'.[1097] Instead, it was argued, Ofcom should work with those filing to see that the projects 'come to fruition' whilst acknowledging that there is also an important need to defend against 'spectrum warehousing'.[1098]

By way of investigating present areas for future development regarding Ofcom's current regulatory approach, it is instructive to observe some of the contributions to the 2022 Space Spectrum Strategy Consultation[1099] from various stakeholders. Although there were numerous suggestions made for the new instrument, there were a number of core recurring themes.

As could be expected, the need for flexibility and adaptability within the regulatory framework was often stressed, particularly amongst industry stakeholders. Whilst it could be expected that a desire to avoid the costly administrative burden often associated with regulatory intervention would be the most frequent objection, there are a number of diverse views on this matter. The EMEA Satellite Operators Association submitted that regulatory flexibility should be a priority in light of emerging technologies such as 5G.[1100] Whilst regulatory certainty was applauded in general, there was also a desire for Ofcom to avoid 'stringent' applications of regulations at a national level so as not to drive satellite operators away from the United Kingdom and towards other

---

1096 SES, 'SES completes acquisition of 100% of o3b networks', 1 August 2016, <https://www.ses.com/press-release/ses-completes-acquisition-100-o3b-networks> accessed 21 June 2024.

1097 Response of o3b to Ofcom's Consultation on Space Spectrum Strategy, 10 June 2016, 4, <https://www.ofcom.org.uk/siteassets/resources/documents/consultations/uncategorised/7813-space-spectrum-strategy/responses/o3b.pdf> accessed 21 June 2024.

1098 *Ibid.* Note, there is due to be a consultation on satellite filings in the 3rd quarter of 2024, see 'Ofcom's Plan of Work, 2024–2025, 26 March 2024, 44, <https://www.ofcom.org.uk/siteassets/resources/documents/consultations/category-2-6-weeks/273274---ofcoms-proposed-plan-of-work-for-2024-25/associated-documents/statement-plan-of-work-2024-25.pdf> accessed 21 June 2024.

1099 N1094.

1100 EMEA Satellite Operators Association ESOA Responses to Ofcom's Consultation on Space Spectrum Strategy, 10 May 2016, 7, <https://www.ofcom.org.uk/siteassets/resources/documents/consultations/uncategorised/7813-space-spectrum-strategy/responses/esoa.pdf> accessed 21 June 2024.

international competitors with less restrictive regulatory environments.[1101] It was also suggested that Ofcom's present satellite filing rules require considerably more detail than is presently required under ITU regulations which could also result in a similar drag factor.[1102] This position was also articulated by SES[1103] who considered it a greater threat to UK satellite operations than that posed by 'paper satellites'.[1104] A practical appeal was also raised in respect of the details required for satellite filings in respect of Low Earth Orbit operations, particularly the need for orbital tolerances 'taking into account the natural variation of orbits over time due to space weather and trace atmosphere combined with the reality of many small NGSO (Non-geostationary orbit) satellites not having propulsive orbit-raising capabilities and instead operating in an ever- decreasing altitude until disposal'.[1105]

Regulatory flexibility and fair spectrum allocations were also regarded as crucial for emergency and disaster relief functions that satellite communications can provide, and a desire for such considerations to be adequately balanced against matters of interference was expressed.[1106] There were also concerns that overregulation could lead to confusion or 'limitation' within the market.[1107] Although the attitude across industry to additional regulation was generally hostile, there was also some support for some additional licence conditions that were being proposed at the time by Ofcom which would help police harmful interference from NGSO downlinks.[1108] Individual licensing in respect of the 'Internet of Things' was met with considerable hostility on

1101 *Ibid*, 9–10. See also the response of Arqiva, 24 May 2022, 2, <https://www.ofcom.org.uk/siteassets/resources/documents/consultations/category-2-6-weeks/233841-space-spectrum-strategy/responses/arqiva> accessed 21 June 2024.

1102 *Ibid*.

1103 SES response to Ofcom's Consultation on Space Spectrum Strategy, 10 May 2016, 4, <https://www.ofcom.org.uk/siteassets/resources/documents/consultations/uncategorised/7813-space-spectrum-strategy/responses/ses.pdf> accessed 21 June 2024.

1104 *Ibid*, 5.

1105 Kepler Communications, Response to Ofcom's Consultation on Space Spectrum Strategy, 10 November 2022, 7, <https://www.ofcom.org.uk/siteassets/resources/documents/consultations/category-2-6-weeks/233841-space-spectrum-strategy/responses/kepler-communications> accessed 21 June 2024.

1106 Access Partnership's response to Ofcom's Consultation on Space Spectrum Strategy, 10 November 2022, 4, <https://www.ofcom.org.uk/siteassets/resources/documents/consultations/category-2-6-weeks/233841-space-spectrum-strategy/responses/access-partnership> 21 June 2024.

1107 Arqiva, Response to Ofcom's Consultation on Space Spectrum Strategy, 24 May 2022, 3, <https://www.ofcom.org.uk/siteassets/resources/documents/consultations/category-2-6-weeks/233841-space-spectrum-strategy/responses/arqiva> accessed 21 June 2024.

1108 *Ibid*, 4.

both technical grounds and the desire to avoid any arising disadvantages to users.[1109] It should be pointed out that praise was given to the satellite licensing system in general from academic quarters[1110] and OneWeb even advocated expansion of the present licensing regime to cover exempt equipment albeit in a way that would not be detrimental to existing licencees.[1111]

Another key theme was that of sustainability, with a number of views expressed as to how effective spectrum management could serve this end. There was a desire to see reform of the licensing regime at both the national and supranational levels in respect of the specific requirements of In-Orbit Servicing (such as Active Debris Removal) which necessitates fluid spectrum usage owing to the need to transcend various orbits.[1112] Owing to the relative infancy of this industry and the advantages it offers in respect of sustainability, adequate support for spectrum access was stated to be of specific importance.[1113] The sustainability advantages for the space environment of such reforms was also championed by CONFERS, the Consortium for the Execution of Rendezvous and Servicing, stressing the benefits of such practices for space debris removal.[1114] These were also detailed at length by the Global Satellite Operators Association who further encouraged Ofcom to prioritise spectrum access in this area.[1115] Inmarsat also suggested that licence conditions

1109 Lacuna Space Ltd, Response to Ofcom's Consultation on Space Spectrum Strategy, 10 November 2022, 2, <https://www.ofcom.org.uk/siteassets/resources/documents/consultations/category-2-6-weeks/233841-space-spectrum-strategy/responses/lacuna-space-ltd> accessed 21 June 2024.

1110 Northumbria University, Response to Ofcom's Consultation on Space Spectrum Strategy, 11 November 2022, 4, <https://www.ofcom.org.uk/siteassets/resources/documents/consultations/category-2-6-weeks/233841-space-spectrum-strategy/responses/northumbria-university> accessed 21 June 2024.

1111 OneWeb, Response to Ofcom's Consultation on Space Spectrum Strategy, 10 November 2022, 1, <https://www.ofcom.org.uk/siteassets/resources/documents/consultations/category-2-6-weeks/233841-space-spectrum-strategy/responses/oneweb> accessed 21 June 2024.

1112 ClearSpace Today Ltd, Response to Ofcom's Consultation on Space Spectrum Strategy, 10 November 2022, 1, <https://www.ofcom.org.uk/siteassets/resources/documents/consultations/category-2-6-weeks/233841-space-spectrum-strategy/responses/clearspace-today-ltd> accessed 21 June 2024.

1113 *Ibid.*

1114 The Consortium for the Execution of Rendezvous and Servicing, Response to Ofcom's Consultation on Space Spectrum Strategy, 6 June 2022, 1–2, <https://www.ofcom.org.uk/siteassets/resources/documents/consultations/category-2-6-weeks/233841-space-spectrum-strategy/responses/confers> accessed 16 October 2024.

1115 Global Satellite Operators Association, Response to Ofcom's Consultation on Space Spectrum Strategy, 11 November 2022, 7, <https://www.ofcom.org.uk/siteassets/resources/documents/consultations/category-2-6-weeks/233841-space-spectrum-strategy/responses/global-satellite-operators-association> accessed 21 June 2024.

on matters of sustainability should be introduced to address space debris,[1116] a position also shared by TechUK.[1117] A further, particularly forward thinking and innovative, intervention came from the Space Energy Initiative, who proposed that Ofcom begin investigating spectrum allocation for Space Based Solar Power operations including the possibility of 'experimental' and 'developmental' licence types for such ventures.[1118] In respect of dark and quiet skies, the Royal Astronomical Society welcomed Ofcom's suggested power limit on satellite downlink transmissions to avoid interference with astronomy operations, and, further, urged the body to examine the agreement between the *Bundesnetzagentur* (the German federal communications agency) and Starlink which seeks to minimise the impact of the transmissions from the latter on analogous operations in Germany.[1119]

In a broader sense, regulatory integration between the CAA and Ofcom on spectrum access and orbital debris was suggested firmly by Lockheed Martin who proposed an 'accelerated discussion' between the two bodies on this topic.[1120] Closer alignment of the spectrum strategy with other space strategies was also advocated by Northumbria University.[1121] Ofcom was also advised to work more closely with other regulators as regards dissuading irresponsible uses of outer space by certain satellite operators.[1122]

1116 Inmarsat, Response to the Ofcom Space Spectrum Strategy 24 May 2022, 1, < https://www.ofcom.org.uk/siteassets/resources/documents/consultations/category-2-6-weeks/233841-space-spectrum-strategy/responses/inmarsat> accessed 21 June 2024.

1117 TechUk, Response to Ofcom's Consultation on Space Spectrum Strategy, 10 November 2022, 3, <https://www.ofcom.org.uk/siteassets/resources/documents/consultations/category-2-6-weeks/233841-space-spectrum-strategy/responses/techuk> accessed 16 October 2024.

1118 The Space Energy Initiative, Response to Ofcom's Consultation on Space Spectrum Strategy, 11 November 2022, 2, <https://www.ofcom.org.uk/siteassets/resources/documents/consultations/category-2-6-weeks/233841-space-spectrum-strategy/responses/space-energy-initiative> accessed 21 June 2024.

1119 Royal Astronomical Society, Response to Ofcom's Consultation on Space Spectrum Strategy, 11 November 2022, 3, <https://www.ofcom.org.uk/siteassets/resources/documents/consultations/category-2-6-weeks/233841-space-spectrum-strategy/responses/royal-astronomical-society> accessed 16 October 2024. For a very comprehensive legislative motion in respect of dark skies generally, see South Africa's Astronomy Geographic Advantage Act, 2007, No. 21 of 2007, <https://www.unoosa.org/documents/pdf/spacelaw/national/safrica/Act21-2007E.pdf> accessed 7 March 2025.

1120 Lockheed Martin, Response to Ofcom's Consultation on Space Spectrum Strategy, 11 November 2022, 2, <https://www.ofcom.org.uk/siteassets/resources/documents/consultations/category-2-6-weeks/233841-space-spectrum-strategy/responses/lockheed-martin> accessed 21 June 2024.

1121 N118, 1.

1122 N1119, 1.

Increasing spectrum access was also a recurring theme. Desire to see regulations enacted to facilitate this was set out by Eutelsat in response to new satellite operations and the ITU's identification of the 51.4–52.4GHz band for Fixed Satellite Services.[1123] Eutelsat further stated that 'A regulatory ecosystem facilitating the access to the Q/V band is essential for the new generation of high throughput satellites.'[1124] There was also a desire to see stronger and coordinated action on interference to EESS (Earth Exploration Satellite Services) sensors on board weather satellites by the Met Office on the basis of ITU recommendations.[1125] SpaceX also advocated for increased spectrum access, also arguing for 'self-coordinated light-licensing for higher-frequency satellite gateway earth stations and inter-service coordination' in addition to "Light-touch' NGSO-NGSO spectrum sharing policies that incentivize private, operator-to-operator coordination on a good faith, timely basis, and reward efficiency, without the need for direct regulator intervention'.[1126] Ofcom was also criticised by one respondent for not prioritising disaster and emergency situations effectively, the justification apparently being that 'satellite systems already have available bandwidth for this purpose.'[1127] This position was shared by SpaceX.[1128]

Whilst criticism was levelled in other areas, Ofcom's international role was met with considerable praise. As regards the prevention of harmful interference, there was broad commendation for Ofcom's efforts on the world stage in addition to the ITU regulatory structure, which was, in one case at least, regarded as effective at keeping interference at a manageable level.[1129] Various stakeholders encouraged the body to support certain ITU initiatives that would

1123 Eutelsat, Response to Ofcom's Consultation on Space Spectrum Strategy, 11 November 2022, 1, <https://www.ofcom.org.uk/siteassets/resources/documents/consultations/category-2-6-weeks/233841-space-spectrum-strategy/responses/eutelsat> accessed 21 June 2024.

1124 *Ibid.*

1125 The Met Office, Response to Ofcom's Consultation on Space Spectrum Strategy, 11 November 2022, 3, <https://www.ofcom.org.uk/siteassets/resources/documents/consultations/category-2-6-weeks/233841-space-spectrum-strategy/responses/met-office> accessed 21 June 2024.

1126 SpaceX, Response to Ofcom's Consultation on Space Spectrum Strategy, 11 November 2022, 2, <https://www.ofcom.org.uk/siteassets/resources/documents/consultations/category-2-6-weeks/233841-space-spectrum-strategy/responses/spacex> accessed 21 June 2024.

1127 Methera, Response to Ofcom's Consultation on Space Spectrum Strategy, 11 November 2022, 2, <https://www.ofcom.org.uk/siteassets/resources/documents/consultations/category-2-6-weeks/233841-space-spectrum-strategy/responses/methera> accessed 21 June 2024.

1128 N117, 2.

1129 N1108, 10–11.

lead to increased competition internationally.[1130] The body was also urged to begin work on formulating regulations in respect of lunar operations in the wake of the Artemis Accords and the forthcoming associated operations.[1131] The United Kingdom Space Agency also advised that a proactive stance on regulation in general was necessary, given that 'updating international radio regulations can take many years'.[1132]

Like many governmental and departmental bodies, Ofcom must manage a range of competing demands. The proliferation of private space activities along with rapid technological advancements in satellite broadcasting and the ever-present need to balance regulatory flexibility and legal certainty presents a serious challenge. Whether or not the present legal regime in respect of telecommunications is robust enough to cope with contemporary space telecommunications is certainly questionable. Although issues such as 'paper satellites' and frequency allocation are certainly nothing new, the Wireless Telegraphy Act 2006 was created at a time when no solid ambitions for a UK space industry existed; space sustainability and radio transmissions from sub-orbital rockets were far from the legislative agenda.

Coupled with the fact that other jurisdictions make specific provision for ITU Regulations within their own space legislation, perhaps the time has come for the United Kingdom to legislate specifically on the matter of space telecommunications. Rather than adding to the existing body of rules, instead such an instrument could serve to consolidate existing provisions. The licensing regime for spectrum usage could be streamlined with particular attention paid to transparency and clarity as per the feedback from the Space Spectrum Strategy consultation. As has been uncovered within this chapter, there are a multitude of different rules and standards weaved throughout the licensing regime, which may or may not apply depending on the individual applicant. A consolidation Act would be an effective way of keeping these important strands together, ensuring greater cohesiveness and ease of use for operators, applicants and other potential stakeholders.

1130 See the response of Amazon to the Consultation on Space Spectrum Strategy as regards NGSO Earth Stations, 10 November 2022, 2, <https://www.ofcom.org.uk/siteassets/resources/documents/consultations/category-2-6-weeks/233841-space-spectrum-strategy/responses/amazon> accessed 21 June 2024. See also the encouragement of Ofcom to implement ECC/DEC (05)01 as regards the 28 GHz band at page 9.

1131 N1118, 2.

1132 The United Kingdom Space Agency, Response to Ofcom's Consultation on Space Spectrum Strategy, 11 November 2022, 6, <https://www.ofcom.org.uk/siteassets/resources/documents/consultations/category-2-6-weeks/233841-space-spectrum-strategy/responses/uk-space-agency-and-beis> accessed 21 June 2024.

As evidence submitted to the Space Spectrum Consultation indicates, this is a very rapidly changing area, with new innovations constantly materialising;[1133] a rigid Act of Parliament may not be the most suitable instrument to ensure effective regulation. Regulation falling behind technological development is almost inevitable, and this is why a proactive approach must be considered at all times when governing this area. Space telecommunications is but one part of Ofcom's remit.[1134] As discussed, it also has responsibility for a number of other important functions as per the Communications Act 2003. Consideration should be given to whether or not a separate body for space telecommunications should be created. Such a body could keep relevant developments under review and, like Ofcom, be empowered to create regulations in response to the rapidly changing space environment.

Although many of the suggestions made by stakeholders in response to the Space Strategy Consultation may indeed have been heeded, there is little evidence to suggest that important matters such as those relating to sustainability have been implemented at the licensing level to any great extent. As far as can be seen, there has been no significant legislative action taken by Ofcom in respect of any of the broad areas of concern that emerged through the consultation process. There is, however, a set of draft regulations which have been prepared in respect of 'spectrum auctioning' in the 26–40 Ghz bands.[1135] At 134 sections and 7 schedules, these would represent a dramatic legislative development. Whilst the legislative impetus is sure to be well-intended, it is difficult to understand why some of the other pressing- and clearly important- concerns raised by stakeholders have not been addressed to anything like this extent. On this note, whilst the actions of Ofcom are clearly well-intentioned, consideration should be given to whether this will be enough to cope with the increasing demands of an ever-more complex space environment.

1133 Space Based Solar Power, for just one example.

1134 Other numerous responsibilities include upholding broadcasting standards, internet usage, ground-based telecommunications and duties connected to the postal service, see Ofcom, 'Ofcom's Plan of Work 2024/2025, 26 March 2024 <https://www.ofcom.org.uk/siteassets/resources/documents/consultations/category-2-6-weeks/273274---ofcoms-proposed-plan-of-work-for-2024-25/associated-documents/statement-plan-of-work-2024-25.pdf> accessed 21 June 2024.

1135 The Draft Electronic Communications Wireless Telegraphy (Licence Award) Regulations [2024], <https://www.ofcom.org.uk/siteassets/resources/documents/consultations/category-2-6-weeks/285288-proposals-to-make-auction-regulations-for-the-mmwave-award/associated-documents/annex-5-draft-wireless-telegraphy-licence-award-regulations-2024.pdf> accessed 21 June 2024.

CHAPTER 9

Sustainability

The Space Industry Act rightly recognises the need to protect the environments of earth and space. At least to some extent, there are efforts made to ensure the associated environmental impact of the industry is minimised. Naturally, there are competing interests at play here. Operators are likely to want as little regulation as possible for reasons of efficiency and economic considerations whilst duties of public protection and safety will be the concern of the Regulator notwithstanding its growth duty. Space activities, whilst being supported by an adequate level of legal infrastructure and facilitated in a manner that is as safe as possible, must also be sustainable.

Before a closer examination of the way in which the Space Industry Act's regime seeks to establish at least some measure of environmental protection, it is instructive to determine what 'sustainability' in this context means. The well-known definition of 'sustainable development' from the Brundtland Report[1136] is 'Development that meets the needs of the present without compromising the ability of future generations to meet their own needs.' A good working definition of regulation being 'the employment of legal instruments for the implementation of social-economic policy objectives'.[1137]

Whilst there is no equivalency of this provision within the UK's space instruments, the Space Industry Act itself states:

> The Regulator must exercise the Regulator's functions under this Act in the way that the Regulator thinks best calculated to take into account … (e) any environmental objectives set by the Secretary of State.[1138]

Although somewhat opaque in respect of what these 'environmental objectives' are, there is at least a foundation here which could have the effect of rendering operators accountable should they act in flagrant disregard of the government's environmental objectives.

1136 The United Nations, World Commission on Environment and Development, *Our Common Future*, (OUP 1987), commonly referred to as the 'Brundtland Report'.

1137 Johan den Hertog, 'Review of Economic Theories of Regulation', Utrecht School of Economics, Discussion Paper Series 10–18 (Tjalling C. Koopmans Research Institute).

1138 N127, s2(2).

 | DOI:10.1163/9789004732551_010

More directly, section 11 (2) of the Space Industry Act 2018 makes the grant of all spaceport and launch operator licences contingent upon the submission of an 'assessment of environmental effects' (AEE). This device represents, if not the environmental teeth of the instrument, then at least the gateway to stronger environmental control by the Regulator.

Under section 11 (3) such an assessment is defined as:

> (a) in relation to a spaceport licence, ... an assessment of the effects that launches of spacecraft or carrier aircraft from the spaceport in question, or launches of spacecraft from carrier aircraft launched from the spaceport, are expected to have on the environment;

and

> (b) in relation to an operator licence authorising launches of spacecraft or carrier aircraft, means an assessment of the effects that those launches are expected to have on the environment.

The actual muscle of the AEE comes from the fact that in deciding whether to approve a licence application or impose conditions, under section 11 (5):

> The Regulator must take into account the assessment of environmental effects.

In theory, if from the AEE it appears that an unacceptable level of environmental harm could arise, under Schedule 2(14)(a) the Regulator could impose:

> Conditions requiring the licencee to conduct the licencee's activities in such a way as—(a) to prevent the contamination of outer space or adverse changes in the environment of the earth.

At the time of writing, this provision has not yet been activated. As will be discussed later, however, a highly praiseworthy AEE was produced by Virgin Orbit in respect of their launch in early 2023. The operator had clearly taken its responsibility seriously in this regard and produced a very comprehensive report. Other than the official guidance, however, there is no set-form which such reports or assessments are required to take. In respect of the comprehensive nature of the Virgin Orbit report – and the clear effort it took to create – there is not necessarily a need under the regulations to submit a new AEE in respect of each new space activity. Under section 11(4) it is stated that:

> … the requirement imposed by subsection (2) to submit an assessment of environmental effects may be met by submitting—
> a. an equivalent assessment prepared previously in compliance with a requirement imposed by or under another enactment, or
> b. an assessment of environmental effects prepared in connection with a previous application.

This is only in instances where the Regulator would be satisfied that no material change had taken place since the previous space activity.

Whilst these measures are clearly important ones, there are some concerns. Not all applicants are required to submit environmental assessment documentation as will also be discussed later. There is also no indication of what is and isn't an acceptable level of environmental harm within this context. Although this could be deemed to sit outside the parameters of the Space Industry Act as essentially an enabling instrument setting out the basic framework for a licensing regime the subsequent regulations themselves are not forthcoming as regards what may or may not be an acceptable level of harm or risk within the context of such operations. Furthermore, the requirement for approval from the Secretary of State is a very broad discretionary hurdle, particularly when it is considered that no specific requirements are put forward as to what this may look like or what may be regarded as a red light in the context of approval being sought.

In respect of operator types who are required to submit an AEE, launch operator or spaceport licences are contingent upon such a submission,[1139] guidance for which can be found elsewhere.[1140] These assessments can be part of a public consultation as was seen with the recent Virgin Orbit launch which makes for good transparency.[1141] However, in respect of other documents, Environmental Impact Assessments are not always publicly available as can be seen from

1139 Space Industry Act 2018, s11(2).

1140 The United Kingdom Civil Aviation Authority, 'CAP 2215: Guidance for the assessment of environmental effects' Guidance for the Assessment of Environmental Effects, 18, <https://assets.publishing.service.gov.uk/government/uploads/system/uploads/attachment_data/file/904454/guidance-for-the-assessment-of-environmental-effects..pdf> accessed 16 October 2024.

1141 The United Kingdom Civil Aviation Authority, Consultations, 'Virgin Orbit and Spaceport Cornwall Joint Assessment of Environmental Effects Public Consultation Responses' <https://consultations.caa.co.uk/corporate-communications/aee-consultation-virgin-orbit-spaceport-cornwall/> accessed 17 October 2024.

the submission of Prestwick Spaceport.[1142] The construction of spaceports has itself been the subject of legal challenge – the most high-profile example of this being the opposition to Spacehub Sutherland which resulted in litigation in the Court of Session.[1143] The case was argued on the basis that the wetlands designated for construction were protected by international treaty, but this claim failed. Another area for exploration for a future legislature could be the question of whether additional regulation is required for sea launches. Section 3(3) for example excludes 'an installation at sea that can be moved from place to place without major dismantling or modification' from the definition of a 'spaceport'.

It was stated further in the UK Spaceflight Regulatory Plenary virtual meeting of 16 March 2021[1144] that '(t)he spaceflight activity is deemed to commence at the launch of the launch vehicle, rather than when the ship carrying the vehicle leaves the port,'[1145] and further, that 'launch from a ship is subject to many variables that will be considered in such a situation. For example, laws of other countries are also likely to be relevant depending on factors such as the location of the ship, flag of the ship and nationality of the operator. In addition, other UK statutes may also apply to launch and other spaceflight activities from the sea, including the Aviation and Maritime Security Act 1990. It is the responsibility of potential applicants to familiarise themselves with any such statutes and to find out whether laws of other countries are relevant.'[1146]

By means of addressing the conundrum of 'installations at sea', it may be wiser to include such artefacts in the definition of 'spaceport' or to create a separate class of 'mobile sea-based spaceports'. Not all sea-going vessels can support a rocket launch and, of those that purportedly are, it would be prudent to require a safety assessment in similar terms to those required for land-based spaceports. As the statement within the plenary meeting holds, there are 'many variables', including potential conflict of law scenarios. For this reason it is submitted that a further degree of legal certainty would be welcome here.

1142 'Prestwick Spaceport Files Environmental Screening Report' (Prestwick Aerospace, 22 July 2021) <http://www.prestwickaerospace.com/prestwick-spaceport-files-environmental-screening-report/> accessed 25 November 2023. Not available at this address as of at least 16 October 2024.

1143 *The Highland Council v Wildland Ltd* (2021) CSOH 87 P901/20.

1144 Launch UK, UK Spaceflight Regulator Plenary, Virtual Meeting, 16 March 2021 <https://assets.publishing.service.gov.uk/media/606c3b5bd3bf7f4011bdb1b3/Plenary_-_Spaceflight_regulator_16_March.pdf> accessed 16 October 2024.

1145 *Ibid,* 6.

1146 *Ibid.*

Presently, sea-based launches are at least partially dealt with under Marine Licensing provisions under section 66(1) of the Marine and Coastal Access Act 2009[1147] which encompasses deposits of 'objects' or substances' within the sea /sea bed from vehicles loaded with such from within any part of the United Kingdom. The marine licensing process is similar in its ambit to the licensing processes in the space legislation. Section 69 of the 2009 Act states that the appropriate licensing authority must have regard to;

a. the need to protect the environment,

b. the need to protect human health,

c. the need to prevent interference with legitimate uses of the sea,

And such other matters as the authority thinks relevant.

It is worth noting that the Marine Management Organisation (MMO) has a track-record of licensing projects which would be considered hazardous or unusual – the Thames Tideway Tunnel, the Hinkley Point C Nuclear Power Station and the London Gateway Port are all examples of this.[1148] However, it seems incongruous that the Marine Management Organisation should have such an influential part of such a process that seems so far removed from their area of expertise. There has been at least one application made to the MMO for a licence[1149]- from Virgin Orbit- and it has been stressed that there will be close collaboration with the CAA on licensing matters 'to avoid duplication'.[1150] As can be seen from the recent Virgin Orbit launch, a 'hazard zone' was requested from the Marine Management Organisation for its operation involving the launch of a rocket from a carrier aircraft over the sea.[1151] The eventual licence issued referred only to the 'deposit of any substance' into the sea by Virgin Orbit as a result of their operations since this came within the remit of section 66 which, as outlined previously, covers such matters insofar as they apply to United Kingdom waters. They were ultimately granted the licence subject to a number of conditions[1152] and specifically instructed that the licence had to

1147 C23.

1148 See The United Kingdom Civil Aviation Authority, Space Launch and Orbit Group, Launch Session July 2022, 35, <https://www.caa.co.uk/media/frmhppj4/july-2022_launch.pdf> accessed 17 October 2024.

1149 *Ibid,* 39.

1150 *Ibid.*

1151 Case ref: MLA/2022/00134/1, Licence ref: L/2022/00477/1, Virgin Orbit Rocket Launch from Spaceport Cornwall.

1152 See the Application and Documents page at the Marine Management Organisation for details of this: <https://www.gov.uk/government/organisations/marine-management-organisation> accessed 17 October 2024.

be read in conjunction with 'the Space Industry Licence issued by the Civil Aviation Authority'.[1153]

As previously recorded, owing to the absence of any treatment of sea launches within the legislation it may be that such launches – in the environmental sense – come within the exclusive preserve of the Marine Management Organisation which may be incongruous with their overall remit.

In addition to the absence of any provisions in respect of sea launches, some other licence types do not require any form of environmental assessment – range control licences, for example, do not require any form of assessment to be submitted and, neither, it seems, do return operator licencees.[1154] Regarding return operator licencees, the published guidance implicitly states the potential for contamination of the earth's environment in respect of 'post-flight hazards':

> An example of a post-flight hazard could be discarded rocket stages that present a continuing hazard, even after they have returned to earth, e.g. if the stage is intact and there is a danger from any residual toxic, flammable or explosive substances or possible rupture of a pressure vessel. Similarly, if a part of the launch vehicle is to be recovered or made safe prior to processing for re-use, then the immediate risks of the initial recovery should be accounted for, especially where any risk is posed to third parties or persons who handle or move the part.[1155]

This may be because, in the case of return operators, it is intended that these licences cover launches from outside the United Kingdom and, therefore, does not involve an actual launch in the United Kingdom itself. Effectively, then, a launch could be conducted in a jurisdiction which has much lower environmental standards than the United Kingdom – and thus lower environmental standards for the operator to follow – and potentially cause greater than nominally acceptable levels of environmental harm to the territory of the United Kingdom on re-entry/return with impunity. If this is the position it does not seem comprehensive enough and although such operations may not occur for a number of years it must be addressed – return operators must be under the same obligations as other types of licencee as regards providing an Assessment of Environmental Effects.

1153 *Ibid.*

1154 Space Industry Act 2018 s11(1)(b).

1155 N192.

Regarding the content of the assessments themselves, there are no strict formal requirements as to what the assessment must contain, but the guidance documents state that the Town and Country Planning (Environmental Impact Assessment) Regulations 2017[1156] along with the Chartered Institute of Ecology and Environmental Management Ecological Impact Assessment Guidelines (EcIA) 2018 are examples of good practice. As regards the former, the list of items contained in Schedule 4 – 'Information for Inclusion in Environmental Statements'[1157] – are likely to be of interest to operators. Section 5 of Schedule 4 states that such information should include:

> A description of the likely significant effects of the development on the environment resulting from, inter alia:
>
> d. the construction and existence of the development, including, where relevant, demolition works;
>
> e. the use of natural resources, in particular land, soil, water and biodiversity, considering as far as possible the sustainable availability of these resources;
>
> f. the emission of pollutants, noise, vibration, light, heat and radiation, the creation of nuisances, and the disposal and recovery of waste;
>
> g. the risks to human health, cultural heritage or the environment (for example due to accidents or disasters);
>
> h. the cumulation of effects with other existing and/or approved projects, taking into account any existing environmental problems relating to areas of particular environmental importance likely to be affected or the use of natural resources;
>
> i. the impact of the project on climate (for example the nature and magnitude of greenhouse gas emissions) and the vulnerability of the project to climate change; [or]
>
> j. the technologies and the substances used.

Although these factors are oriented more towards the construction industry, there are some overlaps with launch operations. Clarity would be welcome as regards point (f) – how, for example, should an operator be required to

1156 SI 2017 No.571.

1157 Chartered Institute of Ecology and Environmental Management Ecological Impact Assessment Guidelines (EcIA) 2018, Version 1.2, Updated April 2022, <https://cieem.net/wp-content/uploads/2018/08/ECIA-Guidelines-2018-Terrestrial-Freshwater-Coastal-and-Marine-V1.2-April-22-Compressed.pdf> accessed 16 October 2024.

measure the impact of any such launch on climate and the potential vulnerability to climate change as the section requests? By what method is the quantification of 'greenhouse gases' to be determined? In the Virgin Orbit Assessment of Environmental Effects there was a range of guidance used for the assessment of greenhouse gases such as the Institute of Environmental Management and Assessment (IEMA) Guide, and the Environmental Impact Assessment Guide to Climate Change Resilience and Adaptation and the Whole life carbon assessment for the built environment.[1158] Whilst it is good to see a range of authoritative sources used for such calculations, some instruction as to a universally agreed standard in this regard, perhaps from the aviation industry would be helpful such as Regulation 18(1) of The Greenhouse Gas Emissions Trading Scheme Order 2020 which states that one 'allowance' is 'an allowance to emit 1 tonne of carbon dioxide equivalent'.[1159] Assuming this amount has not been arrived at arbitrarily, it could then be used to determine the quantifiable environmental impact and allow for consistency across the range of assessments submitted from different operators. In respect of the Climate Assessment undertaken by Virgin Orbit, emissions coming from the carrier aircraft were apparently not considered since this, in the view of those compiling the assessment, would come under activities already licenced at the aerodrome,[1160] specifically, that:

> being a horizontal launch operation utilising a relatively standard Boeing 747 as a carrier aircraft, a number of the activities that form the complete sequence pre-launch, launch, and post-launch fall under existing licenced activities already carried out at CAN (Cornwall Airport Newquay). Those activities that can already be undertaken at CAN or in the appropriate airspace under existing licences have been scoped out of the AEE. As such, this assessment focuses on specific spaceflight operations only. It will exclude embodied carbon in buildings or emissions that are considered as part of other Regulatory processes.[1161]

This is an interesting statement since, under Section 1 of the Space Industry Act, "space activity' means ... launching or procuring the launch or the return to earth of a space object or of an aircraft carrying a space object'.[1162] This

1158 N627, para 5.3.5.
1159 2020 No. 1265 18(2).
1160 N627, 5.2.8.
1161 *Ibid*, para 5.2.8.
1162 Space Industry Act 2018 s1(4).

statement appears on one reading to exclude the carrier aircraft, appearing to be written off as 'a relatively standard Boeing 747'. The launch licence issued to Virgin Orbit by the CAA licences both components of the activity on the face of the document itself – the flight of the carrier aircraft and LauncherOne are both licenced separately within the same document.[1163] Further, at paragraph 1.3 of the Licence:

> The Licenced Activities are as follows ... : launch of the Boeing 747–400 carrier aircraft registration no. N744VG, known as 'Cosmic Girl' ('the Carrier Aircraft') and the launch vehicle type known as 'Launcher One' ('the Launch Vehicle'), by taking off from Spaceport Cornwall, Newquay with the intention of releasing the Launch Vehicle, carrying payloads.

The Act itself also places relevant activities of a carrier aircraft into the specific category of a 'space activity' rather than an activity that could be considered to be 'undertaken under existing licences' – particularly as seeing as the launch operation itself was licenced under UK space law – is it correct, then under an Assessment of Environmental Effects to exclude emissions from carrier aircraft as being 'considered as part of other Regulatory processes'? It is submitted that this cannot have been the approach foreseen by the legislator and could even be perceived as being intellectually dishonest.

Additionally, for the Virgin Orbit launch, guidance was taken from the standards and objectives as set within the Air Quality Standards Regulations 2010[1164] and set out in tabular form as part of the Assessment of Environmental Effects,[1165] in addition to a raft of other legislation and guidance.[1166] Interestingly:

> Aircraft emissions were not considered in detail in the 2014 strategic assessment because the 2013 Air Policy Framework states that 'studies have shown that emissions from aviation related operations reduce rapidly beyond the immediate area around the runway' (Secretary for State for Transport 2013). As a result, the potential air quality effects associated with aircraft emissions are considered to be insignificant.[1167]

1163 N719, 1.
1164 SI 2010 No. 1001
1165 N627, para 4.2.51.
1166 *Ibid*, para 4.2.61.
1167 *Ibid*, para 4.2.58.

Moreover, the effects associated with 'LauncherOne' – the rocket launched from Cosmic Girl, have been stated to be minimal:

> With regards to high altitude (i.e., >10,700 m [35,000 ft] MSL) emissions from the proposed LauncherOne operations, air quality significant effects can only occur where there are sensitive environmental receptors that maybe harmed (or benefit) as a result of changes in air quality. At the altitude where the rocket will be released there are no receptors and so no significant effects can occur. Therefore, any air quality effects associated with the LauncherOne rocket itself are scoped out of this assessment. However, Section 5.2 (Climate) addresses air quality impacts associated with GHG emissions within the affected airspace.[1168]

As Dr Nicholas Ross has indicated,[1169] if the unsuccessful Virgin Orbit venture had carried through: 'over the 8 year, 17 launch proposed operation period of Spaceport Cornwall and Virgin Orbit, there are a total of 5,352 tonnes of carbon dioxide equivalent (tCO2e) emissions, at an average of 315 tCO2e per launch. To put this in context, the UK average carbon footprint is about 10 tCO2e per person per year'. It should be noted that emissions from the space industry in general have been the subject of light touch regulation on the international scale as Ross states, the Montreal Protocol of 1987[1170] completely overlooked the impact of emissions coming from the space industry. This does appear to be reflected in the Virgin Orbit Assessment of Environmental Effects as the most extensive consideration appears to have been given to the increase in road traffic arising in connection with the spaceport's operations.[1171]

Other provisions relevant to environmental impact include Conservation of Habitats and Species (Amendment) (EU Exit) Regulations 2019[1172] as regards the impact on 'terrestrial biodiversity'[1173] in the terms of the Virgin Orbit AEE.

1168 *Ibid,* para 4.2.78.

1169 Dr Nicholas P. Ross, 'The long-term sustainability for the fledgling U.K. Space Sector: Are current regulations and legislation fit for purpose?', Masters Dissertation, <https://img1.wsimg.com/blobby/go/7ecaff53-6d70-4686-a1a6-b3df0238ede9/downloads/SpaceLaw_LLM_dissertation_NRoss.pdf?ver=1688116027623>

1170 1987 Montreal Protocol on Substances that Deplete the Ozone Layer, Signed in Montreal, Canada on 16 September 1987; 1522 UNTS 3; UKTS 1990 No. 19; Cm. 283; ATS 1989 No. 18; 26 ILM 1550 (1987).

1171 N478 at para 4.2.77.

1172 2019 No. 0000.

1173 N627, para 4.2.80.

The 'Impact Assessment' provisions within the EcIA Guidelines[1174] appear comprehensive and useful, although, it is submitted, a discernable objective standard for quantifiable impact should be established by statute or other legislative instrument. However, the guidance requires that the Assessment of Environmental Effects *must* be prepared by 'competent experts'[1175] and there is a suggested format appended to the guidance. It must be stressed too that the interpretation of these requirements in practice has been very comprehensive as can be seen from the detailed approach taken with the Virgin Orbit AEE[1176] which covers a very wide range of potential environmental impacts and the report totals almost 160 pages. For example, potential impacts covered include 'potential for strike from Stage 1 and Fairings Debris' which refers to the potential for injury to a comprehensive range of protected marine wildlife with calculated probabilities of impact for each one, with the striped dolphin being the most likely casualty with a 0.0000500% probability of impact.[1177]

There is inevitably a degree of tension regarding the regulatory aspects of sustainability. On the one hand, there must be a flexible regulatory scheme to enable competition and make for an amenable environment for operators and investors alike. On the other there is the need to protect the environment and for any kind of activity in its own right to be 'sustainable'.

Regarding other criticisms, it is worth noting that the CAA have stated via their Space Launch and Orbit Group, that 'Matters to be covered by the spaceport AEE do not reflect the operating model for horizontal spaceports'.[1178] Further illustration as to the key differences would be welcome.

As will be covered in the next chapter, other legislatures appear to have more robust rules regarding protection of the environment from space activities. It is possible that the relative silence in the United Kingdom regime derives at least partly from the fact that other, more general, legislative provisions cover environmental protection. This is likely to be the case in other jurisdictions too, and it would be desirable to see the formation of a positive duty to protect the environment from the effects of launch as is the case elsewhere, or, at the very least, extend the requirement for an AEE to Large Rocket Permissions albeit on a proportionate scale.

1174 N1165.

1175 N1148, 18.

1176 N627.

1177 *Ibid,* Table 5.4–5, 5–29.

1178 The United Kingdom Civil Aviation Authority, Space Launch and Orbit Group, Launch Session, March 2022, 13 <https://www.caa.co.uk/media/cdujiqmo/mar22-splog_launch-session.pdf> accessed 16 October 2024.

Along with the recent Sustainable Markets Initiative's 'Astra Carta',[1179] itself launched by King Charles III in June 2023, and the 2023 Consultation[1180] on space sustainability within the United Kingdom looks set for further legislative development in the coming years. In particular, with the Astra Carta's emphasis on protection of the environment beyond the Earth itself with a focus on debris mitigation,[1181] it is to be hoped this represents a forthcoming legislative shift. In addition to the Astra Carta, in 2022, the United Kingdom government also released plans for a 'space sustainability standard'.[1182] The growing problem of space debris was acknowledged,[1183] along with the desire to see the completion of Phase 3 of the implementation of the UNOOSA guidelines for the long-term sustainability of outer space.[1184] The United Kingdom government appears to have taken a genuine interest in matters of long-term sustainability, the United Kingdom Space Agency having funded the 3 phases of the Long Term Sustainability project with UNOOSA directly.[1185] True to the ambitions detailed in the press release, Phase 3 was completed in 2023.[1186] There has also been strong progress made in respect of the United Kingdom's Active Debris Removal industry.[1187] Further promising signs are evident from the United Kingdom's acknowledgment of the risks associated with debris re-entering the Earth's atmosphere, with funding granted by the United Kingdom Space

---

1179 The Sustainable Markets Initiative, 'Astra Carta. To Care For The Infinite Wonders Of The Universe', 28 June, 2023 <https://www.sustainable-markets.org/AstraCarta_charter.pdf#:~:text=The%20Astra%20Carta%20is%20a%20collective%20call%20to> accessed 2 October 2024.

1180 N19.

1181 See for instance, Section 1, Articles 3(1), 3(12), 4(13, XIX) and Section 2, Article 5(x).

1182 Press release, The United Kingdom Government, 'Government announces package of new measures to drive space sustainability', 23 June 2022, <https://www.gov.uk/government/news/government-announces-package-of-new-measures-to-drive-space-sustainability#:~:text=Science%20Minister%20George%20Freeman%20has%20today%20(Thursday%2023%20June)%20launched> accessed 3 October 2024.

1183 *Ibid.*

1184 *Ibid.*

1185 Committee on the Peaceful Uses of Outer Space Scientific and Technical Subcommittee Sixty-first session, Vienna, 29 January–9 February 2024, A/AC.105/C.1/2024/CRP.21, 'United Kingdom of Great Britain and Northern Ireland update on its reporting approach for the voluntary implementation of the Guidelines for the Long-term Sustainability of Outer Space Activities', 1 February 2024, <https://www.unoosa.org/res/oosadoc/data/documents/2024/aac_105c_12024crp/aac_105c_12024crp_21_0_html/AC105_C1_2024_CRP21E.pdf> accessed 3 October 2024, 2.

1186 *Ibid.*

1187 *Ibid.*

Agency to those conducting academic studies into this area,[1188] in addition to incubating an Active Debris Removal industry.[1189] Yet more pointedly, as part of the 2024 Regulatory Review, the government recognised that there was no explicit treatment of sustainability within the Space Industry Act in spite of this being such a politically significant driver across the board in terms of overall policy. It henceforth stated that consideration would be given to whether the Act should be changed in light of this omission. With the next round of reform to domestic space legislation, it is to be hoped that concerns around such matters, broadly expressed, can be translated into a narrower form of legislative intent.

1188 N1193, 6.
1189 *Ibid.*

CHAPTER 10

Comparative Perspectives

If international regulation of space activities is a relatively new phenomenon, domestic regulation is even newer. The United Kingdom's first piece of legislation in this area came about in 1986 meaning that domestic regulation is less than 40 years old at the time of writing. More significantly, legislation established to support a domestic space industry based within the United Kingdom did not arrive until 2018. Whilst the United Kingdom has a modest space heritage which is not to be downplayed, it is still far from being sensibly described as one of the world's leading nations in respect of domestic space activities.

Whilst the new legislation may have areas for further development, it represents a commendable effort to provide a legislative basis for the United Kingdom's budding space industry. Owing to the relative lack of experience in this area – both legislatively and in terms of actual space activities carried out – particularly as regards domestic launches, questions should be raised as to whether the approach so far necessarily represents the optimum path.

Within this work, aspects of the United Kingdom's space laws have been critiqued largely with reference to comparable domestic instruments and local jurisprudence across several disparate areas. For this chapter, aspects of the space legislation of the United Kingdom will be compared with the corresponding laws of a selection of other jurisdictions. Unlike other comparative studies which may deal with phenomena such as labour law[1190] or other disciplines common to all if not most jurisdictions, not every jurisdiction has a domestic commercial space program or any significant rules established to facilitate one. Where they have, differing legislative approaches have inevitably been adopted, and it is helpful to this study to observe some of them in order to give further context to the United Kingdom's instruments. It is to be further hoped that this discussion could one day lead to legislative change in some of the areas where it is most needed.

Pacta sunt servanda, all treaties are binding on those who enter into them. As previously mentioned, the United Kingdom generally follows a 'dualist' as

1190 See, for example, Guy Mundlak and Matthew Finklin, *Comparative Labor Law,* (Cheltenham 2015) and Sean Cooney, Darcy du Troit, Roberto Fragale, Roger Ronnie and Kamala Sankaran,'Building BRICs of success?' Comparative Labour Law Eds Matthew Firkin and Guy Mundlak (2015).

 | DOI:10.1163/9789004732551_011

opposed to a 'monist' approach[1191] when implementing such agreements. The experience of creating the domestic space law regime harkens to this, and it is of interest to note how the United Kingdom, as a country with a common law system, has approached the task of safeguarding its international obligations in the formulation of its domestic space law. Regimes such as that of the United States and Australia, also of the common law persuasion, embarked upon this process before the National Space Law Resolution[1192] was passed and prior to the recent strides and extensive ambitions of private actors within the realm of outer space. In the wake of such strides, Professor von der Dunk stated that the implementation of the space treaties is the most important task of domestic legislatures in this realm,[1193] and further that the lack of precision within the treaties themselves could lead to fragmentation of approaches.[1194] Whilst approaches are divergent, there are common threads. Most jurisdictions have attempted to address the overarching aims of the treaties – the need to ensure the peaceful use of outer space has sounded across many legislatures in the form of provisions for security at spaceports and inspection regimes. States have also provided scaffolding for the Liability Convention, requiring private actors to indemnify the state for damage caused by their activities. Protection for damage to the territory of the states themselves – as opposed to that of other states – has also been extended. There are notable differences between how the United Kingdom has pursued its legislative ambitions and the approach of other – mainly civil law – jurisdictions. The UK rules place a considerable emphasis on licensing and certain rules are largely enforced by the imposition of licence conditions at the discretion of the regulator. There is much that is seemingly discretionary and there is a concerning lack of mandatory or directory language as regards key aspects, notably in respect of environmental protection and sustainability. This being written, the United Kingdom has a very comprehensive monitoring, inspection and enforcement program which goes some way to counterbalancing these matters. In other areas where the United Kingdom addresses similar aspects of the international regime to

1191 N10.

1192 Committee on the Peaceful Uses of Outer Space, Legal Subcommittee, Sixty-second session, Vienna, 20–31 March 2023, Item 7 of the provisional agenda, National legislation relevant to the peaceful exploration and use of outer space, 'Schematic Overview of National Regulatory Frameworks for Space Activities' <https://www.unoosa.org/res/oosadoc/data/documents/2023/aac_105c_22023crp/aac_105c_22023crp_28_0_html/AC105_C2_2023_CRP28E.pdf> accessed 24 April 2024.

1193 Frans von der Dunk, *Advanced Introduction to Space Law*, Edward Elgar, 2020, Chapter 6.

1194 *Ibid*, Chapter 6.4.

other jurisdictions, it does so at least as fully in most instances. There are some areas that the United Kingdom – and, in its defence, a number of other jurisdictions too – omits to address in its entirety. There are no provisions made on the exploitation of resources in space in UK space law. The problem of space debris is also much more robustly addressed in the rules of other jurisdictions and there are also definitive mentions of ITU regulations in respect of satellites and broadcasting within the space instruments specifically catered for in others. As seen from the previous chapter, there is an overlap between the role of the CAA and Ofcom as regards certain matters, with ITU regulations falling squarely within the domain of the latter. This can be seen as an inevitable consequence of how United Kingdom telecommunications law has historically developed, but whether it presents the most efficient way of regulating satellites is not entirely evident.

This chapter will firstly focus on the contrast between certain elements of the United States regime and that of the United Kingdom. The United States has the largest volume of domestic legislation and most expansive legal provisions owing to its history and reputation in the field of space flight. Another reason for looking to the United States at first instance, is that like the United Kingdom, it is a common law jurisdiction and although federalist in nature, adopts a somewhat similar approach. The Space Industry Act 2018 applies across all jurisdictions of the United Kingdom and is supported by secondary legislation in a manner not dissimilar to the way in which the United States Code of Federal Regulations[1195] is supported by a large volume of appendices.

Whilst such details are important as regards the similarities between the two jurisdictions, it is hoped that the most valuable contribution of this exercise will lie more with the differences. Whilst the United Kingdom's regime appears expansive, compared with the United States it is anything but. The two are comparable in certain areas – the informed consent principles are broadly similar with some of the phrasing being directly lifted, it seems, from the United States. The United States has a vastly expansive regime in respect of multiple other dimensions of commercial spaceflight, particularly as regards flight-planning and safety implementation. Indeed, one of the striking contrasts is the use of 'mandatory' as opposed to 'permissive' language used in the implementation of the two regimes. This was echoed in the first iteration of the guidance:

> 1.24 Where the guidance uses the term 'must', this refers to a requirement in or under the Act. If applicants / licencees fail to meet that requirement, it could result in the licence not being granted or being revoked or

1195 CFR (U.S.) Title 14.

> suspended. Where it is stated that 'the Regulator expects' applicants to do something, this describes a preferred approach; however, it is not a legal requirement to comply with the Regulator's expectations.[1196]

It is interesting to note that the updated guidance document of May 2024[1197] omits to include a passage to this effect. The new document, in fact, contains much sterner wording than the previous incarnation. As a general matter of law, the expectations of the regulator cannot be expected to equate to the force of statute,[1198] but nevertheless, a demonstrable failure to follow the expectations could certainly result in a finding of negligence on the part of the operator if a court decides that a 'reasonable operator' would have, in the circumstances, chosen to follow such expectations. For example, this kind of language was used in the first generation of guidance documents. Regarding the requirement for a Flight Safety Analysis, it was stated that:

> Regulation 31(1)(b) requires the applicant to identify what could cause or contribute to a hazard. Causes could be processes, physical effects or human factors. For example, in the case of debris from fragmentation, there may be multiple potential causes of fragmentation, such as a manufacturing defect, a process failure such as excessive rapid propellant loading, flight termination or a defective flow rate sensor. The Regulator expects applicants to construct different major accident scenarios for each possible cause.[1199]

One key area where the United States and United Kingdom appear to diverge, it seems, is with respect to the level of authority attached to such regulatory guidance. Much of what is outlined in the statutory guidance provided in the United Kingdom is echoed in actual mandatory rules in the United States. Although this may have been done with the intention of providing a more flexible and attractive commercial environment it is still important that provisions applicable to public safety – and, indeed, the safety of all those involved be they members of the public or not- are furnished with the appropriate level of legal authority.

Significantly there are differences in respect of launch plans as regards the amount of detail required. In short, the US regime requires an extensive amount of detail far in excess of that required in the United Kingdom. In policy terms,

1196 N257, 6.
1197 N368.
1198 See chapter 3 for a discussion of the legal status of guidance generally.
1199 N257, 25.

this is somewhat counter-intuitive given the perceived attitudes to regulation of business on opposite sides of the Atlantic – the US regime demands certain courses of action be taken in respect of certain flight parameters whereas the United Kingdom does not.[1200]

This could be due to the United Kingdom wishing to attract business and investment by promising a low-regulation – and, resultantly, low cost – environment as a unique selling point over what the United States or other jurisdictions may be able to offer in terms of experience and existing infrastructure. Whatever the reason for this may be, the primary objective of the law, whilst attempting to regulate hazardous activities, must surely be to ensure the safety of the public along with those who may be involved in spaceflight activities. Whilst this may be done in a performative sense across certain aspects of the UK regulatory regime, the use of permissive language in addition to a lack of substance relative to the US regime gives cause for concern in respect of both flight safety and other areas.

In other areas there are similarities. Regarding crew-qualifications and training, it is clear that the United Kingdom has undertaken a legal transplant of the corresponding regulations in the United States. The relevant US law is contained in Volume 4 of Title 15 of the US Code of Federal Regulations.[1201] Part 460.5 of the Code of Federal Regulations is broadly the same as Regulation 13 of the UK Space Industry Regulations in respect of the expectations on each crew member to competently undertake their role including 'emergency situations' with the key difference that the US regulations specify that each crew member must complete training so as to avoid the vehicle causing harm to the public[1202] and, moreover, that the training must cover emergency situations[1203] whilst the UK position appears limited to a requirement to 'demonstrate an ability' as regards the same. More similar are the provisions regarding the ability to withstand the physical demands of space flight as outlined in the US Code of Federal Regulations at 460.5 which is mirrored in Regulation 17 of the UK Space Industry Regulations – all flight crew members must be able to show that they can withstand the rigours of space flight – the same stresses are recognised in both instruments as including 'microgravity', 'vibration' and 'high acceleration'. Regarding the latter, the United Kingdom requires that an ability to perform complex tasks whilst experiencing the accompanying physiological affects is specifically tested. Regulation 18 provides that:

1200 There are numerous examples of this as will be seen.

1201 N864.

1202 R13.

1203 CFR (US) 460.5(2)(11).

> 18.—(1) An MFC of a launch vehicle other than a balloon must be able to demonstrate an ability to perform tasks, equivalent in complexity to those which would be performed in flight, while exposed to the mental and physical stresses of rapid acceleration.
>
> (2) Whether the MFC satisfies the criteria in sub-paragraph (1) must be tested in a centrifuge device or an aircraft, or in a combination of the two, that is able to replicate the effects on the human body of the forces of acceleration, the rate of change of those forces and their duration, in conditions equivalent to the periods of the flight when those forces are most acute.

One key difference exists between the UK regime and the US position as regards the training of pilots and remote pilots which could be a result of a drafting error. 460.5(c)(2) of the Code of Federal Regulations states that pilots and remote pilots must:

> (2) Possess aeronautical knowledge, experience, and skills necessary to pilot and control the launch or reentry vehicle that will operate in the National Airspace System (NAS).

Whilst the corresponding UK provision, Regulation 15, drafted in almost identical terms omits any reference to a 're-entry vehicle', instead reading:

> 15.—(1) Pilots and remote pilots must possess the aeronautical knowledge, experience and skills necessary to pilot and control the launch vehicle within airspace having the same classification as the airspace in which the launch vehicle will be operating, including in the vicinity of spaceports and airports.

Under usual rules of statutory construction, 'common sense' could dictate that any reference to a 'launch vehicle' could also include a reference to a 're-entry' vehicle. The UK Regulations themselves are silent on this matter, making no distinction between a launch vehicle and re-entry vehicle for the operating purposes. This could be due to the United Kingdom not envisaging the use of multi-stage spacecraft any time soon but, if so, it seems like an unnecessary limitation, particularly given the ambitious extent of the United Kingdom's plans for a significant market share in this field.

A further interesting difference in respect of training requirements under both instruments is that the UK regime prescribes the appointment of 'Training

Managers'[1204] by launch operators, range control operators and spaceflight operators, for, naturally, the purpose of training certain individuals whilst the US regime does not. The US regime places responsibility on the spaceflight or launch operator directly under 460.7(a) which states that:

> An Operator must train each member of its crew and define standards for successful completion in accordance with § 460.5.

Quite what the justification for the United Kingdom's approach is here is difficult to fathom. It mandates an additional layer of management which it would be incumbent on spaceflight and range operators to implement at their own expense as a licence condition. Whilst on one hand, this could be seen as a diligent and safety conscious approach to this matter, on the other it is important to consider the potential legal advantages such an approach may offer to prospective investors. With the responsibility for training placed upon the shoulders of 'managers', this would bring into play the doctrine of vicarious liability in the event of any failure that could be attributed to deficient training of any individual. For operators, the advantage of this may be that an argument could be mounted in respect of such failure being solely attributable to the assigned manager due to them being on a 'frolic of their own'[1205] as per the English common law in this regard. This could be a valuable way for operators to shield themselves from liability. For such a defence to be successfully pleaded, any such transgression of the training manager would, necessarily as a matter of law, have to be acute in the very least. It is likely that most of a training manager's responsibilities would come within their 'field of activities'[1206] as dictated by their employment relationship and it may be a difficult defence to sustain. Nevertheless, it could offer a potential margin of appreciation re indemnity and contributory negligence. This approach does appear to be reflected in the US regime with the requirement for launch 'directors' mandated under Rule 417 as regards matters of flight safety.

Similarly to the United Kingdom, the United States mandates certain levels of qualification for those in key positions:

> US 417.105 Launch personnel qualifications and certification.
>
> a. General. A launch operator must employ a personnel certification program that documents the qualifications, including education, experience, and training, for each member of the launch crew.

1204 See Regulations 9(3) and 11(e) respectively.

1205 There are various case examples relating to this. See *Mattis v Pollock (t/a Flamingos Nightclub)* [2003] EWCA Civ 887, [2003] 1 W.L.R. 2158 for example.

1206 See *WM Morrison Supermarkets plc v Various Claimants* [2020] UKSC 12.

There are also similar record keeping requirements as regards training documentation such as those under § 417.311.

Interesting differences arise in respect of how factors such as fatigue and their impact on human performance are dealt with. Whilst the UK position is non-directive, the US regime purposefully imposes requirements. Under rule 417.113 (f) it is stated that:

> For any operation with the potential to have an adverse effect on public safety, the launch safety rules must ensure the launch crew is physically and mentally capable of performing all assigned tasks. These rules must govern the length, number, and frequency of work shifts, including the rest afforded the launch crew between shifts.

The UK perspective is not as prescriptive as this, instead requiring relevant information and instructions on fatigue to be contained in the Safety Operations Manual under Regulation 90, Schedule 5. This consists of a requirement to document the measures the operator is taking to mitigate the effects of fatigue rather than a statutory duty. The requirements of Regulation 74(1) are that:

> An individual ('P') may not act as a member of the crew of a launch vehicle or as a remote pilot if P knows or suspects that P's physical or mental condition renders P temporarily or permanently unfit to perform those functions, including unfitness by reason of …
>
> … (e) fatigue.

The key difference here is that whilst the US regime places a positive obligation on operators to ensure there are rules in place providing for adequate rest, the UK regulations do not. Instead, the approach is to place the obligation on the fatigued individual themselves as per Regulation 74 and requiring that information about any rest periods is included in a safety manual. This seems a rather indirect way of enforcing what amounts to a crucial safety aspect of spaceflight from the UK perspective. It perhaps goes without saying that such staff will be protected to an extent by existing provisions such as the Working Time Regulations 1999,[1207] but given the safety critical nature and sensitivity of this area and the potential for widespread harm arising from faulty decision-making, the desirability in making operators directly responsible for ensuring adequate rest et cetera is plain.

1207 SI 1998 No 1833.

It would be more effective if the regulations had been drafted more broadly in a style akin to that found in the Railways and Other Guided Transport Systems (Safety) Regulations[1208] which states:

> 25.—Fatigue (1) Every controller of safety critical work shall have in place arrangements to ensure, so far as is reasonably practicable, that a safety critical worker under his management, supervision or control does not carry out safety critical work in circumstances where he is so fatigued or where he would be liable to become so fatigued that his health or safety or the health or safety of other persons on a transport system could be significantly affected.

UK space legislation refers to fatigue in the context of 'spaceflight duties'[1209] – defined under Part 8 of the Space Industry Regulations as 'duties in connection with the operator's spaceflight activities'[1210] and in the context of crew members of launch vehicles or remote pilots[1211] but should broaden this definition to include other roles which would themselves be 'safety critical' as the railways legislation identifies. There is a question as to the classification of, for example, range control services, which are referred to as 'associated activities' within the Act.[1212] Would these 'associated activities' be classified also as 'spaceflight duties'?

Regarding what could be termed flight safety in general, the UK Regulations are not as exacting as those in the United States. As previously set out, a significant aspect of how the United Kingdom handles these matters is through a 'safety case' approach.[1213] The level of detail required in the safety case is not prescriptive. Under the first iteration of the guidance document, the requirements were that it should:

> be proportionate to the potential consequences of the hazardous events but sufficient to enable the Regulator to have a clear picture of the location, activities and intrinsic hazards associated with the proposed spaceflight activities.[1214]

1208 SI 2006 No. 599.
1209 Schedule 5(3).
1210 R78(1).
1211 R74(1)(e).
1212 N127, S1(1)(a)–(c).
1213 See N512 and the surrounding references for a further discussion of matters relating to the safety case approach.
1214 N257, para 5.9.

The approach may be driven by, amongst other things, a desire to drive down the administrative burden and outline a flexible regulatory framework, but there is a risk of inconsistent safety case design between different operators and members of the regulatory staff who may have different conceptions of terms such as 'proportionate' and different ideas as to how dangerous certain hazards may actually be.[1215] This is also underscored by the fact that the language used throughout the guidance – including specifically within the relevant section of the guidance – is permissive, that is 'the Regulator expects'. As the first edition of the guidance outlined at paragraph 1.24, 'It is not a legal requirement to comply with the Regulator's expectations'. As repeated elsewhere, this statement is not reproduced in the more recent guidance.[1216]

Certain other expectations are very specific, including Schedule 1 of the Regulations whereby it is stated under section 11 that where 'Technical Requirements' are mentioned, that these should have the same, if not a substantially similar meaning, to those in Chapter 6 of the Space Engineering Technical Requirements Specification produced by the European Cooperation for Space Standardisation.[1217]

The US approach appears more elaborate. As identified elsewhere, the UK guidance states that risk must be as low as reasonably practicable with reference to common law principles, importing what may come to be regarded as an objective test in ascertaining flight safety. Whilst part 415.35 (a) of the US Code of Federal Regulations could be construed in broadly similar terms to the UK position, particularly as regards the overall objective, Part 415.35 (b) states that any given launch vehicle must be designed as such to be aligned with the foregoing safety objective. In order to satisfy the requirements of this part, the applicant must provide details regarding 'Launch vehicle structure, including physical dimensions and weight' in addition to identifying 'Hazardous and safety critical systems, including propulsion systems'. The requirement is beyond a mere 'identification' as Part 415.35(c) requires that drawings and schematics be provided of the latter as part of any given application. This approach is also reflected in the 'Safety Review Document' requirements of the part at 415.107 which is drafted with meticulous specificity.

1215 It is also important to observe here that confusion was expressed by industry regarding the meaning of 'acceptable' in a related discussion during the 2024 Space Regulatory Review, see N405, 34.

1216 N368.

1217 European Cooperation for Space Standardisation, Technical requirements specification, ECSS-E-ST-10-06C (6 March 2009) <https://ecss.nl/standard/ecss-e-st-10-06c-technical-requirements-specification> accessed 16 October 2023.

A safety review document must contain such things as a 'glossary of unique terms and acronyms used in alphabetical order', a list of 'all referenced standards, codes and publications', in addition to using 'equations and mathematical relationships derived from or referenced to a recognized standard or text, and must define all algebraic parameters'. Should this be the equivalent of a 'safety case' which is required under the UK Regulations, it appears much more prescriptive. Furthermore, the US Code of Federal Regulations requires that there must be a written description of the launch vehicle provided in addition to the hazardous/toxic elements documented in tabular form.[1218]

One of the most interesting aspects of launch safety when compared to the UK regulations is the amount of detail required about the vehicle's flight-path and trajectory. Under section 415.109(d) drawings of the planned trajectory must be provided, one of which specifies that: 'One drawing must depict the proposed nominal flight profile with downrange depicted on the abscissa and altitude depicted on the ordinate axis. The nominal flight profile must be labeled to show each planned staging event and its time after liftoff from launch through orbital insertion or final impact'.

The same is required for the vehicle's trajectory whereby two drawings must be provided detailing the trajectory – one outlining 'the proposed nominal flight profile' including the projected 'downrange' with parameters depicted graphically via an ordinate axis,[1219] and the other outlining 'instantaneous impact point ground traces' upon a grid which must also include 'the outlines of any continents and islands'. Moreover, paragraph (e) provides that applicants must also outline the timing of any 'staging events' which may occur 'including the predicted impact point and dispersion of each spent stage'.

Under the UK regime, operators must ensure that risks associated with their activities are made as low as reasonably practicable. In doing this, operators will be under a duty to make their enterprises as safe as 'reasonably practicable' in all their circumstances. The guidance document issued by the CAA on 'Assessing ALARP and Acceptable Risk'[1220] includes Asquith LJ's definition of 'reasonably practicable' from the case of *Edwards v National Coal Board*:[1221]

1218 CFR (US) 415.109.

1219 *Ibid*, 109 (1).

1220 The United Kingdom Civil Aviation Authority, 'CAP2220: Principles and guidelines for the spaceflight regulator in assessing ALARP and acceptable risk', 9, <https://www.caa.co.uk/publication/download/18931> accessed 16 October 2024.

1221 [1949] 1 K.B. 704 (EWCA).

> 'Reasonably practicable' is a narrower term than 'physically possible' and seems to me to imply that a computation must be made by the owner, in which the quantum of risk is placed on one scale and the sacrifice involved in the measures necessary for averting the risk (whether in money, time or trouble) is placed in the other; and that if it be shown that there is a gross disproportion between them – the risk being insignificant in relation to the sacrifice – the defendants discharge the onus on them. Moreover, this computation falls to be made by the owner at a point of time anterior to the accident.

It is also worth considering the case of *Adsett v K. and L. Steel Founders and Engineers Ltd*[1222] on the meaning of 'practicable'. 'Practicable' should be taken to mean 'possible' in the context of current levels of knowledge and technology.

In other case law, the concept of 'risk' was explored in the case of *Tomlinson v Congleton Borough Council*[1223] as follows:

> It is a fallacy to say that because drowning is a serious matter there is therefore a serious risk of drowning. In truth the risk of a drowning was very low indeed and there had never actually been one and the accident suffered by the claimant was unique. Whilst broken necks can result from incautious or reckless diving, the probability of one being suffered in the circumstances of the claimant were so remote that the risk was minimal. The internal reports before his accident make the common but elementary error of confusing the seriousness of the outcome with the degree of risk that it will occur.[1224]

Other cases also show how the term has been interpreted in practice. The term was the subject of interpretation by the Scottish Court of Session in *Gillies v Glynwed Foundries*[1225] where the term appeared in section 28(1) of the Factories Act 1961 in relation to factory floors being kept 'as far as reasonably practicable' free from obstruction. It was held that a discarded screw which had been on the floor and had caused an accident did not breach this requirement – the factory had a cleaning system in place and, therefore, it was held that it would not be reasonably practicable to take existing steps. Whether similar reasoning would be employed in a field such as space travel where the stakes would be

1222 [1953] 1 W.L.R. 773 (EWCA).

1223 N858.

1224 *Ibid*, para 79, (Hobhouse LJ).

1225 1977 S.L.T. 97.

notably higher remains to be seen but as *Associated Dairies Ltd v Hartley*,[1226] a case on employer's liability illustrates, every case is judged on its merits. In this case, a Health and Safety Inspector appointed under section 19 of the Health and Safety at Work Act 1974 made a recommendation that all employees be given access to protective footwear.

Following a consideration of several authorities on the meaning of 'reasonably practicable', the Industrial Tribunal found that:

a. The questions for the Tribunal appear to be—
    1. Is the requirement of the inspector practicable?
    2. In the whole circumstances is the requirement reasonable?

b. The question whether in the whole circumstances the requirement is reasonable, should not be determined having regard solely to the proportion which the risk to be apprehended bears to the sacrifice in money, time or trouble involved in meeting the risk, but it is proper to consider whether the time, trouble and expense of the inspector's requirement are disproportionate to the risk involved to the employees if the Tribunal cancel the improvement notice or affirm it with modifications.

In support of this it has also been held that 'what is 'reasonably practicable' depends upon a consideration whether the time, trouble and expense of the precautions suggested are disproportionate to the risk involved'.[1227]

The guidance document on ALARP ('as low as reasonably practicable') principles offers some very practical advice on how to assess reasonable practicability, including measures that could be taken as regards a 'cost-benefit analysis'. As the guidance states:

> There is no expectation for applicants to provide a detailed cost benefit analysis to support their licence application. Where one is provided, the spaceflight Regulator will follow the published guidance on Health and Safety Executive principles for Cost Benefit Analysis (CBA) in support of as low as reasonably practicable decisions when reviewing the cost benefit analysis as part of application process.[1228]

In addition to formulating their own assessments of risk, operators are also encouraged to adopt 'appropriate standards' and 'good practice' with further guidance as to what 'good practice' might objectively resemble.[1229]

1226 [1979] I.R.L.R. 171 (IT).

1227 *Marshall v Gotham* [1954] A.C. 360.

1228 N1228, 9.

1229 *Ibid*, 10.

Although the UK regime is not as detailed or apparently rigid as that from the United States, it is interesting to note that the reports that have been furnished under the rules so far by operators in satisfaction of the rules have been very detailed. As has been outlined elsewhere in this work, there is a risk that such standards may not be followed on a universal basis as different operators adopt different ways and means of accomplishing their goals. This fragmentation may present some difficulty when determining what best practice should look like, particularly as regards inexperienced operators who may adopt standards unsuitable for their particular activities on the basis that they have been tried and tested by others.

As the United Kingdom launch and flight sector grows, it is desirable that appropriate standards be committed to law for the purpose of, firstly, ensuring that high and appropriate standards are uniformly followed in the interests of safety and, secondly, avoiding fragmentation where possible.

Another interesting comparison regarding flight can be made in respect of Launch Plans under Rule 417.111 (4) on trajectory data, which requires a 'description of the launch trajectory' for any given launch. This means:

> For an orbital expendable launch vehicle, the description must include each planned orbital parameter, stage burnout time and state vector, and all planned stage impact times, locations, and downrange and cross-range dispersions. For a guided or unguided suborbital launch vehicle, the description must include each planned stage impact time, location, and downrange and cross-range dispersion.'

In addition, a Launch Plan must also:

> Include a written countdown checklist that provides a formal decision process leading to flight initiation. A countdown checklist must include the flight day preflight tests of a flight safety system required by subpart D of this part and must contain ... (a) ... Record of all critical communications network channels that are used for voice, video, or data transmission that support the flight safety system, during each countdown.[1230]

Such provisions would be welcome within the United Kingdom's framework. Other areas in which the US legislation outstrips the United Kingdom's regime is in respect of rehearsals for space flight. Whilst the UK position refers to

1230 CFR (US) 417.111 (5).

'mission rehearsals' generally[1231] and more specifically in respect of flight termination personnel who have to conduct rehearsals to test 'the flight termination criteria, the flight safety data display integrity and the performance of the MFTPS ('Member of Flight Termination Personnel') for the flight in both normal and abnormal conditions, including emergency situations'.[1232]

Mission rehearsals under the UK rules in a general sense are required to be conducted in a way that:

> must as nearly as possible reproduce the intended spaceflight, spaceport and range control activities which would be carried out on the mission, including—
> a. normal and abnormal situations;
> b. pre-launch, spaceflight and post-launch scenarios; [and]
> c. any conditions in space that could affect the Operator's spaceflight activity.[1233]

This covers all aspects of a spaceflight in a broad sense but the US position is to break these matters down specifically. Rule 417.119 on Rehearsals[1234] is more exacting and requires the specific identification of 'corrective actions needed to ensure public safety'[1235] and the actual assessment of any 'anomalies' identified in the rehearsal process and subsequent incorporation of any changes to the launch or flight arrangements should this be deemed 'material to public safety'.[1236] Very distinctly, the launch operator is directed in mandatory terms to 'inform the FAA of any public safety related anomalies and related changes in operations performed during launch processing or flight resulting from a rehearsal'.[1237] Whether this would come under a general requirement to keep the CAA informed of any relevant changes is also not clear. The US rules on rehearsals go on to require that all those involved with roles pertaining to public safety must have undergone at least one relevant rehearsal prior to a launch whereas this is not a requirement in the United Kingdom. US law also requires a specific 'countdown' rehearsal unlike the United Kingdom along with a 'communications' rehearsal.[1238]

1231 See for example R70(5).
1232 Schedule 3, Part 1, s10.
1233 R70(6).
1234 § 417.119, Rehearsals.
1235 *Ibid.* (a).
1236 *Ibid* s (1).
1237 *Ibid* s (2).
1238 *Ibid* s5(b)/(d).

The difference in drafting style between the US regulations and the UK regime is particularly marked as regards the rules on actual flight and launch. Rule 417.125 has very extensive rules on 'launch of an unguided suborbital launch vehicle' which is backed up by an extensive appendix containing further guidance. The UK position is skeletal by comparison. Under Regulation 26, for example, a flight safety analysis obligates an applicant to:

> carry out a flight safety analysis in which the applicant—
> (a) identifies the major accident hazards that could, whether or not the launch vehicle malfunctions—(i) arise from, or cause a major accident during, the proposed spaceflight activities, or (ii) arise from the launch vehicle, or any part of it, during the proposed spaceflight activities, (b) completes the steps listed in regulation 28(1) for each hazard identified under sub-paragraph (a), and (c) estimates numerically the risk of death or serious injury arising from the hazards mentioned in sub-paragraph (a) to persons who are not human occupants.

Attention must be given, in particular, to the hazards under section 18 of Schedule 1: blast overpressure, fragmentation debris, thermal radiation, toxic release, major accident hazards arising from any discarded part of the launch vehicle and any object, including any payload, released or separated from the launch vehicle, collision with a space object, meteorological or environmental conditions, the use of a carrier aircraft, if applicable, re-entry of the launch vehicle.[1239] Whilst this could seem, at first blush, extensive and exacting, the US position here is, predictably, far more so.

This is also seen as regards provisions pertaining to flight trajectory. Under Regulation 46, Range Control licencees must, on behalf of the operator, take into account the trajectory of the launch vehicle.[1240] It must also form part of the safety case put forward by the operator.[1241] Furthermore, the trajectory of the vehicle must be monitored once it has reached a stable orbit.[1242] The trajectory of the flight must also be communicated on the consent form which is to be signed by certain individuals taking part in space activities.[1243] Notably absent is any detail as to how the trajectory is to be defined and by what parameters.

1239 (a)–(e).
1240 R46(2)(b).
1241 Schedule 1 (1).
1242 R101(1)(A).
1243 R206(2)(D).

The US Code of Federal Regulations is, by stark contrast, much very more exacting in this regard. Under § 417.207, as part of a 'flight safety analysis', a 'trajectory analysis' must also be included which sets out 'the limits of a launch vehicles normal flight'[1244] a 'fuel exhaustion trajectory that produces instantaneous impact points with the greatest range for any given time after liftoff for any stage that has the potential to impact the Earth',[1245] an overall assessment of 'wind effects'[1246] and, divergently, a 'Trajectory Model' which must, in the analysis's final incarnation, 'use a six-degree of freedom trajectory model'.[1247]

There are some caveats in the US regime which can allow operators to avoid following a certain of the guidance should their space activities fall within certain parameters. For example, under rule 417.125 (1) (b), the rules pertaining to a flight safety system must be complied with unless

> (1) The unguided suborbital launch vehicle, including any component or payload, does not have sufficient energy to reach any populated area in any direction from the launch point; or (2) A launch operator demonstrates through the licensing process that the launch will be conducted using a wind weighting safety system that meets the requirements of paragraph (c) of this section.

Owing to its smaller geographical size, the United Kingdom may not be able to import an equivalent provision to exception (1) within the UK rules.[1248] Some equivalent of paragraph (1) of rule 415.125 could be considered in respect of sea-launch capabilities which, as has been noted previously, is lacking. A further distinction between the two regimes here is that there are no provisions directly pertaining to wind under the UK regime, save for those concerned generally with meteorological conditions. Whether or not a similar safety weighting system for wind levels is a best practice standard in respect of determining meteorological safety is also not clear from the guidance documents.

Instead of calling broadly for a flight plan or other information pertaining to trajectory, the US regime specifically calls for operators to provide precise information regarding flight stages, including additional information when a flightpath crosses a populated area, something which is not catered for in such terms under the UK regime. Under Rule 417.217 an 'Overflight gate analysis' is

---

1244 CFR (US) § 417.207 (1).

1245 CFR (US) § 417.207 (2).

1246 CFR (US) § 417.207 (4).

1247 CFR (US) § 417.207 (2)(b).

1248 See Space Industry Regulations 2021, R46(2)(d).

required which establishes 'the portion of a flight safety limit, a gate, through which a normally performing launch vehicle's tracking icon will be allowed to proceed. A tracking icon must enable the flight safety crew to determine whether the launch vehicle's flight is in compliance with the flight safety rules established under § 417.113'.

Regarding particular hazards, the UK regime mentions 'blast overpressure' several times but does not mandate any particular method of analysis for the damage caused. The US regime goes one step further and mandates the terms of such an analysis under rule 417.229. So extensive is the stipulation that it even requires an assessment of the likelihood of broken windows resulting from 'peak incident overpressures below 1.0 psi and related casualties'.[1249] Whilst this work has so far been critical of the relative absence of detail in the UK rules by comparison it is likely that the type of rocket engines envisaged may have been assessed as unlikely to cause such damage. If matters such as broken windows would be a valid consideration, the UK regime arguably absolves an operator from responsibility under section 34(1) of the Space Industry Act whereby:

> No liability arises in trespass or nuisance in respect of spaceflight activities carried out in compliance, or substantially in compliance, with the requirements and conditions imposed by or under this Act.

If 'window damage' is categorised as 'trespass to goods' in this context, then there may be no liability.

Under the US regime there are also requirements for debris analysis which are incorporated into the flight safety analysis. Once again, the requirements for the analysis are stipulated – the analysis must:

> produce lists of debris fragments for each cause of breakup and any planned jettison of debris, launch vehicle components, or payload. The lists must account for all launch vehicle debris fragments, individually or in groupings of fragments whose characteristics are similar enough to be described by a single set of characteristics. The debris lists must describe the physical, aerodynamic, and harmful characteristics of each debris fragment.[1250]

1249 CFR (US) 417.229 (a) (2).

1250 CFR (US) 417.211 (a)–(d).

Whilst the Regulations and the Act adopt a 'safety case' model, in parts the detail as to how safety is to be assessed – particularly as regards the flight itself – is very sparse. In line with what appears to be a 'managerial' approach to the licensing regime, under section 7(1)(B) of the Space Industry Act a Safety Manager must be appointed and is responsible for ensuring that all aspects of the spaceport's licenced activities are carried out safely.[1251] Given the array of technical disciplines and potential hazards associated with the operation of a spaceport this is no small task.

Under section 11(1), a Range Control Licencee must appoint a 'range safety manager'.

One further difference between the US regime and the UK regime is the apparent absence of protection offered to employees of the operator – and implicitly the operator themselves – should they be in the vicinity of the launch site. The strict liability regime under section 34(2) of the Space Industry Act in the absence of negligence applies only to 'Members of the Public' as defined on an exclusionary basis under Chapter 3, Regulation 39 of the Space Industry Regulations 2021 as not including

> ... any person who is—
> d. listed in regulation 40, and
> e. voluntarily in close proximity to a source of danger at a spaceport.

The list of individuals in Regulation 40 is exhaustive, containing employees or other appointees or agents of a licencee,[1252] crew members and spaceflight participants who have given informed consent under section 17 of the Space Industry Act[1253] and individuals 'not falling within sub-paragraphs (a)–(c) who (are) taking part in the operator's spaceflight activities'. This appears likely to include employees, agents or other individuals who, incidentally, may not have given informed consent but may be otherwise involved. It also extends to invitees of the licencee,[1254] employees of the Regulator or those acting on the Regulator's behalf,[1255] and, amongst others, government employees and employees of the emergency services and health and safety authorities and members of the armed forces.[1256] Once again, there is no requirement for such

1251 Space Industry Act 2018 s7.
1252 R40(a).
1253 R40(b)–(c).
1254 R40 (f).
1255 R40 (g).
1256 R40 (h)–(m).

individuals to have given informed consent under section 17 although they could be excluded from the benefit of the strict liability regime should they be detrimentally exposed to hazards which seems at the most an undesirable position.

This position becomes more acute when the risk assessment requirements under the Space Industry Act are contrasted with those under the US regime.

The Space Industry Act provides that a risk assessment must have been carried out in respect of the 'health and safety of individuals who are to take part in a prescribed role or capacity'.[1257] Under section 17(1) only those acting in such a role are required to give informed consent. As previously addressed, those excluded from the strict liability regime encompass a wide range of individuals not required to give informed consent.

The approach regarding risk assessments is seemingly opposed to the US position which holds that, in respect of ground safety, such an assessment must also include 'employee hazard', specifically:

> A hazard to individuals performing a launch operator's work, but not to other people in the area. A launch operator must comply with all applicable Federal, state, and local employee safety regulations. A launch operator's ground safety analysis must identify employee hazards and demonstrate that there are no associated public safety issues.[1258]

Whilst the US regime seems similar in seeking to exempt people not forming part of the public from the assessment, the term 'employee' appears much more inclusive overall. Under the UK regime, 'employees' may not necessarily be deemed to be in a 'prescribed role' or 'capacity'. Under Schedule 2 of the Regulations on Training it is stated that:

> Training regulations may make provision requiring an individual's competence—
>
> (a) to take part in, or otherwise to be engaged in connection with, prescribed activities in a prescribed role or capacity, or (b) to work at a prescribed place, or to work at a prescribed place in a prescribed role or capacity.

There is a distinction inherent in the wording between working *in connection* with a prescribed role or capacity and working *in* a prescribed role or capacity.

1257 S9(2).
1258 CFR (US) 417.405 (3).

The difference could be crucial in determining the extent of a risk assessment and the extent to which informed consent should be given in respect of space activities. Although such individuals could be assumed to be covered by risk assessments under global instruments such as the Health and Safety at Work Act 1974 their apparent exclusion from Space Industry Act specific risk assessments seems arbitrary and unfair.

Unhelpfully in this context, the first iteration of guidance stated that, when compiling a ground safety analysis:

> The ground safety analysis should not include occupational health and safety concerns that arise from conventional hazards covered by existing regulations such as the Health and Safety at Work Act (HSAW 1974) or the Explosives Regulations 2014. However, as stated in regulation 30(6), such regulations must be taken into account.[1259]

This was a drafting error as Regulation 30(6) does not contain any such direction, nor was this present within the draft regulations[1260] It does not even exist. Neither can a 'Section' '30(6)' be found within the Space Industry Act 2018. If the implicit expectation is that an operator is expected to take account of 'such regulations', using the *ejusdem generis* canon of interpretation,[1261] other 'such regulations' could include the Working Time Regulations and others like them, hence incorporating these measures through the back door. In the context of the instruments, this approach would seem unnecessarily opaque. It is of interest to note that the updated guidance document did not repeat this statement in these exact terms, instead providing that: 'You do not need to include occupational health and safety concerns covered by the Health and Safety at Work Act 1974. However, there is likely to be some overlap.'[1262] This is considerably narrower than the original statement, and there is no reference to any provisions, existent or otherwise, within the legislative framework. Some clarity from the regulator would be most welcome as to the correct expectation in this context.

Turning to environmental matters, the requirement for an Assessment of Environmental Effects has been well documented already within this work.

1259 N257, 27.

1260 The draft Space Industry Regulations 2021, UK Draft Statutory Instruments, ISBN 978-0-348-22368-2. Available in full on the legislation.gov.uk website.

1261 See the cases of *Hobbs v Robertson* (CG) [1970] 1 W.L.R. 980 and *Allen v. Emmerson* [1944] K.B. 362 for examples in the context of statutory interpretation.

1262 N368, 26.

It is of note in the comparative context, that the guidance on Assessments of Environmental Effects states that the amount of detail required for each licence type will vary:

> The Regulator will expect more detailed data for a launch operator AEE than for a spaceport AEE as the launch vehicle(s) will be known. The AEE must be based on the actual details of the class, type and detailed requirements of the launch vehicle and must not be based on assumptions.[1263]

The US Code of Federal Regulations appears more prescriptive in respect of the information required:

> An applicant shall provide the FAA with information for the FAA to analyze the environmental impacts associated with a proposed launch. The information provided by an applicant must be sufficient to enable the FAA to comply with the requirements of the National Environment Policy Act, 42 U.S.C. 4321 et seq. (NEPA), the Council on Environmental Quality Regulations for Implementing the Procedural Provisions of NEPA, 40 CFR parts 1500–1508, and the FAA's Procedures for Considering Environmental Impacts, FAA Order 1050.1D.[1264]

Similarly to the UK regime, under § 415.203 there is no need to submit additional environmental documentation where there is already coverage as such. The opinion of the House of Commons Science, Innovation and Technology Committee was that: 'Following the initial launch attempt, it is clear that there are streamlining improvements that should be made to ensure that the Regulatory processes leading up to launch are best aligned'.[1265]

The US Code of Federal Regulations offer some guidance as to how such streamlining could be affected, potentially without harming the overall objective of environmental protection in this regard. '§ 1500.4 Reducing paperwork' incudes various strategies for how this can be done to an extent. These include the use of 'categorical exclusions' for actions that would not ordinarily be expected to have an environmental impact,[1266] an automatic designation of

1263 N1148, 17.

1264 CFR (US) § 415.201 General.

1265 House of Commons Science, Innovation and Technology Committee, UK space strategy and UK satellite infrastructure: reviewing the licencing regime for launch, Seventh Report of Session 2022–23, para 27. <https://committees.parliament.uk/publications/40829/documents/198924/default/> accessed 16 October 2024.

1266 CFR (US) § 1500.4 (a).

'no significant impact'[1267] for activities which patently would not have such an impact and appropriate page limits[1268] among various other measures.

Regarding other potential checks and balances on the likely environmental impact of the operator's activities, as the guidance points out, there is an expectation under the Aarhus Convention[1269] that affected members of the public will be entitled to information as regards decisions relating to the environment. The guidance states that, 'in line with the conventions provisions, the Regulator will consult with the public',[1270] and, further, that '[c]onsultation will enable the public to access the submitted AEE and to express their opinions on the proposals'.[1271] It is further stated that '[t]he Regulator will publish a notice of the submitted AEE and instructions for how people can comment on it and see the AEE on their website. Members of the public and anyone interested in the submitted AEE will be given a specified period of time within which to comment'.[1272] This is further to rights already in place under the Freedom of Information Act 2000[1273] and the Environmental Information Regulations 2004[1274] as the guidance points out.[1275] The Environmental Information Regulations go some way to satisfying the requirements of the Aarhus Convention by importing many of its requirements[1276] as to dissemination and the form/format of the information in question.

Regarding the clarity of such information required by an Assessment of Environmental Effects, it is instructive to observe how the requirement for an Assessment of Environmental Effects has been carried out in practice. The first one of its kind was released in July 2022[1277] in respect of the unsuccessful Virgin Orbit launch. The document is comprehensive but also presented in a user-friendly manner with the Executive Summary pointing out the impact of the mooted effects along with mitigation measures which have been taken.[1278]

1267 *Ibid*, (b).

1268 *Ibid*, (c).

1269 UNECE Convention on Access to Information, Public Participation in Decision-making and Access to Justice in Environmental Matters (Aarhus Convention), 2161 UNTS 447; UKTS 2005 No. 24; Cm. 6586.

1270 N1148, para 4.27.

1271 *Ibid*.

1272 *Ibid*.

1273 C.36.

1274 SI 2004 No. 3391.

1275 N1148, para 4.28.

1276 Part 2 of the Regulations, for example, imports requirements in Article 4 of the Convention.

1277 N627.

1278 *Ibid*, ES-4.

It is interesting to note that, since Virgin Orbit is incorporated in Delaware, it also required a licence from the US Federal Aviation Administration for launching outside the United States[1279] under the Code of Federal Regulations[1280]– a similar requirement to those under the Outer Space Act 1986 for launches outside the United Kingdom it is to be assumed.

A further area of interest across the different regimes is the way in which debris mitigation is approached. The recent Virgin Orbit launch outlined mitigation measures in the report, in particular highlighting some ways in which debris may be impossible to recover.[1281] 'Rocket debris in the marine environment' was also stated to be a 'long term' effect at the report's conclusion.[1282] Whilst there were commendable efforts to account for the creation of terrestrial debris no reference was made to space debris.

This is not to suggest that the United Kingdom is not taking the problem of space debris seriously. It recently joined the United Nations Initiative as regards 'the future sustainability and safety of outer space'[1283] and has been described as a leader in supporting debris mitigation policies and guidelines of the United Nations.[1284] The United Kingdom has debris mitigation measures built into the Space Industry Act 2018 at section 101 which calls for reasonable steps to be taken – on reaching a stable orbit – for the avoidance of releasing space debris in addition to passivation measures and collision avoidance. This is drafted in similar terms to the US Code of Federal Regulations.[1285]

Similarly to the position in the United Kingdom, the US Code of Federal Regulations requires an Assessment of Environmental Effects to be made available for public consultation.[1286] The FAA website sets out a clear procedure for the administration of such assessments including the associated procedural

1279 *Ibid*, 1-1.

1280 CFR (US) § 413.3(c)(1).

1281 See in particular paragraph 3.1.58 on ocean bound debris unable to be recovered.

1282 N828, 8–1.

1283 The United Kingdom Space Agency, 'UN and UK Sign Agreement to Promote Space Sustainability', 2021, <https://www.gov.uk/government/news/un-and-uk-sign-agreement-to-promote-space-sustainability.> accessed 25 November 2023.

1284 See the evidence to the Science and Technology Committee on UK Space Strategy and Satellite Infrastructure, HC 98 Wednesday 9 February 2022 of Dr Paul Bate, CEO of the United Kingdom Space Agency at Q427, 18, <https://committees.parliament.uk/oralevidence/3427/pdf/> accessed 13 November 2023. For further details of the United Kingdom's commitment to debris mitigation, see the end of Chapter 9 on sustainability.

1285 CFR (US) § 417.129 (b)–(c).

1286 See the website of the Federal Aviation Authority, <https://www.faa.gov/space/environmental#erp> accessed 25 November 2023.

rules,[1287] and determines that such assessments may be regarded as being 'of no significant impact' or subject to a 'FONSI' ('Finding Of No Significant Impact') notice.[1288]

As outlined, the UK environmental regime centres around the section 11 Assessment of Environmental Effects which must be submitted in respect of certain space activities. This will be considered by the regulator and environmental conditions may be attached to any licence granted. Most, if not all, jurisdictions, provide at least a degree of environmental regulation in respect of space activities. As has been indicated, the UK regime is somewhat porous in certain regards and could be improved with reference to the practice of other jurisdictions. It appears that there is one further, and crucial, element lacking from the UK regime in relation to space debris – 'end of life' disposal for orbiting space objects. A number of other jurisdictions make at least an outline reference to this. As part of a broader focus on the 'nonpollution of outer space', Argentina requires that information on 'mechanisms for placement in a transfer orbit at the end of the useful life of the space object' along with the 'anticipated date of disintegration' be entered into their national registry.[1289] Several jurisdictions have gone further, adopting the Inter Agency Space Debris Coordination Committee's recommendation[1290] on manoeuvring space objects in low earth orbit near the end of their lifecycles. Denmark stipulates that, '[a]s a general rule, within 25 years of the end date of the functional operating period of the space object, the space object must either safely leave its earth orbit again or safely be placed into an orbit where it is deemed not to constitute a danger to other space activities'.[1291] Finland takes a similar approach, stating that an operator must, 'after the space object has completed its mission, seek to move it into a less used orbit or into the atmosphere'[1292]

1287 *Ibid.*

1288 *Ibid.*

1289 Decree No. 125/95, (Argentina) Art 5.

1290 Inter Agency Space Debris Coordination Committee, 'Space Debris Mitigation Guidelines', 2007, (IADC-02-01 Rev. 3) 5.3.2.

1291 Executive Order on requirements in connection with approval of activities in outer space, etc. pursuant to section 7, section 10(4), section 11(4), section 13(3), section 19 and section 21(3) of the Outer Space Act (Denmark) (Act no. 409 of 11 May 2016 on activities in outer space), Article 6(2), unofficial English translation <https://ufm.dk/en/legislation/prevailing-laws-and-regulations/outer-space/executive-order-on-requirements-in-connection-with-approval-of-activities-in-outer-space-etc-_final.pdf> accessed 25 April 2024.

1292 Act on Space Activities (Finland) (63/2018), Section 10, unofficial English Translation <https://finlex.fi/api/media/statute-foreign-language-translation/53403/mainPdf/main.pdf> accessed 25 April 2024.

and explicitly adopts the '25 year rule' elsewhere.[1293] The '25 year' prescription can also be found beyond Scandinavia such as in Liechtenstein[1294] which references 'graveyard' orbits.[1295]

Regarding the problem of space debris more generally, many jurisdictions adopt a more robust approach to debris mitigation. The UK regulator must take into account 'any space debris mitigation guidelines issued by an international organisation in which the government of the United Kingdom is represented'[1296] and compliance with the same can form a licence condition.[1297] The regulations also require an operator to take 'reasonable steps' to avoid the release of space debris on achieving orbit[1298] and the safety case as submitted must contain information about the debris mitigation measures taken in the construction of the space object.[1299] Debris mitigation in UK space law, then, is governed first of all by proxy under a licensing decision, and then, secondly, under a 'standards' – as opposed to a 'rules' – based formula. There does not appear to be any expansion on this within the guidance documents beyond what is stated in legislation.

According to the COPUOS Legal Subcommittee,[1300] Austria takes the approach to space debris very seriously. Regarding the Austrian Federal Law on the Authorization of Space Activities and the Establishment of a National Space Registry 2011,[1301] 'Particular emphasis is put on the mitigation of space debris so that compliance with the 'state of the art' and 'internationally recognized guidelines for the mitigation of space debris' is required. This commitment can be found under section 5 of the Act, which also states that measures limiting debris release during normal operations have to be taken. The position in

1293 *Ibid*, Section 3.

1294 Ordinance On the Authorization of Space Activities and the Registration of Space Objects, 4 December 2023, (Liechtenstein) Article 4 (g) <https://www.unoosa.org/oosa/en/ourwork/spacelaw/nationalspacelaw/index.html> accessed 25 April 2024.

1295 *Ibid*.

1296 N127, s2(2)(h).

1297 *Ibid*, Schedule 1(1)(g).

1298 N173, Regulation 101, s3(a).

1299 *Ibid*, Schedule 1, (14).

1300 Committee on the Peaceful Uses of Outer Space Legal Subcommittee, 'Status and application of the five United Nations treaties on outer space, and ways and means, including capacity-building, to promote their implementation', Sixty-third session, Vienna, 15–26 April 2024, 4–5/78, https://www.unoosa.org/res/oosadoc/data/documents/2023/aac_105c_22023crp/aac_105c_22023crp_28_0_html/AC105_C2_2023_CRP28E.pdf.

1301 Austrian Federal Law on the Authorization of Space Activities and the Establishment of a National Space Registry 2011 (Austrian Outer Space Act), entered into force on 28 December 2011.

Denmark appears more permissive with Article 6 of the Executive Order made under the Outer Space Act determining that the Danish Agency for Science, Technology and Innovation has the power to demand 'that space activities which involve the launch of space objects into earth orbit meet relevant standards and guidelines for space debris management, such as standards published by the European Cooperation for Space Standardization (ECSS) or the International Organization for Standardization (ISO)'.[1302] This indeed appears permissive – the Agency has the power to stipulate such measures as indeed the UK regulator can impose licence conditions regarding space debris. Finland takes a more direct approach, compelling the operator to '... ensure that the space activities do not generate space debris ... In particular, the operator shall restrict the generation of space debris during the normal operations of the space object'.[1303] Here we see divergence from the UK position of requiring the regulator to consider imposing conditions, or requiring information to be furnished in respect of how a space objects design limits the generation of space debris. Instead, operators are directed to ensure that debris mitigation is conducted. Representing a compromise between the two positions, Liechtenstein, under Article 5(1)(g) of its Act On the Authorization of Space Activities and the Registration of Space Objects[1304] sets out that authorisation of space activities is contingent upon adequate measures being taken to prevent space debris. Ukraine also puts strong emphasis on the avoidance of space debris, stating '[t]he violation of international norms and standards regarding pollution of outer space, in connection with space activities, is prohibited'.[1305] Common law approaches will be addressed later in this chapter but, as can be seen from the approach taken by some European civil law systems, a clearer and more robust approach to the problem of space debris could be taken by the United Kingdom. It would also be desirable for provision to be made for 'end of life' procedures.

The environmental protection regime in UK space legislation is essentially an 'arm's length' approach. There are no direct requirements that an operator refrain from conducting activities in a way which could be environmentally

1302 N1299.

1303 N1300, s10.

1304 Act On the Authorization of Space Activities and the Registration of Space Objects, 5th October 2023 (Liechtenstein) unofficial English translation, <https://www.llv.li/serviceportal2/amtsstellen/amt-fuer-kommunikation/20231212_space-act_en_unofficial-translation.pdf> accessed 25 April 2024.

1305 Ordinance Of The Supreme Soviet Of Ukraine, On Space Activity, Law of Ukraine of 15 November 1996 Art 9.

harmful, but, instead, obtaining a licence may be made conditional upon an operator so refraining. This contrasts with a number of jurisdictions where the responsibilities of the operator are expressed in a more direct manner, often in the form of negative requirements. Austria's federal space law makes obtaining an authorisation conditional on the basis that the activities concerned 'do not cause harmful contamination of outer space or celestial bodies or adverse changes in the environment'.[1306] Although adopting a similar model for authorisation, this appears cast in stronger terms than the UK position. Whilst the Assessment of Environmental Effects in UK space law is left largely to the operator to compile with the assistance of experts chosen by them,[1307] Belgium requires that the environmental impact of 'all' activities covered by the relevant legislation 'shall be assessed by one or more experts designated for that purpose by the Minister'.[1308] Furthermore, '[s]uch an assessment may be carried out at different stages of the activities'.[1309] Whilst such an approach may be desirable in ensuring an independent assessment, it is worth noting that the reports produced for the Virgin Orbit launch of January 2022 and for the SaxaVord spaceport were both highly comprehensive documents apparently conducted by reputable teams of individuals. Within the licensing context of UK space legislation, the Belgian approach could arguably seem overly paternalistic but it is worth noting that the United Kingdom has an extensive regime of inspection and monitoring for other aspects of spaceflight.[1310] Where the Belgian approach maybe fails in respect of efficiency is where it is stated that assessments must be carried out at various stages of the activities concerned. This could seem overly burdensome unless it is reflective of the UK practice of requiring separate AEE's for launches and spaceports.[1311] Article 8 §2 of Belgium's domestic space law requires that an initial study be carried out to assess the 'potential impact on the environment on earth or in outer space of launching or operating the space object' before authorisation is granted. If this is intended to mean *in addition* to the assessments already mentioned

1306 N1309, Article 5.

1307 Although evidence of their qualifications must be presented as part of the AEE per the guidance.

1308 Law of 17 September 2005 on the Activities of Launching, Flight Operation or Guidance of Space Objects consolidated text as revised by the Law of 1 December 2013, Article 8 §1 (B.O.J. of 15 January 2014) <https://www.belspo.be/belspo/space/doc/beLaw/Loi_en.pdf> accessed 25 April 2024.

1309 *Ibid.*

1310 See ss26–33 of the Space Industry Act 2018 and Part 14 of the Space Industry Regulations 2021.

1311 N127, s11(1)(a)–(b).

this could represent a very cumbersome process. This would contrast with the United Kingdom government's policy of trying to foster an efficient legislative background for the fledgling space industry.[1312] The wording of Denmark's environmental provisions also takes an imperative stance, setting out that documentation is required before authorisation is granted demonstrating that 'the space activity which the application concerns is carried out in an environmentally safe manner'.[1313] On one reading, this approach is not too far removed from the UK position – an operator will be granted a licence should the regulator not feel that the activities are likely to cause environmental harm. There is no specific requirement for 'environmental safeness' within the UK regime, only the statement that conditions can be imposed on a licencee to conduct activities so as 'to prevent the contamination of outer space or adverse changes in the environment of the earth'.[1314] The Danish position appears stronger still when taking into consideration Part 4 of the Executive Order on requirements in connection with approval of space activities.[1315] As is stated there in the imperative, 'Space activities must be performed with due consideration for the surrounding environment'[1316] after which follows a number of areas relating to the environment that the Danish Agency for Science, Technology and Innovation can request information about from the operator. The Finnish law also directs operators to carry out activities 'in a manner that is environmentally sustainable and promotes the sustainable use of outer space'[1317] and, further, directs operators to submit an assessment of the environmental effects of its activities in addition to the way in which it proposes to reduce their impact.[1318] This is not a specific requirement under UK legislation. Liechtenstein also provides that authorisation for space activities is conditional on such activities not causing 'harmful contamination' to the environment of Earth or outer space.[1319]

There are also specific reporting requirements under Liechtenstein's December 2023 ordinance that requires documentary evidence to show that

1312 As is reflected in the legislation whereby previously used AEE reports can be used in future applications, thus reducing the administrative burden.

1313 The Danish Outer Space Act (act no. 409 of 11 May 2016) Art 6(5), unofficial translation, <https://ufm.dk/en/legislation/prevailing-laws-and-regulations/outer-space/outer-space-act.pdf> accessed 25 April 2024.

1314 N127, Schedule 1(14)(a).

1315 N1299, Part 4.

1316 *Ibid*, s7.

1317 N1300, s10.

1318 *Ibid.*

1319 N1312, Art 5,1(f).

a space object does not contain 'dangerous or harmful substances that could lead to harmful contamination of outer space or detrimental changes to the environment'.[1320] There are extensive reporting requirements under UK legislation but there is no requirement to directly report on substances harmful to the environment as such. It is to be assumed that the regulator will take such matters into consideration when considering the section 11 Assessment of Environmental Effects.

Kazakhstan directly requires space activities to be 'carried out upon condition of maintenance of health care of people and environment, protection of property of individuals and legal entities'.[1321] Furthermore, operators are directed to 'exercise industrial ecological control of the environment following the procedures established by the ecological legislation of the Republic of Kazakhstan'[1322] and there is provision for ongoing 'state monitoring of environmental matters during space activities'.[1323] Ukraine takes a similar approach, requiring that activities be conducted in a way that complies with existing safety requirements as regards the protection of the environment in addition to compelling operators to establish measures to mitigate environmental harm.[1324]

It is clear from the above that a large number of civil law systems place direct responsibility for environmental protection on the operators themselves, whereas the United Kingdom achieves this through conditions attached to licences. Whilst this nuance may seem insignificant and, indeed, may largely arise from natural contrasts in drafting cultures, it may be an effective method to eradicate lacunae such as that seen in the United Kingdom as regards activities which are not covered by the requirement to provide an Assessment of Environmental Effects.[1325] Imposing a blanket 'duty' to perform activities in a way that causes the least possible harm to the environment and promote the sustainable usage of outer space could be a positive step. If drafting culture or differences in legal culture could be said to be the reason for the absence of such a duty, it is interesting to note the wording of Regulation 101 (c)(III) of the Space Industry Regulations 2021. It states that '[i]f necessary to ensure that an operator's spaceflight activities are carried out safely or to secure

1320 N1302, Art 4(f).

1321 Law of the Republic of Kazakhstan on Space Activities (No. 528-IV of 6 January 2012), Art 27, unofficial English translation.

1322 *Ibid,* Art 29(2).

1323 *Ibid* Art 29 (2).

1324 N1313, Article 21.

1325 Return Operators, Range Control and large rockets not operating above the stratosphere.

compliance with the international obligations of the United Kingdom, the spaceflight operator must after a launch vehicle has reached a stable orbit … prevent contamination of outer space arising from the launch vehicle in orbit or adverse changes in the environment of the earth from that vehicle in orbit'.

This is the only provision within UK space law which places a duty on operators to avoid environmental harm, and it applies only to space objects in orbit. If such duties can arise in respect of objects in orbit, it seems incongruous for them to be absent in relation to other dimensions of space activity.

An interesting contrary observation is that Sweden explicitly excludes 'sounding rockets' from its definition of space activities.[1326] The rocket that is due to launch from SaxaVord spaceport in the Shetland Islands – and which did not require an Assessment of Environmental Effects under section 11 – is described as a 'sounding rocket'. Given the secondary environmental impact of such launches (such as diversion of air traffic) in addition to the associated safety risks any launch necessitates, it is difficult to understand why this is. The Swedish Act is over 40 years old and was created in a pre-Brundtland[1327] era as regards sustainability and many years before the recent proliferation of private space ventures. It will be interesting to see if there are any amendments to this provision in the coming years.

Unsurprisingly, compulsory insurance is a common requirement within jurisdictions which legislate for private space activities. Whilst this practice is broadly adhered to, some jurisdictions offer waivers or reductions for certain space activities. Portugal, for example, provides for this in a number of instances, including the launching and control of 'space objects of small dimensions', operations which are exclusively scientific or educational in nature and operations 'that prove to give rise to reduced risks, as defined by the Space Authority'.[1328] Liechtenstein shares similar provisions but also sets out a broader 'public interest' provision.[1329] There are presently no such provisions in UK law.

Finland also prescribes that insurance can be waived if there is a lower than 1/1000 chance of a collision in orbit and 'if the probability that the space object or its component parts will not burn in the atmosphere is lower than 1/10 000'.[1330] Slovenia too makes an interesting contribution though on

1326 Act on Space Activities (Sweden) s1, (1982:963) unofficial English translation.

1327 N1144.

1328 Decree-Law no. 16/2019, of 22 January, Legal regime of access to and exercise of space activities (Portugal), Article 19(3)(a)–(d) unofficial English translation.

1329 N1312 Art 8 (2)(a).

1330 Decree of the Ministry of Economic Affairs and Employment on Space Activities (Finland) (74/2018), s5, unofficial English Translation <https://tem.fi/documents/1410

different terms. Article 6 of the Space Activities Act[1331] releases an operator from the insurance requirements if they can show that '(a) the space object does not have its own means of propulsion, has a mass of less than 150 kg, is not part of a constellation, is to be launched into an unoccupied low Earth orbit slot and is constructed from materials that ensure that the object will burn up when it re-enters the atmosphere or (b) the space object does not have its own means of propulsion, has a mass of less than 150 kg, is to be launched into orbits above the low Earth orbit, and will remain in orbits that do not encroach upon the geostationary orbit or orbits with an altitude between 19,882 and 20,482 km.' This position seems rather unusual given that any launch carries a risk of disaster whether it is into low Earth orbit or elsewhere. Regarding the second limb of Article 6 there is always a risk of on orbit collision.

Russia makes provision for insurance to be taken out 'for the life and health of the cosmonauts and personnel of space infrastructure facilities'.[1332] Fee-paying spaceflight participants will not likely be covered by the definition of a 'cosmonaut' under this provision but it is interesting to note that UK legislation does not require operators to specifically seek mandatory insurance for spaceflight participants at all, regardless of whether they are participating in spaceflight activities through occupational pursuit or leisure.

The most common thread across all jurisdictions examined is that of licensing or authorisation of space activities. This is unsurprising for a few reasons, chiefly, the imperative nature of ensuring that such activities carried on within national territories are done so in a safe manner. Moreover, it also implements existing obligations in respect of the peaceful uses of outer space. The approaches taken are broadly similar, but the provisions within the UK regime rank amongst the most comprehensive and detailed, particularly when the associated guidance documents are considered alongside them.

Many jurisdictions opt for a form of 'fit and proper person' test to ensure that only individuals with demonstrable financial resources, expertise and

---

877/3227301/Decree+of+the+MEAE+on+Space+Activities/08da7d7b-70e9-4c7e-bd2a-03220d6aa028/Decree+of+the+MEAE+on+Space+Activities.pdf?t=1517303859000> accessed 25 April 2024.

1331 The Space Activities Act (ZVDej) (Slovenia) 16 March 2022.

1332 N381, Art 25. Details as stated by the Committee on the Peaceful Uses of Outer Space, Legal Subcommittee, Sixty-second session, Vienna, 20–31 March 2023, Item 7 of the provisional agenda, National legislation relevant to the peaceful exploration and use of outer space, 'Schematic Overview of National Regulatory Frameworks for Space Activities', 67–68, <https://www.unoosa.org/res/oosadoc/data/documents/2023/aac_105c_22023crp/aac_105c_22023crp_28_0_html/AC105_C2_2023_CRP28E.pdf>accessed 24 April 2024.

reputation are authorised to conduct space activities.[1333] The same approach is taken within UK legislation.[1334] Furthermore, the information to be provided for vetting purposes by potential applicants is considerable. The requirements cannot be found in the legislation, but, instead, can be found in the Regulator's Licensing Rules[1335] and include matters such as projected cash-flow forecasts and profit and loss accounts.[1336] This is in many ways like the Dutch requirements which, contrastingly, are set out in the legislation itself.[1337]

The decision of the United Kingdom not to enshrine the requirements in a formal legislative instrument itself could be indicative of the legal approach that is to be taken as regards the governance of private space activities; where the law is silent or otherwise unclear, the guidance and associated documents have full authority.[1338] Another area where the United Kingdom boasts a comprehensive and detailed regime in contrast to most of its comparators, is in monitoring, inspection and enforcement. Reporting requirements naturally follow licensing ones, and it is no surprise that other jurisdictions also embed these requirements. The UK reporting requirements are much more comprehensive and rigorous in scope by comparison with many other jurisdictions.

By way of overall comparison, the United Kingdom can be said to have a particularly robust and comprehensive legislative regime. Where legislation does not cover a given eventuality, the written guidance almost certainly does. Whilst in a broad sense the United Kingdom covers everything in at least as much detail and care as its civil law comparators – there is certainly a comprehensive address of the United Kingdom's international obligations – there are certain areas which warrant further legislative attention or clarity. Firstly, the provisions around sustainability should be revisited. More robust action

1333 See for example, Article 2 of Austria's Outer Space Regulation- Regulation of the Federal Minister for Transport, Innovation and Technology in Implementation of the Federal Law on the Authorisation of Space Activities and the Establishment of a National Space Registry, (as of 07 June 2022), Article 6 (2) of The Danish Outer Space Act (act no. 409 of 11 May 2016), Section 5 of Finland's Act on Space Activities (63/2018), and Article 4 of Luxembourg's Law of December 15th 2020 on Space Activities.

1334 See the Space Industry Act 2018, Section 8 and the Space Industry Regulations 2021 Regulation 84.

1335 N256.

1336 *Ibid*, 11.

1337 Order of the Minister of Economic Affairs dated 7 February 2008, no. WJZ 7119929, containing rules governing licence applications for the performance of space activities and the registration of space objects, Article 2(2)(b) (Netherlands) translation provided by the Netherlands.

1338 Although, as has been written, the precise legal status of at least some of these documents is difficult to determine.

is required as regards the prevention of space debris and there should also be consideration to including 'graveyard orbit' clauses as per a number of comparators. Furthermore, the existing environmental provisions should also extend to cover 'return' operators as a minimum, and the lacunae regarding AEE's and Large Rocket Permissions should be closed. Secondly, consideration ought to be given to granting indulgences in respect of insurance where the insured activity is one that is being conducted in the public interest as was observed in a number of other jurisdictions. Consideration could also be given to the Finnish approach where elements of risk are a relevant factor in determining exceptions or reductions. As cost factors are undoubtedly one of the main concerns of operators this could lead to a partial offset. Thirdly, matters relating to satellite data and remote sensing could also be enshrined as is the case in other jurisdictions.[1339] There is a paucity of treatment of such matters in UK legislation which seems unusual given the country's history of involvement with the international organisation of space telecommunications. Although not widespread throughout other jurisdictions,[1340] the United Kingdom should also consider legislating for the potential exploitation of space resources. Although it may be fanciful to speculate that the United Kingdom will be launching missions to mine asteroids in the near future, it may nonetheless be home to companies and individuals who have such ambitions.[1341] It should also be noted that whilst there are clearly some areas that have been addressed more completely within other jurisdictions, the United Kingdom has legislated in areas that are completely absent from most, if not all, of the ones observed. The UK informed consent provisions, although there may be certain questions regarding mental capacity and other issues around the administration of an informed consent procedure, are a distinct feature. Whether this is a reflection of the type of activities the United Kingdom wishes to pursue[1342] or, more likely, the result of a legal transplant from the United States, is not clear.

Whilst it has been of interest to observe the UK experience in the context of civil law jurisdictions, some attention should also be given to common

1339 See Germany, for example: Act to give Protection against the Security Risk to the Federal Republic of Germany by the Dissemination of High-Grade Earth Remote Sensing Data (Germany) November 23, 2007 (Satellite Data Security Act – SatDSiG) unofficial English translation, <https://www.unoosa.org/oosa/en/ourwork/spacelaw/nationalspacelaw/index.html> accessed 25 April 2024.

1340 But see Luxembourg, Law of July 20th 2017 on the exploration and use of space resources (Luxembourg), unofficial English translation.

1341 For example, see Asteroid Mining Corporation, one such related entity based in the UK, <https://www.asteroidminingcorporation.co.uk/about> accessed 28 May 2024.

1342 There is not much evidence for this at present.

law jurisdictions beyond the United States. Australia and New Zealand have very comprehensive regimes which are drafted in similar terms to the United Kingdom. A high-level comparative overview of these jurisdictions would be beyond the scope of this work, but some of the pertinent similarities and contrasts will be outlined accordingly.

Australia's full licensing framework for space activities pre-dates that of the United Kingdom by exactly 20 years.[1343] It has a range of separate instruments including general rules[1344] followed by separate ones on matters such as insurance[1345] and 'high powered' rockets.[1346] Similarly to the United Kingdom, these are rules made under a parent Act and also set out a rigorous licensing procedure[1347] which is executed with commendable clarity.[1348] In terms of assessing risk for the purpose of calculating insurance cover, Australia utilises a 'maximum probable loss' methodology whereby operators are expected to calculate potential harm with reference to guidance which is tailored specifically to space activities.[1349] Totaling 40 pages, the guidance contain space activity-specific 'hazard tree' diagrams[1350] and contains a significant amount of 'signposting' for the reader. 'Risk Hazard Analysis' itself is contained in the 79-page spaceflight-specific 'Flight Safety Code',[1351] itself a thorough document.[1352] Although an investigation of the legal status of these documents in Australian law is beyond the scope of this research, it is worth making some general comparisons to the UK approach. As detailed previously, the United Kingdom requires that operators demonstrate that risk is 'ALARP' – as low as reasonably practicable.[1353] Instead of suggesting a prescriptive format for risk assessment,

---

1343 Space Activities Act 1998 (Australia) Act No. 123 of 1998 (as amended). This does not include reference to the 1986 Act as this was not on the same scale.

1344 Space (Launches and Returns) (General) Rules 2019.

1345 Space (Launches and Returns) (Insurance) Rules 2019.

1346 Space (Launches and Returns) (High Power Rocket) Rules 2019.

1347 N1352.

1348 See *Ibid,* Division 3, subdivisions A–D.

1349 Australian Government, Australian Space Agency, 'Maximum Probable Loss Methodology', 1 August 2019 <https://www.space.gov.au/sites/default/files/media-documents/2023-04/iga_maximum_probable_loss_methodology.pdf> accessed 30 May 2024.

1350 *Ibid,* 19, 22, 23, for example.

1351 Australian Government, Australian Space Agency, 'Flight Safety Code' 1 August 2019 <https://www.space.gov.au/sites/default/files/media-documents/2023-04/iga_flight_safety_code.pdf> accessed 30 May 2024.

1352 Which even goes so far as to designate a 'standard person' as a 'hypothetical object of cylindrical shape with a circular base of radius 0.3 metres and linear height of 2 metres' for calculation purposes at page 8 (also referenced within the Maximum Probable Loss guidance.

1353 Space Industry Act 2018 section 9(4)(a).

the approach here is largely to leave the operator much to their own devices by way of demonstrating to the regulator that they have assessed risk in line not just with local space legislation but also 'other relevant health and safety legislation as far as it is within the scope of the licenced activities' and encourages the adoption of other 'appropriate standards where they exist and recognised good practice'.[1354] Whilst the advantage of this approach may be to avoid burdening operators with excessive administrative tasks, it could also serve to make matters more complicated. Which specific industries should the operator look to? What particular standards may be the correct ones to adopt in such circumstances? As previously argued, would allowing operators to choose different standards lead to an undesirable fragmentation of approaches? Could the lack of a defined route to assessing risk be overly burdensome to operators who may not have access to the wide range of expertise required to determine such matters? It is of interest to note here that in the 2024 Space Regulatory Review[1355] concerns were raised by industry in the associated consultations around the term 'acceptable' in section 9(4)(b) in relation to the level of risk. This term was queried as being overly subjective and unclear, highlighting the need for further instruction.[1356] The United Kingdom should consider taking a lead from the Australian approach in this area.

The approach to environmental matters within the Australian legislation also seems more robust, as appears to be the case in respect of many of the civil law jurisdictions examined. An operator must be in receipt of 'all necessary environmental approvals under Australian law' and have presented 'an adequate environmental plan' prior to a licence being granted for construction and operation of a launch facility.[1357] Although this could be the result of a differing culture of environmental regulation generally, making the submission of a plan along with associated 'approvals' as a pre-requisite for the granting of a licence appears more complete than the UK requirement of an Assessment of Environmental Effects – which appears to be the only required document and is sparsely detailed within the legislation itself. It is further stipulated that 'For each launch, the application must include ... evidence that the environmental impact of the launch and any connected return is addressed by the

---

1354 The United Kingdom Civil Aviation Authority, CAP220, 'Principles and Guidelines for the spaceflight regulator in assessing ALARP and Acceptable Risk' July 2021, 3, <https://www.caa.co.uk/publication/download/18931> accessed 30 May 2024.

1355 N405.

1356 *Ibid*, 34.

1357 N1351, 18(b).

environmental plan of the licenced launch facility from which the launch is proposed'.[1358]

This stands in direct contrast to the position in the United Kingdom where an Assessment of Environmental Effects is not required for return operations. Environmental matters in respect of returns are further provided for under section 101 of the Space Activities Act on 'Environment', which states that:

> If the application is for the return of one or more space objects to a place or area in Australia, the application must include information about environmental approvals required for the return or returns under any other law of the Commonwealth or a law of a State or Territory.[1359]

The Act goes further still, providing that, even where there are no local requirements for environmental approval, return applications must 'include an environmental plan that includes ... an assessment of the likely impact of conducting the return or returns on the environment ... arrangements for monitoring and mitigating any adverse effects on the environment from conducting the return or returns [and] mechanisms for reporting on the implementation of those arrangements and for reviewing the plan.'[1360] Quite why return operator licences were made exempt from a section 11 Assessment of Environmental Effects under UK law is difficult to see, although given the sheer size of its territory including large expanses of unpopulated areas in contrast to the United Kingdom, perhaps the Australian government envisaged greater commercial interest in a 'returns' industry.

Australian law also has much more robust requirements in respect of space debris mitigation. The Act requiring applications for launch permits to also include a debris mitigation strategy.[1361] Section 54 of the General Rules[1362] expands upon the requirements for this. The strategy 'must be based on an internationally recognised guideline or standard for debris mitigation, and identify the guideline or standard being used',[1363] and 'must describe any mitigation measures planned for orbital debris arising from the proposed launch or launches (including from payloads)'[1364] which also includes a list of exam-

1358 *Ibid*, 55(a), see also 55 (c) which provides that 'information on how any adverse effects on the environment are to be monitored and mitigated.' is also required.

1359 N1351, s101(1).

1360 *Ibid*, s101(2)(a)–(c).

1361 N1351, s34(2).

1362 N1352, s54.

1363 *Ibid*, s 54(1).

1364 *Ibid*, s 54(2).

ples.[1365] The strategy also requires an 'orbital debris' assessment to be present which is 'based on an internationally recognised model.[1366] As before with observations from the civil law systems, the United Kingdom could adopt a similar approach given the dearth of treatment of this matter.

New Zealand also includes stern provisions on orbital debris mitigation. Under its voluminous Outer Space and High-altitude Activities Act,[1367] a launch licence may only be granted where the relevant Minister 'is satisfied that … the applicant has an orbital debris mitigation plan that meets any prescribed requirements'.[1368] Similarly to Australian law, there are also requirements for the mitigation plan set out in subsequent Regulations.[1369] In addition to an encouragement to formulate such a strategy in line with an identified international standard,[1370] the strategy must specify precisely what the measures are to be taken,[1371] ensure that the release of debris is limited,[1372] that the potential for breakup of the vehicle or payload is minimised along with collision[1373] and also that 'at the end of the activity to which the licence or permit relates, the vehicle or, as the case may be, the payload is disposed of in a way that minimises risks to, or in, Earth's environment and in the space environment (including the risk of collisions)',[1374] the latter being an area which is also under-legislated for in the United Kingdom.

Regarding permits, both Australia and New Zealand specifically require 'overseas payload permits'[1375] whereas there is no direct equivalent in UK space legislation. Applications for overseas payload permits must also be accompanied by an orbital debris mitigation strategy in both jurisdictions.[1376]

Like the United Kingdom, New Zealand employs a 'safety case' strategy in respect of activities[1377] and also makes provision for the safeguarding of

1365 *Ibid*, s54(2)(a)–(e).
1366 *Ibid*, s54(3).
1367 Outer Space and High-altitude Activities Act 2017 Public Act No 29 (New Zealand).
1368 *Ibid* s9(1)(c).
1369 Outer Space and High-altitude Activities (Licences and Permits) Regulations 2017 Order in Council, 21 August 2017, (New Zealand).
1370 *Ibid*, Regulation 13(2)(a)–(c).
1371 *Ibid*, Regulation 13(2)(c).
1372 *Ibid*, Regulation 13(2)(c)(I).
1373 *Ibid*, Regulation 13(2)(c)(II)–(III).
1374 *Ibid*, Regulation 13(2)(c)(IV).
1375 See the Space Activities Act 1998 (Australia) Act No. 123 of 1998 (as amended), Division 5 and the Outer Space and High-altitude Activities Act 2017 Public Act No 29 (New Zealand) s33.
1376 See the Space Activities Act 1998 (Australia) Act No. 123 of 1998 (as amended) s46G(2) and the Outer Space and High-altitude Activities Act 2017 Public Act No 29 (New Zealand) s33(1)(b).
1377 N1377, Schedule 3.

United States Technology under the Technology Safeguards Agreement.[1378] Interestingly, there is specific provision made for the incorporation of 'any standards, requirements, or recommended practices of international organisations' by reference.[1379] This is not specified under UK legislation although under the first and second editions of the CAA Guidance for Launch Operator and Return Operator Licence Applicants and Licencees[1380] there were a raft of external standards regarding the medical criteria of human occupants including from NASA and the FAA.[1381] Under further CAA guidance, applicants for Orbital Operator Licences are also referred to best practice standards as regards operating, designing and operating space craft.[1382] This allows a significant degree of flexibility to operators in respect of how they conduct activities but may also create uncertainty as to the more appropriate strategy or techniques to employ and falls short of being an explicit incorporation by reference as is permitted under the law of New Zealand.

Regarding the definition of space activities, New Zealand law has specific rules on this. This is reflected in the title of the law itself – the Outer Space and High Altitude Activities Act 2017.[1383] A distinction is thus drawn between activities in outer space and 'high altitude activities', with the latter being defined as 'above the higher of- flight level 600 ... and ... the highest upper limit of controlled airspace under the Civil Aviation Act 1990'.[1384] For the sake of clarity, 'flight level 600' is defined as 60,000 feet above the earth's surface[1385] and 'controlled airspace' means 'an airspace of defined dimensions within which an air traffic control service is provided to controlled flights'.[1386] High altitude activities are licenced separately to 'launch' and related activities[1387] and such licences may be dispensed with should the activity be already covered by an existing launch licence.[1388] 'High altitude activities', then, are somewhat anal-

1378 N1377, s63(1)(b).

1379 N1375, s89.

1380 N257 / N368.

1381 *Ibid*, para 6.9.

1382 The UK Civil Aviation Authority, 'CAP 2210: Guidance for Orbital Operator licence applicants and Orbital Operator Licences', 29 July 2021, Annex A, <https://www.caa.co.uk/publication/download/18909> accessed 30 May 2024.

1383 N1375.

1384 *Ibid* s4, (a)–(b).

1385 The Federal Aviation Administration, 'Factsheet- Class E Upper Airspace Traffic. Management (ETM) Concept of Operations (ConOps)' <https://www.faa.gov/sites/faa.gov/files/2022-06/FactSheet_ETM.pdf> accessed 30 April 2024.

1386 S2 Civil Aviation Act 1990, No 98 (New Zealand).

1387 N1375, s45.

1388 *Ibid*, s45(2).

ogous to 'suborbital activities' as defined under the Space Industry Act 2018 although no separate licence scheme exists for these within the Act – activities falling short of this involving rockets are subject to a 'Large Rocket Permission' granted under the Air Navigation Order 2016. Australia includes 'high powered rockets' within its national space law licensing them separately from launches into outer space.[1389]

Although substantially the rules in Australia, New Zealand and the United Kingdom are similar in respect of their aims and follow a broadly synonymous path, the same significant differences emerge as regards matters of sustainability and orbital debris management. Both Australia and New Zealand law specifically require orbital debris management strategies to be formulated by applicants whereas the UK position is less prescriptive. A significant lacuna within the UK regime – that of return operators being exempt from having to provide an Assessment of Environmental Effects – is thrown into sharp contrast by the fact that this is a specific requirement under Australian law.

Having observed the rules across a range of jurisdictions of differing legal families, economic status and stages of space industry development, it can be said confidently that the UK regime, whilst praiseworthy and impeccably considered in the majority of areas, is, nevertheless, somewhat porous in others. The author's main areas of expertise in this field are in the areas of informed consent, sustainability and the UK instruments generally. Should a specialist from a differing background – such as health and safety or human rights – conduct a similar study, it is likely that further areas of concern may come to light. It should be remembered that, like most other jurisdictions in this relatively new field, the United Kingdom is embarking on a new legislative exercise. Largely drawn from experience legislating in similar fields and with a considerable amount of inspiration taken from legislation elsewhere, this is relatively unchartered territory. And it is likely – or at least to be hoped – that many of the areas discussed will be the subject of future legislative amendments.

It is also worth noting finally two further areas that the United Kingdom does not make provision for. Firstly, there is no reference to ITU Regulations within UK space specific instruments. Demonstrating compliance with ITU requirements as regards orbital positions and frequencies is a precondition for authorisation in Liechtenstein[1390] and there are similar requirements in Finland.[1391] It is also an explicit registry requirement in Austria.[1392] Interest-

1389 Space (Launches and Returns) Act 2018 No. 123, 1998 (Australia), Part 3.

1390 N1312, Art 5(1)(h).

1391 N1300, s5

1392 N1309, § 9(4).

ingly, Sweden excludes 'receiving signals or information in some other form from objects in outer space' from the definition of 'space activities'.[1393] The only direct mention of these matters in related UK instruments comes in the form of the radio frequency question set[1394] which is set out in a guidance document. This is a form which is to be completed seemingly as part of an application for an orbital operator licence, and is to be shared with Ofcom, 'the UK authority for managing the civilian use of radio spectrum, for the purposes of ensuring the correct ITU filings have been made (i.e. that the frequencies to be used will not cause interference issues).'[1395] Other than this, there is no direct or detailed mention of such requirements within the rules.

In common with many other jurisdictions, the United Kingdom does not place an exact figure on where the boundary between airspace and outer space lies. Others that do have used 100 km as the invisible boundary.[1396] Denmark, for example, defines 'outer space' as 'Space above the altitude of 100 km above sea level'.[1397] According to a note to UNOOSA from the Danish Ministry of Higher Education and Science,[1398] the motivation was to 'clarify the scope of the Act to launches or attempted launches up to a clearly defined point and, thus, provide certainty to industry' as opposed to a statement on where outer space should be defined as a matter of international law.[1399] Given the largely fragmented approach to this question across a range of jurisdictions it is not particularly unusual to observe that the United Kingdom has not endeavoured to place its own exact figure on this boundary.

1393 N1334, s1.

1394 The United Kingdom Civil Aviation Authority, 'SRG2229 Radio Frequency/Spectrum Question Set', 1 November 2021, <https://www.caa.co.uk/publication/download/21873> accessed 14 June 2024.

1395 *Ibid.*

1396 See Kazakhstan (Art. 1 Kazakhstan Space Law) and the Malaysian Space Board Bill 2022.

1397 N1321, Art 4(4).

1398 Note to UNOOSA from Danish Ministry of Higher Education and Science, 14 June 2018, <https://www.unoosa.org/documents/pdf/spacelaw/national/denmark/Danish-Outer-Space-Act_Note-on-Scope-of_ApplicationE.pdf> accessed 25 April 2024.

1399 *Ibid*, 13.

CHAPTER 11

Conclusions

From the foregoing review of varying dimensions of the United Kingdom's new space law regime, it is apparent that although it represents a commendable legislative effort, there are some areas for development or at least consideration by the legislature.

Evidence from various stakeholders submitted to the Science and Technology Select Committee amongst other channels have proposed various reforms. Skyrora, for example, a Scottish based rocket manufacturer[1400], have suggested that better co-ordination and input from environmental agencies on – particularly secondary – legislation is desirable given both the environmental impact of space activities as well as the highly valuable information that can be gleaned from space activities themselves.[1401] They also proposed a significant modification of section 36 of the Space Industry Act 2018 as regards indemnification of the government for any claims arising out of loss or damage associated with space activities along with Regulation 220 requiring a limitation being placed on liability.

Skyora's claim is that:

> the normal position in most space faring nations is to specify a cap, with governments then taking on any additional risk. If this approach is not replicated in the United Kingdom, it may stall industry before it has a chance to properly start.

Furthermore, they suggest that a stricter timeframe should be introduced for the CAA processing satellite launch operations – 100 days – 80 below the US Federal Aviation Authority.[1402] Other measures include, notably, streamlining licensing application procedures in addition to greater levels of automation as regards applications and associated reportage. Whilst this may be desirable to some extent, no suggestion is made as to how this can be best achieved. Moreover, criticism of the CAA being sluggish as regards licensing processes generally was contradicted in other evidence submitted by Black Arrow Technologies

1400 See <https://www.skyrora.com> accessed 18 October 2024.

1401 N379, 5.

1402 *Ibid.*

 | DOI:10.1163/9789004732551_012

Ltd. who suggested that a rushed approach would also have been met with criticism.[1403]

Whilst the CAA's approach to such licensing matters could certainly be improved, the desirability of this should be fully appraised taking into consideration associated matters of public safety. In addition, 80 days less than the US Federal Aviation Authority's targets may be slightly ambitious given the far greater experience the FAA presumably has over and above the CAA in such matters.

One further concern which arises regarding regulatory activity is that of an absence of an effective voice for stakeholders as regards the processes. Satellite Applications Catapult have called for a 'regulation innovation group'[1404] whilst Airborne Engineering have called for 'a Regulatory body that understands the engineering and science in this field'.[1405] One contribution to the debate which is certainly worth taking note of is the submission by Lockheed Martin who proposed that:

> The U.S. National Space Council has a Users' Advisory Group, to provide a means for industry and others to provide specialist input to policies, laws, regulations, and programmes. A similar approach should be adopted in the UK.[1406]

Regarding future space operations, it is likely that 'point A to point B' suborbital flights are likely to be considered as a means of quicker – and possibly more environmentally friendly – global transportation. It was stated in the first edition of the guidance for launch and return operator licence applicants and licencees:

1403 House of Commons Select Committee on Science and Technology, Written Evidence Submitted by Black Arrow Technologies Ltd (SPA0105), <https://committees.parliament.uk/writtenevidence/119104/pdf/> accessed 16 October 2024.

1404 House of Commons Select Committee on Science and Technology, Written Evidence Submitted by Satellite Applications Catapult (SPA0037) <https://committees.parliament.uk/writtenevidence/37202/pdf/> accessed 16 October 2024.

1405 House of Commons Select Committee on Science and Technology, Written Evidence Submitted by Airborne Engineering Limited per Dr Peter Shaw, Senior Lecturer in Astronautics, Kingston University, London (SPA0044) <https://committees.parliament.uk/writtenevidence/37223/pdf/> accessed 16 October 2024.

1406 House of Commons Select Committee on Science and Technology, Written Evidence Submitted by Lockheed Martin UK (SPA0050), para 14, <https://committees.parliament.uk/writtenevidence/37239/pdf/> accessed 16 October 2024.

> No additional legislation has been drafted regarding Point A to Point B suborbital spaceflight operations and orbital and interstellar spaceflight operations with human occupants. It is not currently intended to licence these activities. These are technically complex and difficult to regulate activities, and by their very nature will require global collaboration on common standards to a much higher threshold than is achievable with current technologies.[1407]

Presumably, the reason for there being no current intention to licence these sorts of activities stems more from the present state of our technological capabilities rather than the desire to see such activities go unlicenced when they become viable. It does not seem helpful to conflate 'interstellar spaceflight operations' with point A to point B suborbital flights here – this seems like a slightly throwaway remark on the part of the drafter – such suborbital operations will possibly form part of the next technological wave of space activities and it would certainly be wise to begin considering how regulations would look in principle. It has also been suggested that, along with point A to point B suborbital/orbital travel, orbital manufacturing should also be the subject of legislative consideration.[1408] As with the former, this is far more likely to need attention sooner than any prospect of interstellar travel. Furthermore, where such activities are considered viable there must be further consideration as regards the implementation of the 1929 Warsaw Convention[1409] in respect of the regulation of the vehicles used. There is presently no authority on such matters – overall the best approach could be an international move to change the Convention itself so that such travel is covered rather than campaign for domestic reform.

Should such journeys be considered in the near future, the debate over whether the CAA should indeed be the designated Regulator may well return. Should there be no ventilation of the old concerns in respect of this before then, it is submitted that, in any eventuality, consideration should at least be given to whether or not the present scope of legislative duties placed on the CAA are indeed compatible with regulation of an experimental and hazardous industry. As outlined previously, the CAA has to take into consideration both the 'Regulators Code' and considerations of 'risk' along with section

1407 N257, para 2.23.

1408 House of Commons Select Committee on Science and Technology Written Evidence Submitted by UK Research and Innovation (UKRI) (SPA0024) <https://committees.parliament.uk/writtenevidence/37178/pdf/> accessed 16 October 2024.

1409 N538.

108(1) of the Deregulation Act 2015 which imposes a duty to 'have regard to the desirability of promoting economic growth'. This dichotomy is almost a perfect distillation of the regime itself – a tension between risk management and commercial flexibility. Public safety should be the priority for licensing regimes such as the one envisaged and it is hoped that this consideration will prevail over competitive advantage where the impact to the latter is not grossly disproportionate. Whether the balance has been struck between safety and commercial flexibility within the Regulations themselves is certainly open to question. There are certain areas which seem unusually lenient towards operators in the context of safety duties – or responsibilities associated with such duties. The record keeping requirements in respect of training records and other documents are highly questionable, particularly where the mandated length of retention is the equivalent of a personal injury limitation period. It is difficult to see the motivation for such slim requirements being any other than to stifle the chances of successful litigation in the wake of an accident or other alleged transgression. In the present age of computing and hard drives, what would be the objection to such records being kept for 6 years in total or even 10?

As has been outlined, security in the context of domestic space infrastructure is a key area in terms of securing the peaceful uses of outer space. As pointed out in chapter 5, there are some areas where it would probably be, on balance, desirable to introduce further rules regarding security matters such as designating the kind of payloads which an operator can and cannot reasonably believe they are able to inspect. As mentioned, without further clarity in this area, operators may be confused as to what sort of payloads they can and cannot request a closer examination of. Whilst it is likely that any payloads being launched on behalf of the government are likely to be accompanied by some form of order as regards secrecy from the relevant Secretary of State and, hence, straightforward to observe, this will not be the case as regards private actors. It would not be unwise to expect that many – if not all – private entities wishing to launch payloads will likely claim some form of 'proprietary sensitivity' as per the wording in the guidance or otherwise claim commercial confidentiality. It would be unfair to expect an operator to have to judge which cases are 'genuinely' sensitive and which are not and could lead to unnecessarily increased levels of cost and inefficiency as regards launch proceedings, particularly if there is some form of protracted disagreement potentially involving court proceedings. It is submitted, therefore, that the regulator should be required to assess whether the veil of proprietary sensitivity should attach itself to any given payload. Although this will add to the administrative burden it is surely more effective – and potentially safer – than what may lie in the alternative.

Other security matters worthy of consideration are whether the guidance for what is and is not allowed into a spaceport is fit for purpose. Presently this is judged by the CAA guidance pertaining to airports with no extension for those which support space activities or vertical spaceports themselves. This is similar to the policy on prohibited articles which is also silent as regards spaceports. Specific changes that should be made here are beyond the author's expertise but consideration should at least be given to this, particularly as regards any crewed spaceflights – such matters are clearly beyond the existing experience of the United Kingdom CAA. Furthermore, there does not seem to be a unified approach to the most desirable security policy to follow, with licencees encouraged to borrow from existing areas of practice. This may be attractive for operators who may wish to source the most cost-effective security solution but is this necessarily the best policy to pursue in respect of public safety and security (or for securing the peaceful uses of outer space?).

Proposals for changes to the licensing rules have also come from the CAA itself. These include rules on qualifications and employment – 'Narrow the scope of these requirements to reduce the number of individuals required to provide information/Change certificates requirement to a listing of relevant qualifications',[1410] less 'prescriptive financial listing' and a review of which prescribed roles must be assigned at the time of applications.[1411] The CAA has carried out a review of the more limited licensing requirements under the Outer Space Act 1986, being of the view that: 'Greater alignment between the OSA and SIA will also help to streamline and simplify the UK licensing process, reducing the Regulatory differences UK licencees face when operating from the UK or from overseas'.[1412] A three phased alignment was proposed between the Outer Space Act and the Space Industry Act which would bring together common elements for licensing whilst also taking into consideration the geographical differences between licensing under the Outer Space Act and the Space Industry Act.[1413] The potential drawbacks it was held would be for those applying for Outer Space Act licences who would, under these proposals, be

1410 The United Kingdom Civil Aviation Authority, Space Launch and Orbit Group, Orbit Session November 2022, 25, <https://www.caa.co.uk/media/5yklgyq2/november-splog-master_orbit_published.pdf> accessed 16 October 2024.

1411 *Ibid.*

1412 The United Kingdom Civil Aviation Authority, Space Launch and Orbit Group, Orbit Session November 2021, 11, <https://www.caa.co.uk/media/p4feumza/nov-2021-orbit-session.pdf> accessed 16 October 2024.

1413 *Ibid*, 12.

required to submit additional documentation on 'corporate checks' – presumably on the status of 'fit and proper persons' but that this may be mitigated by additional streamlining measures for corporate checks overall.[1414] The changes were judged as neutral or positive for applicants under the Space Industry Act.[1415] From the foregoing research in this work along with that provided by the CAA[1416] there are many differences between the two regimes, mainly due to the Space Industry Act laying down a comprehensive licensing framework whereas the Outer Space Act was never designed for these objectives. Such a review and resulting changes, therefore, would be welcome but at the time of writing there have not been any legislative changes made to this or any other aspect of the legislation. What's more, it would be desirable in the interests of sustainability for environmental assessments to be made mandatory for licensing under the Outer Space Act since presently this is not a requirement due to it catering for licences for launches overseas. This seems uncoordinated with global initiatives regarding the environment generally,[1417] and a degree of proactivity on part of the legislator would certainly be welcome in this regard.

Other areas to legislate for include, as referred to when examining the Appeals Regulations, a clarification of Schedule 10(6) on circumstances where an appeal can be made. There is ambiguity here regarding whether or not appeals can be lodged which fall outside the strict interpretation of the rules. Moreover, the phrasing of Schedule 10(6) could lead to arbitrariness and unnecessary fragmentation as regards decisions which are permitted to go to appeal. Refusals to allow appeals in such instances could, in turn, could lead to public law litigation on the basis of irrationality following the case of *Associated Provincial Picture Houses Ltd. v Wednesbury Corporation*[1418] should the panel be deemed a 'public body'.

In respect of space traffic management, some areas of concern have come from evidence given to the Science and Technology Select Committee on UK Space Strategy and Infrastructure, where there have been calls for a formal space traffic management system to be established which would also be

1414 *Ibid.*

1415 *Ibid.*

1416 *Ibid*, 14.

1417 United Nations, The Guidelines for the Long-term Sustainability of Outer Space Activities (LTS Guidelines), adopted by the Committee on the Peaceful Uses of Outer Space (COPUOS) in 2019. <https://spacesustainability.unoosa.org/content/the_guidelines> accessed 16 October 2024.

1418 [1948] 1 KB 223 (EWCA).

responsible for debris removal.[1419] There may be some merit in the United Kingdom making unilateral strides in this area but such a suggestion was posed by the Director General of the European Space Agency so a multi-lateral approach may be worth considering. The United Kingdom considers space traffic management to be at the heart of its ambitions, with this responsibility presently handled by the UK National Space Operations Centre,[1420] and there has been a considerable amount of progress towards formalising 'Space Domain Awareness' (SDA)[1421] which space traffic management feeds into.[1422] As at present, there are a number of requirements for SDA to unify the approach across the range of stakeholders in space activities, governmental and non-governmental but no formal legislation as such.[1423] Some of the requirements relate to UK-licenced space objects and orbital parameters with requirements for risk assessments[1424] but there is apparently no linkage between this and the broader UK space law regime. There have not yet been any space objects launched from the United Kingdom that have reached orbit, but even the 1986 Outer Space Act pertaining to objects launched from overseas contains no such provisions relating to space traffic management or space domain awareness. It is also regrettable that the United Kingdom no longer plays a role in the European Union Space Surveillance and Tracking program following the withdrawal from the European Union and whilst an international approach to matters of space traffic management would be desirable, there seems to be resistance to this in some quarters.[1425] With these issues in mind and considering the importance of this area, it would be a helpful step to see some legislative action taken to cement policy goals as regards space traffic management

1419 See the Science and Technology Committee Oral evidence: UK Space Strategy and UK Satellite Infrastructure, HC 98 Wednesday 12 January 2022 at question 288 per Josef Aschbacher, Director General of the European Space Agency.

1420 Department for Science, Innovation and Technology, Ministry of Defence, Policy Paper, 'National Space Strategy in Action', 19 July 2023 <https://www.gov.uk/government/publications/national-space-strategy-in-action/national-space-strategy-in-action> accessed 16 October 2024.

1421 United Kingdom Space Command, 'Cross Government Space Domain Awareness (SDA) Requirements Publication, Version 2.0, 2024, <https://assets.publishing.service.gov.uk/media/65fd8c7365ca2f00117da8e7/Space_domain_awareness_-_requirements.pdf> accessed 16 October 2024.

1422 United Kingdom Space Agency Space Domain Awareness Study, 20 May 2022, 10 <https://www.ukspace.org/wp-content/uploads/2022/07/UKSA-SDA-Study-Report_v2.4.pdf> accessed 16 October 2024.

1423 *Ibid.*

1424 *Ibid*, 5.

1425 European Space Policy Institute, 'ESPI Report 71 – Towards a European Approach to Space Traffic Management – Full Report'.

so as to put them on a similar position to the management of air traffic. International partnerships and cooperation should also be embraced.

Consideration must also be given to creating charging guidelines in respect of paying spaceflight participants. In the context of 'space tourism', it does not seem like an equitable outcome for the forfeiture of the entire purchase price of a 'seat' to depend wholly on the outcome of an aeromedical examiner's decision, particularly where present legislation gives no means of formal redress. Given what will certainly be large sums of money being tendered in respect of such services, it seems unconscionable for an operator to be allowed to profit twice – given the high levels of appeal for such services, there will almost certainly be another paying spaceflight participant in line to take the place of another who has been deemed unfit to fly.

In respect of sustainability requirements, there are number of ways in which these could be improved/clarified overall. Firstly, where a licencee has its registered office in another country there may be a need for two environmental assessments or consultations to be carried out as was the case with Virgin Orbit. Even though Virgin Orbits space activities were taking place in the United Kingdom, its United States licence required the FAA to also enter into consultations regarding the potential environmental impact. Whilst on some levels this could be welcome, it would seem like a sensible measure to standardise such requirements – or at least an exercise whereby the approaches are sufficiently similar in order to avoid duplication. Such an arrangement could be arrived at by means of a Memorandum of Understanding or a more formal agreement between the respective states. On a similar note, there should be extensive praise given to Virgin Orbit in respect of its highly comprehensive Assessment of Environmental Effects which appeared to exceed the strict requirements of the Regulations and guidance. The range of legislation and guidance that was used in respect of formulating predictions about possible effects and for assessments generally was nothing short of impressive but this leaves open the question, once again, of whether or not this could lead to a potential fragmentation of standards should different operators choose to use different guidance by way of formulating their assessments. Without taking away the freedom of operators or their agents – the primary authors of the report were Wardell Armstrong LLP and ManTech Advanced Systems International – to observe a range of best practice, consideration should be given to specifying minimum standards for any given report. Whilst – subject to the

January 2020, 6, <https://www.espi.or.at/wp-content/uploads/2022/06/ESPI-Public-Report-71-Towards-a-European-Approach-to-Space-Traffic-Management-Full-Report.pdf> accessed 16 October 2024.

common law principles relating to discharge of duty – *maxim omne majus continet in se minus* (the greater includes the less) – this could potentially lead to a 'box-ticking' or 'bare minimum' approach, it could also streamline matters whilst crucially ensuring consistency and also be of assistance for operators in respect of cost-planning if minimum standards were known.

Other issues regarding sustainability could also be advanced through the legislation. If the United Kingdom is to be seen to be taking its obligations seriously as regards reduction and mitigation of space debris, the definition of 'environment' – and the requirements for the Assessment of Environmental Effects – could be changed to mean both the environment of earth *and* of space. Regulation 101, echoing the language of the Outer Space Treaty, states that, on reaching a stable orbit, a spaceflight operator must take reasonable steps to 'prevent contamination of outer space arising from the launch vehicle in orbit or adverse changes in the environment of the earth from that vehicle in orbit'. Given that 'contamination' and 'change' are patently 'environmental', the Assessment of Environmental Effects should require an assessment of such effects pertaining to both. The Virgin Orbit Assessment of Environmental Effects did not consider the space environment. There are numerous other international matters that could be fully ratified and implemented to make a practical difference. Under the United Kingdom's 'dualist' approach to international law, specific legislation has to be brought in by Parliament to give effect to any international instruments. Under the Secretary of State's guidance to the regulator under section 2(2)(e) of the Space Industry Act 2018,[1426] it is made clear that the United Kingdom is associated with various international instruments pertaining to sustainability – many of which concern space debris.[1427] Whilst it is stated that such instruments are not legally binding, it is made clear that the Secretary of State has the power to impose conditions on operators ensuring compliance where necessary. This would seem to strengthen

1426 The Department for Transport, 'Guidance to the regulator on environmental objectives relating to the exercise of its functions under the Space Industry Act 2018 Given by the Secretary of State under section 2(2)(e) of the Space Industry Act 2018' (London, 2021) <https://assets.publishing.service.gov.uk/media/60d06eb88fa8f57ceec3ca03/guidance-to-the-regulator-on-environmental-objectives-relating-to-the-exercise-of-its-functions-under-the-space-industry-act-2018.pdf> accessed 16 October 2023.

1427 *Ibid*, 5. Listed as Space Debris Mitigation Guidelines of the Committee on the Peaceful Uses of Outer Space. Guidelines for the Long-term Sustainability of Outer Space Activities, European Code of Conduct for Space Debris Mitigation, Inter-Agency Debris Coordination Committee Space Debris Mitigation Guidelines, Space Debris Mitigation Requirements BS ISO 24113-2019, Disposal of orbital launch stages BS ISO 16699:2015, Requirements on Space Debris Mitigation for European Space Agency Projects.

the argument for including issues in space debris in an Assessment for Environmental Effects. The Secretary of State would then be more informed as to whether such conditions are necessary.

As mentioned, there are other matters not covered by the legislation, including exploitation of space resources which numerous other jurisdictions have now provided for. There are other areas such as the need to avoid harm arising from the introduction of 'extra-terrestrial matter' to the environment as set out in Article IX of the Outer Space Treaty. This may go hand in hand with the former provisions on resource exploitation should the United Kingdom desire a future in such an area and wish to bring material from other celestial bodies such as asteroids back home. Whilst this may initially seem far-fetched, it is important to note that a budding asteroid mining enterprise with far-reaching links to UK academia and the UK Space Agency is based at Canary Wharf in London.[1428]

The present domestic legislation lays down a specific licence and safety case regime which seeks to cover all bases of the United Kingdom's space industry ambitions. Licence applicants must meet strict criteria and the conditions can, to an extent, be exacting. There are certain areas which require clarification and what could be regarded as potential 'loopholes' within the rules, whether there by legislative intent or not. For example, a range licencee does not require a safety case and a return operator licencee is not required to submit an assessment of environmental effects. It is worth noting the first guidance document issued on return operator licences:

> This is the type of licence needed if a person or organisation wants to return a launch vehicle, launched elsewhere than the United Kingdom, to land in the UK or within the UK's territorial waters. A person or organisation holding a return operator licence is referred to as a spaceflight operator, or in some circumstances, return operator licencee.[1429]

Whilst these requirements may have been dispensed with in the interests of streamlining or reducing a potential administrative burden, there may be other more productive – and safety conducive/environmentally responsible – ways in which any perceived administrative burden may be reduced.

From the outset it should be mentioned that the apparent regulatory gulf between 'permissions' granted under the Air Navigation Order 2016 and 'licences' granted under the Space Industry Act 2018 is a considerable one.

1428 N1349, Asteroid Mining Corporation.
1429 N257, 11.

As noted, the SaxaVord Large Rocket SR75 permission granted by the CAA falls outside the Space Industry Act – the launch is not regulated in the same way although it concerns a suborbital rocket. Although such permissions are granted subject to conditions and have to submit safety cases, they apparently forgo the requirement for a monitoring and oversight agreement. Further, there does not seem to be the same requirement for as regards environmental considerations. Article 96 of the Air Navigation Order 2016 does not make any mention of permission for the launch of a large rocket being subject to any Assessment of Environmental Effects. Moreover, the permission granted by the CAA is at no stage conditional regarding environmental matters. In view of the weight given to environmental matters in the Space Industry Act, Regulations and recent developments as regards environmental matters and concerns generally, this seems to be a troubling contradiction. The SaxaVord rocket is not covered by the Space Industry Act regime since the rocket used will not travel beyond the stratosphere as per section 1(5)(a), but to a maximum ceiling of 45 km.[1430] According to the original guidance document for launch and return operator licence applicants and licencees:

> ... the Regulator proposes to use the International Standard Atmosphere (47km) as the stratopause (i.e. the upper limit of the stratosphere) for the purposes of determining whether an activity is 'suborbital'.[1431]

It will remain to be seen whether the majority of flights operating from SaxaVord will be similar in terms of their maximum ceiling. Whilst the law must observe a 'cut-off' point as it must in many areas, given the importance of environmental matters as discussed, this would appear to make a mockery of the statutory regime should such activities be excluded owing to a difference of 2 km.

It is fair to say that, owing to the relative lack of space launch experience, the United Kingdom's legal framework could not be expected to be overly comprehensive as regards spaceflight itself at this stage. The rules of the United States can certainly offer much in the way of inspiration. Some of the legislative concepts and provisions have been taken almost verbatim from the US regime but by the same measure there are other areas which the UK drafters appear to have overlooked. To some extent this may be to do with the fact that existing

1430 HyImpulse Airspace Change Proposal Stakeholders Engagement Report, Version 1.0, 14 April 2022, 35.

1431 N257, 9. It is of interest to note that the figure of 47km was not included in the updated guidance document. See N368.

legislation outside the UK space regime covers these matters – the Working Time Regulations[1432] for example could be taken to supplant any requirement for 'adequate rest' of employees as is provided for in the United States,[1433] but it is submitted that a more consolidated approach would be more helpful – and potentially less costly. Reference should be made to existing legal provisions where the legislation itself is silent on such matters.

The UK approach appears very much insistent on layers of 'management' to shoulder any burden and retain accountability in the event of misfortunes. This appears inconsistent with other jurisdictions examined which do not insist on such requirements. Whilst this may be due in some part to the prevailing legislative culture, it would perhaps be wise to consider whether or not such an approach is desirable.

Another significant matter within the UK legislation is the apparent uncoupling of liability as regards individuals who are not classed as 'members of the public'. The effect of the legislation is to essentially remove liability towards all those in the presence of the space operator's activities on the part of the government itself, leaving a large class of individuals potentially denied a straightforward claims process in the event of personal injury or death. Individuals who are not classed as 'members of the public' include police officers and military personnel.

The desirability of such an approach is questionable given the abrogation of important rights that it involves, not only to those voluntarily in a place of danger, but others also, such as CAA employees and the like. Whilst closely aligned with the US position, the rules relating to 'informed consent' as regards human occupancy of spacecraft which are aimed at regulating instances of 'space tourism', whilst more satisfactory now than under the draft instrumentation, could still be improved to ensure that valid consent is truly obtained. The 24-hour period information should be furnished to prospective occupants within under Regulation 213 is a significant improvement to the previously proposed 12-hour period. It is debateable whether the updated time is indeed sufficient for an individual to be deemed fully appraised and cognisant of the risks they are undertaking. Moreover, there is insufficient treatment of the situation vis-à-vis those who may lack mental capacity to give informed consent. This could potentially lead to discrimination claims or misleading business practices as regards the provision of space tourism opportunities and thus requires consideration and reform prior to any such transactions. Whilst this particular area of the rules formed the basis for extensive discussions, it is

1432 N1215.
1433 CFR (US) 417.

worthy of some final considerations. The extent to which the informed consent regime is compatible with the Unfair Contract Terms Act 1977 – as both regards 'space tourists' and employees/individuals in other capacities – should be addressed. The Act makes no attempt to say that informed consent leads to the complete forfeiture of the right to claim compensation, but it is important to indicate that nowhere does it specify that informed consent given is given without prejudice to any future legal proceedings. This means that the giving of consent will be – in the absence of any express statutory provision or other rule of evidence – admissible in proceedings to illustrate a party's state of mind. It is likely that the thrust of such submissions would be that the party was aware of the risks involved and thusly may not be as deserving of compensatory measures as they may otherwise have been. Whilst this is understandable as a rule of logic – and of law to some extent – it could prove unduly harsh in some circumstances.

Regarding sustainability there is much that could be done to facilitate this and factor in more environmental protection in addition to potential streamlining. As has been pointed out, the fact that some licences do not require assessments of environmental effects to be submitted – return operator licensing for example – is problematic, as are some of the broader concerns in this regard. The fact that space operations appear completely divorced from domestic emissions trading frameworks is perplexing, particularly when the potential damage arising from such emissions is significant. Whilst flexibility and agility in the regulatory framework may be a priority for industry, this must be balanced against broader issues of public interest as regards the environment and sustainability. It is submitted that, should the Regulator or Parliament wish to undertake any kind of 'streamlining' exercise as regards environmental provisions of UK space law, an appropriate place to begin would be by looking at the US approach to reducing paperwork and implementing some of the less 'substantive' measures rather than eliminating necessary environmental safeguards. It is also worth stating again that whilst initial environmental assessments may be time consuming, they can be used in subsequent applications for licences which should prove less of an administrative burden. Further developments could be achieved under sustainability goals more generally in the respect of licensing costs. As previously outlined, licensing under the Space Industry Act was carried out completely free of charge up until 2024 in order to facilitate development within the sector. There is no reason such incentivisation could not be factored into future pricing regimes so as to facilitate a more sustainable approach to launching activities. For example, a requirement could be factored in which would reduce the cost of satellite operator licences if it could be shown that the launch system chosen was the most environmentally friendly option or that passivation measures or 'end of life' measures for the satellite have been adopted so as to avoid adverse effects to the environment of earth or space.

Rahim Talibzade, graduate of the London School of Economics, legal professional and former member of the Space Generation Advisory Council, notes that, from a sustainability perspective, the adoption into national legislation of the COSPAR guidelines[1434] will be necessary at some stage and at the very least desirable as the United Kingdom embarks upon a comprehensive launch schedule. On this note, it may also be desirable to transpose the spirit and content of ISO 24113:2023 on Space Debris Mitigation Requirements into national legislation as regards manufacturing of space objects in pursuance of sustainability. As noted previously, this could be at least partially accomplished by expanding the definition of 'environmental' within domestic legislation to cover both the environment of earth and of space.

On a broader scale, it is worth noting that a number of jurisdictions have legislated specifically for the exploitation of space resources. As Talibzade has noted in written advice to the Science and Technology Select Committee,[1435] both Luxembourg and the United Arab Emirates have such provisions. The United Kingdom, with its emphasis on the establishment of a comprehensive licensing regime may wish to consider legislation of this kind in future as the exploitation of space resources, for good or ill, may be something on the minds of future investors and operators contemplating the United Kingdom as a base.

Whilst the foregoing has been largely concerned with broad amendments being made to existing provisions, there are some areas which are presently not the subject of any direct regulation. For example, regarding flight trajectories and the information that should be provided, the US regime greatly outshines that of the United Kingdom. The US rules on trajectory analysis are far more flight-specific than anything observed within the UK counterpart. There are also rules regarding 'overflight gate analysis'[1436] in the US regime which is aimed at ensuring safety when flying over populated areas as part of a space operation. The United Kingdom takes a much more general approach to this matter. It is submitted that some form of legal transplantation of such rules

---

1434 COSPAR Policy on Planetary Protection, Prepared by the COSPAR Panel on Planetary Protection and approved by the COSPAR Bureau on 17 June 2020. <https://cosparhq.cnes.fr/assets/uploads/2020/07/PPPolicyJune-2020_Final_Web.pdf> accessed 16 October 2024.

1435 United Kingdom As A Space Nation: a Snapshot of Current Capabilities And Lessons From Other Countries, Written Evidence Submitted by Rahim Talibzade, (SPA0066) <committees.parliament.uk/writtenevidence/37274/pdf/> accessed 16 October 2024.

1436 CFR (US) 417.217.

should be affected before launch operations become more frequent, particularly given the dearth of experience in such operations from UK soil and relative lack of operations. If such requirements are incorporated by reference into the United Kingdom's rules – which does not appear to be apparent – this must be made much clearer.

The flight safety analysis for the United Kingdom appears to be much more comprehensive than in the United States and potentially more cumbersome as a result – there seems to be much ground to cover and potentially too many avenues to go down as a result of the wording. The specific aspects outlined in the US legislation should be adopted so that, at the very least, these important dimensions of space flight are covered and not at the expense of more mundane detail which could prove to be distracting and time-consuming.

On a similar note, whilst it is clear that other jurisdictions such as the United States will have more in terms of domestic regulation than the United Kingdom, a blind legal transplant of such provisions would not be advisable. It is essential that, where any rules from other jurisdictions are to be incorporated, such rules themselves do not fall below standards already operative in the United Kingdom in other areas, health and safety being arguably the most important. As has been observed from the Virgin Orbit experience, some operators may decide that they wish to adopt certain rules from other jurisdictions so as to inform their own practices regarding a range of activities that the United Kingdom simply could not reasonably be expected to have considered in a legislative sense – moving payloads around spaceports was the activity in question as regards Virgin Orbit. As stated previously, this is both praiseworthy and slightly concerning for a number of reasons. In a positive sense it is encouraging to see best practice from other jurisdictions being considered and adopted and it is to be assumed that such rules would be reasonable ones to follow. In a negative sense, in addition to there being no guarantee that such rules will be in conformity with domestic standards elsewhere, there is also a real possibility of fragmentation if different operators choose to follow different standards for various activities. This could potentially prove confusing and dangerous or at the very least make for inefficiencies as national spaceport networks become farther integrated. In this area it would be desirable for a full review to be taken of all possible subsidiary rules – such as those related to payload handling – which could be adopted following the early experiences of Virgin Orbit and subsequent operators. Such rules could then either be transplanted in full if deemed in compliance with the domestic regime or augmented accordingly to ensure uniformity of standards.

Another area which requires at least some legislation it is submitted, would be that of seaborne launches. At present these are not covered by the definition of 'spaceport' in spite of the fact that they could pose as large a threat to safety or the environment as any land-based launch. The absence of any or any significant treatment of seaborne launches within the legislation begs the question of how such a launch should be defined in the first place. For example, would a launch from a vessel 10 or 100 metres from the coast near a residential area be classified as a 'seaborne launch' and, therefore, avoid the need for formal licensing? Presently, an operator considering a seaborne launch has to contact the Regulator prior to engaging in any such activity but there is no information beyond this.

The comparative exercise taken in respect of the UK and US regimes, as has already been set out, uncovered a huge gulf in the respective regulatory expertise. As some concerns regarding the UK regime – particularly as regards safety – have comprehensive treatment in the United States, it would be wise for there to be closer alignment between the two bodies of law. The United Kingdom could borrow much of what is set out in the US legislation as regards the calculation of blast zones and other danger areas, in addition to specifying the particular type of information that is required for determining flight – paths, azimuths, nodal points and other parameters. Putting such matters on a statutory footing would give major advantages in respect of legal certainty for all concerned parties.

CHAPTER 12

Afterward: 'RFA ONE'; the United Kingdom's First Vertical Launch Licence – a 'Brave New World'

Shortly before this work was first sent to press, news broke of the first grant of a vertical launch licence under the Space Industry Act 2018.[1437] In the spirit of completeness, the author deemed it necessary to comment upon this important development despite the delay incurred to the publication process. The only previous authorisation granted to date for a vertical launch was to HyImpulse for the launch of a sounding rocket.[1438] As should be recalled, the launch was authorised under the Air Navigation Order 2016 by means of a 'large rocket permission' as opposed to the Space Industry Act 2018. The rocket in question fell outside the parameters of the Space Industry Act 2018 since it was not 'capable of operating above the stratosphere'.[1439]

The licence in question here, was granted to another German rocket firm, Rocket Factory Augsburg[1440] in respect of the RFA ONE rocket. Standing at 30 metres tall and boasting 9+1 engines,[1441] it is designed for orbital flights.[1442] This will be its intended purpose when it launches from SaxaVord spaceport, possibly as early as late 2025.[1443]

Representing a crucial development in the history of the space legislation of the United Kingdom, it is only right that this work covers it to the extent that the available information allows. Firstly, the terms of the issued licence will be examined along with the reporting plan, and secondly, the same will be done for the Assessment of Environmental Effects. It is hoped that an analysis of this licence, given its importance and scope as a 'true' vertical launch licence, will be a veritable 'proving ground' for the licensing regime set forth under

1437 BBC News, 'UK first as vertical rocket launch Licence granted', 16 January 2025 <https://www.bbc.co.uk/news/articles/c4gzl9dz5rdo> accessed 17 January 2025.

1438 N678.

1439 N1430.

1440 N1437.

1441 Rocket Factory Augsburg, 'RFA ONE Flexible Launch System' <https://www.rfa.space/rfa-one/> accessed 17 January 2025.

1442 Adrian Bell, 'German startup Rocket Factory Augsburg successfully performs critical tests ahead of 2022 debut', 30 August 2021, <https://www.nasaspaceflight.com/2021/08/rocket-factory-augsburg-tests-2022-debut/> accessed 17 January 2025.

1443 N1437.

 | DOI:10.1163/9789004732551_013

the Space Industry Act and Regulations. Comparisons will also be drawn with the licence granted to Virgin Orbit and the associated reporting plan in addition to some exploration of surrounding materials such as spaceport licenses by means of observing any potential intersections. Comparing the licences should offer a significant insight into the Regulators licencing practices under the Act and Regulations allowing for further examination of how they are implemented in practice.

1 The Licence

The licence[1444] is stated on its face to be a 'Spaceflight Operator Licence' for the launch of the RFA ONE rocket referred to above. As anticipated, the licence is granted subject to conditions stipulated within which must 'have been met to the satisfaction of the Regulator'.[1445] The licenced activities are the launch of the RFA ONE rocket including the carrying and deployment of payloads[1446] *in addition* to the carrying out of orbital activities "in so far as those activities are necessary to comply with Regulation 101 until the Launch Vehicle has been positioned to the satisfaction of the Regulator".[1447] As detailed previously within this work,[1448] Regulation 101 compels a spaceflight operator to monitor the trajectory and basic orbital parameters of a launch vehicle after it has reached a stable orbit and 'take reasonable steps' to 'avoid the launch vehicle interfering with the space activities of other persons in the peaceful exploration and use of outer space … limit or prevent major accident hazards to the health, safety and property of persons arising from the launch vehicle in orbit … and … prevent contamination of outer space arising from the launch vehicle in orbit or adverse changes in the environment of the earth from that vehicle in orbit'.[1449] The loading of 'dangerous goods' onto the Launch Vehicle and their carriage is also permitted.[1450]

1444 The United Kingdom Civil Aviation Authority, 14 January 2025, 'Space Industry Act 2018, Spaceflight Operator Licence for Launch of RFA ONE (Licence ref: SR-APP – 001180)' <https://www.caa.co.uk/publication/download/23976> accessed 20 January 2025.

1445 *Ibid,* para 1.2.

1446 *Ibid,* para 1.3.1–1.3.3.

1447 *Ibid,* para 1.3.4.

1448 p138.

1449 Regulation 101(1)(a)–(d).

1450 N8, para 1.4.

Under section 1.5 of the licence, the amount of launches permitted in accordance with the Assessment of Environmental Effects (which will be discussed later) is limited to 10 within a 12 month period[1451] and no more than two launches per month[1452] or one within a 24 hour period.[1453] Launch trajectories are also limited "along azimuths between 330° to 030° relative to true north except as otherwise agreed in writing by the Regulator".[1454] As with other issued licenses, the Interpretation Act 1978[1455] applies here. Perhaps the most crucial aspect of the licence is under sections 3 to 6 which pertain to the various conditions the licence is granted subject to. If licensing is where 'the rubber meets the road'[1456] the conditions represent the 'checks and balances' upon a given licenced activity, whatever its nature, and may be regarded as the 'teeth' of the regime along with the reporting plan.

Section 3 consists of a list of 'Conditions Precedent'[1457] which must be met prior to 'each occasion'[1458] the licenced activities are to be carried out which include the taking out of insurance for the activity,[1459] informing the regulator of the 'range' along with having carried out hazard identification in accordance with the submitted safety case,[1460] maintaining in place a 'data sharing agreement' between the licencee and the National Space Operations Centre'[1461] in addition to the conclusion of any relevant arrangements with other countries regarding the activities.[1462]

Section 4, which immediately follows, is entitled 'General Conditions'[1463] although they are not necessarily more cumbersome than those in the preceding section. These conditions include compliance with the requirements of the reporting plan,[1464] and the rendering of 'reasonable assistance' to the Regulator where required to assist the discharge of its functions under the licence, Act or Regulations.[1465] There is also the requirement to provide a 'new

1451 *Ibid*, para 1.5.1.
1452 *Ibid*, para 1.5.2.
1453 *Ibid*, para 1.5.3.
1454 *Ibid*, para 1.6.
1455 C30.
1456 p27.
1457 N1444, para 3.
1458 *Ibid*, para 3.1.
1459 *Ibid*, para 3.1.1.
1460 *Ibid*, para 3.1.2.
1461 *Ibid*, para 3.1.3.
1462 *Ibid*, para 3.1.4.
1463 *Ibid*, para 4.
1464 *Ibid*, para 4.1.
1465 *Ibid*, para 4.2.

or revised' Assessment of Environmental Effects should there be a material change at any stage in the licensing process[1466] and relatedly the submission of a new Assessment of Environmental Effects upon any variation of the licence or, alternatively, a written justification as to why the old one should prevail.[1467]

Section 5 on 'Insurance Conditions', although concerned with a narrower aspect of the licence, is more voluminous. It initially states the requirement for third party insurance cover to be in place which extends to His Majesty's Government and the Regulator and other third parties 'in the United Kingdom or elsewhere as a result of or in connection with the licenced Activities'.[1468] Section 5.2 further stipulates that the cover must further extend to 'Shetland Space Centre Limited, any person procuring the launch of a payload on the Launch Vehicle' and their respective governments unless otherwise contractually agreed.[1469] Section 5.2.2 also stipulates that the licencee's contractors and subcontractors, those covered by cross-waiver agreements and contracted range control service providers must also be covered. This is in addition to those listed in section 36(2) of the Space Industry Act which are '(a) an appointed person; (b) the Health and Safety Executive; (c) the Health and Safety Executive for Northern Ireland; (d) the office for Nuclear Regulation; (e) a body or person prescribed under section 21(2); (f) a public authority with whom arrangements are made under section 64'. An 'appointed person' is defined under section 16 of the Act as a person appointed under regulations by the Secretary of State 'to exercise any function conferred on or by this Act that is expressed (in whatever way) to be a function of the regulator.[1470] The Act states that an appointed person 'may be appointed – (a) to exercise a function for particular purposes, in relation to particular activities or services or in relation to particular areas; (b) to exercise a function instead of, or concurrently with, the Secretary of State; (c) to exercise a function subject to conditions; (d) to exercise a function for a particular period.' As stated, the implications of this for the licencee are that their insurance will have to cover such appointed individuals although it is largely unclear from the Act who such appointed persons may be. It could be reasonably expected that such individuals may be drawn from bodies similar in scope to the Civil Aviation Authority or perhaps from the private sector as part of an outsourcing exercise. Whatever the source of such individuals, it is to be hoped that they are identified and communicated to the licencee ahead

1466 *Ibid*, para 4.3.
1467 *Ibid*, para 4.4.
1468 *Ibid*, para 5.1.
1469 *Ibid*, para 5.2.1.
1470 The Space Industry Act 2018 s16(1).

of time to ensure full coverage is in place.[1471] The 'body or person prescribed under section 21(2)' presumably relates to 'a prescribed body or person whose functions consist of or include functions of a public nature relating to safety' under 21(2)(c), as 21 (a) and (b) refer to the agencies listed under 36(2)(b), (c) and (d). As such, this appears to be a 'catch-all' provision to ensure that prescribed persons or agencies in attendance at a launch or other related, insured activity are also given the benefit of insurance protection. Other important provisions in Section 5 include the provision of insurance documentation and evidence of payment to the Regulator,[1472] the authorisation of the Regulator or Secretary of state to seek confidential advice in relation to the insurance without the need to resort to a non-disclosure agreement in certain circumstances[1473] and a requirement that no provisions or terms must be varied by the licencee during the material period the insurance covers unless authorised in writing by the Regulator.[1474] There is also a requirement that the licencee notify the Regulator in writing should any incident occur that could result in a claim under the insurance policy.[1475]

Building upon Section 5, Section 6 refers to 'Indemnity Conditions', and specifies the limitation on liability in respect of injury or damage as outlined in section 34(2) of the Space Industry Act 2018. Section 34(2) of the Act refers to:

> ... injury or damage ... caused to persons or property on land or water in the United Kingdom or in the territorial sea adjacent to the United Kingdom, or to aircraft in flight over any such land, water or sea, or to persons or property on board any such aircraft—
>
> a. by any craft or space object being used by a person ("the operator") for spaceflight activities,
> b. by anything falling from such a craft or object, or
> c. by any person in such a craft

As previously stated within this work, damages in respect of such harm are recoverable on a strict liability basis requiring no proof of negligence or willfulness on the part of the operator.[1476] It is also important to remember that

1471 Although such coverage could presumably be effective if it purports to cover the 'Secretary of State and his/her agents' or other such phrasing.

1472 N1444, para 5.4.

1473 *Ibid,* para 5.5.

1474 *Ibid,* para 5.6.

1475 *Ibid,* para 5.7.

1476 p76.

this provision does not apply to individuals of a 'prescribed description'[1477] nor those who contribute to the injury or damage through their own negligence.[1478]

Although Section 34(2) appears to cover all conceivable individuals within the United Kingdom who could potentially be injured, it is very interesting to note that Section 6.1.2. of the licence also appears to extend the licencee's liability to "any third party liability arising out of spaceflight activities which may be incurred by the licencee in respect of the death of or bodily injury to any person or damage to property not covered by section 34(2) of the Act". Given that section 34(2) appears to plug the gap in the Liability Convention insofar as that instrument only applies to damage to other states, Section 6.1.2 appears to extend liability to those outside of the jurisdiction of the United Kingdom as also appears to be stated within Section 5.1 which states that the insurance must cover 'all liabilities that may arise in respect of death, personal injury, damage or loss suffered by third parties in the United Kingdom or elsewhere'. A more fanciful interpretation may suggest that it extends liability to individuals of a 'prescribed description' in contravention of the Act but it is not likely that such an argument would be sustainable given the emphasis the Act places on excluding these persons. However, there may be an inherent contradiction within the terms of the license elsewhere. As mentioned above regarding paragraph 5.2.2, the insurance must cover, unless agreed contractually or with the Regulator, contractors and subcontractors of the licencee. Such individuals may be those of a 'prescribed description' per Section 34(3)(a) of the Space Industry Act 2018 and these individuals are not entitled to receive compensation for injury or damage on a strict liability basis. As addressed elsewhere in this work, the distinction between those entitled to claim on a strict liability basis and those so excluded is an area of tension within the regime. It is possible that the extent of liability as contained in the License terms mitigates the apparent harshness to some degree.

Section 6.1.3. includes His Majesty's Government and the bodies referred to in Section 36 of the Act referred to above in the formulation of the total sum.

The total limit on the liability of the operator is 'limited to £10.5 million (or such other sum as may be stipulated in writing by the Regulator from time to time)'[1479] on a 'per launch' basis. As to be expected, this limitation will not apply where gross negligence or wilful misconduct is proven on the part of the operator[1480] and it is likely that litigation, prospective or otherwise, would ensue in

---

1477 The Space Industry Act 2018 s34(3)(a).

1478 *Ibid*, s34(3)(b).

1479 N1444, Section 6.1.3.

1480 *Ibid*, Section 6.2.

the event of damage caused exceeding this amount. Section 6.2.2 also provides that the limitation will not apply where damage is caused as a consequence of non-compliance with licence conditions[1481] or otherwise with the requirements of the Space Industry Act 2018 or regulations made under it.[1482] Whether or not non-compliance with other regulations such as those applicable to matters of health and safety would also give rise to a raising of the liability cap is not addressed. Given that Section 6.2.1. refers only to 'gross negligence' or 'wilful misconduct'[1483]- as previously established, a high threshold- it would seem inconsistent with other terms of the licence specifically and the thrust of the statutory regime in general to allow adjustments to the liability cap in cases of 'mere' negligence. This is compounded by Section 34(1) of the Space Industry Act which states that 'no liability arises in trespass or nuisance in respect of spaceflight activities carried out in compliance, or substantially in compliance, with the requirements and conditions imposed by or under this Act'. Section 6.3 completes Section 6 by stating that the licencee shall bear any costs incurred by the Regulator in connection with the indemnity including legal costs.

As would be expected, Section 7 reserves the right of the Regulator to 'revoke, vary or suspend the licence' and its conditions 'where it appears to the Regulator' that there has been material changes to information provided to them before or after the licence application or grant of the licence,[1484] where the licencee has entered administration or gone into insolvency or liquidation[1485] or where they have breached a licence condition.[1486]

Although drafted in similar terms to the licence granted to Virgin Orbit for Cosmic Girl and LauncherOne,[1487] there are a number of significant differences between them. This may be at least in part due to the fact that the RFA ONE licence was granted in respect of a vertical launch whilst the Virgin Orbit licence was granted in respect of a horizontal launch involving a carrier aircraft.[1488] At first glance, however, the most striking difference appears in respect of the amounts of insurance liability. Unlike the RFA ONE license, the liability sums in the Virgin Orbit License are divisible, with separate amounts

1481 *Ibid,* Section 6.2.2 (I).
1482 *Ibid,* Section 6.2.2. (II).
1483 p76.
1484 N1444, Section 7.1.1.
1485 *Ibid,* Section 7.1.2.
1486 *Ibid,* Section 7.1.3.
1487 N709.
1488 *Ibid.*

stipulated for pre-flight ground operations[1489] and actual spaceflight activities.[1490] The RFA ONE licence contains only one sum for matters arising out of spaceflight operations. The divisible nature of the sum is far from the most striking contrast, however. Under Section 5.1, liability for spaceflight activities 'is limited to the sum of $US 250,000,000, a significantly larger sum than that of £10.5 million[1491] for the RFA ONE licence, itself much closer to the sum of $US 3,000,000 stipulated in respect of ground operations alone under the Virgin Orbit License.[1492] However, whilst the cost of recouping expenses such as legal fees to remedy a breach of any licence conditions or the Act/Regulations themselves appears, within the terms of the RFA ONE licence, to be unlimited, the Virgin Orbit licence places a maximum limit of '$US 250,000,000' on these also. Assuming that this sum is distinct from the insurance liability for the spaceflight activity, the total cost to the insurer in the absolute worst-case scenario for the Virgin Orbit Launch could have been $US 500,000,000 including the costs referred to in Section 5.2. It could be safely assumed that the cost of an insurance premium in the case of the Virgin Orbit launch would have been considerably higher than is likely to be the case for RFA ONE.[1493] The reason for this contrast is unknown, but it could be speculated that this may have been due to the flightpaths of the respective vehicles and the more public launch profile[1494] perhaps in addition to the involvement of the FAA and 'US Technology'.

Another difference between the 'conditions precedent' across both documents is the absence of a requirement in the Virgin Orbit license to provide for 'a data sharing agreement for launch information between the Licensee and the National Space Operations Centre'[1495] but this is due to the fact that this body was launched on 14 May 2024,[1496] almost a year and half after the Virgin Orbit License was granted.

1489 N709, Section 4.2.

1490 *Ibid,* Section 5.1.

1491 N1444, Section 6.

1492 N709, Section 4.2.

1493 Although, theoretically, since there is no limit on liability stated under Section 6.3 of the RFA ONE Licence, the technical amount recouped by the operator could be far in excess of the limit of $USD 250,000,000 stipulated for the same within the Virgin Orbit Licence.

1494 See the terms of the Virgin Orbit Licence at N709 and reported attendance at the launch itself at page 40 of this work.

1495 N1444, Section 3.1.3.

1496 Kylie Bielby, 'UK launches National Space Operations Centre and regulatory review', May 20, 2024, <https://www.unmannedairspace.info/latest-news-and-information/uk-launches-national-space-operations-centre-and-regulatory-review/> accessed 24 January 2025.

Very interestingly, there are provisions in the 'Conditions Precedent' in the Virgin Orbit licence regarding space site security which are absent from the RFA ONE licence. Under Section 3.1.3 of the Virgin Orbit licence, prior to carrying out licenced Activities, the Regulator had to be satisfied that the Licensee had "made a proposal to the Secretary of State for the designation of a space site security restricted area and controlled area in accordance with Regulation 174 and that the areas have been so designated by the Secretary of State in accordance with that Regulation". Under Regulation 174, such an application has to be made if the licencee intends to carry out the activities under Regulation 174 (2) (a)–(c) which are, respectively, 'assembling and integration of launch vehicles or carrier aircraft ... the mating of launch vehicles or carrier aircraft to their payloads, and ... mission management or range control services where such activities require restricted access.'. Within Volume 1 of the Non-Technical Summary of the Assessment of Environmental Effects[1497] submitted by Rocket Factory Augsburg to the Civil Aviation Authority there are several statements which imply that at least some degree of 'assembly' will be taking place at integration hangars at SaxaVord spaceport.[1498] Whilst references to Regulation 174 are wholly absent from the RFA ONE Launch licence, the requirement for a proposal for the designation of a space site security restricted area is replicated in the Oversight and Monitoring Plan for SaxaVord spaceport.[1499] Rather than reflecting a drafting omission or oversight on the part of the Regulator, this may be due to contractually agreed allocations of responsibility and risk between the parties and possibly to avoid duplication of efforts and administrative burden. However, there are additional requirements in the Oversight and Monitoring Plan for the Virgin Orbit Launch that appear to be 'operator' specific in relation to security matters, such as the requirement at Section 4.1.3. to provide a copy of the 'operator security programme upon a copy of the operator security programme upon its annual review, as required

1497 Rocket Factory Augsburg, Launch Operator Licence Application Assessment of Environmental Effects (RFA SaxaVord AEE V4.1) 19 January 2024, <https://consultations.caa.co.uk/++preview++/space/rocket-factory-augsburg-rfa-public-consultation/user_uploads/rfa-saxavord-aee-v4.1_vol-i-nts_vol-ii-chapters.pdf> accessed 24 January 2024.

1498 See *Ibid,* paras 1.2.7, 1.3.6, 1.5.4, 2.5.4, 2.5.8, 3.4.2, 3.7.9, 8.4.4, 8.4.29, 8.7.1. See also, 'Volume III, AEE Technical Drawings, (RFA SaxaVord AEE V4.1) 19 January 2024, <Drawing 3.2 <https://consultations.caa.co.uk/++preview++/space/rocket-factory-augsburg-rfa-public-consultation/user_uploads/rfa-saxavord-aee-v4.1-vol-iii-drawings.pdf> accessed 24 January 2025. 'Assembly, Integration and Storage Hangars' are clearly marked on Drawing 3.2.

1499 The United Kingdom Civil Aviation Authority, Reporting Plan v 1.0 for SaxaVord Spaceport Issued to Shetland Space Centre Limited, 16 December 2023, <https://www.caa.co.uk/publication/download/20953> accessed 30 January 2025.

by Regulation 171(5)'.[1500] Regulation 171 decrees this where there is a requirement to appoint a security manager. Regulation 9(3) applicable to spaceflight operators states that this is a requirement for launch operators.

Another anomaly which arises between the two licences is the condition in the Virgin Orbit licence that the Regulator must be satisfied that the Licencee: 'has appointed an individual, or individuals, to undertake the roles of accountable manager, launch director, safety manager, security manager and training manager'.[1501] This was not included in the RFA ONE licence, perhaps with good reason since licencees are already bound to appoint such individuals under the Space Industry Regulations 2021.[1502]

It is possible that the identified omissions may be part of a shift in the drafting ethos towards letting the Regulations speak for themselves in the context of Spaceflight Operator licences. After all, operators are under myriad duties to report to and inform the Regulator of a wide range of changes and listing them all as licence conditions or conditions precedent may appear overwhelming. It is also possible that the seemingly inconsistent approach could arise from the Regulator being satisfied that evidence provided of RFA ONE's operations discharged numerous obligations under the regulatory regime and, hence, there was no need to impose conditions compelling the operator to comply.

2 The Oversight and Monitoring Plan

The associated Oversight and Monitoring Plan for RFA ONE[1503] is broadly drafted in similar terms to the one issued to Virgin Orbit save for a number of specific maters. Both Plans require information to be furnished to the Regulator ensuring engagement with Launch Collision Avoidance requirements,[1504] but, unique to the RFA ONE Plan, there is a requirement that a 'lessons learned report on the integrated stage test anomaly at SaxaVord Spaceport on 19 August 2024'[1505] be provided. This, of course, refers to the recent static engine test fire at SaxaVord[1506] and it is promising from a safety standpoint to see that historical incidents arising from the activities of the same operator are incorporated

1500 Section 4 also contains a number of other such requirements not mirrored in the RFA ONE Licence.
1501 N709, Section 3.1.2
1502 See Regulation 8(1) and 9(3)(a)–(c).
1503 N1499.
1504 *Ibid*, Section 2.1.1, 3.3.4, (Section 2.4.4. Virgin Orbit OMP, infra).
1505 *Ibid* 2.1.2.
1506 N507.

into future authorisations. Another difference is that, under the RFA ONE Plan, there is a requirement to furnish the Regulator with copies of NOTAMS[1507] issued to 'any States affected by a proposed Launch as required by ICAO Annex 11'[1508] in addition to marine notifications.[1509] These requirements were also absent from the Virgin Orbit Plan. The reason for this is not immediately apparent since such matters arise out of international obligations which were clearly common to both endeavours. Also not featuring in the Virgin Orbit Plan was the requirement to provide the Regulator with 'evidence of compliance with the most up-to-date and published Inter-Agency Debris Coordination Committee (IADC) Debris Mitigation Guidelines'.[1510] Under Schedule 1 (1)(g) of the Space Industry Act 2018, conditions as to compliance with 'space debris mitigation guidelines' can be included in a licence at the Regulators discretion. This could appear to be a blurring of the boundaries between licence conditions and Oversight and Monitoring Plans as regards Regulatory practice, but, in any case, the Regulator has a duty to exercise its functions in a general sense to 'take into account … any space debris mitigation guidelines issued by an international organisation in which the government of the United Kingdom is represented'.[1511] This does not cast any light on the absence of space debris-related matters in either the Virgin Orbit licence or Oversight and Monitoring Plan, but its inclusion in the RFA ONE Plan should be welcomed given the urgent need to address such matters.

Other common matters include the requirement to notify the Regulator of the launch window and trajectory so as to enable it to 'facilitate the issue of a notification under the Hague Code of Conduct against Ballistic Missile Proliferation (HCoC)'[1512] and the requirement to provide the Regulator with 'post launch' information on objects placed into orbit to enable it to meet its international obligations under the Registration Convention.[1513]

1507 'Notices to Airmen'
1508 N1503, Section 3.3.6.
1509 *Ibid,* Section 3.3.7.
1510 *Ibid,* Section 3.3.8.
1511 The Space Industry Act 2018, Section 2(2)(h).
1512 N1503, Section 3.4. This requirement refers to Article 4(a)III of the Hague Code of Conduct which requires that Staes with Ballistic Missile and Space Launch Vehicle prgrammes:' exchange pre-launch notifications on their Ballistic Missile and Space Launch Vehicle launches and test flights. These notifications should include such information as the generic class of the Ballistic Missile or Space Launch Vehicle, the planned launch notification window, the launch area and the planned direction'.
1513 N1503, Section 4.1.3. (II).

3 Environmental Matters and the Assessment of Environmental Effects

The Virgin Orbit licence had significantly higher environmental expectations than the licence for RFA ONE. Whilst both documents state the right of the Regulator to require a new or revised Assessment of Environmental Effects,[1514] the Virgin Orbit licence dedicates an entire section to 'Environmental Conditions'.[1515] In addition to the duplicate section regarding updates or revisions, the Virgin Orbit licence states that the Licensee 'must purchase credits from a recognised offset provider for projects that have been independently verified as meeting an accredited carbon offsetting code in the United Kingdom and are sufficient to offset the calculated greenhouse gas emissions attributable to the carrying out of the Licensed Activities … in that year.'[1516] The reason for the discrepancy here may be that the relevant activities covered by the RFA ONE licence, namely the actual launch of the rocket, may not qualify for carbon off-setting per-se whilst the Virgin Orbit launch involved a carrier aircraft which, by definition, would do. According to one source, RFA ONE is fueled by a mixture of 'rocket-grade kerosene known as Rocket Propellant 1 … oxidized [sic] by liquid oxygen'.[1517] Under the United States Environmental Protection Agency's 'Emission Factors for Greenhouse Gas Inventories',[1518] 'Kerosene' and 'Kerosene-Type Jet Fuel' appear to return very similar values for CO_2 emissions to 'Aviation Gasoline'. Unless the burning of Rocket Propellant 1 yields significantly lower values than that expected by the flight of Cosmic Girl, it would seem strange that its use in the context of a rocket launch would not qualify for any carbon off-setting scheme. However, the Assessment of Environmental Effects submitted by Rocket Factory Augsburg[1519] states that:

> Offsetting is not currently under consideration as a mitigation strategy. The Proposed Project has no scope for direct offsetting as it is a transient activity with no physical footprint where land use change could be explored.

1514 See N1444, Section 4.3–4.4 and N … Section 7.2.

1515 N709, Section 7.

1516 *Ibid,* Section 7.1.

1517 Adrian Beil, 'German startup Rocket Factory Augsburg successfully performs critical tests ahead of 2022 debut', August 30, 2021 < https://www.nasaspaceflight.com/2021/08/rocket-factory-augsburg-tests-2022-debut/> accessed 24 January 2025.

1518 Environmental Protection Agency, 'Emission Factors for Greenhouse Gas Inventories', June 5, 2024 <https://www.epa.gov/system/files/documents/2024-02/ghg-emission-factors-hub-2024.pdf> accessed 24 January 2025.

1519 N1497.

> The purchase of third-party carbon credits is not considered to offer a guarantee of genuine additive GHG savings in the current market.[1520]

Regarding the specific environmental impact of the rockets fuel source, the AEE goes on to state:

> Nitromethane and nitrous oxide are used as a bipropellant mixture to provide impulse for the third stage of the RFA ONE NOM Launch Vehicle. Reaction products are likely to be mixed but are assumed to be primarily composed of carbon dioxide, water and nitrogen. The RFA ONE NOM Launch Vehicle will have reached the thermosphere before third stage firing takes place, and this layer of the atmosphere is not associated with enhanced greenhouse effects from emitted gases such as carbon dioxide. However, it has been included in the overall GHG[1521] budget for a launch on a precautionary basis.[1522]

The author lacks the relevant expertise to critique the veracity of these statements. What they may tell us, however, is that the scientific and technical assessment of the associated greenhouse gases presented to the Regulator in the AEE documentation persuaded them that the inclusion of licence conditions pertaining to carbon off-setting in this instance was not necessary, hence the omission of such a condition.

Despite the statements within the AEE, however, the Regulator saw fit to require that an assessment of 'calculated greenhouse gas emissions' be included in a 'Post-Launch Report' under the Oversight and Monitoring Plan.[1523] There is also a mandatory obligation for the licencee to produce and submit an Annual Report which covers, *inter alia*, 'information on progress to reduce greenhouse gas emissions, including the implementation of the measures outlined in the Assessment of Environmental Effects'.[1524] The Regulator also maintains a discretionary power under the Plan to 'require the Licensee to contribute to a separate report addressing the combined environmental effects of these operations alongside a variety of Operator launch vehicles operating at SaxaVord Spaceport over time'.[1525]

1520 *Ibid*, s 4.2.17.

1521 'Greenhouse gas'.

1522 *Ibid*, s 4.2.18.

1523 N1444, Section 4.2.7, but note that under Section 4.2, the use of the word '*may*' in relation to whether such a report is required.

1524 *Ibid*, Section 5.5.6.

1525 *Ibid*, Section 5.9.

As was the case with Virgin Orbit, the AEE presented by Rocket Factory Augsburg[1526] is incredibly detailed and comprehensively sets out the likely impact of its launch activities. Appropriately, the 'Environment' is considered broadly and holistically. In addition to climate change,[1527] the report also recounts the expected impact on wildlife,[1528] air quality,[1529] levels of noise and vibration,[1530] the marine environment[1531] and other mandated areas.[1532] Like the Virgin Orbit AEE, the report was compiled by a number of highly qualified experts as detailed by the technical appendix[1533] and it is clear that Rocket Factory Augsburg have taken their duty to provide the assessment under Section 11 of the Space Industry Act 2018 very seriously. As written elsewhere in this work, however, it would be germane to the thrust of the United Kingdom's international responsibilities[1534] as regards the mitigation of space debris and the magnitude of the problems caused by it for such reports to also require, as a statutory obligation, reference to the environment of outer space as well as that of the Earth.

4 Conclusions

There are many observations that can be made from comparing the licences and Reporting Plans issued to operators under the Space Industry Act 2018. Firstly, there is the inconsistency. As indicated above, there is at least one instance where a particularly important security requirement has been promulgated as a licence condition for a spaceflight operator in one case and part of the Oversight and Monitoring Plan for a spaceport operator in another.[1535] Another omission in respect of security matters appears to be the absence of any condition compelling RFA to appoint a security manager as per the requirements of the Regulations for launch operators. As outlined, such omissions could be

1526 N1497.

1527 *Ibid,* Chapter 4.

1528 *Ibid,* Chapters 5–6.

1529 *Ibid,* Chapter 7.

1530 *Ibid,* Chapter 8.

1531 *Ibid,* Chapter 10.

1532 Such as 'visual impact' of the proposed activities, see s1.2.2.

1533 RFA SaxaVord AEE V4.1, Volume IV, AEE Technical Appendices, 19 January 2024, <https://consultations.caa.co.uk/++preview++/space/rocket-factory-augsburg-rfa-publiYash@#123456c-consultation/user_uploads/rfa-saxavord-aee-v4.1-vol-iv-technical-appendices.pdf> accessed 31 January 2025.

1534 And, indeed, those of the Regulator under Section 2 of the Space Industry Act 2018.

1535 N1502.

due to the Regulator being satisfied that these requirements have already been met by the operator in question or otherwise satisfied that such requirements have been met by another Licensee. As before, should such an undertaking have been made proactively by the operator it may be that the Regulator feels uncompelled to stipulate the same as a licence condition where the operator is seen to be discharging its duties. This could also have been the case with the requirement in the RFA ONE licence to provide evidence of compliance with internationally agreed space debris mitigation guidelines which was also absent from the Virgin Orbit documentation. However, this matter was not commented upon in Virgin Orbit's Assessment of Environmental Effects and the author is not aware of other documentation which evidenced Virgin Orbit's compliance with such standards ahead of the issuance of their spaceflight operator licence.

Overall, the licencing and reporting documentation for these launches are as revealing of regulatory practices as they are opaque. There could be any number of reasonable explanations for many of the inconsistencies observed but it is to be hoped that such an approach will not be conducive of role confusion for operators when applying for licences or otherwise lead to a fragmented approach. Both outcomes could be damaging to both commercial certainty and, at the risk of sounding hyperbolic, national security in the worst-case scenario. There may likewise have been similar compelling reasons not to include reference to space debris mitigation in either the licence or Reporting Plan for Virgin Orbit in contrast to the expectations of Rocket Factory Augsburg. Given the importance of space debris mitigation and the duty of the Regulator under Section 2 of the Space Industry Act 2018 in respect of the same, consistent and regular inclusion of requirements to ensure that operators actively pledge to engage in debris mitigation and report regularly on such matters would be desirable.

List of Documents

International Instruments

The Artemis Accords; Principles for Cooperation in the Civil Exploration and Use of The Moon, Mars, Comets, and Asteroids for Peaceful Purposes.

Agreement on the Constitution of a Provisional European Telecommunications Satellite Organisation, Paris, 13 May 1977; UKTS 1990 No. 15; Cm. 956; Cmnd. 9069.

Agreement establishing Interim Arrangements for a Global Commercial Communications Satellite System and Special Agreement, Washington, 20 August 1964; 514 UNTS 25; TIAS 5646; 15 UST 1705; 1966 UKTS 12; 3 ILM 805 (1964).

Agreement relating to the International Telecommunications Satellite Organization 'INTELSAT', Washington 20 August 1971; 1220 UNTS 21; TIAS 7532; 23 UST 3813; UKTS 1973 No. 80; Cmnd. 4799; ATS 1973 No. 6; 10 ILM 909 (1971).

Agreement on the Rescue of Astronauts, the Return of Astronauts and the Return of Objects Launched into Outer Space ("Rescue Agreement"), UNGA Res 2345 (XXII) (22 Apr 1968).

Convention relating to the regulation of Aerial Navigation (with additional Protocol), signed at Paris, October 13, 191.

Convention for the Protection of the Marine Environment of the North-East Atlantic (OSPAR) 22 September 1992.

Convention Establishing the European Telecommunications Satellite Organization, Paris, 15 July 1982.

Convention on International Civil Aviation, signed at Chicago, 7 December 1944.

Convention on International Liability for Damage Caused by Space Objects ("Liability Convention"), UNGA Res 2777 (XXVI) (29 Mar 1972).

Convention on the International Maritime Satellite Organisation, London, 3 September 1976.

Convention on the Rights of Persons with Disabilities, Treaty Series vol. 2515, December 2006.

Convention for the Unification of Certain Rules relating to International Carriage by Air (Warsaw Convention) (as amended at the Hague, 1955, and by Protocol No. 4 of Montreal, 1975).

Constitution and Convention of the International Telecommunication Union, Geneva, 22 December 1992.

Convention on Registration of Objects Launched into Outer Space, UNGA Res 3235 (XXIX) (14 January 1975).

The Declaration on International Cooperation in the Exploration and Use of Outer Space for the Benefit and in the Interest of All States, Taking into Particular Account the Needs of Developing Countries', UNGA Res 51/122 (13 December 1996). Directive 2014/53/EU of the European Parliament and of the Council of 16 April 2014 on the harmonisation of the laws of the Member States relating to the making available on the market of radio equipment and repealing Directive 1999/5/EC.

The International Telecommunications Union, Radio Regulations Articles, Edition of 2020.

The International Telecommunications Union, Recommendation S.465-6 (01/2010).

The International Telecommunications Union, Recommendation ITU-R S.580-6, (01/2004).

The Principles Governing the Use by States of Artificial Earth Satellites for International Direct Television Broadcasting', UNGA Res 37/92 (10 December 1982).

The Principles Relating to Remote Sensing of the Earth from Outer Space', UNGA Res 41/65 (3 December 1986).

The Principles Relevant to the Use of Nuclear Power Sources in Outer Space', UNGA Res 47/68 (14 December 1992).

Treaty banning nuclear weapon tests in the atmosphere, in outer space and under water, No 6964 Moscow, 10 October 1963.

Treaty on Principles Governing the Activities of States in Exploration and Use of Outer Space, including the Moon and Other Celestial Bodies ("Outer Space Treaty") (adopted 27 Jan. 1967, entered into force 10 Oct 1967) 610 UNTS 205.

Resolution 68/74 adopted by the General Assembly on 11 December 2013, Recommendations on national legislation relevant to the peaceful exploration and use of outer space.

Space Debris Mitigation Guidelines of the Committee on the Peaceful Uses of Outer Space, UNOOSA, 2007, endorsed by the United Nations General Assembly by Resolution 62/217.

General Assembly Resolution 1721 on equitable global access to satellite communications (XVI) December 20, 1961.

European Union Instruments

Commission Regulation (EU) No 185/2010 of 4 March 2010 laying down detailed measures for the implementation of the common basic standards on aviation security.

Convention for the establishment of a European organisation for the exploitation of meteorological satellites ("EUMETSAT"), Geneva, 24 May 1983.

Convention for the Establishment of a European Space Agency (CSE/CS(73)19, rev.7) 31 December 1975.

Council Directive 93/13/EEC of 5 Apr. 1993 on Unfair Terms in Consumer Contracts.

Council Directive 2013/59/EURATOM of 5 December 2013 laying down basic safety standards for protection against the dangers arising from exposure to ionising radiation, and repealing Directives 89/618/Euratom, 90/641/Euratom, 96/29/Euratom, 97/43 /Euratom and 2003/122/Euratom.

Directive 2014/53/EU of the European Parliament and of the Council of 16 April 2014 on the harmonisation of the laws of the Member States relating to the making available on the market of radio equipment and repealing Directive 1999/5/EC.

European Union Product Liability Directive 85/374/EEC.

Regulation (EC) No 300/2008 Of the European Parliament and of the Council of 11 March 2008 on common rules in the field of civil aviation security and repealing Regulation (EC) No 2320/2002.

Regulation (EC) No 549/2004 of the European Parliament and of the Council of 10 March 2004 laying down the framework for the creation of the single European sky (the framework Regulation).

Regulation (EU) 2016/679 on the protection of natural persons with regard to the processing of personal data and on the free movement of such data, and repealing Directive 95/46/EC (Data Protection Directive).

Regulation (EU) 2018/1139 of the European Parliament and of the Council of 4 July 2018 on common rules in the field of civil aviation and establishing a European Union Aviation Safety Agency, and amending Regulations (EC) No 2111/2005, (EC) No 1008/2008, (EU) No 996/2010, (EU) No 376/2014 and Directives 2014/30/EU and 2014/53/EU of the European Parliament and of the Council, and repealing Regulations (EC) No 552/2004 and (EC) No 216/2008 of the European Parliament and of the Council and Council Regulation (EEC) No 3922/91.

Inter-state Agreements and Memoranda of Understanding

Agreement in the form of an exchange of notes between the government of the United Kingdom of Great Britain and Northern Ireland and the government of the United States of America on technology safeguards associated with United States participation in space launches from the United Kingdom, Washington 16 June 2020.

Headquarters Agreement between the Government of the United Kingdom of Great Britain and Northern Ireland and the International Maritime Satellite Organisation, London, 15 February 1980; 1203 UNTS 131; 1980 UKTS 44, Cmnd. 7917.

The International Code of Conduct Against Ballistic Missile Proliferation, 2002.

Memorandum of Understanding between The United Kingdom Space Agency of the Government of the United Kingdom and the Algerian Space Agency of the Government of the People's Democratic Republic of Algeria Concerning Collaboration on Civil Space Activities, 17 March 2014, Algiers.

Memorandum of Understanding between the Comision Nacional de Actividades Espaciales and the British National Space Centre on co-operation in the field of space activities, 27 October 1998, London.

Memorandum of Understanding between the Government of Great Britain and Northern Ireland And the Government of the Faroe Islands On Cooperation on Space Launches From the United Kingdom of Great Britain and Northern Ireland, 4 June 2020 London.

Memorandum of Understanding Between the Saudi Space Commission in Saudi Arabia And United Kingdom Space Agency in the United Kingdom of Great Britain and Northern Ireland on Peaceful Uses of Outer Space, Riyadh, 27 June 2022.

Acts of Parliament, Statutory Instruments and Orders

Adults with Incapacity (Scotland) Act 2000.

The Air Navigation (Cosmic Radiation: Protection of Air Crew and Space Crew and Consequential Amendments) order 2019.

The Air Navigation Order 2016.

The Air Navigation (Amendment) Order 2021.

The Airports Act 1986.

The Air Quality Standards Regulations 2010.

The Aviation Security Act 1982.

The Civil Aviation Act 1971.

The Civil Aviation Act 1982.

The Civil Aviation Authority Regulations 1991.

The Civil Contingencies Act 2004.

The Communications Act 2003.

The Consumer Protection from Unfair Trading Regulations 2008.

The Control of Major Accident Hazards Regulations 2015.

The Data Protection Act 2018.

The Deregulation Act 2015.

Disability Discrimination Act 1995.

The Employment Rights Act 1996.

The Energy Act 2016.

The Environmental Information Regulations 2004.

The Equality Act 2010.

The European Union (Withdrawal Agreement) Act 2020.

The Explosives Regulations 2014.

The Freedom of Information Act.

The Health and Safety at Work Act 1974.

Land Reform (Scotland) Act 2003.

The Interpretation Act 1978.

The Law Reform (Contributory Negligence) Act 1945.
The Legislative and Regulatory Reform Act 2006.
The Limitation Act 1980.
The Local Authority and Social Services Act 1970.
The Marine and Coastal Access Act 2009.
The Marine Works (Environmental Impact Assessment) Regulations 2007.
The Mental Capacity Act 2005.
The Mental Capacity Act (Northern Ireland) 2016.
The Mental Health Act 1983.
The National Lottery (Imposition of Penalties and Revocation of Licences) Procedure Regulations 1999.
The Network and Information Systems Regulations 2018.
The Occupiers Liability Act 1957.
The Offshore Installations (Offshore Safety Directive) (Safety Case etc.) Regulations 2015.
The Outer Space Act 1986.
The Petroleum Act 1998.
The Planning (Hazardous Substances) Act 1990.
The Railways (Safety Case) Regulations 2000/2688.
The Railways and Other Guided Transport Systems (Safety) Regulations 2006.
The Space Industry Act 2018.
The Space Industry Regulations 2021.
The Space Flight Activities (Investigation of Accidents) Regulations 2021.
The Space Industry (Appeals) Regulations 2021.
The Town and Country Planning (Environmental Impact Assessment) Regulations 2017.
The Air Navigation (Amendment) Order 2021 & The Air Navigation Order 2016.
The Unfair Contract Terms Act 1999.
The United Kingdom Space Agency (Transfer of Property etc.) Order 2011.
The Working Time Regulations 1999.
The Wireless Telegraphy Act 2006.
The Wireless Telegraphy (Limitation of Number of Licences) (Amendment) Order 2006.

Cases

Abrams v United States (1919) 250 US 616.
Adsett v K. and L. Steel Founders and Engineers Ltd [1953] 1 W.L.R. 773.

Allcard v. Skinner, 36 Ch.D. 145.

Associated Dairies Ltd v Hartley [1979] I.R.L.R. 171.

Associated Provincial Picture Houses Ltd. v Wednesbury Corporation [1948] 1 KB 223.

Aster Healthcare Ltd v Shafi (The Estate of) [2016] 2 All E.R. 316.

Bainbrigge v Browne (1881) 18 Ch. D.

Bank of Credit and Commerce International SA v Aboody [1990] 1 Q.B. 923.

Bank of New York Mellon (International) Ltd v Cine-UK Ltd [2021] EWHC 1013 (QB).

Banque de l'Indochine et de Suez SA v Euroseas Group Finance Co Ltd [1981] 3 All ER 198.

Bolam v Friern Hospital Management Committee [1957] 1 WLR 582.

Botta v Italy 21439/93, [1998] ECHR 12, [1996] ECHR 83.

Byrne v Kinematograph Renters Society Ltd [1958] 1 WLR 762 (EWHC).

Callow v Tillstone (1900) 64 JP 823 322.

Cardiff County Council v Peggy Elizabeth Ross (by her litigation friend the Official Solicitor), Case No. 12063905.

Cassley's case, [2015] EWHC 722.

Chapter of Ely v Bliss (1842) 49 ER 700.

Churchwardens and overseers of West Ham v Fourth City Mutual Building Society [1892] 1 QB 654 (EWHC).

Clyde Cycle Co v Hargreaves (1898) 78 L.T. 296.

Coles v Reynolds [2020] EWHC 2151 (Ch), [2021] 1 P. & C.R. DG8.

Commission of the European Communities v. United Kingdom of Great Britain and Northern Ireland. [1997] EUECJ C-300/95.

Cutter v Powell 101 ER 573 (KB).

Datec Electronic Holdings Ltd v United Parcels Service Ltd [2007] UKHL 23, [2007] 1 W.L.R. 1325.

Diamond v Royal Devon and Exeter NHS Foundation Trust [2019] P.I.Q.R. 12.

Donoghue v Stevenson, (1932) SC (HL) 31.

Duce v. Worcestershire Acute Hospitals NHS Trust [2018] P.I.Q.R. P18.

Dunhill v Burgin [2014] 1 W.L.R. 933.

Edwards & Others v The Secretary of State for Justice Appeal No. UKEAT/0123/14/DM.

Edwards v Flamingo Land [2013] Eq. L.R. 888.

Edwards v National Coal Board [1949] 1 K.B. 704.

Exxon Corpn v Exxon Insurance Consultants International Ltd [1981] 3 All ER 241.

Faccanda Chicken v Fowler [1986] 3 W.L.R. 288.

Fehily v Atkinson [2017] Bus. L.R. 695.

Fenwick v Schmalz (1867-68) L.R. 3 C.P. 313.

Fountaine v Chesterton (1968) 112 Sol Jo 690.

FX v A Local Authority [2017] EWCOP 36.

Gillies v Glynwed Foundries 1977 S.L.T. 97.

Glor v Switzerland (Application no. 13444/04).
Greenwich RLBC v EOA [2021] EWCOP 20.
Hamilton v Bennett (1930) 94 J.P.N. 136.
Hart v Prater (1837) 1 Jur. 623.
Holyoake v Candy [2017] EWHC 3397 (Ch).
Hutton v Warren, Clark 150 E.R. 517 (Ex).
Imperial Loan Co v Stone [1892] 1 Q.B. 599.
JH Rayner (Mincing Lane) Ltd v Department of Trade and Industry [1990] 2 A.C. 418, 500 (HoL).
Liverpool City Council v CMW (By her litigation friend, the Official Solicitor) Case No: 13699739, Court of Protection.
Local Authority X v MM [2009] 1 F.L.R. 443.
London Borough of Tower Hamlets v PB (by his litigation friend, the official solicitor) [2020] EWCOP 34.
Loudon v Elder's, 1923 CB.
Makin v London & North Eastern Railway [1943] K.B. 467.
Maredelanto Compania Naviera S.A. v Bergbau-Handel G.M.B.H (The Mihalis Angelos) [1971] 1 Q.B. (EWCA) 164, 205.
Markham v Karsten [2007] EWHC 1509 (Ch).
Marshall v Gotham [1954] A.C. 360.
Maylin v. Dacorum Sports Trust (t/a XC Sportspace) [2017] EWHC 378 (QB).
McInnes v Onslow Fane [1978] 1 WLR 1520 (EWHC).
Mitchell v Homfray (1881) 8 Q.B.D. 587.
Montgomery v Lanarkshire Health Board [2015] A.C. 1430.
Muir v Glasgow Corporation 1943 SC(HL).
Nash v Inman [1908] 2 K.B. 1. (EWCA).
National Westminster Bank Plc v Morgan [1985] A.C. 686.
O'Byrne v. Secretary of State for Environment, Transport and the Regions [2001] EWCA Civ 499.
Paulley v FirstGroup Plc [2017] 2 All E.R. 1.
Pearce v. United Bristol Healthcare NHS Trust [1999] PIQR 53.
PC v City of York [2014] 2 W.L.R. 1.
Perrett v Collins [1998] 2 Lloyds Rep 255.
Poppleton v. Trustees of the Portsmouth Youth Activities Committee [2009] P.I.Q.R. P1.
R v Barnsley Metropolitan Borough Council, ex p Hook [1976] 1 WLR 1052 (EWCA).
R. v Bateman (Percy), (1927) 19 Cr. App. R. 8.
R v Islington Borough Council, ex parte Rixon (1998) 1 CCLR 119 (EWCA).
R (Munjaz) v. Mersey Care NHS Trust [2006] 2 A.C. 148 (EWCA).
R. (on the application of X) v Tower Hamlets 2013 WL 617504 (EWHC).

Re A (An Adult) [2019] 3 W.L.R. 59.
Re Rhodes, (1890) L.R. 44 Ch. D. 94.
Re T (Adult) [1992] 4 All ER 649.
Re Williams (1887) 36 Ch D 573.
Rodney Crossman v. St George's Healthcare NHS Trust [2016] EWHC 287.
Rogers v Whittaker (1992) 175 CLR (Aus) 479.
Royal Bank of Scotland Group Plc v Allen (2010) 112 B.M.L.R. 30.
Ryder v Wombwell (1868) L.R. 3 Ex. 90.
Rylands v Fletcher (1868) LR 3 HL 330.
Sayers v Harlow UDC [1958] 1 WLR 623.
Senteges v. The Netherlands (2002) 27677/02.
Seward v 'Vera Cruz' (1884) 10 App Cas 59.
Sidaway v. Board of Governors of the Bethlem Royal Hospital [1985] A.C. 871.
Southampton Port Health Authority v Seahawk Marine Foods [2002] EWCA Civ 54.
Spurling v Bradshaw [1956] 1 W.L.R. 461.
Stratton v. Hughes, unreported, 17 Mar. 1998.
The Chagos Marine Protected Area Arbitration (Mauritius v United Kingdom) (Award) 18 March 2015, (PCA Case No 2011-03) ICGJ 486.
The Highland Council v Wildland Ltd (2021) CSOH 87 P901/20.
The Sea Angel [2007] 2 Lloyd's Rep.
Thoburn v Sunderland City Council [2002] All ER (D) 223.
Tomlinson v Congleton Borough Council [2004] 1 A.C. 46.
UCB Corporate Services Ltd v Williams [2002] 3 F.C.R. 448.
Watson v British Boxing Board of Control [2001] 2 W.L.R. 1256.
Wattleworth v Goodwood [2004] P.I.Q.R. P24.
WM Morrison Supermarkets plc v Various Claimants [2020] UKSC 12.
Zehnalová and Zehnal v Czech Republic (38621/97) May 2002.

Acts and Instruments of Other Jurisdictions

Act On the Authorization of Space Activities and the Registration of Space Objects, 5th October 2023 (Liechtenstein).
Act on Space Activities (Finland) (63/2018).
Act on Space Activities (Sweden) s1, (1982:963).
Act to give Protection against the Security Risk to the Federal Republic of Germany by the Dissemination of High-Grade Earth Remote Sensing Data, November 23, 2007 (Satellite Data Security Act – SatDSiG) (Germany).
Austrian Federal Law on the Authorization of Space Activities and the Establishment of a National Space Registry 2011 (Austrian Outer Space Act), entered into force on 28 December 2011.

Civil Aviation Act 1990, No 98 (New Zealand).

The Danish Outer Space Act (act no. 409 of 11 May 2016).

Decree-Law no. 16/2019, of 22 January, Legal regime of access to and exercise of space activities (Portugal).

Decree No. 125/95, (Argentina).

Decree of the Ministry of Economic Affairs and Employment on Space Activities (Finland) (74/2018).

Executive Order on requirements in connection with approval of activities in outer space, etc. pursuant to section 7, section 10(4), section 11(4), section 13(3), section 19 and section 21(3) of the Outer Space Act (Denmark) (Act no. 409 of 11 May 2016 on activities in outer space).

Federal Law No. (12) of 2019 Issued on 19/12/2019 On The Regulation of the Space Sector (United Arab Emirates).

French Space Operations Act 2008.

Law of 17 September 2005 on the Activities of Launching, Flight Operation or Guidance of Space Objects (Belgium).

Law of 20 July 2017 on the Exploitation and Use of Space Resources (Luxembourg).

Law of 15 December 2020 on Space Activities (Luxembourg).

Law of the Republic of Kazakhstan on Space Activities (No. 528-IV of 6 January 2012) 1329.

Commercial Space Launch Competitiveness Act of 2015 51 USC 10101(US).

Commercial Space Launch Act of 1984 51 USC Ch. 509, 50923 (US).

National Aeronautics and Space Act, Section 51, USC S 40302.

Order of the Minister of Economic Affairs dated 7 February 2008, no. WJZ 7119929, containing rules governing licence applications for the performance of space activities and the registration of space objects (Netherlands).

Ordinance Of The Supreme Soviet Of Ukraine On Space Activity, Law of Ukraine of 15 November 1996.

Ordinance On the Authorization of Space Activities and the Registration of Space Objects, 4 December 2023, (Liechtenstein).

Outer Space and High-altitude Activities Act 2017 Public Act No 29 (New Zealand).

Outer Space and High-altitude Activities (Licences and Permits) Regulations 2017 Order in Council, 21 August 2017, (New Zealand).

Russian Law on Space Activities, Federal Law No. 5663-1[2].

Space Activities Act 1998 Act No. 123 of 1998 (as amended), (Australia).

Space Affairs Act 1993 [No. 84 of 1993] G 14917. S.1 (xv) (South Africa).

The Space Activities Act (ZVDej) (Slovenia).

Space (Launches and Returns) (General) Rules 2019 (Australia).

Space (Launches and Returns) (Insurance) Rules 2019 (Australia).

Space (Launches and Returns) (High Power Rocket) Rules 2019 (Australia).

The United States Code of Federal Regulations.

Other Documents

Access Partnership's response to Ofcom's Consultation on Space Spectrum Strategy, 10 November 2022, https://www.ofcom.org.uk/siteassets/resources/documents/consultations/category-2-6-weeks/233841-space-spectrum-strategy/responses/access-partnership.

Arqiva, Response to Ofcom's Consultation on Space Spectrum Strategy, 24 May 2022, https://www.ofcom.org.uk/siteassets/resources/documents/consultations/category-2-6-weeks/233841-space-spectrum-strategy/responses/arqiva.

Australian Government, Australian Space Agency, 'Flight Safety Code' 1 August 2019 <https://www.space.gov.au/sites/default/files/media-documents/2023-04/iga_flight_safety_code.pdf>.

Australian Government, Australian Space Agency, 'Maximum Probable Loss Methodology', 1 August 2019 https://www.space.gov.au/sites/default/files/media-documents/2023-04/iga_maximum_probable_loss_methodology.pdf.

BBC, 'BBC Response to Ofcom's Space Spectrum Strategy' 10 May 2016, https://www.ofcom.org.uk/siteassets/resources/documents/consultations/uncategorised/7813-space-spectrum-strategy/responses/bbc.pdf?v=212879.

Written evidence of Thomas Cheney submitted to Parliament in respect of the Space Industry Bill https://publications.parliament.uk/pa/cm201719/cmpublic/space/memo/sib01.htm.

ClearSpace Today Ltd, Response to Ofcom's Consultation on Space Spectrum Strategy, 10 November 2022, 1, https://www.ofcom.org.uk/siteassets/resources/documents/consultations/category-2-6-weeks/233841-space-spectrum-strategy/responses/clearspace-today-ltd.

Committee on the Peaceful Uses of Outer Space (COPUOS) Scientific and Technical Subcommittee, Forty-ninth session, Vienna, 6-17 February 2012, 'Active Debris Removal – An Essential Mechanism for Ensuring the Safety and Sustainability of Outer Space. A Report of the Interntional Interdisciplinary Congress on Space Debris Remediation and On-Orbit Satellite Servicing, 30 – 31, https://www.unoosa.org/pdf/limited/c1/AC105_C1_2012_CRP16E.pdf.

Committee on the Peaceful Uses of Outer Space Scientific and Technical Subcommittee Sixty-first session, Vienna, 29 January–9 February 2024, A/AC.105/C.1/2024/CRP.21, 'United Kingdom of Great Britain and Northern Ireland update on its reporting approach for the voluntary implementation of the Guidelines for the Long-term Sustainability of Outer Space Activities', 1 February 2024.

Committee on the Peaceful Uses of Outer Space Scientific and Technical Subcommittee Long-term sustainability of outer space activities: implementation experiences, opportunities for capacity-building and challenges, 'Working paper by the Chair of the Working Group on the Long-term Sustainability of Outer Space Activities', A/AC.105/C.1/L.410/Rev.1, 7 May 2024.

Committee on the Peaceful Uses of Outer Space Legal Subcommittee, 'Status and application of the five United Nations treaties on outer space, and ways and means, including capacity-building, to promote their implementation', Sixty-third session, Vienna, 15–26 April 2024, 4–5 /78.

The Consortium for the Execution of Rendezvous and Servicing, Response to Ofcom's Consultation on Space Spectrum Strategy, 6 June 2022, https://www.ofcom.org.uk/siteassets/resources/documents/consultations/category-2-6-weeks/233841-space-spectrum-strategy/responses/confers.

COSPAR Policy on Planetary Protection, Prepared by the COSPAR Panel on Planetary Protection and approved by the COSPAR Bureau on 17 June 2020. https://cosparhq.cnes.fr/assets/uploads/2020/07/PPPolicyJune-2020_Final_Web.pdf.

Council of the International Civil Aviation Organisation, 36th Session, Legal Committee Working Paper on Commercial Space Flights, Montréal, 30 November to 3 December 2015, https://www.icao.int/Meetings/LC36/Working%20Papers/LC%2036%20-%20WP%203-2.en.pdf.

DAP 1916 'Statement of Need', submitted by Shetland Space Centre Limited in respect of application ACP-2017-79, 30 June 2018, UK Civil Aviation Authority, Airspace Change, https://airspacechange.caa.co.uk/PublicProposalArea?pID=92.

Department for Business, Energy and Industrial Strategy, Department for Transport, Civil Aviation Authority, United Kingdom Space Agency, 'Call For Evidence: Space Industry Act 2018 – Government Response', 28 May 2019, https://assets.publishing.service.gov.uk/government/uploads/system/uploads/attachment_data/file/804375/Government_Response_to_Call_for_Evidence_-_Spaceflight_liabilities_-_Final_190528.pdf.

Department for Business, Energy and Industrial Strategy, 'Growth Duty: Statutory Guidance, Statutory Guidance under Section 110(6) of The Deregulation Act 2015', https://assets.publishing.service.gov.uk/government/uploads/system/uploads/attachment_data/file/603743/growth-duty-statutory-guidance.pdf.

Department for Business, Innovation and Skills, Better Regulation Delivery Office, 'Regulators Code', April 2014, https://assets.publishing.service.gov.uk/media/5f4e14e2e90e071c745ff2df/14-705-regulators-code.pdf.

The Department for Business, Innovation and Skills, The United Kingdom Space Agency, 'Review of the Outer Space Act 1986', Impact Assessment, 20 June 2013, https://assets.publishing.service.gov.uk/government/uploads/system/uploads/attachment_data/file/493187/OSA_Impact_Assessment_FINAL_BIS0067.pdf.

Department for Constitutional Affairs, 'Mental Capacity Act Code of Practice', Issued by the Lord Chancellor on 23 April 2007 in accordance with sections 42 and 43 of the Act, 24, https://assets.publishing.service.gov.uk/government/uploads/system/uploads/attachment_data/file/921428/Mental-capacity-act-code-of-practice.pdf.

Department for Culture, Media and Sport, 'The UK Spectrum Strategy; Delivering the best value from spectrum in the UK', 10 March 2014 https://assets.publishing.service.gov.uk/government/uploads/system/uploads/attachment_data/file/287994/UK_Spectrum_Strategy_FINAL.pdf.

Department for Science, Innovation and Technology, Ministry of Defence, Policy Paper, 'National Space Strategy in Action', 19 July, 2023 https://www.gov.uk/government/publications/national-space-strategy-in-action/national-space-strategy-in-action.

The Department for Transport, 'Guidance to the regulator on environmental objectives relating to the exercise of its functions under the Space Industry Act 2018 Given by the Secretary of State under section 2(2)(e) of the Space Industry Act 2018' (London, 2021) https://assets.publishing.service.gov.uk/media/60d06eb88fa8f57ceec3ca03/guidance-to-the-regulator-on-environmental-objectives-relating-to-the-exercise-of-its-functions-under-the-space-industry-act-2018.pdf.

Department for Transport, Space Industry Bill, Spaceflight Impact Assessment, 30 September 2016 https://www.legislation.gov.uk/ukpga/2018/5/pdfs/ukpgaodssss_20180005_en_001.pdf.

The Draft Electronic Communications Wireless Telegraphy (Licence Award) Regulations [2024], https://www.ofcom.org.uk/siteassets/resources/documents/consultations/category-2-6-weeks/285288-proposals-to-make-auction-regulations-for-the-mmwave-award/associated-documents/annex-5-draft-wireless-telegraphy-licence-award-regulations-2024.pdf.

ECSS Q70C Rev.1 on Materials, Mechanical Parts and Processes, and ECSS-E-ST-20C on Electrical and Optical Engineering - Electrical and Electronic.

EMEA Satellite Operators Association ESOA Responses to Ofcom's Consultation on Space Spectrum Strategy, 10 May 2016, https://www.ofcom.org.uk/siteassets/resources/documents/consultations/uncategorised/7813-space-spectrum-strategy/responses/esoa.pdf.

Environmental Protection Agency, 'Emission Factors for Greenhouse Gas Inventories', June 5, 2024 https://www.epa.gov/system/files/documents/2024-02/ghg-emission-factors-hub-2024.pdf.

Equality Act Statutory Code of Practice, Equality and Human Rights Commission, 'Equality Act Statutory Code of Practice', https://www.equalityhumanrights.com/sites/default/files/servicescode_0.pdf.

European Space Policy Institute, 'ESPI Report 71 - Towards a European Approach to Space Traffic Management - Full Report' January 2020, https://www.espi.or.at/wp-content/uploads/2022/06/ESPI-Public-Report-71-Towards-a-European-Approach-to-Space-Traffic-Management-Full-Report.pdf.

EUTELSAT, Response to Ofcom's Consultation on Space Spectrum Strategy, 11 November 2022, 1, https://www.ofcom.org.uk/siteassets/resources/documents/consultations/category-2-6-weeks/233841-space-spectrum-strategy/responses/eutelsat.

The Federal Aviation Administration, 'Factsheet- Class E Upper Airspace Traffic Management (ETM) Concept of Operations (ConOps)' https://www.faa.gov/sites/faa.gov/files/2022-06/FactSheet_ETM.pdf.

The Federal Aviation Administration Office of Commercial Space Transportation, Guidance on Informing Crew and Spaceflight /headquarters_offices/ast/regulations /media/Guidance_on_Informing Participants of Risk, (Version 1.1 Arpil 4 2017) https://www.faa.gov/about/office_org/headquarters_offices/ast/regulations /media/Guidance_on_Informing_Crew_and_Space_Flight_Participants_of_Risk.pdf

The Federal Aviation Administration, Recommended Practices for Human Space Flight Occupant Safety, Version 1.0 August 27 2014, https://www.faa.gov/about /office_org/headquarters_offices/ast/media/recommended_practices_for_hsf _occupant_safety-version_1-tc14-0037.pdf.

The General Medical Council, 'Consent: Patients and Doctors Making Decisions Together', (2008), https://www.gmc-uk.org/static/documents/content/Consent _-_English_0617.pdf.

Global Satellite Operators Association, Response to Ofcom's Consultation on Space Spectrum Strategy, 11 November 2022, https://www.ofcom.org.uk/siteassets /resources/documents/consultations/category-2-6-weeks/233841-space-spectrum -strategy/responses/global-satellite-operators-association.

Walter Flury, Jean-Michel Contant, 'IAA Position Paper on Orbital Debris, Proceedings of the Third European Conference on Space Debris', 19-21 March 2001 https:// conference.sdo.esoc.esa.int/proceedings/sdc3/paper/7/SDC3-paper7.pdf.

Health and Safety Executive, 'Our role as a regulator', https://www.hse.gov.uk/enforce /our-role-as-regulator.htm.

House of Commons Select Committee on Science and Technology, Written Evidence Submitted by Airborne Engineering Limited per Dr Peter Shaw, Senior Lecturer in Astronautics, Kingston University, London (SPA0044) https://committees .parliament.uk/writtenevidence/37223/pdf/.

House of Commons Select Committee on Science and Technology, Written Evidence Submitted by Black Arrow Technologies Ltd (SPA0105) https://committees .parliament.uk/writtenevidence/119104/pdf/.

House of Commons Select Committee on Science and Technology, Written Evidence Submitted by Lockheed Martin UK (SPA0050) https://committees.parliament.uk /writtenevidence/37239/pdf/.

House of Commons Select Committee on Science and Technology, Written Evidence Submitted by Satellite Applications Catapult (SPA0037) https://committees .parliament.uk/writtenevidence/37202/pdf/.

House of Commons Select Committee on Science and Technology Written Evidence Submitted by UK Research and Innovation (UKRI) (SPA0024) https://committees .parliament.uk/writtenevidence/37178/pdf/.

House of Commons Science and Technology Committee, 'UK Space Strategy and Satellite Infrastructure; Second Report of session 2022–2023' HC 100, 4 November 2022, https://committees.parliament.uk/publications/31490/documents/176763 /default/.

House of Commons Science, Innovation and Technology Committee, UK space strategy and UK satellite infrastructure: reviewing the licencing regime for launch, Seventh Report of Session 2022–23, https://committees.parliament.uk/publications/40829/documents/198924/default/.

Georgina Hutton, 'The Space Industry Bill 2017–2019' (2018) Briefing Paper Number CBP 8197, online https://commonslibrary.parliament.uk/research-briefings/cbp-8197/.

ICNIRP Guidelines For Limiting Exposure to Electromagnetic Fields (100 KHZ TO 300 GHZ) Health Phys 118(5): 483–524, 2020, https://www.icnirp.org/cms/upload/publications/ICNIRPrfgdl2020.pdf.

Inmarsat, Response to the Ofcom Space Spectrum Strategy 24 May 2022, 1, <https://www.ofcom.org.uk/siteassets/resources/documents/consultations/category-2-6-weeks/233841-space-spectrum-strategy/responses/inmarsat>.

INTERIM REPORT REALITIES AND TENDENCIES IN EUROPEAN TELEVISION : PERSPECTIVES AND OPTIONS (Report from the Commission to the European Parliament), 127, COM/1983/0229 final.

The International Civil Aviation Organisation, International Standards and Recommended Practices, Annex 13 to the Convention on International Civil Aviation, Aircraft Accident and Incident Investigation, http://www.airsafe.com/downloads/icao-annex-13.pdf.

The International Civil Aviation Organisation, 'Manual of Civil Aviation Medicine', Annex 1, Requirements of Mental Fitness, Chapter 9.1.3, (Third Edition 2012, Quebec) https://www.icao.int/publications/documents/8984_cons_en.pdf.

The International Telecommunications Union, Radio Regulations Articles, Edition of 2020, <https://www.itu.int/en/publications/ITU-R/pages/publications.aspx?parent=R-REG-RR-2020&media=electronic>.

HyImpulse Airspace Change Proposal Stakeholders Engagement Report, Version 1.0, 14 April 2022.

ISO 14302:2002 on Space systems – Electromagnetic compatibility requirements and ISO 14303:2002 on Space systems – Launch-vehicle-to-spacecraft interfaces.

Kepler Communications, Response to Ofcom's Consultation on Space Spectrum Strategy, 10 November 2022, https://www.ofcom.org.uk/siteassets/resources/documents/consultations/category-2-6-weeks/233841-space-spectrum-strategy/responses/kepler-communications.

Lacuna Space Ltd, Response to Ofcom's Consultation on Space Spectrum Strategy, 10 November 2022, https://www.ofcom.org.uk/siteassets/resources/documents/consultations/category-2-6-weeks/233841-space-spectrum-strategy/responses/lacuna-space-ltd.

The Law Commission, 'Mental Incapacity' (1995) Law Com No 231, 28 February, 33.

License template issued by Ofcom pursuant to the Wireless Telegraphy Act 2006 for Earth Station Networks, https://www.ofcom.org.uk/siteassets/resources/documents

/manage-your-licence/satellite-earth-stations/templates/esn-licence-template .pdf.

License template issued by Ofcom pursuant to the Wireless Telegraphy Act 2006 for GNSS Repeater licenses <https://www.ofcom.org.uk/siteassets/resources/documents /manage-your-licence/satellite-earth-stations/templates/gnss-repeater-licence -template.pdf>.

License template issued by Ofcom pursuant to the Wireless Telegraphy Act 2006 for Non-Fixed Satellite Earth Stations, <https://www.ofcom.org.uk/siteassets /resources/documents/manage-your-licence/satellite-earth-stations/templates /non-fixed-satellite-earth-station-licence-template.pdf>.

License template issued by Ofcom pursuant to the Wireless Telegraphy Act 2006 for Non-Geostationary Earth Stations, https://www.ofcom.org.uk/siteassets/resources /documents/manage-your-licence/satellite-earth-stations/templates/non-geos tationary-earth-station-licence-template.pdf.

License template issued by Ofcom pursuant to the Wireless Telegraphy Act 2006 for Transportable Earth Station Licenses, <https://www.ofcom.org.uk/siteassets /resources/documents/manage-your-licence/satellite-earth-stations/templates /transportable-earth-station-licence-template.pdf?v=328907>.

Written Evidence Submitted by Lockheed Martin UK to the House of Commons Select Committee on Science and Technology (SPA0050), https://committees.parliament .uk/writtenevidence/37239/pdf/.

Lockheed Martin, Response to Ofcom's Consultation on Space Spectrum Strategy, 11 November 2022, https://www.ofcom.org.uk/siteassets/resources/documents /consultations/category-2-6-weeks/233841-space-spectrum-strategy/responses /lockheed-martin.

Methera, Response to Ofcom's Consultation on Space Spectrum Strategy, 11 November 2022, 2, < https://www.ofcom.org.uk/siteassets/resources/documents/consultations /category-2-6-weeks/233841-space-spectrum-strategy/responses/methera>.

The Met Office, Response to Ofcom's Consultation on Space Spectrum Strategy, 11 November 2022, https://www.ofcom.org.uk/siteassets/resources/documents /consultations/category-2-6-weeks/233841-space-spectrum-strategy/responses /met-office.

The Ministry of Defence, Defence Standard 00-56 Part 1, Safety Management Requirements for Defence Systems, Part 1: Requirements, 28 February 2017, 26, https:// s3-eu-west-1.amazonaws.com/s3.spanglefish.com/s/22631/documents/safety -specifications/def-stan-00-056-pt1-iss7-28feb17.pdf.

The Ministry of Defence, The UK Civil Aviation Authority, Safety and Airspace Regulation, CAP761 'Operation of IFF/SSR interrogators in the UK: Planning principles and procedures' 4 January 2019, 12, https://www.caa.co.uk/publication/ download/13116.

National Aeronautics and Space Administration, HUMAN INTEGRATION DESIGN HANDBOOK (HIDH), NASA/SP-2010-3407/REV1, January 2010, 1st Revision 2023, <https://www.nasa.gov/wp-content/uploads/2023/03/human-integration-design-handbook-revision-1.pdf?emrc=671267bcc12f1>.

Note verbale dated 27 March 1998 from the Permanent Mission of the United Kingdom of Great Britain and Northern Ireland to the United Nations (Vienna) addressed to the Secretary-general, UN Doc ST/SG/SER.E/333.

Note to UNOOSA from Danish Ministry of Higher Education and Science, 14 June 2018, https://www.unoosa.org/documents/pdf/spacelaw/national/denmark/Danish-Outer-Space-Act_Note-on-Scope-of_ApplicationE.pdf.

Notification of RECOGNISED SPECTRUM ACCESS (RSA) grant by the Office of Communications ('Ofcom') under section 18 of the Wireless Telegraphy Act 2006 ('the Act') template issued by Ofcom, <https://www.ofcom.org.uk/siteassets/resources/documents/manage-your-licence/satellite-earth-stations/templates/receive-only-earth-station-rsa-grant-template.pdf.

Northumbria University, Response to Ofcom's Consultation on Space Spectrum Strategy, 11 November 2022, 4, https://www.ofcom.org.uk/siteassets/resources/documents/consultations/category-2-6-weeks/233841-space-spectrum-strategy/responses/northumbria-university.

o3b, Response of o3b to Ofcom's Consultation on Space Spectrum Strategy, 10 June 2016, 4, https://www.ofcom.org.uk/siteassets/resources/documents/consultations/uncategorised/7813-space-spectrum-strategy/responses/o3b.pdf.

Ofcom, 'Apply for a satellite earth station license', 30 October 2023 https://www.ofcom.org.uk/spectrum/space-and-satellites/earth-stations.

Ofcom, 'Booklet OfW 597 Wireless Telegraphy Licence Conditions', 20 January 2023, <https://www.ofcom.org.uk/siteassets/resources/documents/spectrum/emf/emf-glc-licence-conditions-booklet.pdf?jsn_mobilize_preview=1>.

Ofcom, 'Guidance on EMF Compliance and Enforcement' 18 May 2021 https://www.ofcom.org.uk/siteassets/resources/documents/spectrum/emf/guidance-emf-compliance-enforcement.pdf.

Ofcom, Permanent Earth Station Licence Template, https://www.ofcom.org.uk/siteassets/resources/documents/manage-your-licence/satellite-earth-stations/templates/permanent-earth-station-licence-template.pdf.

Ofcom, 'Space Spectrum Strategy', 10 November 2022, https://www.ofcom.org.uk/siteassets/resources/documents/consultations/category-2-6-weeks/233841-space-spectrum-strategy/associated-documents/statement-space-spectrum-strategy.pdf.

Ofcom, 'Space Spectrum Strategy- Consultation', 15 March 2022, https://www.ofcom.org.uk/spectrum/space-and-satellites/space-launch-uk.

Ofcom, 'UK Interface Requirement 2022', January 2018, https://www.ofcom.org.uk/siteassets/resources/documents/spectrum/interface-requirements/ir_2022.pdf.

OneWeb, Response to Ofcom's Consultation on Space Spectrum Strategy, 10 November 2022, 1, https://www.ofcom.org.uk/siteassets/resources/documents/consultations/category-2-6-weeks/233841-space-spectrum-strategy/responses/oneweb.

The Regulators Licensing Rules, 2 July 2020, 8, Table A, https://assets.publishing.service.gov.uk/government/uploads/system/uploads/attachment_data/file/904463/the-regulators-licensing-rules.pdf.

Royal Astronomical Society, Response to Ofcom's Consultation on Space Spectrum Strategy, 11 November 2022, https://www.ofcom.org.uk/siteassets/resources/documents/consultations/category-2-6-weeks/233841-space-spectrum-strategy/responses/royal-astronomical-society.

SaxaVord UK Spaceport, 'SaxaVord Spaceport Permanent Airspace Reservation', 12 June 2023, https://consultations.airspacechange.co.uk/saxavord-spaceport/saxavord-spaceport-airspace-reservation/.

SES response to Ofcom's Consultation on Space Spectrum Strategy, 10 May 2016, 4, https://www.ofcom.org.uk/siteassets/resources/documents/consultations/uncategorised/7813-space-spectrum-strategy/responses/ses.pdf.

Science, Innovation and Technology Space Strategy Sub-Committee, Written Evidence Submitted by the Department for Business, Energy and Industrial Strategy (BEIS) (SPA0026) https://committees.parliament.uk/writtenevidence/37181/pdf/.

Science, Innovation and Technology Space Strategy Sub-Committee, Written Evidence Submitted by Newton Launch Systems, (SPA0107) https://committees.parliament.uk/writtenevidence/119106/pdf/.

Science and Technology Committee Oral evidence: UK Space Strategy and UK Satellite Infrastructure, HC 98 Wednesday 12 January 2022.

Science, Innovation and Technology Committee, 'UK Space Strategy and UK satellite infrastructure, reviewing the licensing regime for launch', Written Evidence Submitted by Skyrora, (SPA0064), https://committees.parliament.uk/writtenevidence/37269/pdf/.

Space Debris Mitigation Guidelines of the Committee on the Peaceful Uses of Outer Space. Guidelines for the Long-term Sustainability of Outer Space Activities, European Code of Conduct for Space Debris Mitigation, Inter-Agency Debris Coordination Committee Space Debris Mitigation Guidelines, Space Debris Mitigation Requirements BS ISO 24113-2019, Disposal of orbital launch stages BS ISO 16699:2015, Requirements on Space Debris Mitigation for European Space Agency Projects.

The Space Energy Initiative, Response to Ofcom's Consultation on Space Spectrum Strategy, 11 November 2022, https://www.ofcom.org.uk/siteassets/resources/documents/consultations/category-2-6-weeks/233841-space-spectrum-strategy/responses/space-energy-initiative.

Space Industry Bill [HL] Explanatory Notes, 29 November 2017, https://publications.parliament.uk/pa/bills/cbill/2017-2019/0137/en/18137en.pdf.

SpaceX, Response to Ofcom's Consultation on Space Spectrum Strategy, 11 November 2022, https://www.ofcom.org.uk/siteassets/resources/documents/consultations/category-2-6-weeks/233841-space-spectrum-strategy/responses/spacex.

United Kingdom As A Space Nation: a Snapshot of Current Capabilities.

And Lessons From Other Countries, Written Evidence Submitted by Rahim Talibzade, (SPA0066) <committees.parliament.uk/writtenevidence/37274/pdf/.

TechUk, Response to Ofcom's Consultation on Space Spectrum Strategy, 10 November 2022, 3, https://www.ofcom.org.uk/siteassets/resources/documents/consultations/category-2-6-weeks/233841-space-spectrum-strategy/responses/techuk.

UK-Australia Space Bridge Framework Agreement, 23 February 2021.

The United Kingdom Civil Aviation Authority, 'CAP1616 Airspace change: Guidance on the regulatory process for changing the notified airspace design and planned and permanent redistribution of air traffic, and on providing airspace. information' https://publicapps.caa.co.uk/modalapplication.aspx?appid=11&mode=detail&id=8127.

The United Kingdom Civil Aviation Authority, Air Navigation Order 2016, ANO Large Rocket Permission granted for HyImpulse Technologies GmBh, ORS10 2023-001, https://www.caa.co.uk/publication/download/20588.

The United Kingdom Civil Aviation Authority, 'CAA Cyber Security Oversight Process for Aviation', https://www.caa.co.uk/publication/download/17492.

The United Kingdom Civil Aviation Authority, 'The CAA Safety Plan – our approach to protecting UK citizens and the general public from aviation risk' <https://www.caa.co.uk/safety-initiatives-and-resources/how-we-regulate/safety-plan/the-caa-safety-plan/>.

The UK Civil Aviation Authority, Consultations, 'Virgin Orbit and Spaceport Cornwall Joint Assessment of Environmental Effects Public Consultation Responses' https://consultations.caa.co.uk/corporate-communications/aee-consultation-virgin-orbit-spaceport-cornwall/results/virginorbitandspaceportcornwalljointassessmentofenvironmentaleffectspublicconsultationresponses.pdf.

The United Kingdom Civil Aviation Authority, 'Guidance for Airport Operators Designating Known Suppliers of Airport Supplies', CAP 1260, https://www.caa.co.uk/publication/download/15044.

The United Kingdom Civil Aviation Authority, 'Guidance on Appealing Decisions made Under the Space Industry Act 2018 and the Outer Space Act 1986', https://assets.publishing.service.gov.uk/government/uploads/system/uploads/attachment_data/file/904910/guidance-on-appealing-decisions-made-under-the-space-industry-act-2018.pdf.

The United Kingdom Civil Aviation Authority, 'Guidance on Applying for a License' https://assets.publishing.service.gov.uk/government/uploads/system/uploads/attachment_data/file/904285/guidance-on-applying-for-a-licence.pdf.

The UK Civil Aviation Authority, 'Guidance for the assessment of environmental effects' Guidance for the Assessment of Environmental Effects, https://assets.publishing.service.gov.uk/government/uploads/system/uploads/attachment_data/file/904454/guidance-for-the-assessment-of-environmental-effects..pdf.

The United Kingdom Civil Aviation Authority, Guidance on duties for all licensees under the Space Industry Act 2018 including monitoring and enforcement by the Regulator, https://www.caa.co.uk/publication/download/18935.

The United Kingdom Civil Aviation Authority, Guidance on the Investigation of Spaceflight Accidents, https://www.caa.co.uk/publication/download/18927.

The United Kingdom Civil Aviation Authority, 'Guidance for Launch Operator and Return Operator License Applicants and Licensees' 1st edition, https://assets.publishing.service.gov.uk/government/uploads/system/uploads/attachment_data/file/904911/guidance-for-launch-and-return-operator-licence-applicants-and-licensees.pdf.

The United Kingdom Civil Aviation Authority, 'Guidance for Launch and Return Operator Licence Applicants and Licensees', (CAP2213), 2nd Edition, 31 May 2024, https://www.caa.co.uk/publication/download/18943.

The United Kingdom Civil Aviation Authority, Guidance for Orbital Operator Applicants and Licensees, 1st edition, https://assets.publishing.service.gov.uk/government/uploads/system/uploads/attachment_data/file/904448/guidance-for-orbital-operator-licence-applicants-and-licensees.pdf.

The United Kingdom Civil Aviation Authority, 'Guidance for Oribtal Operator Licence Applicants and Licensees', 2nd edition, 31 May 2024, https://www.caa.co.uk/publication/download/18909.

The United Kingdom Civil Aviation Authority, Guidance for Range Control Applicants and Licensees, <https://assets.publishing.service.gov.uk/government/uploads/system/uploads/attachment_data/file/904472/guidance-for-range-control-licence-applicants-and-licensees.pdf>.

The United Kingdom Civil Aviation Authority, Guidance on Security Matters, https://assets.publishing.service.gov.uk/government/uploads/system/uploads/attachment_data/file/904451/guidance-on-security-matters-for-applicants-and-licensees.pdf.

The United Kingdom Civil Aviation Authority, Guidance for Spaceport Licence Applicants and Licensees, (CAP2212) https://www.caa.co.uk/our-work/publications/documents/content/cap2212/.

The United Kingdom Civil Aviation Authority, HyImpulse Sounding Rocket Launch from SaxaVord Spaceport – Shetland, Airspace Change Proposal documentation, https://airspacechange.caa.co.uk/PublicProposalArea?pID=402.

The United Kingdom Civil Aviation Authority, 'Launch Collision Avoidance Analysis', https://www.caa.co.uk/space/guidance-and-resources/launch-collision-avoidance-analysis-lcola/.

The United Kingdom Civil Aviation Authority, 'Licensing of Aerodromes', (CAP168) 14 January 2022, https://www.caa.co.uk/our-work/publications/documents/content/cap-168/.

The United Kingdom Civil Aviation Authority, 'Our Regulatory Principles', (CAP2185) https://www.caa.co.uk/publication/download/18804.

The United Kingdom Civil Aviation Authority, Oversight and Monitoring Plan v.1.0 for Cornwall Airport Limited, https://www.caa.co.uk/publication/download/20109.

The United Kingdom Civil Aviation Authority, Oversight and Monitoring Plan v.1.0 for Virgin Orbit LLC in relation to its Spaceflight Operator License, https://www.caa.co.uk/publication/download/20113.

The United Kingdom Civil Aviation Authority, 'Principles and guidelines for the spaceflight regulator in assessing ALARP and acceptable risk', https://www.caa.co.uk/publication/download/18931.

The United Kingdom Civil Aviation Authority, 'Radio Frequency / Radio Question Set', November 2021, https://www.caa.co.uk/publication/download/21873.

The United Kingdom Civil Aviation Authority, Space Industry Act, Spaceflight Operator License for the Launch of the Carrier Aircraft Cosmic Girl and Launch of the Launch Vehicle Type LauncherOne, 20 December 2022, Licence ref: SR-APP-001002, 3, https://www.caa.co.uk/publication/download/20111.

The United Kingdom Civil Aviation Authority, 'Space Launch and Orbit Group (SPLOG), remit, members and terms of reference' https://www.caa.co.uk/space/about-us/space-launch-and-orbit-group-splog/.

The United Kingdom Civil Aviation Authority, Space Launch and Orbit Group, Launch Session July 2022, https://www.caa.co.uk/media/frmhppj4/july-2022_launch.pdf.

The United Kingdom Civil Aviation Authority Space Launch and Orbit Group, Launch Sessions July and November 2022, https://www.caa.co.uk/media/l2mmf50w/november-splog-master_launch_published.pdf.

The United Kingdom Civil Aviation Authority, Space Launch and Orbit Group, Launch Session, November 2022, https://www.caa.co.uk/media/l2mmf50w/november-splog-master_launch_published.pdf.

The United Kingdom Civil Aviation Authority Space Launch and Orbit Group, Launch Session March 2023 <https://www.caa.co.uk/media/xm4budq0/march-2023-launch.pdf>.

The United Kingdom Civil Aviation Authority, Spaceport License Granted to Cornwall Airport, November 2022, https://www.caa.co.uk/publication/download/20107.

The United Kingdom Civil Aviation Authority, 'SRG2229 Radio Frequency / Spectrum Question Set', 1 November 2021, <https://www.caa.co.uk/publication/download/21873>.

The United Kingdom Civil Aviation Authority, 'Technical Question Set', v2, 16 February 2024, https://www.caa.co.uk/publication/download/19252.

The United Kingdom Government, Committee on the Peaceful Uses of Outer Space (COPUOS): UK statement on legal mechanisms relating to space debris and remediation measures at the 61st Legal Sub-committee.

The United Kingdom Government, 'Draft proposals for exempting defence-related activities from the Space Industry Act 2018' 16 September 2024, https://www.gov.uk/government/consultations/draft-policy-proposals-for-exempting-defence-related-activities-from-the-space-industry-act-2018/draft-policy-proposals-for-exempting-defence-related-activities-from-the-space-industry-act-2018#:~:text=Open%20consultation.%20Draft%20policy.

The United Kingdom Government, Department for Science, Innovation and Technology, 'Space Regulatory Review 2024; A targeted review of space regulations', Research Paper Number 2024/007, May 2024.

https://assets.publishing.service.gov.uk/media/6644d26fb7249a4c6e9d3597/space_regulatory_review_2024.pdf.

The United Kingdom Space Agency, 'Consultation on Orbital Liabilities, Insurance, Charging and Space Sustainability', 14 September 2023, https://www.gov.uk/government/consultations/consultation-on-orbital-liabilities-insurance-charging-and-space-sustainability.

The United Kingdom Space Agency, Response to Ofcom's Consultation on Space Spectrum Strategy, 11 November 2022, https://www.ofcom.org.uk/siteassets/resources/documents/consultations/category-2-6-weeks/233841-space-spectrum-strategy/responses/uk-space-agency-and-beis.

The United Kingdom Space Agency, 'UK Registry of Space Objects; To comply with international obligations and section 7 of the Outer Space Act 1986' May 2021.

The United Kingdom Space Agency, Department for Transport, Department for Business, Energy and Industrial Strategy, The UK Civil Aviation Authority, 'Unlocking Commercial Spaceflight for the UK consultation on draft insurance and liabilities requirements to implement the Space Industry Act', 2020, 18, https://assets.publishing.service.gov.uk/media/5f8e8bbfe90e0727c3edba6b/unlocking-commercial-spaceflight-for-the-uk-consultation-on-draft-insurance-and-liabilities-requirements-to-implement-the-space-industry-act.pdf.

United Kingdom Space Command, 'Cross Government Space Domain Awareness (SDA) Requirements Publication, Version 2.0, 2024, https://assets.publishing.service.gov.uk/media/65fd8c7365ca2f00117da8e7/Space_domain_awareness_-_requirements.pdf.

United Kingdom Space Agency Space Domain Awareness Study, 20 May 2022, <https://www.ukspace.org/wp-content/uploads/2022/07/UKSA-SDA-Study-Report_v2.4.pdf.

United Nations Committee on the Rights of Persons with Disabilities Eleventh session 30 March–11 April 2014 Item 10 of the provisional agenda General comments and days of general discussion, General comment on Article 12: Equal recognition before the Law, https://digitallibrary.un.org/record/779679.

United Nations, The Guidelines for the Long-term Sustainability of Outer Space Activities (LTS Guidelines), adopted by the Committee on the Peaceful Uses of Outer Space (COPUOS) in 2019. https://spacesustainability.unoosa.org/content/the_guidelines.

UNCOPUOS AC.105/891, Report of the Legal Subcommittee on its forty-sixth session held in Vienna from 26 March to 5 April 2007.

US Department of Transportation, Federal Aviation Administration, Guide 437.53-1, <https://www.faa.gov/about/office_org/headquarters_offices/ast/regulations/media/Guide-Cal-of-Safety-Clear-Zones.pdf>.

Virgin Orbit (and multiple authors), 'Assessment of Environmental Effects Virgin Orbit LLC LauncherOne Operations from Spaceport Cornwall, Cornwall Airport Newquay, United Kingdom, July 2022, https://consultations.caa.co.uk/corporate-communications/aee-consultation-virgin-orbit-spaceport-cornwall/user_uploads/virgin-orbit-spaceport-cornwall-aee--13jul22--1.pdf.

Books

Diggory Bailey and Luke Norbury, *Bennion, Bailey and Norbury on Statutory Interpretation*, 8th Edition Supplement, November 2022.

Frans von der Dunk and Fabio Tronchetti, (eds), *Handbook of Space Law* (Edward Elgar, 2015).

Frans von der Dunk, *International Space Law*, 29, in Frans von der Dunk, Fabio Tronchetti, *Handbook of Space Law*, (Edward Elgar, 2017).

Frans von der Dunk, *Advanced Introduction to Space Law* (2020), Cheltenham, UK, Edward Elgar Publishing.

James Eberle and Helen Wallace, *British Space Policy And International Collaboration*, Royal Institute of International Affairs, Routledge, 1987.

European Space Policy Institute, *Yearbook on Space Policy; 2008.2009:Setting New Trends*, SpringerWienNewYork, 2010.

Thomas Gangale, *How High The Sky?,* Brill Nijhoff 2018.

Daniel Greenberg (ed), *Stroud's Judicial Dictionary*, 11th Edition.

Charles N. Hill *Vertical Empire, A: History Of The British Rocketry Programme*, World Scientific Publishing Company 2nd Ed, 2011.

S. Houston Lay and Howard J. Taubenfeld, *The Law Relating to Activities of Man in Space*, University of Chicago Press/ American Bar Association, 1970.

Francis Lyall, *Law and Space Telecommunications,* Dartmouth, 1989.

Francis Lyall, *Space Law: A Treatise*, Routledge, 2nd edition.

Patricia McCormack, Murray J. Mechanick (eds), The Transformation of Intergovernmental Satellite Organisations: Policy and Legal Perspectives, Brill Niijhoff, 2013.

Peter Morton, *Fire Across the Desert; Woomera and the Anglo Australian Joint Project* (1989) Commonwealth of Australia, Defence Science and Technology.
Guy Mundlak and Matthew Finklin, *Comparative Labor Law*, Cheltenham 2015.
Dave Scott & Alexei Leonov, *Two Sides of the Moon*, Bedford Square Books, London 2004.
Guenter Treitel QC, *Frustration and Force Majeure*, 2nd Edition, Sweet and Maxwell, 2004.
The War Office, *Report on "Operation Backfire* (1946) Volume 1.

Articles

Jonathan Amos, "Muscular' United Kingdom Space Agency Launched', BBC News, 23 March 2010.
Owen Anderson, Mike Wearne, 'Informed consent for elective surgery--what is best practice?' J R Soc Med. 2007 Feb, 100(2), 97.
Anna Arstein-Kerslake & Eilionóir Flynn (2016) 'The General Comment on Article 12 of the Convention on the Rights of Persons with Disabilities: a roadmap for equality before the law', The International Journal of Human Rights, 20:4.
BBC News, 'UK first as vertical rocket launch Licence granted', 16 January 2025.
Colin Burgess, Shattered Dreams: The Lost and Cancelled Space Missions, (Lincoln, University of Nebraska Press 2019) 147.
Ed Cape, 'Modernising Police Powers – again?', Crim. L.R. 2007, Dec, 934.
Bin Cheng, 'The Commercial Development of Space: The Need for New Treaties' (1991) 19 J Space L 17, 38–39.
Barnali Choudhury, 'Balancing Soft and Hard Law for Business and Human Rights' International and Comparative Law Quarterly 67, 2018, 961–986.
Cliona de Bhailis and Eilionoir Flynn, 'Recognising legal capacity: commentary and analysis of Article 12 CRPD', Int. J.L.C. 2017, 13(1).
Frans von der Dunk, 'Billion-dollar questions? Legal aspects of commercial space activities', June 2018, Uniform Law Review, Vol 23, 2, 418–446.
Frans Von der Dunk, 'The 1972 Liability Convention: Enhancing Adherence and Effective Application' (1998). Space, Cyber, and Telecommunications Law Program Faculty Publications 371.
Frans von der Dunk, Towards 'Flags of Convenience' in Space?", in Proceedings of the International Institute of Space Law 2012 (IISL)(2013), 811–30.
Frans von der Dunk, 'Liability for Damage Caused by Small Satellites – A Non- Issue?' (2016) Space, Cyber and Telecommunications Law Program Faculty Publications, 99.
Oliver Dunnett, 'Geopolitical Cultures of Outer Space: The British Interplanetary Society, 1933-1965' Geopolitics, 22(2), (2017).

Jaye Ellis, 'Shades of Grey: Soft Law and the Validity of Public International Law' Leiden Journal of International Law, 25 (2012), 313–334.

Eugene M. Emme, Aeronautics and Astronautics Chronology, 1955–1957.

Thomas Gangale, 'The Non Karman Line: An Urban Legend of the Space Age', 41 J. Space L. 151 (2017).

Andrew G. Haley, 'Space Exploration: The Problems of Today, Tomorrow and in the Future', 2 PROC. ON THE L. OF OUTER SPACE(1959) 49.

Johan den Hertog, 'Review of Economic Theories of Regulation', Utrecht School of Economics, Discussion Paper Series 10-18 (Tjalling C. Koopmans Research Institute).

Stephan Hobe, 'Legal Aspects of Space Tourism' 86 (2007) Neb. L. Rev. 441.

Ram Jakhu, Bhupendra Jasani, Jonathan McDowell, 'Critical Issues Related to Registration of Space Objects and Transparency of Space Activities', Acta Astronautica 143 (2018) 406.

Stephen Jones, 'The Police and Criminal Evidence Act 1984', Modern Law Review, 1985-11, Vol 48(6), 679.

Otto Khan Freund, 'On uses and misuses of Comparative Law' (1974) Modern Law Review 37.

Tracey Knutson, What Is Informed Consent for Space-Flight Participants in the Soon-to-Launch Space Tourism Industry, 33 J Space L 105.

Ben Livings, 'A Different Ball Game – Why the Nature of Consent in Contact Sports Undermines a Unitary Approach' JCL 71 (534).

Catriona Mackenzie and Wendy Rogers, 'Autonomy, vulnerability and capacity: a philosophical appraisal of the Mental Capacity Act', Int. J.L.C. 2013, 9(1), 37–52.

Bertrand de Montluc, 'The Changing Face of the European Sector: The policies of Germany, Italy and the United Kingdom' Space Policy 1997 13(1).

Darrell Martin-Lawson, Stefania Paladini, Krishnendu Saha and Erez Yerushalmi, 'The cost of (Un)regulation: Shrinking Earth's orbits and the need for sustainable space governance', (2024) Journal of Environmental Management, 349.

Zeledine Niamh O'Brien, 'To boldly go? Private contracts for the carriage of persons in space, exclusion clauses and inter-party waivers of tortious liability' (2007) 29 D.U.L.J., 341.

Makoto Seta, 'The contribution of the International Organization for Standardization to ocean governance', July 2019, Review of European, Comparative, and International Environmental Law.

Alex Simmonds, 'The UK Perspective on Informed Consent in Commercial Space Travel', (2020), 45, Air and Space Law, Issue 4, 367.

Jill Stavert, 'Glor v Switzerland: article 14 ECHR, disability and non-discrimination', Edin. L.R. 2010, 14(1), 141.

Harry Street, 'Justice in the Welfare State', (2nd edn, 1985) Hamlyn Lectures; Williams 'Control by Licensing' (1967) CLP, 70.

Melanie Walker, Suborbital Space Tourism Flights: An Overview of Some Regulatory Issues at the Interface of Air and Space Law, 33 J Space L 375, 384 (2007).

Colin Warbrick, Robin Churchill, Robin White, John Woodliffe and Brian Yeomans, 'The Outer Space Act 1986' (1986) 35(4) ICLQ 986.

Other Sources

Tom Acres, 'Virgin Galactic's first space tourism flight launches today - here's what you need to know', Sky News, 10 August 2023, https://news.sky.com/story/amp/virgin-galactics-first-space-tourism-flight-launches-today-heres-what-you-need-to-know-12936619.

Alliance Scotland, 'Incorporating the United Nations Convention on the Rights of Disabled People in Scotland' November 2020 https://www.alliance-scotland.org.uk/wp-content/uploads/2020/11/ALLIANCE-Inclusion-Scotland-CRPD-Incorporation-in-Scotland-Main-Report-Nov-2020.pdf.

Jonathan Amos, BBC News, "Muscular' United Kingdom Space Agency Launched', BBC News, 23 March 2010, http://news.bbc.co.uk/1/hi/sci/tech/8579270.stm.

Jonathon Amos, BBC News, 'The UK bids farewell to EU's Galileo System', 14 January 2021, https://www.bbc.co.uk/news/science-environment-55665537.

Jonathon Amos, BBC News, 'UK Space Launch: Historic Cornwall Rocket Launch Ends in Failure' 10 January 2023, https://www.bbc.co.uk/news/science-environment-64218883.

Astroscale, 'Building the Future of Space, Sustainably', https://astroscale.com/.

Adrian Bell, 'German startup Rocket Factory Augsburg successfully performs critical tests ahead of 2022 debut', 30 August 2021, https://www.nasaspaceflight.com/2021/08/rocket-factory-augsburg-tests-2022-debut/.

Kylie Bielby, 'UK launches National Space Operations Centre and regulatory review', May 20, 2024, https://www.unmannedairspace.info/latest-news-and-information/uk-launches-national-space-operations-centre-and-regulatory-review/.

Center for Science Education, 'The Stratosphere' https://scied.ucar.edu/shortcontent/stratosphere-overview.

Clearspace, 'The Clear Mission', https://clearspace.today/missions/clear.

Department for Transport, Corporate report, 'A Guide to UK spaceports' 18 April, 2018, https://www.gov.uk/government/publications/brochure-a-guide-to-the-uks-commercial-spaceports/a-guide-to-the-uks-commercial-spaceports.

Eastern Daily Press, 'Norfolk-built rocket launches from Outer Hebrides', 27 August 2021, https://www.edp24.co.uk/news/20644373.norfolk-built-rocket-launches-outer-hebrides/.

Eutelsat Group press release, 'EUTELSAT AND ONEWEB COMBINATION HERALDS NEW ERA IN SPACE CONNECTIVITY AS WORLD'S FIRST GEO-LEO OPERATOR', 28

September 2023, https://www.eutelsat.com/en/news/press.html#/pressreleases/eutelsat-and-oneweb-combination-heralds-new-era-in-space-connectivity-as-worlds-first-geo-leo-operator-3276261.

The Federal Aviation Administration, 'About the Office of Commercial Space Transportation', https://www.faa.gov/about/office_org/headquarters_offices/ast.

Jeff Foust, 'Launch Industry asks Congress for Regulatory Reforms', Spacenews, October 19, 2023 https://spacenews.com/launch-industry-asks-congress-for-Regulatory-reforms/#:~:text=Gerstenmaier%20and%20other%20witnesses%20called,to%20the%20office.

Michael Hepfler, Tom Coyne, 'Successful 'rockoon' launch makes space more accessible to microsatellites', Purdue University School of Industrial Engineering, https://engineering.purdue.edu/IE/news/2019/hepfer-leo-rocket-launch.

Ofcom, 'Space Launch UK', 16 March 2023, https://www.ofcom.org.uk/spectrum/space-and-satellites/space-launch-uk.

Richard Hollingham, BBC.com, 'Apollo in 50 numbers: The rocket', 26 June 2019, https://www.bbc.com/future/article/20190626-apollo-in-50-numbers-the-rocket.

The Institution of Engineering & Technology, 'UK Commits to Continuing Membership of European Space Agency,' The Institution of Engineering & Technology, November 29, 2019.

Sarah Knapton, 'Meet the British 'space inspectors' working for a safe blast-off', The Telegraph, March 2024, https://www.telegraph.co.uk/news/2024/03/09/space-inspectors-rocket-shetland-technology-caa-economy/.

Launch UK, UK Spaceflight Regulator Plenary, Virtual Meeting, 16 March 2021 https://assets.publishing.service.gov.uk/media/606c3b5bd3bf7f4011bdb1b3/Plenary_-_Spaceflight_regulator_16_March.pdf.

Steven Morris, UK air accident officials to investigate failure to get satellites into orbit, The Guardian, 10 January 2023, https://www.theguardian.com/science/2023/jan/10/uk-rocket-launch-failure-virgin-orbit-second-mission.

G. Nield et al., 'Informed Consent in Commercial Space Transportation Safety', Federal Aviation Administration doc IAC-13-D5. 1.4, https://www.faa.gov/sites/faa.gov/files/space/additional_information/international_affairs/Informed_Consent_paper_IAC_Sept_2013_FAAfinal.pdf.

Ofcom's Plan of Work, 2024-2025, 26 March 2024, https://www.ofcom.org.uk/siteassets/resources/documents/consultations/category-2-6-weeks/273274---ofcoms-proposed-plan-of-work-for-2024-25/associated-documents/statement-plan-of-work-2024-25.pdf.

Ofcom, 'Satellite filings; Satellite filing submissions', 17 January 2024, https://www.ofcom.org.uk/spectrum/space-and-satellites/satellite-filings/.

Rocket Factory Augsburg, Launch Operator Licence Application Assessment of Environmental Effects (RFA SaxaVord AEE V4.1) 19 January 2024, https://consultations

.caa.co.uk/++preview++/space/rocket-factory-augsburg-rfa-public-consultation/user_uploads/rfa-saxavord-aee-v4.1_vol-i-nts_vol-ii-chapters.pdf.

Rocket Factory Augsburg Assessment of Environmental Effects, 'Volume III, AEE Technical Drawings, (RFA SaxaVord AEE V4.1) 19 January 2024, <Drawing 3.2 https://consultations.caa.co.uk/++preview++/space/rocket-factory-augsburg-rfa-public-consultation/user_uploads/rfa-saxavord-aee-v4.1-vol-iii-drawings.pdf.

Rocket Factory Augsburg Assessment of Environmental Effects RFA SaxaVord AEE V4.1, Volume IV, AEE Technical Appendices, 19 January 2024, https://consultations.caa.co.uk/++preview++/space/rocket-factory-augsburg-rfa-public-consultation/user_uploads/rfa-saxavord-aee-v4.1-vol-iv-technical-appendices.pdf.

Rocket Factory Augsburg, 'RFA ONE Flexible Launch System' https://www.rfa.space/rfa-one/.

Paul Rodger, 'Skylark Nano: Shetland propelled into the rocket age with first launch', The Times, June 16 2020, https://www.thetimes.com/uk/scotland/article/skylark-nano-shetland-propelled-into-the-rocket-age-with-first-launch-mvptwtdll.

Royal Institute of Navigation, 'Withdrawal of EGNOS for UK Users', 11 July 2021, https://rin.org.uk/news/572850/Withdrawal-of-EGNOS-for-UK-users.htm.

Marti Sarigul-Klijn, Nesrin Sarigul-Klijn, 'Flight Mechanics of Manned Sub-Orbital Reusable Launch Vehicles with Recommendations for Launch and Recovery' (Spacefuture.com, January 2003) http://www.spacefuture.com/archive/flight_mechanics_of_manned_suborbital_reusable_launch_vehicles_with_recommendations_for_launch_and_recovery.shtml.

SES, 'SES completes acquisition of 100% of o3b networks', 1 August 2016, https://www.ses.com/press-release/ses-completes-acquisition-100-o3b-networks.

The Missile Technology Control Regime https://mtcr.info/.

R. Siebold, R. Young & N. Demidovich, 'Safety of Spaceflight Participants Aboard Suborbital Reusable Launch Vehicles – Background Research, NTRS/NASA', 2019, https://ntrs.nasa.gov/api/citations/20190025274/downloads/20190025274.pdf.

Radioactivity.eu.com, 'MilliSievert; A unit for low doses of radioactivity', https://www.radioactivity.eu.com/site/pages/MilliSievert.htm.

Dr Nicholas P. Ross, 'The long-term sustainability for the fledgling U.K. Space Sector: Are current regulations and legislation fit for purpose?', Masters Dissertation, https://img1.wsimg.com/blobby/go/7ecaff53-6d70-4686-a1a6-b3df0238ede9/downloads/SpaceLaw_LLM_dissertation_NRoss.pdf?ver=1688116027623.

SaxaVord UK Spaceport, 'SaxaVord and HyImpulse announce launch plans', SaxaVord website, November 15 2023, https://saxavord.com/saxavord-and-hyimpulse-announce-launch-plans/.

Skyrora, 'Skyrora attempts first rocket launch to space with Icelandic mobile spaceport' https://skyrora.com/skyrora-attempts-first-rocket-launch-to-space-with-icelandic-mobile-spaceport/#:~:text=Langanes%2C%2008%20October%202022%20

-%20Skyrora%20has%20attempted,vertical%20orbital%20launch%20from%20 UK%20soil%20in%202023.

Thomas Seal, 'U.K. Launches First Satellites With New Space Partner India,' BloombergQuint, December 18 2020 https://www.bloombergquint.com/business /u-k-launches-first-satellites-with-new-space-partner-india.

The Sustainable Markets Initiative, 'Astra Carta. To Care For The Infinite Wonders Of The Universe', 28 June, 2023 https://www.sustainable-markets.org/AstraCarta _charter.pdf#:~:text=The%20Astra%20Carta%20is%20a%20collective%20 call%20to.

The United Kingdom Civil Aviation Authority, Air Accidents Investigation Branch, 'Statement on an investigation into why launch vehicle LauncherOne did not reach orbit following its launch from Cornwall Spaceport on 9 January 2023', 3 October 2024, https://assets.publishing.service.gov.uk/media/66feaae73b919067bb482bed /Boeing_747-400__modified__LauncherOne_Spaceflight.pdf.

The United Kingdom Civil Aviation Authority, 'Appeal a decision the CAA has made affecting your organisation' <https://www.caa.co.uk/our-work/make-a-report-or -complaint/challenge-a-caa-decision/appeal-a-decision-the-caa-has-made-affect ing-your-organisation/>.

The United Kingdom Civil Aviation Authority, CAA Regulation, Space, 'Space Licensing in the UK', https://www.caa.co.uk/media/kbfjgbx0/space-licensing-in -the-uk.pdf#:~:text=There%20are%20no%20fees%20for%20spaceport%2C%20 range%2C%20launch,no%20current%20charging%20scheme%20for%20 these%20licensing%20activities.

The United Kingdom Civil Aviation Authority, 'Guidance and Resources', https://www .caa.co.uk/space/guidance-and-resources/.

The United Kingdom Civil Aviation Authority, Licences Granted Under the Space Industry Act 2018, https://www.caa.co.uk/space/about-the-space-team/licences -granted-and-registers-of-space-objects/.

The United Kingdom Civil Aviation Authority, 'Monitoring and Oversight', https:// www.caa.co.uk/space/what-happens-next/monitoring/.

The United Kingdom Foreign, Commonwealth and Development Office, 'International Treaty; UK–US Technology Safeguards Agreement for Spaceflight Activities: Understanding the TSA', https://www.gov.uk/government/publications/ukusa -agreement-in-the-form-of-an-exchange-of-notes-between-the-united-kingdom-and -the-united-states-of-america-on-technology-safeguards-associated/uk-us-technology -safeguards-agreement-tsa-for-spaceflight-activities-understanding-the-tsa.

United Kingdom Government, Air Accidents Investigation Branch, 'Air Accidents Investigation Branch appointed as Space Accident Investigation Authority for the United Kingdom', 29 July, 2021, https://www.gov.uk/government/news/air

-accidents-investigation-branch-appointed-as-space-accident-investigation-authority-for-the-united-kingdom.

The United Kingdom Government, Air Accidents Investigation Branch, 'SAIA and FAA to jointly oversee Virgin Orbit investigation', 13 January 2023, https://www.gov.uk/government/news/saia-and-faa-to-jointly-oversee-virgin-orbit-investigation.

The United Kingdom Government, 'Government announces package of new measures to drive space sustainability', 23 June 2022, https://www.gov.uk/government/news/government-announces-package-of-new-measures-to-drive-space-sustainability#:~:text=Science%20Minister%20George%20Freeman%20has%20today%20(Thursday%2023%20June)%20launched.

The United Kingdom Government, 'Space Bridge' across the world will help UK and Australia get ahead in global space race, 23 February 2021 https://www.gov.uk/government/news/space-bridge-across-the-world-will-help-uk-and-australia-get-ahead-in-global-space-race.

The United Kingdom Hydrographic Office, 'Our Role in Government', https://www.admiralty.co.uk/government.

The United Kingdom Civil Aviation Authority, 14 January 2025, 'Space Industry Act 2018, Spaceflight Operator Licence for Launch of RFA ONE (Licence ref: SR-APP – 001180)' https://www.caa.co.uk/publication/download/23976.

The United Kingdom Civil Aviation Authority, Reporting Plan v 1.0 for SaxaVord Spaceport Issued to Shetland Space Centre Limited, 16 December 2023 https://www.caa.co.uk/publication/download/20953.

The United Kingdom Civil Aviation Authority, 'Space; Information on rocket launches, space flight and associated activities', <https://www.caa.co.uk/space>.

The United Kingdom Space Agency, 'UN and UK Sign Agreement to Promote Space Sustainability', 2021, https://www.gov.uk/government/news/un-and-uk-sign-agreement-to-promote-space-sustainability.

The United Kingdom Space Agency and UK Civil Aviation Authority, 'Applying for a license under the Space Industry Act 2018', 29 July 2021, https://www.caa.co.uk/publication/download/18919.

The United Kingdom Space Agency, Corporate report, 'Size and Health of the UK Space Industry 2023', 26 July 2024, https://www.gov.uk/government/publications/the-size-and-health-of-the-uk-space-industry-2023/size-and-health-of-the-uk-space-industry-2023#state-of-the-uk-space-industry.

The United Kingdom Space Agency, '(First) Pathfinder Launch Lessons Learned report', 14 December 2023, https://www.gov.uk/government/publications/uk-pathfinder-launch-lessons-learned-report/pathfinder-launch-lessons-learned-report-html.

The United Kingdom Space Agency, 'Strengthening Space Ties between the UK and Japan,' 25 June 2021 https://space.blog.gov.uk/2021/06/25/strengthening-space-ties-between-the-uk-and-japan/.

The United Kingdom Space Agency, 'UK working with global partners to clear up dangerous space debris' 26 October 2021 https://www.gov.uk/government/news/uk-working-with-global-partners-to-clear-up-dangerous-space-debris.

The United Kingdom Space Agency, United Kingdom Space Agency Blog https://space.blog.gov.uk/2022/03/16/on-the-ground-with-space-hub-sutherland-and-orbex/.

The United Kingdom Space Agency, Consultation on Orbital Liabilities, Insurance, Charging and Space Sustainability, 14 September 2023, https://www.gov.uk/government/consultations/consultation-on-orbital-liabilities-insurance-charging-and-space-sustainability/consultation-on-orbital-liabilities-insurance-charging-and-space-sustainability.

The United Kingdom Parliament, Early Day Motions, 'Skyrora and UK's first rocket launch test in 50 years', 20 May 2020, https://edm.parliament.uk/early-day-motion/57003/skyrora-and-uks-first-rocket-launch-test-in-50-years.

United Nations Office for Outer Space Affairs, 'Compendium of space debris mitigation standards adopted by States and international organizations', https://www.unoosa.org/oosa/en/ourwork/topics/space-debris/compendium.html.

United Nations Office for Outer Space Affairs, 'Online Index of Objects Launched into Outer Space', https://www.unoosa.org/oosa/osoindex/search-ng.jspx?lf_id=.

United Nations Office for Outer Space Affairs 'Status of International Agreements Relating To Activities in Outer Space As At 1 January 2020', (2020) United Nations, https://www.unoosa.org/documents/pdf/spacelaw/treatystatus/TreatiesStatus-2020E.pdf.

Joanne Wheeler, 'In review: space law, regulation and policy in United Kingdom', Lexology, online https://www.lexology.com/library/detail.aspx?g=ae61ea3b-c17c-4c60-8a7c-2364f7b60f1c.

Index

www.ingramcontent.com/pod-product-compliance
Lightning Source LLC
LaVergne TN
LVHW102105300926
849161LV00001B/25
* 9 7 8 9 0 0 4 7 3 2 5 4 4 *